DIVO

Also by Helena Matheopoulos:

MAESTRO: Encounters with Conductors of Today

DIVO

GREAT TENORS, BARITONES AND BASSES
DISCUSS THEIR ROLES

HELENA MATHEOPOULOS

1817

HARPER & ROW, PUBLISHERS, New York
Cambridge, Philadelphia, San Francisco, Washington
London, Mexico City, São Paulo, Singapore, Sydney

This book was originally published in Great Britain under the title *Bravo*.

FIRST U.S. EDITION

Library of Congress Cataloging-in-Publication Data

Matheopoulos, Helena.
  Divo: great tenors, baritones, and basses discuss their roles.

  Bibliography: p.
  Includes index.
  1. Singers.   I. Title.
ML400.M36 1986   782.1′092′2   86-45127
ISBN 0-06-015634-1

86 87 88 89 90 HC 10 9 8 7 6 5 4 3 2 1

To my angelic mother who nurtured and encouraged my nascent love of music and opera with enthusiasm and verve, in memory of so many happy musical journeys and performances in my childhood, adolescence and beyond.

CONTENTS

Contents

ILLUSTRATIONS

ACKNOWLEDGEMENTS

First and foremost I should like to thank Lord Weidenfeld, whose idea it was to write this book – and its twin volume on female singers, which will follow shortly – who didn't take 'no' for an answer and whose unswerving support, patience and kindness – and that of John Curtis, Editorial Director, and my editor Linden Lawson – far surpassed the normal author-publisher bond and made it possible for me to work free from any of the usual aggravations that beset such relationships and did much to lessen the equally usual doubts and angst that writers experience on the way ... I look forward to working with them on the next volume with great joy. Also Kevin McDermott, for copy-editing the manuscript; and Hugh Van Dusen for his unstinting support.

Second, my deepest gratitude goes to my friend Olivier Maitland Pelen, First Councillor at the French Embassy in Lagos, whose infinitely perceptive, always interested and often critical remarks were instrumental in defining, in my own mind, the direction I wanted this book to take. For the endless trouble he took, by correspondence, by telephone, indeed almost by pigeon post, and for his many helpful suggestions and improvements I am deeply thankful.

Third, to my friends Richard Byron, Sarah Granito di Belmonte, Alexandra Eversole, Oliver Gilmour, Willie Hancock, Peter Katona, Sir Emmanuel Kaye, Victor Sebek, Augustin von Paege and Daphne Voelin, very many thanks for their vital support during those hard months of hard writing.

I would also like to thank the following:
Peter Adam; Peter Alward; Dietlind Antretter, the Salzburg Festival Press Office; Lies Askonas, of Lies Askonas Ltd, for her help and encouragement; Joanna Beckerlegg, Assistant, the Opera Press Office, Covent Garden; Joel Block; Claire Burring, Assistant, Press Office, English National Opera; Edward Butcher, House Manager, English National Opera; Jeremy Caulton, Director of Opera Planning, English National Opera; John Coast, Caroline Woodfield and Penelope Marland at John Coast Agency, for constant and extra-special help; Martin Engstrom; Piero Faggioni; Carol

Felton, Press Officer, Philips Classics; Johanna Fiedler, Press Officer, the Metropolitan Opera; Ubaldo Gardini; Peter Gelb of Columbia Artists Management; Michael Geliot; Peter Girth; Tom Graham of Harrison Parrott; Patricia Greenan; Helen Greenwood, Press Officer, English National Opera; Sir Peter Hall, Director, the National Theatre and Artistic Director, Glyndebourne Festival Opera; Frau Dina Hausjell, the Salzburg Festival Press Office; John Hunt, who helped steer so much helpful material my way; Sue Hyman;

Peter Jonas, Managing Director, English National Opera; Trevor Jones, House Manager, the Royal Opera House, Covent Garden; Denise Kantor; Tony Kaye; Doctor Eddie Khambatta; Lothar Knessl, the Press Office of the Vienna State Opera; Marguerite Werner-Kollo; Luisa Lasser-Petrov; Robert Leslie; Mary Jo Little, Classic A & R, Deutsche Grammophon; James Lock, Chief Engineer, Decca Records; James Lockhart; Leone Magiera; Barry Malcomber, International Press Officer, EMI International; Professor Albert Moser, President, the Salzburg Festival; Elijah Moshinsky; Helen O'Neill, Press Officer, Glyndebourne Festival Opera; the Press Office of the Bavarian State Opera; the Press Office of La Scala; Robert Rattray of Lies Askonas Ltd; Janine Reiss; Vera Rosza; John Schlesinger; Klaus Schulz; Maggie Sedwards, Director of Publicity, English National Opera; Hilary Sheard of PolyGram;

Alan Sievewright, of whose almost peerless knowledge and understanding of the voice I was the constant beneficiary; David Sigall of Ingpen & Williams; Nicholas Snowman, Artistic Administrator, the South Bank; Jochen Sostman, Betriebsdirektor, the Vereinigte Städtische Bühnen, Krefeld und Monchengladbach; Margheritta Stafford and David Law; Clifford Starr, Assistant House Manager, the Royal Opera House, Covent Garden; Sir John Tooley, General Director, the Royal Opera House, Covent Garden, for being so generous with his time and thoughts over the past three years; Edgar Vincent and Cynthia Robbins of Edgar Vincent Associates, New York City; Nina Walker; Catherine Waltrafen, Press Officer, Paris Opéra; Dr Hans Widrich, Press Officer, the Salzburg Festival; Katharine Wilkinson, Opera Press Officer, the Royal Opera House, Covent Garden, for her unstinting support and friendship; Serena Woolf, formerly Classical Press Officer, Decca Records; and Gun Brinson at the *Sunday Times Magazine*.

Once again, my thanks go to Herbert von Karajan, James Levine and Riccardo Muti, whose inspired remarks about the voice, singing, the present and future of opera in my previous book *Maestro: Encounters with Conductors of Today* I have made extensive use of in appropriate places.

FOREWORD

The aim of this book – the first of two volumes covering the leading male and female singers of our day – is to explore in detail the relationship between the singer and the role, and to analyse each artist's approach, both vocal and dramatic, to some of the roles they are usually associated with. What vocal problems are posed by a particular role and how does each singer experience it emotionally? In some cases singers singing the same roles have totally different dramatic viewpoints: for instance, Placido Domingo considers Cavaradossi in *Tosca* a remarkable man in his own right – not just 'Mr Tosca as he is sometimes portrayed' – while José Carreras finds him uninteresting. Samuel Ramey sees Don Giovanni as an elegant, romantic man passionately in love with the female form while Thomas Allen and Ruggero Raimondi invest him with different, more dangerous overtones. In other cases the vocal approach itself differs: Nicolai Ghiaurov believes the title role in *Boris Godunov* should be sung musically while Paata Burchuladze prefers a more declamatory approach. Renato Bruson considers the Conte di Luna in *Il trovatore* the hardest of all Verdi roles while for Piero Cappuccilli it poses no vocal problems.

In some cases, though, all singers agree about specific difficulties in certain roles. All the tenors I spoke to singled out the Duke of Mantua's aria 'Parmi veder le lagrime' as one of the most difficult in the entire tenor repertoire, and all the baritones agree that the difficulties in the title role of *Rigoletto* are not specifically vocal but also scenic, i.e. have to do with the hunchback position they are forced to adopt on stage, which makes it hard for them to make proper use of their diaphragms.

All of the artists included have been asked to explain the stylistic demands of various composers – and kinds of singing – and how they can be mastered. They also discuss their training and vocal development and offer helpful suggestions for young singers, so direly in need of good advice at a time when good teachers are the exception rather than the rule. They also discuss some of the plagues besetting opera today and offer useful remedies. All the singers in this book are still active on the operatic stage itself. Singers now devoting all their time to *Lieder* alone are not included.

As the chapters were written to be read individually as well as continuously, some general points about operatic life today recur from time to time. The choice is personal, though almost all the artists included are obvious choices because of the distinction and the importance of their careers. Restrictions of space *alone* have prevented the inclusion of some singers I admire – like Evgeny Nesterenko, Giuseppe Taddei, Gabriel Bacquier, Martti Talvela, Rolando Panerai and Peter Schreier – and other, younger singers who have reached prominence in recent years – notably Giorgio Zancanaro, the excellent Italian baritone, the British tenor David Rendall, now enjoying an important international career, the Swedish baritone Håkan Hågegard, the Finnish baritone Jorma Hynninen, the Italian baritone Leo Nucci – are omitted for the same reason. Jon Vickers is omitted because he is writing his own book and did not wish to be included.

*

Some other greatly promising singers have emerged since the book was conceived:

William Shimell, the British baritone with a beautiful, melodious voice and dark, tense, wiry good looks who excelled as Count Almaviva at Glyndebourne in 1984 and in the 1985–6 Jonathan Miller production of *Don Giovanni* at English National Opera. There is no doubt in my, or anybody's, mind that Shimell will become one of the great Don Giovannis of the next decade, and probably also one of the great Onegins, though there are no specific plans for him to sing this role as yet. Noteworthy also is **John Tomlinson**, a bass excelling in a wide variety of roles, from the title role in Rossini's *Moses*, which he sang with distinction at English National Opera, to Mephistopheles in Gounod's *Faust*, as well as Wagnerian roles like Hagen and Mozartian roles like Leporello.

From Italy **Claudio Desderi**, an excellent bass-baritone whose Figaro won high acclaim at Glydebourne and whose Don Alfonso in *Così* was highly praised at Covent Garden. He was poised to sing the three Mozart-Da Ponte operas in succession under Barenboim in Paris. Also **Ferruccio Furnaletto**, an Italian bass who has sung Leporello in Karajan's recording of *Don Giovanni* and will do so in his Salzburg 1987 Easter Festival production, and who also distinguished himself when he stood in for José Van Dam in the 1986 Salzburg Easter Festival production of *Don Carlos*.

Dimitri Kavrakos is a Greek bass currently singing at the Metropolitan Opera, New York. He was a remarkable Pimen in Covent Garden's revival of *Boris Godunov* in 1984 and Commendatore at Glyndebourne.

Gino Quilico, an excellent, attractive Canadian baritone whose portrayals of Valentin in *Faust*, Belcore in *L'elisir d'amore*, Marcello in *La Bohème* and Escamillo in *Carmen* at Covent Garden drew high critical praise and impressed with their musicality, tonal beauty and stylistic sense.

Gary Lakes, an American tenor with, apparently, a gift for Heldentenor roles, excelled as Siegmund in Barenboim's concert performances of *Die Walküre* in Paris. If he is careful and paces his expansion into the Wagnerian *Fach* cautiously, he might become the Heldentenor the operatic world is waiting for.

GLOSSARY

appoggiatura: a term derived from the Italian verb 'appoggiare' (to lean or support). A grace note inserted before a note but to be sung equal length, to support or emphasize a melodic or harmonic progression

bel canto: literally 'beautiful singing'. A term associated with singing in the eighteenth and early nineteenth centuries when a beautiful vocal performance was more important than the dramatic. *Bel canto* composers most often referred to in this book include Bellini, Donizetti and Rossini

cabaletta: in nineteenth-century opera, the fast concluding section of an aria or ensemble. In the early part of that century, a separate aria in lively tempo

cantabile: literally 'songful' – denotes *legato*, expressive singing

da capo: return to the beginning

a cappella: unaccompanied singing

cavatina: technically a short aria but now used to describe widely differing types of song and therefore virtually meaningless

coloratura: elaborately embellished singing. The term later came to apply to singers specializing in roles needing great vocal agility

'covering' a note: singing it with a 'closed' throat, i.e., as Dr Ardeshir Khambatta explains, allowing the larynx to float downwards rather than upwards. For a full explanation see p. 128

fioritura: florid vocal embellishment

legato: from the Italian verb 'legare', meaning to bind or tie. Refers to the smooth passage from one note to another, as opposed to *staccato*

lirico-spinto: from the Italian verb 'spingere', meaning to push. Identifies a lyric voice leaning towards the dramatic

messa di voce: a crescendo and diminuendo on a phrase or note

mezza voce; literally 'half voice'. Denotes singing softly, but not as softly as *piano*. A special way of singing as if under the breath, referring not only to the amount of volume but to a different quality from that when singing full voice

passaggio: the notes E, F and G which lie between the head and the chest registers

piano: term applying to volume meaning soft; also

　　pianissimo: very soft
　　forte: loud
　　fortissimo: very loud

portamento: from the Italian verb 'portare', meaning to carry. A practice by which singers slide from one note to another without a break

recitative: declamatory passages imitating speech which precede arias, duets and ensembles. Particularly common in eighteenth-century opera

register: a term used to denote a certain area or vocal range – 'chest', 'middle', 'head'

rubato: literally 'stolen time'. A way of performing without adhering strictly to musical time

solfège: an elementary method of teaching sight reading and ear training whereby the names of the notes (*do, re, mi* . . .) are pronounced while the notes are sung unaccompanied. The intervals have to be learned by ear. A common teaching method in France and Italy, known in English as 'tonic solfa'

tessitura: literally 'texture'. A term used to designate the average pitch of an aria or role. A part can be taxing despite the absence of especially high or low notes due to the prevailing range or *tessitura*

verismo: literally 'realism'. The opposite to *bel canto*, where drama is as important as beautiful singing. A term applied to the works of Italian composers after Verdi including Puccini, Mascagni, Leoncavallo, Zandonai and Giordano. Can also be used as an adjective, *veristic*, meaning realistic and applied to the way in which the works of these composers are sung – i.e. more freely and less precisely than those of composers such as Mozart

vocalize: exercise the voice. Can be a specifically composed wordless song or exercise

INTRODUCTION: OPERA TODAY

Not since the days of Verdi, when it was the genuine, living theatre of the time, has opera been as popular as it is today. Opera houses are proliferating, new festivals – like Buxton, Santa Fe, Hohenems, Pesaro and Macerata, to name but a few – are springing up regularly in both Europe and America and recent years have seen an explosion of public interest in all things operatic. Within a fortnight of this book going to press, three plays with opera as their subject opened in London's West End (*Lend me a Tenor, After Aida* and *Café Puccini*). Films of opera, like Losey's *Don Giovanni*, Zeffirelli's *La traviata* and Rosi's *Carmen* have enjoyed, and some are still enjoying, long, profitable runs in the cinemas of most major cities, while Zeffirelli's new film of *Otello* proved to be a major attraction at the 1986 Cannes Film Festival. Sales of operatic recordings and videos are booming and opera is receiving considerable exposure on television, in the form of live transmissions, studio films and masterclasses conducted by famous singers. In the opera house itself, audiences are getting younger and include significant numbers of 'first timers'.

Several factors are responsible for this massive public interest: nostalgia for an art form now essentially dead – for few new operas have joined the general repertoire since the war; modern marketing techniques; and the efforts of megastars like Luciano Pavarotti and Placido Domingo to break away from the confines of the established operatic public through recitals and performances in venues like parks and stadiums with a 20,000 – 50,000 capacity. The result has been that millions of people whose geographical or other circumstances might preclude a visit to the theatre are now eager to experience the uniqueness, excitement and magic of opera. As Peter Jonas, Managing Director of English National Opera, points out, 'it is rare nowadays to encounter anyone who does not know what opera is, whereas twenty years ago it was perfectly possible to find people, both in Britain and America, who had never even heard of opera'.

But the main reason for today's operatic boom is the improved quality of the product itself. Opera would never have survived, let alone thrived, in this age of essentially cinematic criteria of dramatic credibility had it not undergone a thorough transformation in the fifties and early sixties: the Callas/Visconti/Wieland Wagner revolution that dispelled the notion that opera is 'just singing', in costume and against some crude naturalistic backdrop, turned it into believable theatre and invested it with the musical-dramatic unity essential to it as an art form. Maria Callas achieved this through performances of maximum dramatic intensity in which she experienced the characters body and soul, always using the music, the score, as her guide and inspiration; Luchino Visconti through the then unprecedented realism of his productions; and Wieland Wagner, the great composer's grandson, by 'smashing all the bombastic symbolisms and conventions of the nineteenth century at a stroke', in the words of Rolf Liebermann, former Intendant of the Hamburg State Opera and the Paris Opéra, and setting the works free to speak to our time – first, as usual, to scandalized derision and eventually to eulogies.

This is necessarily an over-simplification, because tomes could be written about this revolution and its perpetrators and also because, decades before Callas, opera had its first great singing-actor in the person of Feodor Chaliapin (1873-1938), the Russian bass whose performances apparently displayed the same dramatic credibility and searing intensity. But he was a solitary beacon of light in a dramatically primitive operatic age when audiences consisted mostly of canary-fanciers. (They're still around – mercifully on the decline!) What enabled the Callas/Visconti/Wieland Wagner revolution to have such a profound and lasting impact on the development of opera was the fact that it happened simultaneously and at a time when other great artists were also thinking alike. These three geniuses were pivotal points in a wider movement that also included producers as inspired and influential as Günther Rennert and Walter Felsenstein and singing-actors of the calibre of Tito Gobbi, Hans Hotter and Boris Christoff, to name but a few, all of whom played a crucial role in spreading the new image of opera to all corners of the musical world.

The time was ripe. As Rolf Liebermann rightly points out, the German opera houses had been destroyed by bombing, their sets and costumes had been burnt and their audiences, stunned by their recent experiences, sat, wrapped up in mufflers, in draughty, unheated theatres. The collective unconscious was therefore more than receptive to the stark realism of the new productions and to the probing, psychological approach of the new producers. They and their much-maligned successors, the producers of today, have changed Everyman's concept of what opera is about. 'The great thing about a work of art is that it transcends its time and its fashion and speaks down the ages,' says Michael Geliot in *Opera*. 'Do we want Shakespeare to be performed in replica Globe theatres and spoken in the accents of the time? Do we want Verdi to be fossilized in the nineteenth century, because we have among us critics who can research the "authentic" presentation styles? Do we want Mozart musicologically decorated according to prevailing eighteenth-century whim?'

I don't think so. We have reached a point where most of us would agree with Elijah Moshinsky's premise that 'the performance of opera must be drawn from some essential dramatic thread inside it. In order to make the work live for the audience, for the artists, for oneself, one must feel free to interpret: otherwise one would end up a dead repetition of tradition. When one looks at the D'Oyly Carte Company or the Berliner Ensemble, one sees the dangers. So, I resist the current tidal wave saying you merely have to reproduce the composer's instructions. That's not the point. What you have to do is to perform the opera! You can easily perform the instructions and miss the opera altogether. I derive great inspiration from a letter of Wieland Wagner's, where he wrote that, living in the age of Picasso and Matisse, he didn't feel compelled to adhere to the visual taste of his grandfather!'

Yet some, including Sir Peter Hall, Director of the National Theatre and Artistic Director of Glyndebourne Festival Opera, feel there is a reverse side of the coin and that the giant dramatic strides opera has made in our day have resulted in too much dominance on the part of producers who often take unwarranted liberties and do not always express or follow the music closely enough: 'I am a militant classicist. I believe we have to journey to the words through the music and that the job of the producer and of the conductor is to try to reveal the piece to the audience. I don't think it's their job to publicize their own personal fantasies, induced in them by the music. There's a lot of that about and I don't like it. It doesn't hurt me but it bores and sometimes amuses me, because it's much easier to set opera in some jazzy new period and make it have some kind of historical resonance that never crossed the composer's or the librettist's mind, than it is to realize the piece. So, in this sense, the excessive dominance of the producer has resulted in a certain loss.'

Most of the singers in this book echo Sir Peter Hall's misgivings and refer to our age as 'the scourge of the producer', to which phenomenon – along with the disappearance of the old-fashioned type of vastly experienced operatic conductors, like Tullio Serafin, Vittorio Gui and Antonino

Votto, who knew opera, understood the voice and had the patience, foresight and will to act as glorified coaches, nurture young singers and guide their vocal development to fruition – they attribute some of the responsibility for the sad vocal decline that has accompanied, in inverse proportion, the dramatic advances made by opera in our time. The claim is unjustified. For although producers *are* sometimes guilty of violating the spirit of the works they interpret, they are certainly not guilty of causing the vocal decline we are witnessing. The only legitimate *vocal* complaint singers can hurl at producers is their suggestion that singers sometimes adopt positions not conducive to the best singing they're capable of. But this is a detail that can be, and usually is, resolved at rehearsals. 'What singers are *really* bitching about is the producers' preference for working with artists who do not just sing well, but also act well and look good,' says Peter Jonas.

'I think it is probably true that we live in the age of the producer, but I do not think it is necessarily a scourge,' he continues. 'It all depends very much on whether we are talking about opera as a whole. It goes back to what one really believes opera is. If you believe opera is theatre, if you believe the English National, or the Vienna State or the Metropolitan Opera is a theatre, a theatrical institution, then production is of paramount importance. To make the conductor God in opera is actually false from the musical-dramatic point of view and I think the composers would agree.★ The composers – Mozart, Verdi and Puccini – were practical men of the theatre and quite commercially minded. Rather like the Jerome Kernses of their day, they were concerned with putting on a good show which people would want to go and see and which would make money. In fact the closest equivalent to the great composers of the past are not, I regret to say, the modern operatic composers but people like Stephen Sondheim and others writing new musical theatre. I think it's important for opera to have good conductors, great conductors, the best one can get. But if one is going to put on opera with any sense of honesty about what it is about – and not just mount a concert performance in costume – then obviously the producer of "the show" must be the most important person.'

Before going on to discuss the vocal decline plaguing opera today, it is worth dwelling for a moment on an important point brought up by Peter

★Verdi certainly did and, in a letter dated 18 March 1899, shortly after the premiere of *Falstaff*, complained that 'When I began to shock the music world with my sins, there was the calamity of the primadonna. Now there is the tyranny of the conductor! Bad, bad, still less bad the former!' Plus ça change....

Jonas: the alienation of today's operatic composers from the mainstream of contemporary operatic life – a phenomenon unique in the history of music theatre. The German tenor René Kollo is also deeply concerned about this dangerous trend and fears it may condemn opera to a slow death by atrophy. 'With very few exceptions, like Britten's *Peter Grimes*, which is not all that recent, nobody is writing "real operas" any more, and especially not real *singers*' operas,' he laments. 'If this situation continues, combined with the rapid disappearance of sufficient great voices, it will result in the death of opera as an art form.'

Sir Peter Hall agrees, but is more optimistic about the eventual outcome: 'When you think of opera a hundred years ago, there was Wagner and there was Verdi, both of whom were absolutely modern and popular. Between the wars, there were Richard Strauss and Alban Berg. Since the war, few modern operas have really entered the repertoire. But I believe this will change. I think it should be possible to write modern operas about life as it is lived now. And when you consider the popularity of a great deal of music, I feel sure a way will be found to bring the two together. Of course, the real, basic problem is not so much to do with opera as with the crisis in modern music. In the past thirty to forty years most composers, when they sit down to write, almost re-invent music and the gulf between them and the public is enormous and unique. I am sure this cannot go on because no artist can exist without an audience.'

Personally, I feel convinced that some of the masterpieces among today's 'musicals'– like Bernstein's *West Side Story* and Gershwin's *Porgy and Bess* – are indeed contemporary operas which, within the space of a decade or so, will join the standard operatic repertoire. The fact that both the Metropolitan Opera and Glyndebourne Festival Opera mounted ambitious full-scale productions of *Porgy and Bess* within the past two years and Deutsche Grammophon recorded *West Side Story* with the best of operatic casts – José Carreras, Kiri Te Kanawa and Tatiana Troyanos – is a step in the right direction, indicating that these great works are finally being recognized for what they are. I am convinced that the future of opera lies, as Peter Hall mentioned, in bridging the gap between it and the popular music theatre.

Far more dangerous for the future of opera is the serious vocal decline we have witnessed in the past twenty years, and the tragic shortage of sufficient singers for some sections of the repertoire: Verdi baritones, Verdi mezzos and Heldentenors in particular are in such short supply that one has to make do with substitutes (i.e. Donizetti baritones taking on Verdi roles and lyric tenors tackling the Wagnerian repertoire), while top-flight tenors are also hard to come by. Placido Domingo's recent cancellation of his operatic engagements for six months following the Mexican earthquake, for instance, played havoc with the plans of every major international opera house. While, twenty years ago, one could think of at least a dozen top tenors for the Italian repertoire alone, the number has now dwindled to half – and half of *that* meagre figure consists of veteran singers now in their late fifties or early sixties! As Peter Katona, Artistic Administrator of The Royal Opera, observes, 'the vocal decline and shortage of sufficient singers seems to get more acute with each half-generation', while James Levine, Music and Artistic Director of the Metropolitan Opera, recently complained to the *New York Times* that 'whereas in the fifties a good performance of Puccini's *Madama Butterfly* could be taken for granted, today it would be the exception rather than the rule'.

He is dead right. For the title role in *Madama Butterfly* and its male lead, Pinkerton, both demand superb vocalism – something very, *very* rare in our day, except from veterans like Carlo Bergonzi, Nicolai Gedda and Alfredo Kraus, or from the very cream of today's singers when they are in top form and not too exhausted from doing too much. So rare, in fact, is it that when one does encounter it – as in Samuel Ramey's recent rendition of Mephistopheles in Gounod's *Faust*, and of Assur in Rossini's *Semiramide* at Covent Garden – one is left literally spellbound at rediscovering the exhilaration that note-perfect, vocally brilliant performances can arouse, even when, as was the case with *Faust*, they occur in archaic productions.

The reasons for the vocal decline we have experienced in recent years are manifold: too much singing, too much travelling, too little time devoted to vocal training and consolidation, a dearth of good teachers, the disappearance of the old breed of knowledgeable operatic conductors already mentioned, and the need for operatic managements and the industry to exploit emerging talents beyond their capacities by asking them to sing the wrong roles or even the right roles at the wrong time. In short, the plague besetting opera today and endangering the vocal longevity of both young and established singers is due both to musical and to economic factors.

'The market for everything is different and, in order to live, these people have to lead different lives, as we all do', says Peter Jonas. 'We are required to earn a large living and to keep up, to a certain extent, with certain "de rigueur" things, all of which demands a certain turnover, and the need to keep going. The advent of the jet plane, the ease of travel, the popularity of opera, modern marketing techniques, modern theatre-going habits, modern theatre-going appetites and the way opera is consumed, have all resulted in a new breed of opera singer.' The eminent French coach and accompanist Janine Reiss concurs and explains that we have, perhaps, come to expect too much from our opera singers. 'Instead of letting them concentrate on their vocal development and the need to sing as beautifully and as perfectly as possible, we also demand that their acting is of a standard comparable to that of the Comédie Française or the Royal Shakespeare Company, that their dancing matches that of the starlets of *A Chorus Line*, and that their looks compare with those of matinee idols in other branches of show business. It's a lot, you know!'

The result, as Peter Jonas points out, is that conservatoires are no longer necessarily producing the right kind of operatic material we need, but tend to dish out 'people who are better actors than singers'. As a veteran operatic conductor who would rather remain anonymous recently remarked, 'the operatic stage is getting full of stage-struck strumpets who would be just as happy lifting a leg in a West End musical!'. Clearly, there is an acute need for this to be counterbalanced by a sufficient number of well-trained voices and of artists serious and dedicated enough to devote adequate time to the arduous, continuous hard work it takes to become a really great opera singer. Thank goodness such artists do emerge (like excellently trained, vocally dazzling and hard-working American sopranos June Anderson and Kathleen Battle) – but not in sufficient numbers to service the needs of the relentlessly expanding operatic world.

While there is no shortage of beautiful voices, every artist I talked to in this book stressed that the problem lies in the fact that most of them are prematurely ruined. As Carlo Bergonzi and Graziella Sciutti – who now gives master-classes all over the world – observe, there are and there will always be plenty of good voices. But, as Sciutti explains, 'the problem is that these young people, some of whom are also well-prepared musically (especially in the United States and in Britain), are quickly taken up by theatres, managements and the recording industry and pushed into rapid stardom before they really know what it's all about and before their vocal cords have had time to settle down. Because the voice is a physical thing, part of one's anatomy, and singing is a bit like a sport: the muscles in question must be allowed time to grow and become elastic and resilient. This is why, when a promising young singer is immediately asked to sing roles that are too big and too taxing for his or her age, although the voice *itself* can do it, i.e. can sing the notes, the body doesn't yet have the necessary resilience to sustain such an effort. The voice thus loses its "bloom" and can also be permanently damaged. The misuse of the available material lies at the heart of the vocal problem besetting opera today.' The well-known coach and accompanist Nina Walker never tires of stressing this point too; and Bernd Weikl and Kurt Moll refer to the same problem in their chapters.

Those responsible for casting could therefore do a great deal to remedy the situation; in fact, as Nina Walker points out, the success or otherwise of any given production is already decided by the judiciousness or otherwise of the casting director or committee. But their task is not as simple as it might seem to outsiders. For while most managements do have endless discussions about individual singers and, in the case of ensemble theatres like the English National or the Welsh National Opera, try to map out a future for their young artists that takes into account both the latters' vocal development and the needs of the theatre, it is sometimes impossible to satisfy both. 'There are instances when managements are so hard-pressed economically and have such difficulties in making ends meet, especially in Britain, that we sometimes end up using young people too ruthlessly,' says Peter Jonas. 'But this is nothing new. If one reads the memoirs of the man who ran the Met at the beginning of the century, one comes across many instances where he admits to exploiting singers beyond what he knew to be their natural capacities. Managements then were, if anything, even more ruthless and commercial than now. Singers were always asked to sing the wrong roles. We just hear of those who survived, and there are plenty surviving now. The problem is that we tend to look back on the whole period of 1900-40 as a single generation which, of course, it was not. If we look back on the period 1945-85 in the same way, we will find just as many great singers, especially up to the early sixties, when the jet plane began to influence things adversely.'

Those in charge of the big international houses also bear in mind the acuteness of this problem for the future of opera. According to Sir John Tooley, General Director of the Royal Opera House, Covent Garden, 'we think a lot about this and take a great deal of care in our casting and we *do* have sensible regard for the artists' development and possible damage to their voices. But of course, as far as repertoire is concerned, the choice is ultimately theirs. There are singers who have a very clear idea of what to sing and what not to sing and who are not afraid of saying "no" to managements. But there are others who are less sure of themselves and terrified because they are worried that if they refuse to sing a specific role, they might not be asked to sing at this particular house again – which is essentially untrue, if they are talented! So, the reasons for the very real vocal decline we have experienced and are still experiencing are not just due to the jet plane but lie much nearer home: the succumbing to economic pressures. Very few singers can afford *not* to sing a great deal.'

The rewards are certainly substantial: twenty thousand Swiss francs a performance for the top-flight singers (and more in some Continental opera houses), lucrative recording, film and video contracts, recitals in mass venues for which the most popular opera stars may receive fees as high as fifty thousand dollars or more. But all this should be viewed against the precarious background of insecure, short-lived careers during which opera singers must more or less make provision for the rest of their lives. So the pressures are great indeed.

Yet, despite these pressures and the temptations they are continuously exposed to, the most dedicated artists do find it in them to say 'no', 'even to Karajan', according to soprano Ileana Cotrubas, and to adhere to a repertoire suitable to their voices. Among the great singers of the past generation, for instance, Elisabeth Schwarzkopf, for one, is known to have eschewed the role of Violetta in *La traviata* after she heard Maria Callas singing it, while Carlo Bergonzi, Alfredo Kraus and Nicolai Gedda have preserved their voices into their sixties by singing only the right repertoire. Of the younger generation, British baritone Thomas Allen is known to be particularly good at saying no, because, being exceptionally intelligent, he realizes it's the only way to maintain the quality of his voice and ensure its longevity.

This increased awareness on the part of singers is one of several encouraging signs that we may be on the way to stalling, if not eliminating, today's vocal decline. Another hopeful development is the desire of most of the singers in this book – and of their female counterparts in volume two – to spend their retirement years teaching and coaching. Indeed, some of them, like Bergonzi, Kraus, Prey and, more recently, Pavarotti, have already begun giving masterclasses, while Moll would eventually like to become a full-time voice teacher. This should go a long way towards alleviating the shortage of good teachers that all young singers complain about.

The third promising factor is the determination of conductors in charge of operatic institutions, like James Levine – who, according to the testimony of singers as distinguished and experienced as Sherrill Milnes, is fast becoming as knowledgeable about the voice as the Serafins, Guis and Vottos of yesterday – to spend as much time as possible in their theatres and devote considerable personal effort to the discovery and development of young voices. Levine is exceptionally conscientious in this way and is largely responsible for the careers of Kathleen Battle, Maria Ewing, Neil

Shicoff and Catherine Malfitano. If Riccardo Muti, who will shortly take up his appointment as Artistic Director of La Scala and is a renowned expert on the voice, follows suit – a recent interview in *The Times* in which he paid tribute to Serafin seems to indicate he has every intention of doing so – and if Claudio Abbado, the new Music Director of the Vienna State Opera and Bernard Haitink, the new Music Director of the Royal Opera House, Covent Garden decide to do the same, this will be a giant leap forward in the battle to arrest declining vocal standards and ensure a better future for opera. James Levine sums up the situation as follows: 'Originally, we had a period when vocal development triumphed, but opera was often dramatically ridiculous. This was followed by a time when there were great dramatic strides, but opera was vocally inadequate. Now, the pendulum has begun to swing somewhere in the middle and this balance is essential for the future of opera.'

A recent concert performance of *Semiramide* at Covent Garden, in which the thrilling vocal virtuosity of Marilyn Horne was matched by that of the younger generation in the persons of Samuel Ramey and June Anderson, made me feel that Levine's remark may well be justified.

THE TENOR

The tenor is the highest natural register of the male voice, with a compass of about two octaves, on either side of middle C. The term derives from the Latin verb 'teneo', to hold, because in the Middle Ages and the Renaissance the tenor held, took and kept the plainsong or other melody used as canto fermo *in sacred polyphonic composition. The high notes at the top of the tenor register – the B flat, B natural, the high C and in some very rare cases the D flat or D natural – used to be sung falsetto until 1837, when the French tenor Gilbert Louis Duprez sang the first full-chested high C in musical history in a performance of Rossini's* Guillaume Tell *at the Paris Opéra.*

Rossini himself was horrified and likened the sound to 'the squawk of a capon having its throat cut', while Berlioz records in his memoirs that 'silence reigned in the stupefied house . . . amazement and admiration blended in an almost fearful mood'. Since then, the more dramatic, full-blooded kind of operas that were fast replacing the grace and decorum of the classical and the bel canto *styles of composition all required this new kind of robust, full-chested sound at the top of the register and it became de rigueur that all high notes be sung with full chest.*

The tenor voice is usually classified into the following five categories: the tenore leggiero *or light-lyric, possessing extreme facility in the upper register plus considerable agility (corresponding to that of* coloratura *sopranos); the* tenore lirico; *the* lirico–spinto, *a lyric tenor leaning towards the dramatic (from the Italian verb 'spingere', to push); the* tenore robusto *or dramatic; and the Heldentenor or heroic tenor specializing in Wagnerian roles.*

GIACOMO ARAGALL

Catalan-born Giacomo Aragall has a mellifluous, highly individual lyric voice with an instantly identifiable timbre and clear, ringing top notes that delight audiences and arouse the admiration of fellow tenors, who tend to hold him in high esteem. Yet, at forty-five, he is neither as famous nor as widely popular as some of his contemporaries. His relatively low profile is due largely to an acute lack of self-confidence and consequently of some of the bravura and star quality of a Pavarotti, a Domingo or a Carreras. Yet, as Sir John Tooley, General Director of the Royal Opera House, Covent Garden, rightly points out, Aragall is 'a very appealing artist and audiences, once they get to know him, become strong supporters of his. Offstage, he is a withdrawn and intensely private man, but his personality becomes more evident on stage and this, coupled with a very committed approach to roles, wins him a lot of support.'

Aragall's career began in 1963, when, aged only twenty-three, he made his Scala debut and was immediately offered a three-year contract which soon led to a string of highly successful international debuts in the great opera houses, where he was hailed as one of the finest and most promising tenors of his generation. This period of intense activity and international success was followed by a brief lull in the late seventies caused by nervous exhaustion, from which he nevertheless re-emerged, in top form, with a voice still as fresh yet richer and more substantial than in his early years.

Aragall is not bothered about being less well-known than some of his colleagues and professes himself fully satisfied with his career 'such as it is', built without recourse or concessions to publicity. His model has always been Alfredo Kraus, 'whose public is always there for him wherever he happens to sing, despite his total disregard for publicity. I think I can say that throughout my twenty-two-year career I, too, have been singing to full houses in the greatest theatres in the world.'

It was interesting to learn that Aragall consciously modelled his career on Kraus, because the two tenors have several characteristics in common:

both sing a limited number of performances, usually a maximum of fifty to fifty-five a year, and both share a small repertoire consisting of about twenty roles which range from *bel canto* parts to some of the lighter Verdi roles. But Aragall's voice has a richer, more luscious timbre and is rounder, 'grainier' and more dramatic than that of Kraus, which is smooth, beautifully modulated yet slightly dry. This has made it possible for him to sing with distinction some of the heavier Verdi parts, like the title role in *Don Carlos* and Riccardo in *Un ballo in maschera* as well as verismo roles like Rodolfo in *La Bohème* and Cavaradossi in *Tosca*, which lie beyond Kraus's vocal means.

Aragall is conscious of the fact that, with a voice like his and top notes which, in the words of Placido Domingo, 'are always there, clear as a bell', he could have had a wider and possibly more adventurous repertoire. 'But I am too severe with myself and not very confident. No role is easy for me. Everything is difficult. I have to be ninety-nine percent sure I can do a role justice before I attempt to sing it.' This insecurity and lack of self-confidence, which are typical of him, are his principal weaknesses as an artist. Unlike Alfredo Kraus, who has found a way of never showing any obvious sign of nerves, Aragall has still not managed to master this weakness of his fully. When he appears in well-rehearsed productions with congenial colleagues and conductors, he excels. But when, for whatever reason, justifiable or not, he feels insecure he can deliver uneven performances even of roles he may have sung with distinction a hundred times in the past.

Of course, as Sir John Tooley points out, some artists are better than others at mastering their nerves. The great Franco Corelli, for instance, never managed to do so at all, even in his heyday. Indeed the toll of living in this constant state of tension and apprehension became too much and caused him to retire prematurely with his voice still intact. 'I have always been afraid,' confided Corelli to *Newsweek* in 1976, offering a rare glimpse of the strain of a top-flight international career. 'I wasn't born to be a singer. In the beginning I didn't have the high C so I was afraid. Then I did have the B and the C but was afraid I would lose them. Sometimes I get up in the morning and the voice doesn't answer. If I'm on holiday and not singing I worry if it's still there. I tape every performance. I then spend three hours listening to the tapes. I am exhausted. I need rest but I can't sleep. If the performance was good I can't sleep for joy. If not, I cannot sleep for despair. What is this life? It is the life of a prisoner, in a hotel room, in front of the television or playing solitaire. I was born free, you know, fifty meters from the sea, in Ancona.'

The nervous strain is even greater when, as in Aragall's case, a singer begins his career right at the top, at La Scala, before he has had time to mature emotionally and come to terms with the pressures and demands it imposes on his nerves. And although Aragall admits that 'my worst enemy is my nerves', his immense dedication to his art has enabled him to overcome them sufficiently for him to continue his career with considerable success.

Apart from his, perhaps excessive, conscientiousness and rigorous perfectionism, 'he is an artist who always wants to give of his best', according to Sir John Tooley. Another reason why Aragall's repertoire remained as limited as it has is lack of imagination on the part of the various opera houses who keep asking him to sing the same roles over and over again. Having now tackled Riccardo successfully, Aragall would one day like to sing Alvaro in *La forza del destino*, Des Grieux in *Manon Lescaut* and especially, one day, the title role in *Andrea Chénier*. When the French magazine *Opéra International* pointed out that, with a top as easy as his, it was strange he shouldn't have attempted to sing Manrico in *Il trovatore*, he replied that he was scheduled to do so at Karajan's 1977 Salzburg Festival production, and went through the rehearsals successfully. But a severe cold – which, he fears, may have been mistaken for cold feet – compelled him to cancel before the opening night.

He would still like to have the opportunity to sing Manrico one day. But although he doesn't really need to transpose the very exposed high C at the end of the famous aria 'Di quella pira' down half a semitone, he says that he will probably do so, because 'I would then feel more secure. If I sang it in the original tessitura I would spend the whole evening worrying about the high C and thus ruin my entire performance' (the reason why he now also transposes the high C at the end of 'Che gelida manina' in *La Bohème* down to a B natural). Yet Aragall points out that his perhaps excessive caution and diffidence as far as repertoire is concerned have brought their own rewards in the shape of a voice which, after twenty-two years on stage, retains a fresh and youthful timbre yet is now mature enough for some of the spinto roles.

Perhaps more important than vocal maturity is the psychological maturity which Aragall has attained and which now enables him to cope with the stress and tensions of an international operatic career. As Alfredo Kraus points out in his chapter, this psychological maturity is as essential to a singer as his vocal and purely artistic equipment – which is why it is often preferable for careers to begin slowly and gather momentum gradually, thus allowing young singers to mellow both as artists and human beings. Aragall's career began early and developed very fast. Although at the time he found the hurly-burly of operatic life exciting, this left him little time to adjust to the loneliness, insecurity, pressures and sacrifices that are part and parcel of such a life.

In his case those sacrifices were greater than usual because he was born into a very poor family who sometimes scarcely had enough to eat. His father had 'an extraordinary' tenor voice and had begun to study music. But after the Civil War, he found himself unable to continue his studies and was forced to earn a living as a middleman in the fish market in Barcelona. Yet, despite these difficult circumstances, Aragall remembers his father always singing. 'He sang all day long and I can still hear the sound of his beautiful tenor voice in my mind.'

As a child, Aragall sang in the children's choir of his local church and took elementary music lessons from a young piano student who was a family friend and who felt sure his pupil had a good tenor voice. He decided to take him along to audition for Professor Jaime Francisco Puig, a highly respected voice teacher who later also taught José Carreras.* Professor Puig's verdict was that Aragall, who was eighteen at the time, possessed a small voice of particularly beautiful quality. Knowing him to be very badly off, he offered to take him on as a pupil *gratis* and immediately set about the task of building Aragall's voice through a series of vocal exercises. After a year it had developed sufficiently for him to contemplate a professional career as an operatic tenor and, on completing his military service, he decided to take Bruno Prevedi's advice and continue his studies in Milan, with Professor Vladimiro Badiali.

This was 1963 and, armed with blind faith and little else, Aragall arrived in Milan by train on a freezing January night, in the middle of a snowstorm, with virtually no money and nowhere to stay. He had struck up an acquaintance with an Italian family on the train, and they took pity on him and drove him to a church near the station, where the priest was a friend. He agreed to help by allowing the penniless young voice student to sleep in a corner of the presbytery for a fortnight. He also fed him once a day and Aragall remembers feeling so hungry that he 'almost ate the

---

*Aragall remembers being summoned by Professor Puig – in 1965, when he was back in Barcelona between performances at La Scala – to hear 'a young tenor whose voice greatly resembles yours'. Somewhat displeased at the prospect, for he liked to think his was a unique voice, he went along. After hearing the young tenor, whose name was José-Maria Carreras, he had to admit that their voices were, indeed, similar in many ways. In recent years, though, Carreras's voice has grown darker than Aragall's, probably because he has been singing a heavier and more varied repertoire. Aragall remains a great admirer of Carreras and found himself completely carried away by the latter's 'grandiose' performance of the title role in *Andrea Chénier*.

plate as well'. Meanwhile, he located some Spanish friends who, in turn, found him cheap lodgings with a Milanese family.

He also managed to contact Professor Badiali, who recognized and confirmed the young tenor's exceptional potential and agreed to teach him for a pittance. (The money was provided by Aragall's two brothers in Barcelona.) His faith was not misplaced: within six months Aragall won first prize at the world-famous 'Voci Verdiane' singing competition at Busseto and within less than a year he made his debut at La Scala, which was followed by performances of *La Bohème, L'amico Fritz* and Hindemith's *Cardillac*. Thus, nine months after his dramatic arrival in Milan as a penniless student, Aragall had embarked on a fully fledged international career. Granted his extreme youth and financial predicament, it is even more remarkable that he should have resisted the temptation to do too much and to embark on the wrong repertoire. Fortunately, he was sensible and realistic about his vocal potential: 'Youth is a physical, biological reality that has everything to do with the timbre, weight and colour of the voice. At the time, my voice was light and ideal for *bel canto* roles like Edgardo in *Lucia*, Fernando in *La favorita* and the Bellini Romeo plus some of the lighter Verdi roles like Alfredo and the Duke of Mantua. Slowly and gradually it developed to a point when, a decade later, I could take on heavier roles like Don Carlos and Cavaradossi for which my voice had previously lacked the necessary weight.'

Although a long and difficult role that contains no arias of the rabble-rousing kind, Don Carlos is a favourite and, vocally, a comfortable role for him. Aragall is not in favour of performing the uncut version – even though vocally this makes little difference to the tenor, apart from changing the placement of his aria slightly and giving him an extra duet – because 'it makes a long opera even longer and tiring for both singers and public. From the vocal point of view Act I, which contains Don Carlos's only aria, situated uncomfortably near the beginning of the opera, is the hardest and Act IV, which is wholly lyrical, the easiest. After his aria in Act I, the tenor has to compete with four principals – the Queen, Princess Eboli, Rodrigo and King Philip II – who all have wonderful, "bravura" arias designed to ensure instant success, in terms of which Don Carlos is an unrewarding role for the tenor. Its reward lies in Verdi's score, one of the most beautiful he ever wrote, through which Don Carlos emerges as a noble and endearing character. The historical Don Carlos was quite different – a hunchback, an epileptic and not quite right in the head. Fortunately, my task is to interpret Verdi's. And the first time this character ever came alive for me was when I heard Placido Domingo singing it.* He found things in it I had never heard before.' Don Carlos is now one of Aragall's most successful roles. He first sang it at the onset of his 'mature' period, and has since taken it to most great theatres in the world.

'But there are two sides to every coin. For as my voice grew bigger, it lost some of its lightness and agility in the upper register and suddenly, I found that singing the Duke of Mantua was not all that easy anymore. After singing more than three hundred performances of this role, it was becoming more difficult, as a result of the natural vocal development that comes with the years. Of course, the Duke of Mantua is a "young" role par excellence and most tenors who sing it with distinction in their youth and early prime tend to abandon it as soon as their voices grow bigger and darker.' (Not Alfredo Kraus, however.)

Aragall first sang the Duke of Mantua in Verona in 1965 and it soon became his calling card. He sang it at Covent Garden in 1966 and subsequently at the Metropolitan and the Vienna State Opera. In fact for a long time he says he was asked to sing little else besides this role! (This is understandable when one considers the chronic shortage of tenors capable of doing it full justice.) Aragall's view of the Duke is that, from the dramatic point of view, it is an uninteresting role because 'In *Rigoletto* the dramatic weight undoubtedly rests on the baritone's shoulders. The tenor's sole task is to stand there and sing supremely well! This is not as easy as it might seem. For although the Duke's music sounds debonair and carefree it is extremely difficult to sing, contains plenty of high notes – B flats and B naturals – and is written largely in the *passaggio* zone. In fact it is so full of pit falls that it would be true to say that I have neither heard nor myself delivered a perfect performance of this role. Something is always bound to go wrong somewhere!'

As usual Aragall was being over-modest for he *has* delivered excellent performances of this role. From his point of view, the easiest of its four acts is Act I. (Pavarotti, on the other hand, considers the Duke's Act I duettino with the Countess of Ceprano, 'Partite crudele', to be one of the trickiest spots in the opera.) For him the real difficulties begin in Act II, where the tenor has to sing a duet with Gilda that demands 'the same quality of legato that you have to give to *bel canto* roles plus several high notes'. Act III contains the aria 'Parmi veder le lagrime' which all tenors I

*Domingo and Aragall are close friends and the latter was present, together with Domingo's father, at the former's Metropolitan Opera debut, when he was summoned from the City Opera across the road to substitute for Franco Corelli, who happens to be Aragall's ideal tenor, 'magnificent, grandiose, titanic!'

have spoken to consider one of the most difficult in the entire tenor repertoire. 'It must be sung absolutely perfectly,' says Aragall, stressing the point also made by Carlo Bergonzi. 'The slightest flaw sticks out a mile. Yet getting it right is exceedingly hard, because it contains some typically Verdian sustained *andantes* which *must* sound flawless yet cannot be properly supported from the diaphragm. And in Act IV you have the well-known aria, "La donna è mobile" which contains a B flat and, in its second repeat, a B natural. As soon as you have finished that you have to sing the quartet "Bella figlia dell'amore" which, although admittedly beautiful, is nevertheless a very hard sing: consistently high, containing several *passaggio* notes and culminating in a B flat, all at the end of a very tiring evening where the tenor doesn't get even a short respite.'

Aragall hasn't sung this role on stage since 1978. Yet when he recorded it, in 1984, for Ariola (with Bernd Weikl as Rigoletto and Lucia Popp as Gilda), much to his surprise, the vocal problems he had anticipated failed to materialize! Although he now sings it with a bigger and somewhat 'shorter' voice, all those B flats and B naturals were there, effortlessly. He also succeeded in singing them with the same colour as the rest of the music, which gave him great satisfaction because he considers it especially important for the voice not to change colour at the top of the register. In addition, as he explained to *Opéra International*, the success of the Ariola engineers' effort to capture the quality of his voice deeply gratified him. He felt that all previous commercial recordings distorted his sound by endowing it with a 'faraway' quality whereas pirate discs mysteriously managed to convey his vocal colour accurately. His future plans therefore include two further recordings with Ariola: a recital record comprising one side of French and one of Italian arias and a recording of *Un ballo in maschera*.

The role of Riccardo – or Gustavus III, depending on which setting of the opera is used – in *Un ballo in maschera*, which contains several famous arias and duets, is one of the most beautiful in the tenor repertoire, as well as being 'difficult from start to finish', and certainly *the* most demanding in Aragall's. 'It is written for a lyric tenor with a certain volume, long breath and a capacity for sustained legato. I don't have particularly long breath and consequently find the sustaining of certain tessituras particularly arduous. It is true that my top notes are always accurate as far as position is concerned. But I suffer from low blood pressure and my build is not of the hefty barrel-chested kind. Consequently I sometimes lack stamina, tire easily and fail to sustain certain notes and certain tessituras properly. Riccardo's tessitura, which is consistently high and written largely on the *passaggio*, is a case in point: hard to sustain and, after you have succeeded in doing so for some time, it becomes especially difficult to climb up to the top notes. (For I am sure you know that the relative ease or difficulty of high notes depends on how you have to approach them. Approaching them after singing in the *passaggio* zone for some time is hard.) But despite its considerable difficulties, I always enjoy singing Riccardo's beautiful music, with its showcase arias. From the dramatic point of view, though, I cannot say that I warm to his character.'

Aragall's favourite role is Cavaradossi and he says that if one were to wake him up and ask him to sing his favourite aria first thing in the morning, it would be 'Recondita armonia', from Act I of *Tosca*. The reason he finds this role so satisfying both vocally and dramatically is because 'it is marvellous for a singer to have to portray a painter and a revolutionary to boot. All tenors love Cavaradossi' (with the exception of José Carreras, who sings the role marvellously yet finds it dramatically unrewarding), 'who is *simpatico* and never fails to make an impact on the public. From the moment he walks on stage with his brush and easel, the public are on his side. And if he sings "Recondita armonia" well, he has already won ninety per cent of the battle. I must say that although I find the beginning of *any* opera – breaking the ice – difficult, I confront the beginning of *Tosca* with something approaching serenity.'

Yet he points out that although singing 'Recondita armonia' beautifully is more than half the battle, there is still the rest of the opera to be got through, especially Act III, which contains 'music so well-known and loved, so beautiful and emotion-packed that you risk becoming so wrapped up and carried away by its emotion that you lose part of your vocal control. "E lucevan le stelle", for instance, always brings tears to my eyes, as do certain passages in *La Bohème*, the opera which, I feel, is closest to my own life. ... But this is dangerous because although "E lucevan le stelle" does not contain any tightrope high notes, it is written in a more delicate way than "Recondita armonia" that requires extremely precise and subtle breath control.'

Aragall disagrees with those who consider Puccini dangerous for the voice. 'He is such a great genius that all you have to do is follow his instructions as faithfully as possible.' And despite some difficult moments in *Tosca* – the phrase 'la vita mi costasse, lo salvero', for instance, which demands a lot of voice – the role is generally so well-written that, in Aragall's opinion, a tenor who cannot sing Cavaradossi well has to be ill! He himself sings it superbly, with ease, deep feeling and utmost vocal beauty. It is, in fact, as Sir John Tooley confirms, one of his best roles and his recent recording of it under Sir Georg Solti (with Kiri Te Kanawa as Tosca) is therefore eagerly awaited.★

The other reason Aragall disagrees with the view that Puccini's loud and dense orchestrations constitute a danger for the voice is that, on the contrary, their substance and volume helps support and blend it with the whole, whereas 'thin' orchestrations can leave singers feeling very exposed. As an example he cites the title role of *Werther*, which he considers 'the Otello of the French repertoire, full of manifold difficulties, both musical and dramatic. Even Alfredo Kraus, who sings everything with consummate ease, admits that Werther is not easy! From the dramatic point of view, it takes a lot out of you, because you have to bear the weight of a character who carries death inside him. Musically, you have just the problem I referred to, of never being properly *accompanied* by the orchestra, in the true sense of the word. A lot of the time – during several monologues and phrases – they are playing something different from what you are singing while at other times, which include most of Act I, you have to sing rhythmically difficult music to a very thin orchestral accompaniment, sometimes consisting merely of a couple of violins. Even Werther's "Hymn to nature", after his first appearance, is very exposed indeed and it is not until the end of the Act, where he sings "Charlotte je vous aime" that you are finally accompanied by a full and loud orchestra and can give all the volume you're capable of. Until then, Act I is lyrical and should be sung with a light voice.'

For Aragall's particular voice, the most difficult of all four acts is Act II, with a tessitura written for a high tenor with a good top and particularly hard to sustain for reasons similar to the ones he referred to apropos Riccardo in *Un ballo in maschera*. Vocally, the ideal acts for him are III and IV. But they, in turn, present him with a different kind of problem. How to maintain full vocal control and contain his emotion vis à vis the drama, 'which is so strong and the music, which is unbearably poignant. In Act III Werther has first a recitative, then a wonderful, heart breaking aria, "O souffle du printemps", followed by an even more poignant and tragic duet which never fails to bring me to the verge of tears and make my heart pound. I have this image, fixed forever in my mind, of Werther walking out of the French window to his death and although I try

---

*Aragall says that one of the greatest joys of this recording was the opportunity to work with Sir Georg Solti, 'the kindest and most generous conductor I have ever come across, with a heart even greater than his prodigious energy. He *really* cares about singers and takes the time to nurture, protect and help us. I am sad I had to wait twenty-two years before working with someone like this!'

desperately hard to control myself at this point, I just cannot. . . . I know singers should find the right balance between involvement and detachment and distance themselves slightly from the role in order to maintain full control over both their vocal production and the pace of their performance. But I confess that I still haven't learnt to do this to a satisfactory degree.' Yet Aragall's deeply felt commitment to the roles he sings is what makes his performances so convincing. He is neither a remarkable nor an indifferent actor, from the purely scenic point of view. His greatest qualities as a singer are the natural beauty of his voice and his wholehearted emotional response to the roles he portrays. Of Act IV of *Werther* he remarked that 'as it depicts a dying man, it should be sung rather softly, but with great feeling and perfect enunciation'.

Aragall's French repertoire, which in earlier years also included the Massenet Des Grieux, 'an ideal role for a young tenor with a light voice and an easy top', now consists, in addition to Werther, of Roméo and Faust. The latter has always been considered one of his best interpretations and he feels it is still getting better every time he sings it. He points out that it takes time to absorb and master all the subtle nuances as well as the elegance and lightness of touch demanded by the French style of singing. It is impossible for a tenor used to singing Italian opera to absorb this style right away. Aragall understood a great deal about French singing when he sang Faust under Georges Prêtre, 'a wonderful conductor for French opera, whose extraordinary *rubato* keeps you constantly on your toes'.

'Faust should be sung in a very elegant, typically French way, with great elegance, sinuous *legati* and without *ever* pushing the voice. From the vocal point of view, one of the trickiest moments occurs in the very dramatic last-act trio between Faust, Marguerite and Mephistopheles, where the ensemble is very high and one note follows another in rapid succession without any suitable gaps for breathing.' Unlike Kraus, who uses a different vocal colour for the old Faust of the prologue, Aragall indicates the switch from the old to the young Faust through scenic means: posture, gestures, movements. Indeed, so successful is he in conveying the difference between the two Fausts that a friend who once attended a performance enquired who the tenor singing the old Faust had been and took some convincing before he believed Aragall had sung both the old and the young Faust.

As far as the dramatic content of the work is concerned Aragall says that although he has read Goethe's text three or four times, he still finds it mystifying, but is fascinated by 'this wrinkled old man who still has enough of the Devil in him to want to be young again! If only that were possible', he sighs. 'Everyone would want to do it, even if it meant making the same mistakes that Faust made. It would all be worthwhile, if one could have one's youth back. You say I am in my prime and that life is at its most interesting for a man in his forties. But it was equally interesting for a man in his twenties! The problem with life is that it simply goes by too fast. Five, ten, fifteen years go by without one realizing it.... Still, I am content with my life and especially with my work, which I love passionately. I couldn't conceive of life without, or away from, the theatre. I *need* the theatre at the moment and cannot function without it. Last year, for instance, I took a short, two-week holiday with my family, which we spent near Verona. Although I was delighted to be with them, I found myself getting bored after a few days. Something was missing: the excitement, tumult, the wracking tensions and moments of exultation that make up our world of opera.'

A few years ago, Aragall went through a stage when he could no longer bear life as an opera singer, perpetually living out of a suitcase, in new surroundings, different hotel rooms, always away from his family. This disenchantment, coupled with the considerable strain his constant stage fright and self-doubts impose on his nervous system, brought about a nervous breakdown, which he calls 'the disease of the century. We artists, with our ultra-sensitive nervous systems, are particularly prone unless we have learnt to develop strong, in-built defence systems. I stopped working for a while and took a deep rest. [He recovered completely, and resumed his career with added zest.] Fortunately, one changes and matures during the course of one's life, and now I see things in a different perspective. I feel well again and, thank God, everything I do at present seems to turn out well.'

Francisco Araiza

'Good heavens, he sings as if he had no idea how difficult it is!' exclaimed the Principal Flute of the Berlin Philharmonic Orchestra as soon as Francisco Araiza began Tamino's 'Portrait Aria' 'Dies Bildnis' at the sessions for the Deutsche Grammophon recording of *Die Zauberflöte* under Karajan. It was a compliment that delighted the young Mexican 'heroic-sounding lyric tenor', now one of the foremost lyric tenors of our day. ('One of the most significant Mozart voices there has ever been', confirmed Sir John Tooley, General Director of the Royal Opera House, Covent Garden. 'The best Mozart tenor in the world', enthused *The Times*.) For he had, by then, reached the stage of feeling so completely in command of the Mozart style of singing and of the technique needed to achieve the absolute, crystalline perfection it demands, that he could simply let the part sing for him. 'Which meant that I had come full circle,' he explained.

For Tamino, along with Ferrando in *Così fan tutte*, had been one of the first Mozart roles Araiza ever studied as a masterclass student with Richard Holm in Munich and performed in public at the Karlsruhe Staatstheater in 1975. He recalls that, at the time, his experience of both roles had been 'that of a young singer who has a technique but doesn't need it. Everything happened naturally, every note was in the right place, seemingly by itself.' But as he began to merge into the life of a repertory theatre where he often had to sing three times a week and sandwich his Mozart parts between other roles, he realized the enormous responsibility entailed in being a Mozart singer.

'Singing Mozart means using your voice as a musical instrument: with the evenness of colour, the exactitude in every range, the similarity of every note evident in ordinary musical instruments which attack notes directly and have the same colour throughout the scale. This instrumental use of the human voice is unique to Mozart and different from Bach's which doesn't demand *quite* the same degree of perfection. In this sense the composer nearest to Mozart is Verdi, who demands greater vocal purity

14

and precision than all the other Italian composers. But you can sing Verdi
with three different colours and always rescue yourself out of a tight spot
with a *portamento* or a gasp – neither of which are allowed in Mozart. So,
Mozart singers have to be even more careful, look after their voices even
more diligently than Italian singers, and try to have adequate rest before
tackling Mozart roles.'

But after a while, Araiza discovered that by being *over*-careful and
singing almost exclusively Mozart, his interpretations risked becoming
too 'safe and sterile'. In fact Sir John Tooley, who happened to hear him
at the time, was 'struck by the beauty of his light lyric tenor voice but
thought there was such a passive quality about it that it was uninteresting'.
In addition, Araiza became afraid that, by singing almost only Mozart, he
might lose his top notes. For, with the exception of the tenor version of
Idamante in *Idomeneo*, which contains two high Cs, Mozart doesn't take
the tenor voice any higher than an A. His solution was to begin singing
some Italian roles like Nemorino in *L'elisir d' amore* which allowed him
'to breathe and open up the voice a bit'. And much to his surprise and
despite his initial apprehension, the experience of 'something different'
proved highly beneficial to his singing of his Mozart roles, which he now
approached with new insights and in which he discovered a host of detail
that could be tackled differently, phrases that could be sung more fully
and not *quite* as instrumentally as he had been singing them before.
'Because,' he explains, 'every Mozart role should first be put into a tight
corset, squeezed as much as possible and then opened up and filled out.
But I only realized this after singing my first Verdi *Requiem*. I had felt
nervous about returning to a Mozart role after a week of letting my voice
out a bit. But to my astonishment, everything happened with the same
naturalness I had known in my first Taminos and Ferrandos. It's funny
that you should have to come full circle before arriving at the same result.
But the difference is that by the time I came to record Tamino, I knew
how to *fabricate* this feeling, this product that used to come so naturally
and effortlessly. Before, it had been spontaneous. Now, it was conscious.'
Sir John Tooley was quick to notice this difference when he next heard
Araiza sing, and was highly impressed 'by this voice of tremendous quality,
a truly beautiful instrument which he used, and uses, with great artistry'.

Araiza is a highly musical and intelligent singer with an engaging stage
presence (like baritone Thomas Allen, he has the knack of getting the
audience on his side whatever role he happens to be singing), excellent
acting ability and a serious and analytical approach to the craft concealed
within the art of singing. While studying, he marks his scores extensively

by entering the breathings, noting where his break is and which notes he has to 'cover'. After he has found it necessary to 'cover' a note once, he will always try to do so, 'because it means that for *my* voice, this is the right way to tackle this particular note'. Then he plays the score through on the piano before starting to work with a professional coach, and prefers not to listen to recordings just before learning a role. 'I prefer to come to it fresh.' Luckily, he has a gift for easy and rapid memorization and travels around with masses of scores which he reads, even for relaxation, instead of books. And once he has finished his technical preparation and knows exactly what and where the difficulties of the role are, he concentrates on interpretation and 'lets the part sing' for him.

And so it was with Tamino, 'one of Mozart's strongest parts, a hero'. But the heroic element in Tamino's character, the fact that it is not really a lyric, but more of a heroic, part constitutes one of its main difficulties. For, even though Tamino may be a hero, he is still a Mozart character and cannot be sung like a Siegmund. The heroic side of his nature must be expressed within the exigencies of the Mozart style, which is not easy. The second major vocal problem in this role is the 'Portrait Aria' which is not really an aria but more of a 'sung recitative' and shouldn't therefore be sung as an aria. Yet it has come to be known as an aria over the years and to demand a line and melody that, strictly speaking, don't belong to it. The tenor must therefore find the correct balance between the two.

He considers the *Sprecherszene* (scene with the Speaker), which lasts about twelve minutes and encapsulates all the shapes of phrase contained in the whole opera, to be the neuralgic point of the work. This scene should therefore be developed to its full dramatic potential and treated as a real dialogue rather than a scrap of conversation, which would spell instant sterility and boredom. But if the singers concerned succeed in injecting real drama into it, it becomes a powerful conflict of generations with all that this implies: the younger generation's refusal to accept the values of the old unquestioningly. And in this sense the interpretational problems facing the tenor singing Tamino are even greater than the vocal difficulties. For there are two different ways of viewing both the role and the opera as a whole. One is a naturalistic approach epitomized by August Everding's Munich production, which happens to be Araiza's favourite. 'A production full of life from the first moment, with real fright, real surprise, real anger, and in which Tamino is portrayed as a young man emerging from puberty to adulthood with all the problems inherent in this progress to maturity. Alternatively, both Tamino and the work as a whole can be interpreted in a symbolic way, like a very long marriage ceremony, but for the kind of marriage that has long been programmed.' The real difficulty is to understand Mozart's intentions and reasons for composing the work in this particular way and to grasp what Tamino and all the other symbols stand for. And Araiza admits he has not yet made up his mind about this. Which is why, although he would certainly be prepared to sing in a 'symbolic' production, his own view leans towards the naturalistic approach. Apart from these specific vocal and interpretational difficulties, the role presents no problems either of *tessitura* or of length: it amounts to about forty-five minutes' singing – the same as Belmonte and Idamante.

The longest Mozart tenor role – one full hour's singing in its uncut version – is Ferrando in *Così fan tutte*, a role in which Araiza has always scored big personal successes: in Karlsruhe where he made his debut to notices rhapsodizing 'this wonderful new lyric tenor voice', in Munich, in the now famous Muti/Hampe Salzburg Festival production, recorded live by EMI, and in London. Ferrando is not only the longest, but also one of the more difficult Mozart roles, mainly because it requires two different kinds of tenor voice: a lyric tenor for the first quintet and the first big aria, 'Un' aura amorosa', and a much heavier voice for the second aria, ''Tradito, schernito' (an Italian-type outburst heavy both because of its placing near the end of the opera and its tessitura), and for most of the trios, especially the 'laughing trio', which should be handled with kid gloves. 'For if you are not careful and laugh *too* much, you risk compressing your diaphragm and thus getting a slight tremolo in "Un' aura amorosa", the beautiful, long-breathing aria that immediately follows this trio. In fact this is one of the trickiest spots in all Mozart and one wonders why he chose to place the laughing trio before such an aria.'

Another vocal difficulty is that in *Così fan tutte* the tenor leads in all the ensembles – which is fine if the baritone singing Guglielmo and the bass singing Don Alfonso have fairly light, lyric voices. The tenor is then in for a comfortable sing, can use the opening trio to warm up and maintain a light, springy voice for the rest of the evening. But, if faced with heavier voices, he is in for a hard time because reasons of balance compel him to start *really* working and give out more right from the opening ensemble. And after working hard in *all* the ensembles, he must still be able to sing 'Un' aura amorosa' impeccably. (In fact Araiza was faced with just such a situation in Salzburg where his partners were James Morris as Guglielmo and José Van Dam as Don Alfonso.) So although Ferrando is *always* a difficult role, just *how* difficult depends partly on the rest of the cast.

The easiest and shortest Mozart role – forty minutes' singing – is Don Ottavio in *Don Giovanni*, again a part Araiza has always been successful with, not just for vocal reasons but also because of his unusual dramatic conception, which prompted a German critic to exclaim 'at last, here is a Don Ottavio with balls!' Araiza feels that Ottavio is not the person he pretends – or is made out – to be but a much colder, stronger and more calculating character, a real opportunist out to marry the Commendatore's daughter no matter what. It is the position that matters to him, not her feelings. But as he wants to be acceptable in the eyes of society, he has to discover if Giovanni really raped Anna. He admits that the only snag in the validity of this conception is Ottavio's aria 'Dalla sua pace', which expresses much more sincere feeling. But this was added by Mozart later, after Ottavio's character had been conceived and the rest of his music composed, at the request of a specific tenor. Therefore Araiza's solution is to remove it out of the dramatic context of the role and sing it as a straightforward, beautiful, lyric aria. But despite the fact that this aria is vocally difficult because it consists of big, long phrases with little time between them for recovery, that Ottavio's other aria 'Il mio tesoro' is one of the most difficult in all Mozart, and that the role as a whole demands plenty of physical stamina, it is still a very comfortable part for him.

'The hardest of all Mozart roles is Belmonte in *Die Entführung aus dem Serail* which must be sung one hundred per cent perfectly or else you miss the boat completely. Firstly because Mozart composed it in a special way that allows the orchestra to play parallel to the singer, something he seldom did. Secondly because it has a very high *tessitura* and requires a feathery, springy voice with a lot of agility, especially in Belmonte's second aria, "O, wie ängstlich", which has a lot of coloratura.' But Araiza stresses that this kind of Mozart coloratura is especially difficult to sing in style, because it's different from a Rossini or a Bach coloratura: 'The Mozart coloratura is an instrumental coloratura – in fact hardly a coloratura at all, but a sort of spinning line, yet with every note clearly articulated. It is also much more *legato* than a Rossini coloratura, which has to be more supported and have its notes just a bit more separated, like the beads of a rosary.' (A splendid example of what he means is his outstanding performance as Almaviva in the Philips recording of *Il barbiere di Siviglia* which, according to Harold Rosenthal, Editor of *Opera*, 'outshines the recorded performances by Cesare Valletti and Ugo Benelli on earlier sets'.) 'Thirdly because Belmonte has to begin with this murderous aria, "Hier soll ich dich denn sehen" the very moment he goes on stage, with no chance to warm up' (something all singers hate to have to do).

Araiza finds the interpretative side of this role equally problematic and has not yet settled on a definitive way of portraying Belmonte convincingly: he can be viewed either as a young lover, a young hero who tries his best, but fails, to rescue his beloved, is captured and ends up a broken figure in a finale which is 'pure vaudeville with moral implications'. But at least he is prepared to die, which brings a touch of greatness to all this vaudeville. Or he can be portrayed as a Spanish nobleman who does not behave in a very noble way, who goes to rescue Constanze but immediately proceeds to hurt her by doubting her fidelity before trying to rape and kidnap her – not the noblest way of rescuing anybody – and then 'cuts a bad figure' by getting himself captured. 'In either case he is a loser and I don't much care for him. It's curious but true that Mozart always tried to insert a flaw into his characters. No Mozart character – apart from Idamante – is flawless. And as he is the greatest of all musical geniuses and can presumably see deeper into human nature than any other composer, perhaps he is trying to say that perfection is not part of the human condition and that we must accept and love ourselves as we are.'

Mozart's single flawless character, Idamante in *Idomeneo*, is Araiza's special favourite among the roles in this repertoire. 'It is a lyrical yet, at the same time, a dramatic role portraying a highly idealistic character, a role into which you can pour *everything*! Sometimes a singer finds a role that seems to fit him perfectly and with which he can identify totally and wholeheartedly. And the one for me is Idamante, although I have only sung the part four times – once in a concert performance in 1977, and three times during the Munich Mozart Bicentennial Festival. It's strange, but in this opera Mozart composed music years ahead of his time and conceived a different kind of drama, akin to what Verdi was to do later.'

Vocally, Idamante is a very difficult part – the widest Mozart role from the point of view of *tessitura*, which spans over two octaves of register and includes two high Cs. At the other end of the scale, the fact that it was originally composed for mezzo-soprano and only later adapted for tenor, means that it is quite low. And all its heroic cadenzas and arias crowned by high Bs – 'from which you then have to climb down on a dominant and a tonic, usually in E flat major' – demand an almost 'Italian' singing technique and the ability to sing very wide phrases.

Araiza claims that his exceptional musical understanding, technical knowledge and mastery of the Mozart style, and super-analytical approach to roles stem from an effort to compensate for the fact that, by nature, his voice is not one hundred per cent ideally suited for Mozart, whose music – with the exception of Idamante's – fits one and a half octaves perfectly.

'But the centre, the balance point, of this range lies one and a half semitones too high for my voice, which is heavier and therefore tends to "pull" downwards in the same way that Fritz Wunderlich's used to. Which means that voices like ours have to work extra hard to sustain an even line in Mozart and that, to sing his music perfectly, we have to know three times as much, both musically and technically, as a "natural" Mozart tenor.'

In fact Araiza was quite astonished to find himself being classified as a Mozart tenor to begin with. It happened when he first arrived in Europe in 1974, aged twenty-three, to participate in the ARD (German Television Channel One) Singing Competition in Munich. Until then, he had specialized mainly in the Italian *spinto* repertoire, and having already sung Rodolfo and the Massenet Des Grieux, was in the process of learning Calaf, Florestan and Andrea Chénier, extracts of which he had prepared for the competition, along with some Verdi and Puccini arias. The only Mozart he had sung to date was one of Tamino's arias, prepared for his first audition and 'Un' aura amorosa', planned for a later stage in the competition, which explains why his Mozart style was not yet pure enough and why, although the jury (which included such famous past Mozart singers as Anton Dermota and Richard Holm) immediately recognized his potential as a Mozart singer, he ended up with third prize.

As Araiza observed with surprise when recently hearing some tapes dating back to those days, his voice was much heavier at the time. It still leant heavily towards the Italian repertoire. He has since reduced it further, to its present level, which he feels is just about right: light and lyrical enough for Mozart, yet full-bodied enough to be comfortable in his Italian roles, which include Rossini parts like Almaviva in *Il barbiere di Siviglia*, Don Ramiro in *La Cenerentola* and Idreno in *Semiramide*; *bel canto* roles like Nemorino in Donizetti's *L'elisir d' amore* and Ernesto in *Don Pasquale*, Arturo in Bellini's *I puritani* and Elvino in *La sonnambula*; Verdi roles like Fenton in *Falstaff* and Zamoro in *Alzira*; Rodolfo in Puccini's *La Bohème*, and a great many Monteverdi roles. His only French roles to date are Des Grieux in Massenet's *Manon* and the title role in *Faust*, and the German repertoire is represented by the title role in Handel's *Saul* and the Steuermann in Wagner's *Der fliegende Holländer*. Plans for the immediate future included Alfredo in *La traviata* and the Duke in *Rigoletto*; towards the end of the eighties he would like to try the title role in *Don Carlos* and more French roles like Werther, a particular dream of his for which his voice would seem ideally suited, and Roméo. And the heroic undertones in his voice may make it feasible for him to expand further into the German repertoire – Loge, Walther von Stolzing, Florestan and Max in *Der Freischütz* – in the nineties, 'which explains why I feel it would be out of the question to reduce my voice any further'. As his mention of a conscious and systematic 'reduction' is a particularly interesting aspect of voice-building, I asked him to explain the procedure step by step and to trace his vocal development from his student days to the present.

Araiza expressed no interest in studying music until his mid-teens, although his father, himself a tenor 'with a voice similar but much more beautiful than mine', taught him how to read music and play the piano at an early age, and took him to Sunday matinees at the Mexico Opera, where he was Chorus Master in the golden days when Callas and Del Monaco were annual visitors. His father, who could have had an international career had he not felt obliged to support his widowed mother, was instrumental in guiding his son towards the career he himself never had. He had a theory that too much free time is bad for teenagers and only leads them to mischief, and, as school only took up half a day, he always ensured that his sons had plenty of extra-curricular interests and studies. In 1966, when Francisco was fifteen and had already been studying English for some time, he was offered the choice of three spare-time activities: more English, computer studies or music. He opted for music and enrolled in the organ class of the Escuela de Musica, where he was also required to attend a secondary class. As the cello class was full, the cello being an especially popular instrument, he chose first the drums, then the flute and lastly the violin. And only after he had exhausted all other possibilities and the cello class was still full, did he finally and reluctantly join a singing class. The chorus master of the school choir, in which Araiza sang at the time as a bass (!) – 'and I could *really* reach the lowest of low notes' – and several other people had been urging him to study singing for some time. But he neither liked singing, nor was he interested in being a singer. Indeed, he says that, but for this chance requirement in the school curriculum, he might never have taken it up. Yet the experience of so many different musical instruments may partly account for his unusual musicality.

At the time, he wasn't even sure what kind of voice he had and approached his first teacher thinking he might be a bass-baritone or maybe just a baritone 'with a good bottom'. However, when the teacher sat at the piano and began taking him up the scale, he found that Araiza could reach up to the high B flat. Enthused, he got up and embraced his pupil declaring that he was 'a dramatic tenor in embryo!'. He asked him to prepare some arias from *Fedora* and *La fanciulla del West* for his next lesson. Not surprisingly for someone who had never before sung in the tenor register, Araiza had trouble with the high B flat in Dick Johnson's aria from *Fanciulla*. The teacher hastily concluded that he must be 'a short tenor', i.e. a tenor with a short *tessitura*, meaning a not very good top, to which Araiza replied that if, with no technique at all, he could still reach up to the high B flat when vocalizing, a good vocal technique would certainly enable him not only to consolidate this note but to reach up to a high C as well.

But to acquire such a technique meant finding the right teacher, and the dearth of such people is a problem facing most young singers. Araiza's experience with his first teacher demonstrates all too clearly the potential harm that can be caused by inadequate or short-sighted teachers. The problem is even more acute for tenors because 'tenor-singing is an unnatural thing and the tenor range is one of the most unnatural registers of the male human voice' (as his colleague José Carreras also points out). 'Which is why the building-up of a tenor is such an incredibly difficult process and why there are so few teachers with the knowledge, foresight and patience for the task. My father never managed to find such a teacher. I was luckier.'

But before finding Irma Gonzalez, and after his disenchantment with his original teacher, Araiza studied for a while with a professional baritone who was due to leave for Europe, as well as working on repertoire with a coach. He was eighteen at the time and already studying business administration at University. But both the coach and he himself felt he was now ready for a professional recital, which consisted of Schumann's *Dichterliebe* and, at his father's instigation, was attended by Irma Gonzalez, a well known voice teacher from the Conservatoire. Impressed both by his voice and his musicality, she urged him to continue to study singing, and when he told her that his teacher was about to leave and asked her if she would take him on, she readily accepted but pointed out that he would have to leave the Escuela de Musica and enrol as a full-time voice student at the Conservatoire.

During the next six years (1968-74) she guided Araiza from the 'short dramatic tenor' he was supposed to be, to the 'heroic-sounding lyric voice' that was to be instantly recognized as that of a potential Mozart singer in Munich. What he had at the time was a good middle range and few top notes. For, while he could reach up to the high B flat when vocalizing, when singing in full voice and strength he could barely reach an A. So the first task, declared Gonzalez, was to acquire a top, and the only way this could be done was by reducing the middle range by 'putting it into a sort of corset' with special vocal exercises. It was a lengthy process, and for the first two semesters Araiza was desperately unhappy and afraid he might be losing his voice altogether, for he could neither feel any strength in it nor open it wide anymore. But she persisted and kept urging him to trust her, because this was the only way to acquire a top. Once he had, the voice would then start branching off from there, exactly like a tree. The main trunk of the tree, on the other hand, could not be forced and would only develop with time. He trusted her reluctantly but soon found that his trust had not been misplaced.

After the end of the second semester he noticed that, suddenly, he could sustain arias without breaking or getting tired. At the beginning of the third semester, the first thing she asked was whether he had had a good rest. Yes, he replied and she immediately sat at the piano and began to take him up and up and up the scale. 'It was thrilling: all the notes were coming, except the high C.' And when, a few days later, he was in the middle of Faust's 'Salut demeure', and prepared the high C, it didn't come, Gonzalez calmly remarked that she *knew* he had the note but that some kind of inhibition was preventing it from coming out. So, she suggested they try singing the aria together. 'And when it came to the point, I could *feel* myself singing the high C without actually being able to hear it, as she was singing along with me. But suddenly, she stopped, and there I was, in the middle of my high C! I could hear it, and it didn't sound forced, it was good and well-placed and sounding. And to me, acquiring a top was like discovering a new world!'

'Let's do it again, but this time without accordion,' added his teacher. She was referring to Araiza's problem with his prominent Adam's apple, which in those days was apt to move upwards while he was singing thus closing up the pharynx – a big mistake, bound to cause difficulties in breathing. An Adam's apple should either not move at all or, if it does, it should be *downwards*, so that it has the opposite effect, of *opening* up the pharynx. So she taught him special exercises for achieving total control of every muscle – mouth, head, neck, throat – for breathing and resonance. 'Because', explains Araiza, 'you can make your whole body "sound" by creating cavities and then projecting your voice into those cavities.' As always, Gonzalez's method was not to make him repeat something he was doing wrong in the hope that he would once get it right, but to wait until she felt he *could* do it right, repeat it once to make sure he really *had* mastered it, and then leave it. 'And,' Araiza adds, 'there is a solution for every vocal problem that has been correctly diagnosed.'

After acquiring a top and getting rid of the problem caused by his

Adam's apple, it was time for his teacher to begin strenghening and building up his voice, by taking him up and down the scales and through all the vowels, beginning with 'u' which if sung correctly 'leaves your throat muscles in peace and reaches down to the visceral centre. The vowel "e" does just the opposite, reaching up towards the "a"; and I had to learn how to open up to an "a" from the position of the "e".' Irma Gonzalez's method was the work of a very fine trainer who always knew exactly what she was doing and who could discern, right from the beginning, what the end product would be and how best to achieve it.

During his fourth semester as a voice student, in 1970, Araiza – who was also studying some of the German operatic, concert and *Lieder* repertoire with a Viennese teacher resident in Mexico City named Erika Kubacsek – made his operatic debut as the first prisoner at a concert performance of *Fidelio* for Beethoven year. Shortly afterwards, he graduated to singing Jaquino in the same opera, plus the 'Choral Fantasia'. He feels that, in many ways, Beethoven fits his voice better than Mozart and does not fully agree with those who claim that Beethoven didn't really understand the voice.

'Beethoven is not easy to sing, but he is not technically wrong. He heard, in his mind's ear, what his music *could* sound like, granted the necessary technical skills. When compared to Wagner, whose orchestrations are also massive, Beethoven does emerge as a less than accommodating orchestrator. For Wagner allows a singer first to sing a phrase, then to colour it, and only then does he under-line it with orchestra, usually with instrumental combinations that blend well with the voice. But Beethoven expected his singers to be superhuman, and wrote for very advanced people, centuries ahead of his time, and for today's orchestras, which is why his music will always sound better and better, with time. Yet, *if* you can sing him, the kindest composer of all for the voice is Mozart. No one can hurt their voice singing Mozart.'

After Araiza won third prize at the ARD Competition and was classified as a Mozart singer, the jury reached the agreement that he should either return to Mexico and continue training in the Italian repertoire for two whole years before returning to Europe, or stay in Germany and concentrate entirely on Mozart for the time being. He chose to stay, and as the Karlsruhe Staatstheater was in the throes of planning a full Mozart cycle stretching over several seasons, the Director of the competition arranged for Araiza to audition for them. The day after a very successful audition – and 'the art of auditioning, of abstracting themselves from the present situation so as to achieve the result they would on stage, is something all young singers should master' – he was offered a two-year contract with an option for a third. But luckily, the engagement was not due to begin until six months later, the following March, with a new production of *Così fan tutte*, preceded by a five-week rehearsal period and two weeks' prior preparation – which left him six months in which to learn German and perfect his Mozart style. In fact at the time of the competition he had been both fed up and sceptical about 'this Mozart style' everybody seemed to be talking about and enquired who could teach it to him. The answer was, two people only: Anton Dermota and Richard Holm, both of whom were on the jury. The latter agreed to enlist Araiza in his, and also in pianist Erik Werba's, masterclasses at the Munich Hochschule für Musik. And every day for six months they worked on the Mozart style, on acting technique and on thoroughly preparing the first two roles Araiza was to sing in Karlsruhe: Tamino and Ferrando plus the Duke in *Rigoletto*, because Holm rightly judged that his pupil was also ideally suited for the Italian repertoire, and that he should never give it up completely in favour of Mozart.*

The results of these six months were obvious at the premiere of *Così fan tutte* in Karlsruhe, where Araiza was so enthusiastically acclaimed that, while still in costume, he was visited by the Intendant who proceeded to tear up his existing contract and replace it with a new, three-year one at an extra 1,000 marks per annum. During those three professionally fulfilling years Araiza also made his debut, as Don Ottavio, in the Ponnelle production of *Don Giovanni* at the Cologne Opera – his first chance of singing the role in Italian. In 1977 he moved to the Zurich Opernhaus (after getting married to his wife Vivian, a young mezzo-soprano with whom he now has two children) where he spent a frustrating first six months singing roles like Idreno, Arturo and Cassio, 'unrewarding because they are merely difficult technically, but have no scope for dramatic development', before tackling Mozart again. Since 1978 he has had a permanent guest-contract with the Bavarian State Opera in Munich and has also appeared at the Bayreuth and Aix-en-Provence Festivals, the Hamburg Opera, the Houston and the San Francisco Opera, the Deutsche Oper in Berlin, the Chicago Lyric Opera, the Royal Opera House, Covent

---

* This was wise and prophetic advice. For Araiza's performances in Italian roles have been as highly praised as those in Mozart. An example is the reaction of the music critic of *Opera* to his performance of Ernesto in *Don Pasquale* at the Bavarian State Opera in Munich: 'Francisco Araiza with his relaxed Mozart voice moved most purposefully into the Italian style; this was *bel canto* of the most melting kind – particularly in "Com' è gentil". His voice combines polish and fire with warm sensitivity. What more can one ask for?'

Garden, La Scala, the Vienna State Opera and the Metropolitan Opera.

But he feels that the highlights of his career, the experiences that enriched and fulfilled him most as an artist, are the performances he sang under Herbert von Karajan: the recording of *Die Zauberflöte* mentioned earlier, the role of Fenton in both the recording and the Salzburg Summer Festival performances of *Falstaff*, several oratorios, including *Die Schöpfung*, the Mozart *Requiem*, the Bruckner *Te Deum* and the Mozart C Minor Mass at the Salzburg Easter Festival. His first audition for Karajan took place in Berlin, in 1977; but Karajan's serious illness in October 1978 and subsequent postponement of the recording until 1979, plus the fact that by then he was looking for a Fenton as well as a Tamino, meant auditioning for him again, this time in Salzburg: and, not surprisingly, Araiza recalls the occasion vividly:

'After singing Tamino's big aria *pianissimo* – something Karajan is known to enjoy – the Maestro seemed pleased and remarked, "Yes, this is how it has to be".' Araiza later learnt that he whispered to the recording executive sitting beside him that he thought that 'this is him, but let's see'. 'So he asked for Fenton's "Serenade" at the end of which he exclaimed, "Yes, we will do it like this, exactly like this." Then he walked up to me, squeezed my hand and said: "Now, you belong to me. You are a Karajan singer. Don't go signing any exclusive contracts with any of the recording companies because they are all gangsters and will never free you for any project I might be planning with one or the other of them. Being a Karajan singer means you are free and *they* will have to come to you and ask you, everyone will now have to ask *you*." You can imagine my exhilaration! And I put all my energy, everything I had at the time, into this recording. The whole experience was a very special challenge because from the moment Karajan appears to the moment he leaves, it's high voltage, high tension! No one, however famous, is ever totally relaxed in the Maestro's presence and, needless to say, neither was I. And this makes you give more than you are used to, or believe yourself capable of, as anyone who has worked with him will testify.' (José Carreras makes precisely the same point in his chapter.) 'Of course, he doesn't teach you anything purely vocal – for he correctly assumes that by the time you come to work for him, you have the necessary technique – but a great deal about interpretation. And his interpretations are so special that everyone should think of them as models, to be emulated and imitated. I particularly like the recording of *Die Zauberflöte* and the kind of Tamino he and I created together. It's different from any past interpretations of this role. In fact I remember that when I returned to sing it in the last three performances of the Everding production under Sawallisch in Munich after having completed my recording with Karajan, I did all the new things Karajan had just taught me; and I looked down into the pit and saw Sawallisch visibly relishing my "new" interpretation. It was Karajan who had brought it all out of me. And if my career had ended after that recording, I'd still be happy to have been a singer.'

Since then, Araiza has begun a very successful expansion into the Italian lyric repertoire, with Leicester in *Maria Stuarda*, Richard Percy in *Anna Bolena*, Alfredo in *La traviata*, the Duke of Mantua in *Rigoletto* and Rodolfo in *La Bohème*. He sang the title role in *Faust* at the Vienna State Opera, which proved an experience comparable to his recording of *Die Zauberflöte*, and was greatly looking forward to singing the title role in *Les Contes d'Hoffmann* and, most especially, in *Werther* at the San Francisco Opera. He had been dreaming of singing this role for at least six years. 'I've always, always had a special feeling about Werther', so those performances should prove quite a landmark in the career of this musical, intelligent singer.

CARLO BERGONZI

'All students of tenor-singing should, as an obligatory part of their education, listen as often as possible to Alfredo Kraus singing the French repertoire and Carlo Bergonzi singing Verdi', declares London-based laryngologist Dr Ardeshir Khambatta, a connoisseur of the art of singing and a highly critical observer of the international operatic scene. His remark rightly singles out Bergonzi's excellence, indeed uniqueness, as a Verdi interpreter and stylist whom Magda Olivero has called 'a superior vocal civilization' and Jon Vickers labelled 'a miracle'. For although Bergonzi is also a first-class singer of *verismo* and some of the *bel canto* repertoire, it is as a Verdi tenor that he has earned his place among the immortals of the operatic pantheon.

When Bergonzi sings Verdi, one is aware of a fusion between composer and interpreter and an unshakeable conviction that everything about his singing is right: the size, timbre and colours of his voice, the accents, the special way of singing *legato* and of declaiming the words, the proud, noble virility of his Verdian phrasing. 'He only has to open his mouth and sing a single phrase for all the instinctive impulses that bind me to Verdi to spring alive', writes Italian musicologist Rodolfo Celletti, author of *Le grandi voci*, the definitive volume on the great singers of that period and of the past published in 1964.

Bergonzi's flair for creating an instant Verdian atmosphere seems even more remarkable when one considers that, far from being a consummate singing-actor in the Domingo mould, he is rather static on stage. Yet, in his case alone among great singers whose acting is rudimentary, this hardly seems to matter! For unlike Pavarotti, who tends to remain himself no matter what role he is singing, Bergonzi, through the vividness, power and sheer commitment of his vocal characterizations, succeeds in convincing us we are in the presence of whatever character is being portrayed. In short, his interpretations ring true, as colleagues are quick to point out: 'What does it matter what he does, or does not do, on stage when his stupendous *legato* phrases and delectable singing in the *mezza voce* create such an enchanted atmosphere that you instantly find yourself inside the characters and the drama?', confided a mezzo-soprano to Celletti, who adds that Bergonzi brings to his interpretations of all, but especially of Verdi, roles 'a constant inner tension, a spontaneity, a vibrant, broad sound and a knack for an emphasis here or an inflection there, which, although barely perceptible, are such as to create a style of expression genuinely romantic and even more genuinely Verdian'.

Despite his wholehearted identification with Verdi, Bergonzi maintains that this greatest of Italian operatic composers is not kind to tenors! 'Yes, his operas are well-written, yes, he has given us roles with which to score big successes and yes, he ensured that no tenor can be said to have "made it" until he shows what he can do with the great Verdi warhorses like Manrico, Alvaro, the Duke of Mantua, Riccardo or Radames. Yet Verdi has ruined as many tenors as he has made. First, because he forgives nothing, tolerates no imperfections or deviations from his style and is vocally and stylistically the most exacting of all Italian and, after Mozart, of all composers, full stop. Second, because his roles are so well known and loved that the public won't tolerate hearing them badly or unidiomatically sung, either! When they hear the bravura of that wonderful, typically Verdian sound in the orchestra they expect the voice on stage to respond with the right colours! If it doesn't they can get very stroppy, especially in Italy, and make no secret of their disappointment. This has happened to many singers, many of them great artists, whose voices didn't sound "Verdian". For those reasons, I believe a singer has to be *intelligent* to sing Verdi!'

What Bergonzi means is that a tenor who aspires to sing the Verdi repertoire should be an artist astute, resourceful, willing and hard-working enough to acquire the technical awareness and expertise that will enable him to solve, or circumvent, the many problems he will encounter in every Verdi role, from the earliest operas to *Falstaff*, and the sensitivity that will help him pinpoint and master the specific stylistic nuances and inflections that constitute this composer's signature. *Verismo* roles are not as difficult and don't require as perfect a technique, as all tenors point out. 'You need voice, plenty of voice, but then, you need that for everything! But you can indulge in more *portamenti* and are less dependent on purity of line. A singer who sings Verdi well will certainly acquit himself with distinction in *verismo* roles. The opposite is very far from true!'

Bergonzi, whose Verdian phrasing Celletti rightly calls 'the most authentic to be heard in the last forty years – since the days of Pertile – not only among tenors but also among baritones and basses', has sung the entire Verdi lyric and *lirico-spinto* repertoire with equal ease. He has never sung Otello on stage, because he considers it too dramatic for his voice. He explains that the reason he never sang Otello has nothing to do with vocal size and everything to do with vocal colour. 'I just never found the right colours I feel Otello should have. For, to my mind, there has never been a real, "right" Otello since Ramón Vinay. Many singers have sung and still sing Otello admirably. But only Vinay's colour convinced me Otello was the commander he was supposed to be.' But he included Otello's arias in an exemplary recording, for Philips, of thirty-one Verdi tenor arias. This monumental achievement gave him enormous satisfaction and won the *Deutscher Schallplattenpreis* and the *Premio della critica discografica Italiana* in 1976 and the 1977 *Stereo Review* 'Record of the Year' Award in the United States. Still active at sixty-one – his and Kraus's vocal longevity is another valuable lesson for young singers – Bergonzi recorded Verdi's first opera, *Oberto*, in 1984.

Therefore he knows what he is talking about when he stresses that there is no such thing as an easy Verdi role. *All* Verdi roles are difficult, including those in his early operas like *Oberto*, *Attila*, *Il corsaro*, *I masnadieri* and *Ernani*. As one approaches Verdi's middle years, the roles get progressively more difficult, especially Alfredo in *La traviata* and the Duke in *Rigoletto*, which Bergonzi always recommends to young singers, 'because these are operas that actually teach you how to sing!'. Alfredo, which is often dismissed as an unimportant role, probably because it contains no rabble-rousing arias, is, according to Bergonzi, important, both vocally and dramatically.

'Alfredo is *simpatico*, very appealing, much easier to interpret than to sing!' (Kraus, on the other hand, thinks it's very difficult to make something of this character from the dramatic point of view.) 'Precisely *because* it contains no blockbusting aria which, if well sung, would ensure an instant triumph, it is the kind of opera that requires the tenor to sing well the *whole* time, if he is to score a discreet success. The entire performance hinges on the duets and *cabalettas*, all of which should be sung perfectly. If the tenor fluffs a single one, his whole evening will have been wasted and he will have laboured in vain.' (The recent experience of an uneven performance of this role instantly reminded me of Bergonzi's words.) 'Vocally, the role is full of difficulties, written largely on the *passaggio* zone but leaning towards a lyric line, which is much harder than *dramatic* singing in this zone, when you place the sound in the mask and support it from the diaphragm. In Alfredo's case, you still have to do this, but, as he is a very young man, you have to keep the breathing lighter in order to produce a consistently light sound; because, as always, the role is written in a certain way because of the character it depicts, which is the clue to everything. For all those reasons, I always think that a tenor who makes a success of Alfredo is a very good singer.' Bergonzi's superb singing in the RCA recording of this opera – especially in the recitative 'Lunge da lei per me non v'ha diletto' and aria 'De'miei bollenti spiriti' at the beginning of Act II – is rightly singled out by Celletti as a lesson in how to achieve authentic Verdian phrasing through technical expertise: total, meticulous breath control and the judicious 'closing' of the sound in places and 'covering' of certain notes, in fact of all the *passaggio* notes.

The skilful, super-intelligent use and management of his vocal resources, which is a major contributing factor to Bergonzi's greatness as a singer, is very much in evidence in his interpretation of the Duke in *Rigoletto* which, along with Radames in *Aida*, is one of the most difficult roles in the Verdi, indeed the entire tenor, repertoire. All tenors who sing this role – Domingo, Pavarotti, Kraus and Aragall – agree that this is so. But while all of them consider the Duke of Mantua difficult from start to finish, Bergonzi singles out as the main difficulty in this part the aria 'Parmi veder le lagrime' which immediately follows the recitative 'Ella mi fu rapita,' in Act III.

'This aria, which is beyond the reach of most tenors, requires a perfect voice and perfect singing. You have to attack on a G flat – *Par*mi veder le lagrime – a *passaggio* note which should be sung *piano*, as Verdi marked it, but very seldom is, for the simple reason that this is extremely difficult, because both this note and the whole line of the aria are written in G and A flat, i.e. in and around the *passaggio* zone, but should have pulp, substance, as should the last note, a G flat also marked *piano*. Usually they are sung loudly, because very few tenors know how to sing *piano* or even *mezza voce* in the *passaggio* zone.' The ability to do just that and to bring a great variety of colours and nuances into his *piano* and *mezza voce* singing is one of Bergonzi's greatest gifts.

He applies it to excellent effect in his singing of Radames, a *spinto* role bordering on the dramatic, which represents the limits of Bergonzi's vocal possibilities. Yet with his characteristic ability to pinpoint, surmount or circumvent technical difficulties – which, in conversation, sometimes makes him sound more like an expert voice teacher than a singer – he has found solutions to all the problems that abound in this role, which is 'difficult from the first note to the last'.

'Radames is undoubtedly the most difficult of all my Verdi roles, both vocally and musically. In Act I, the moment you walk on stage, you start off with "Celeste Aida" which, along with "Parmi veder le lagrime" in *Rigoletto*, is one of the most difficult arias in all Verdi. You ask why, when there are thirty-two B flats in this role, the one all tenors are nervous about is the one at the end of "Celeste Aida" – the phrase "Un trono vicino al *sol*". The reason is that the aria is written in such a way that you suddenly have to spring up to this B flat, and this sort of leap is always dangerous. The best way to illustrate what I mean is by comparing the tenor to a diver who has to plunge into the sea from a great height. He has a split second to take stock and brace himself and then hop, he dives. Sometimes the plunge is perfect and sometimes the water gets a bit ruffled – exactly like the B flat in "Un trono vicino al *sol*", which sometimes comes out perfectly and sometimes less so.

'But this B flat is by no means the only stumbling block. There are those other thirty-one B flats. Although they are not as difficult as the one at the end of "Celeste Aida", you still have to sing them: those in "Im*men*so Fthà" in Scene 2 of Act I, for instance, or in "Sacerdote, io resto a te" in Act III, by which time you have consumed seventy-five per cent of your energy. Yet this entire act demands a lot of voice and expression, but without ever forcing your voice, always using your natural sound.'

After this challenging act comes Act IV with its two scenes, both of which are difficult in very different ways and, as Bergonzi explains (and Carreras also points out in his chapter), require two different kinds of voice: 'Scene 1, Radames's highly dramatic encounter with Amneris, is written quite low. You have to sound like a heroic tenor, but if you force those dramatic sounds you won't be able to cope with Scene 2 and its duet "O terra addio", which should have a light-lyric and transfigured sound. You should think of the situation, of finding yourself in this tomb with the woman you love, knowing you will both die, and everything will then happen naturally, by itself. If you haven't forced your voice in the previous scene and have kept it elastic by singing a lot of Nemorinos, you will find the necessary lightness of sound, which many of the big voices that used to sing Radames didn't. In fact few of them were good in the last scene. But a tenor who sings *all* of Radames well is qualified to be called great.'

This is probably why it is becoming almost impossible to find tenors capable of singing the role. But, Bergonzi adds, it is becoming just as difficult to find a tenor who can sing Alvaro in *La forza del destino*. Again, the reason is the tenor's aria 'O tu che in seno agl' angeli', in Act III which is 'almost but not *quite* as difficult as "Celeste Aida", because you have had a chance to warm up with the duet in Act I. You have to attack on A flat, and if you are to sing as Verdi wished and as the words themselves demand, you should sing this attack *piano*. But as I have already explained apropos *Rigoletto* this is very, very difficult. This is why it has become so hard to find tenors able to cope with Alvaro, or indeed, with any Verdi roles. There are no more Verdi voices around. Only voices capable of coping with *verismo* which, of course, is much easier.'

The causes for this sad state of affairs require 'careful reasoning', according to Bergonzi. 'Because it is not true that there are no longer any good voices. There are, and there always will be, good voices. The trouble is that they are always being asked to sing the wrong things, roles which, twenty years ago, no one would *dream* of proposing to a young singer! It is enough for a singer to sing a single good B flat for him to be instantly rung up by La Scala and asked to sing Radames! Naturally, he doesn't refuse and thus a promising voice is ruined at a stroke. We have arrived at a corrupt situation where theatres, agents and conductors alike no longer care about developing, nurturing and protecting voices or even about the art of singing itself. If a singer can get through a role, no matter how, thus enabling them to stage the work in question, they are satisfied. It makes no difference to them that a voice designed to sing a good Almaviva is being made to sing Manrico and thus heading for certain ruin. For in two years' time, they will find someone else to do the same thing. And needless to say, he, too, will be ruined. In the process, quality, excellence and the art of singing itself have, with very few exceptions, vanished.'

Bergonzi believes this tragic situation could be righted in five years, if managements all over the world were to decide to stage *only* those operas for which there exist the right voices. 'If we don't have the right voices for *Aida* or *Il trovatore* or *Rigoletto*, then we simply don't stage them for a while. We stage *La traviata*, *Il barbiere di Siviglia*, *Don Pasquale* and *L'amico Fritz*, all of which can be sung by light-lyric voices. If, in five years' time, with the development that comes from experience and maturity, one of those tenors grows into a *lirico-spinto* capable of singing Radames, *then* we can stage *Aida*. And if this tenor is then not pushed into singing *only* heavy roles but also allowed to sing *Manon*, *Rigoletto* and *La Bohème*, during the *next* five years he may develop into an Otello and so in ten years from now we will have *Otello*. It's all a question of long-term policies rather than wrong short-term planning. If such policies were to be universally adopted, the desperate situation and even bleaker future facing opera today would be remedied, and there will, once again, be Verdian voices: Verdi tenors, Verdi baritones and most especially Verdi mezzos, who have seemingly ceased to exist!'

Yet every great singer is the result of both acquired and innate qualities. There are voices with a natural timbre and colour that predispose them towards French or German roles, just as there are voices naturally suited for the Italian repertoire in general and Verdi in particular. In Bergonzi's case nature, or fate, played a decisive role in preordaining and shaping him to be a Verdi tenor. He was born on 13 July 1924, in the hamlet of Vidalenzo, four kilometres from Verdi's villa at Sant' Agata and equally close to his birthplace of Busseto, where Bergonzi now owns a hotel, *I due Foscari*, run by the younger of his two grown up sons, Marco. Thus he grew up steeped in the atmosphere and breathing the same air as the great composer. A small, stocky, robust and affable man, Bergonzi has the sharp, earthy wit, vigour, forthrightness and tenacity characteristic of Emilians and the spontaneous charm and human warmth typical of Italians in general and especially of those Italians whose roots are close to the earth. (Pavarotti, a fellow Emilian, shares some of the same characteristics.) These qualities are reflected in the sunny timbre of Bergonzi's beautifully modulated lyric voice, devoid of any hint of metal and possessing a warmth and radiant luminosity that caresses rather than scorches the ear, and which makes him, in the words of Harold Rosenthal, editor of *Opera*, 'the most winning Italian tenor of his time'. Celletti, who, like Rosenthal, was writing in the mid-seventies, states that if asked to name the leading tenor of the preceding thirty years he would name Franco Corelli, but if asked which tenor he *liked* best, he would answer: Carlo Bergonzi.

Like most Emilians, Bergonzi's father, a cheesemaker by profession, was an ardent opera-lover and introduced his little son to the joys of opera when the boy was only six, by taking him to see a performance of *Il trovatore* at the local theatre in Busseto. The boy was instantly taken by the proceedings, and especially by the tenor and the aria 'Di quella pira'. Next morning he was found in the family kitchen, singing what he could remember of the aria, brandishing pasta-making utensils in lieu of Manrico's sword. During his growing years, he sang 'countless *Ave Marias*' in local churches and as an extra in performances of *La Bohème* and *Andrea Chénier* at the theatre in Busseto. People were always telling him he should have his voice assessed by a professional and he vividly remembers the decisive day in 1938 when, at the age of fourteen, he decided he wanted to be a professional singer:

'It was a hot August morning and, as usual in the school holidays, I was working in the same cheese factory as my father, pushing a wheelbarrow full of coal for the steam machines used in those days for making cheese – and singing. The boss, called Romeo, stopped me and said: "One cannot do two things at once. One either works or one sings." Hot, tired and exasperated, I replied that, in that case, I'd much rather sing! I flung away the wheelbarrow and rushed to the shed where my poor father was turning the cheese moulds. Surprised, he looked up and enquired what I was doing there. I told him what had just happened. He smiled and replied: "Good, now go home". Next morning, with his blessing, I went to audition for the baritone Edmondo Grandini, who was currently singing Rigoletto during the theatre's summer season at Busseto.'

Grandini thought Bergonzi had a promising voice but classified him as a baritone. As he was about to retire, he offered to give the fourteen-year-old boy singing lessons if the latter were willing to come with him to his home town of Brescia. Bergonzi agreed, and remained there until the onset of the war, when he became an active anti-Nazi. In 1943, while doing his military service in Mantua, he was captured by the Germans and spent the rest of the war in a German prisoner-of-war camp. At the end of the war, his passion for singing stronger than ever, he returned to Italy and enrolled as a full time student at the Boito Conservatoire in Parma, where he studied for three years. (Thanks to the thoroughness of his musical training, he has always been able to study his roles alone.)

His professor of singing at the Conservatoire was Ettore Campogalliani, whose students have included Tebaldi, Scotto, Freni, Raimondi and Pavarotti. Campogalliani also mysteriously classified him as a baritone, as did the famous operatic conductor Tullio Serafin, for whom Bergonzi auditioned at La Scala in 1947. Even though he himself always felt he was a tenor, he didn't wish to contradict or antagonize his teachers and began his training as a baritone with conscientious verve. He dismisses this puzzling classification as a baritone of a singer destined to become a tenor with a very good top as 'one of those things' and points out that many young voices have an ambiguous character. In any case he considers his training as a baritone a bonus in the long run, because he happened to stumble upon teachers who taught him a first-class breathing technique and thus helped him 'build an edifice on such strong foundations that it didn't matter if the number of storeys to be constructed was five or six'.

Bergonzi made his professional debut as a baritone singing Figaro in *Il barbiere di Siviglia* at Lecce in 1948, and during the next three years sang the baritone roles in *Lucia di Lammermoor, Don Pasquale, L'elisir d' amore, La traviata, L'Arlesiana, Adriana Lecouvreur, La fanciulla del West* and *Rigoletto* (where he replaced Gobbi in the title role), often next to famous tenors like Schipa, Tagliavini and even Gigli, then at the end of his career. The only vocal difficulties he seemed to encounter in the baritone register were with the top notes F and F sharp. This, he explains, was hardly surprising, because these top notes for the baritone coincide with the tenor's *passaggio* notes, which are E, F and G above middle C. This was enough to make an intelligent and technically aware singer like Bergonzi realize that, despite favourable reviews, there was something fundamentally wrong about his vocal production.

This 'something' was, as he discovered on a day historic both for his own career and for the annals of operatic history, 12 October 1950, the fact that he was indisputably a tenor. As a bet with himself, he had decided to try and reach up to a high C while vocalizing in his dressing room before singing Sharpless in a production of *Madama Butterfly* in Livorno; and he succeeded in doing so, effortlessly! It was therefore obvious that a singer who cracks on an F but sails up to high C is not a baritone. In the light of this heady discovery, Bergonzi began to re-train his voice, by himself, for the tenor register. His only aids were the recordings of four of the greatest singers of the past and of the day: Beniamino Gigli, Aureliano Pertile, Tito Schipa and 'the incomparable voice of Enrico Caruso, which sounded as if it had never needed any training at all'.

His aim was not to copy those great artists but to learn, through their superb techniques, how to solve his own vocal problems. 'When hearing Gigli's amazing use of the *mezza voce*, for instance, I would ask myself, "How does the man *do* it?" Then I would try singing the same phrase with my own voice until I found the position used by Gigli. When listening to one of Caruso's pulpy, powerful yet never forced notes, I tried to figure out exactly how he supported it. From Pertile I learnt the very important fact that even the most dramatic passages are based on alternating singing *piano* with singing *forte*, and how to shape broad, soaring phrases. From Schipa I learnt another fundamental thing which, I think, forms an essential part of my technique: how to produce light, soft sound even at the top of the register and how, through a hidden and highly skilful recourse to the nasal cavities, to blend the chest and head sounds in the *passaggio* zone.' (This is indeed the secret of Bergonzi's magical singing in the *mezza voce* and ability to observe all the *piano* markings in Verdi scores.) 'When you consider the natural and acquired qualities of these four artists, it is obvious that Schipa and Pertile did not possess voices as naturally beautiful as those of Gigli and Caruso. Yet, through their exemplary vocal and interpretational techniques, they succeeded in raising them to the level of the latter two and in making them heard as clearly from the last row of the gallery as from the first row of the stalls. This is what vocal technique is all about: to enable an artist to arrive at a level of excellence where it is impossible to guess which qualities are acquired and which are innate.' James Levine, Music Director of the

Metropolitan Opera, agrees and stresses that this should also be the aim of every voice teacher.

At the basis of all great singing lies the technique of correct breathing. Bergonzi considers his own phenomenal breath control to be the secret of his success. 'I breathe', he always replies when asked to describe his singing technique. Watching his substantial thorax at work during rehearsals or recording sessions is a singing lesson in itself. Yet Bergonzi is not an advocate of artificial methods of breath support of the 'self-conscious, muscle-flexing, shoulder-raising kind', which he considers dangerous for young singers because 'it gives them a complex, makes them self-conscious and leads them to adopt mistaken positions. I understand why they are taught to do it – in order to open up the sound. But in so doing they are basing their technique and their whole future as singers on completely wrong foundations. I believe in breathing naturally and singing normally, with my vocal possibilities, without forcing and without recourse to artificial breathing and mistaken positions. I breathe naturally, like a normal person.'

Bergonzi explains that the process of achieving total, meticulous breath control is long and laborious. The ideal way of breathing is to store the greatest possible amount of air through a simultaneous maximum contraction of the diaphragm and expansion of the rib cage during inhalation, and during exhalation to use the stored air carefully and intelligently for sound production, when the column of air set in motion should push the sound towards the resonating cavity that best responds to the position and colour of the particular note being sung at the moment. If the singer has to sing a musical phrase that requires a variety of colours, then he should exhale slowly and regulate the pressure of air released extremely carefully. Any sudden increases or decreases in the pressure of air immediately disturb the flow of a *legato* line. An abrupt increase in air pressure causes a jerky, shrill, uneven sound, while a decrease produces a dim, dull kind of sound. Both play havoc with intonation.

Even the stylistic differences between the various composers boil down to the way a singer uses and controls his breath: in *bel canto*, for example, even though the voice needs agility and a capacity for *fioriture*, Bergonzi stresses that 'it is vital for it never to lose its position, which should be sustained throughout and remain supported from the diaphragm, but lightening the sound through a skilful manipulation of the pressure of air. The colour should stay uniform throughout' (a point Pavarotti also makes in his chapter), 'but the timbre should be lighter and clearer. It's a question of luminosity, of how much light one lets into the voice, not of volume.

This is the secret of all singing which young singers should bear in mind: one doesn't sing a Donizetti role like, for example, Edgardo in *Lucia di Lammermoor* in the same way that one sings a Verdi role like Alvaro or a *verismo* role like Chénier. When you declaim a word on the note, in the right position, you then have to find the right *colour* for the word. The colour and timbre change according to the style of each composer, not the technique of singing which is the same for all styles.'

Bergonzi's dependence on his amazing degree of breath control and on keeping his diaphragm as elastic as possible is such that, every single day of his life, he does breathing exercises, for half an hour. 'Nothing spectacular, like trying to push pianos with my stomach [twinkle], but just breathing naturally, inhaling and exhaling rhythmically, for half an hour, to keep the diaphragm muscles elastic. Because vocal sound is the result of a huge muscle apparatus. Therefore the best way to warm up the voice is to warm up those muscles.' Bergonzi repeats his breathing exercises in his dressing-room before a performance, when he vocalizes only minimally and just the *passaggio* notes, 'because if those are in place everything else will happen naturally, by itself' (an interesting contrast to Domingo's way of warming up, which consists of taking the voice a little higher than he will have to during each particular performance). He loves illustrating the futility of excessive vocalizing before performances with an anecdote, in fact a real story that happened to him when, a few years ago, he attended a performance of *Il trovatore* in which Manrico was sung by a famous colleague whom he refuses to name, but who could be heard rehearsing the high C in 'Di quella pira' in his dressing-room during the interval. 'Every two minutes, out came the heavy artillery, "O *teco* almeno, O *teco* almeno etc.". I counted no less than ten high Cs, one more perfect than the other. But would you believe it, came the third act in the theatre, and he cracked on the high C! And I couldn't help thinking that if, instead of wasting those ten perfect high Cs in his dressing-room at the interval, he'd saved at least one for the performance, he'd be home and dry!'

Three months after deciding to switch to the tenor register – a courageous decision for a young man recently married whose wife was expecting their first baby – Bergonzi was ready to make his debut singing the title role in *Andrea Chénier* at the Teatro Petruzzelli in Bari. Chénier is a heavy *spinto* role which most tenors are not ready for until at least a decade after their debuts; but because of its central 'baritonal' *tessitura*, it was an obvious first choice for a tenor who had just switched from the baritone register. Next came his first two Verdi tenor roles: Riccardo in *Un ballo in maschera* and Alvaro in *La forza del destino* at the Teatro Nuovo in Milan. Then Bergonzi began a conscious effort to lighten his voice by singing lyric as well as *spinto* roles: in 1952 he sang Faust in Boito's *Mefistofele* at the Terme di Caracalla in Rome and Alvaro in Catania, displaying the prodigious ease at switching from the lyric to the *spinto* repertoire that was to remain with him throughout his long career. In 1953, he made his Scala debut in a new work, Napoli's *Masaniello*, and his London debut as Alvaro at the Stoll Theatre (where Alfredo Kraus and Renata Scotto also made their British debuts). At the same time, he sang Nemorino in *L'elisir d'amore*, Ernesto in *Don Pasquale* and Edgardo in *Lucia di Lammermoor* in various provincial Italian cities and Nero in *L'incoronazione di Poppea*, Gabriele Adorno in *Simon Boccanegra*, Carlo VII in *Giovanna d' Arco* and Alvaro for Italian radio, as well as many roles in new operas that were to remain unknown.

His big international break came in 1955 when he made his American debut at the Chicago Lyric Opera in *Cavalleria rusticana*, *Il tabarro* and *L'amore dei tre re*, and in 1956-7 when he sang Radames and Manrico at the Metropolitan Opera. He returned to the Met regularly until the mid seventies and has continued to sing there in the past decade. At the same time, he began to make regular annual – mostly triumphant – appearances at the Verona Arena. In 1962, he made his Covent Garden debut as Alvaro and has returned to sing most of his Verdi and Puccini roles there. La Scala lagged behind, as it has often done in the case of exceptional singers: Alfredo Kraus only made his Scala debut, as Werther, in 1976, after twenty years' career as a top singer. Pavarotti was brought to La Scala in 1967 by Karajan, who had previously invited him to the Vienna State Opera. In Bergonzi's case, although he had sung a few performances of *La forza del destino* (after di Stefano) in 1955 and some of *Simon Boccanegra* in January 1956, it was not until 1963 when he sang Radames, followed by the Verdi *Requiem* under Karajan, that La Scala began to realize his true worth. The rest is operatic history.

Yet, in terms of our own decade, Bergonzi's relatively slow ascent to world fame seems hard to understand. Now, he would probably have been asked to sing Radames and Otello soon after his first Chénier! (Indeed he was asked to sing *Pagliacci* earlier than he felt ready for it, and refused, thus alienating some important conductors.) Perhaps the fact that this was still the heyday of del Monaco and di Stefano and of the clarion voice of Franco Corelli, phenomenal while it lasted, explains why managements, and especially La Scala, were slow to recognize Bergonzi's true worth. Yet the six years between his debut as a tenor and his Metropolitan Opera debut in 1956 gave him the necessary time to learn the repertoire and acquire the knowledge that turned him into the great stylist and technician we know. A valuable lesson for our own generation of singers, at a time when style has all but vanished from the operatic stage.

In an effort to remedy this sad state of affairs, Bergonzi has begun giving annual masterclasses during which, he stresses, he doesn't talk! 'Instead, I listen to the young singers, suggest they might, perhaps, try singing this phrase or aria in this or that way, and then proceed to demonstrate what I mean. I show them how to breathe and produce the sound, how to place, support and round it, how to sing *piano* and *a mezza voce*, how to soften the sound of a phrase begun *forte*, and how to strengthen the sound in a phrase begun *piano*. Then I ask them to repeat what I've just demonstrated. Right away, I can tell if they've understood, and also hear the qualities and possibilities of each individual voice. Because one should never forget that the student makes the teacher, and that the latter should adapt his teaching methods to the former. If they *imposed* their technique indiscriminately on every student, they would risk ruining some voices in a couple of lessons. My aim is to teach them to use my technique of correct breath control and support with *their* vocal possibilities.'

Bergonzi – who in 1981 was presented with the 'Caruso Prize' at the Villa Bellosguardo at Lastra a Signa, Caruso's Italian residence from 1904 to 1921, by Gino Begni, who named the tenor 'the ambassador of Italian *bel canto* throughout the world' (previous winners were Galliano Masini and Mario del Monaco) – admits that it takes great dedication, hard work, tenacity and an even greater enthusiasm and passion for music to be an opera singer, carve an important career, and especially put up with the sacrifices required. Of course, there are compensations, 'beautiful things, too. The satisfaction of feeling the public with you during a good performance, for instance.' (Bergonzi says that one of the proudest moments in his career was singing Edgardo in *Lucia di Lammermoor* at Covent Garden in April 1985, with Dame Joan Sutherland, to endless ovations and universal critical eulogies. 'The attack and accuracy of his tenor remain undimmed and the way Bergonzi started the sextet should be a model for all aspirant Edgardos,' wrote John Higgins in *The Times*, a verdict echoed by Harold Rosenthal in *Opera*, who felt all young singers should make a point of seeing this performance as part of their education. 'Well, to be able to pull this off at my age *was* satisfying, I must say,' beamed Bergonzi a few days after the premiere.)

'But this satisfaction lasts only two hours. Because after the performance, you automatically begin to criticize and mentally correct what you did and to think about the next role. So, on this level at least, the sacrifices far outweigh the satisfaction; because when you have a premiere, for instance, you should never go out after the dress rehearsal if the weather is cold or damp. Ideally, you shouldn't even talk, because you talk in the wrong position and use unsupported breath (i.e. you use your throat rather than your lungs). So it's best to keep completely silent on the day before a performance. If the weather permits you could go and see a film; if not, then you should stay in your hotel room and read, write or watch television. It's a great sacrifice, because it means you hardly ever get to really explore the cities you sing in and thus lose the train of life of a normal person. And the only thing that makes this bearable is love for your work and for music. If you don't feel this love, to an extraordinary degree, you *cannot* make those sacrifices. There are many people with very beautiful voices whose careers lasted only a very short time, because they weren't prepared to make sacrifices – which is why I never insisted that my eldest son, Maurizio, who had a good voice and is now a doctor, take up singing. It's something you must, yourself, feel with every fibre of your being. If you do feel yourself a singer, then you simply throw yourself at it. And if you have this passion plus a good voice then you will succeed. This is the secret.'

JOSÉ CARRERAS

'The tenor voice is by far the most difficult in the whole range,' sighed Catalan-born José Carreras, fresh from a triumphant run of performances in the title role of Giordano's *Andrea Chénier* at Covent Garden. 'For the tenor sound is not a natural sound. It has to be *fabricated*,' he explained, reiterating the same fundamental point about tenor-singing made by his Mexican colleague, Francisco Araiza. 'Yet it has always electrified opera-goers more than any other kind of voice, male or female. Something about the physical quality of this sound and of its vibrations, to say nothing of those high notes right at the top of the register [the B flat, the B natural and the high C, which *Time* aptly labelled 'the tenor's money notes'], seem to arouse an instant, visceral excitement in the audience. And of course the tenor is usually the protagonist, the romantic hero, of most operatic plots.'

Carreras's own highly individual, richly coloured lyric tenor voice, instantly recognizable on tape or record and possessing the dark colour often associated with male Spanish singers ('which can be dangerous because at times it makes me seem to have a bigger voice than I really do'), has propelled him to the front rank of today's younger generation of tenors headed by Domingo and Pavarotti. His attractive stage presence, musical sensitivity and remarkable expressive gifts – which mean that he can inject drama and characterization into his singing through his delicate shaping and colouring of phrases – go a long way to compensate for an indifferent acting ability which, at the beginning of his career, often resulted in somewhat wooden, albeit sympathetic portrayals. This, according to Sir John Tooley, General Director of the Royal Opera House, had something to do with a failure to *energize* his singing. 'Right from the beginning, José's was a voice of particularly beautiful quality, a voice with a call to it and also a very well-centred voice. But for a long time it was rather passive and lacked energy, because although you can have a beautiful voice and sing a beautiful line, this beautiful line will become *twice* as

42

beautiful if you energize it. This is an obvious point, yet something José wasn't doing very much in the early days. There was absolute application to the notion of spinning a beautiful line and a lack of awareness that there was more to it, possibly because he is almost self-taught and there was no one around to tell him. Yet gradually he did become aware that he must, somehow, find the intensity needed for a full portrayal of most roles, and slowly he discovered it. How he did it, I don't know. But it happened. His recent performances of Andrea Chénier were totally committed, as well as showing a vocal development: i.e. he was more secure in the "bigger" way he was singing than he had ever been before.'

This significant improvement in Carreras's acting ability began after his gradual expansion from a hitherto basically lyric repertoire – which included the Rodolfos in *La Bohème* and *Luisa Miller*, Cavaradossi in *Tosca*, Alfredo in *La traviata*, the Duke in *Rigoletto*, Edgardo in *Lucia di Lammermoor* and Nemorino in *L' elisir d' amore* – into heavier, *spinto* roles like Andrea Chénier, Don Carlos, Don José in *Carmen*, Manrico in *Il trovatore*, Alvaro in *La forza del destino*, and Calaf in *Turandot*, which satisfy and excite him more than any of his lyric roles, with the exception of Rodolfo in *La Bohème*. 'Of all the roles I sing, Rodolfo is most like the real me as well as being ideal for my voice,' he says. 'No one could quibble about it being too lyrical or too dramatic or too light for my voice: it just fits it perfectly.' The critics concur: 'Puccini might have tailored the part for him,' wrote *The Times*.

Yet this expansion of an essentially lyric voice into the heavier, *spinto* repertoire was originally greeted with misgivings and plenty of head-shaking, lest it should damage the exquisite Carreras lyric sound which, after his debut at the New York City Opera as Pinkerton in *Madama Butterfly*, was described as 'a honeyed lyric tenor, richly coloured, clear and true and possessing a sensual beauty that is quite extraordinary' (*Ovation* Magazine). Yet Carreras – a born gambler in more ways than one – to whom routine spells anathema, reckoned this was a calculated risk worth taking. 'I couldn't bear a boring career consisting of going around the world year after year with a repertoire of half a dozen roles even if I were to sing them near-perfectly,' he explained (an opposite view to that of his compatriot, Alfredo Kraus). 'This way, when my career is over, I will, at least, have sung what I wanted to sing.'

The results of this gamble, which include one of the finest interpretations of Andrea Chénier and Don José in living memory and an interesting, moving and refreshingly different interpretation of Don Carlos, have largely proved him right and confounded the gloomy forecasts. If his attempt at Manrico was less than wholly satisfying in the role's meatier moments and his singing of Radames under Karajan plainly a mistake – well, as every gambler knows, you win some, you lose some. What is certain, though, is that singing the heavier repertoire has not damaged his voice, which, according to a recent edition of *Ovation*, 'remains amazingly sensual and completely individual'. The successive runs of five performances each of Rodolfo and Andrea Chénier at Covent Garden in February 1984 proved this beyond doubt. And, although it is true that his voice has grown somewhat darker and slightly less agile in recent years, this is due to age rather than anything else.

Carreras is now forty, and the last few years have seen him grow into one of the finest tenors of our age. It is a well-known fact that tenor voices change and develop dramatically between the ages of twenty-five and thirty, and again between thirty and thirty-five. And naturally, as the voice gains volume and acquires greater weight and a darker, more important timbre, it loses some of that feathery lightness and agility characteristic of very young voices. 'Ideally,' he sighs, 'one should possess all those qualities at the same time! But, alas, it doesn't often work out that way. And when anything in your voice changes, it affects simply everything in your way of singing, which has to be reconsidered and, possibly, relearnt.' This is confirmed by Nina Walker, the eminent voice coach. 'All muscles, including those controlling the larynx and diaphragm, have memory built into them. And if anything in your body changes, you have to re-learn a role with your new muscular pattern.'

There are, however, two important points Carreras feels lyric tenors should bear in mind when singing *spinto* roles. The first is never to try and change the basic nature of their voice. 'Even when singing roles more dramatic than you are used to, you should approach the drama through interpretation rather than trying for a vocal size you don't have. For there are many Italian roles, like Alvaro in *La forza del destino*, for instance, which lyric voices can sing by adding dark colours and the right accents rather than volume, in short through various forms of expressiveness. And this is the secret of the art of singing, something so many singers who sing, like *papagalli*, in languages they don't understand, fail to realize.' The second important point lyric tenors should remember is to balance their repertoire and ration the more arduous *spinto* roles. If they have been singing a run of six Chéniers or Alvaros or Don Josés they should, as Carreras always tries to do, return to something lighter like Rodolfo, Edgardo or Nemorino, 'to freshen up the voice again'.

Observing these safeguards rigorously may explain why, although he says that vocally the role of Andrea Chénier stretches him to his utmost limits, he surprised even his critics by singing it gloriously, seemingly without effort, with total conviction and no signs of forcing his voice in any way. It soared loud, clear and thrilling in the dramatic climax of Act III, while retaining the warm, melting lyrical sound typical of Carreras at his best in the more intimate moments. 'Switching effortlessly from the lyric poet Rodolfo in *La Bohème* a few weeks ago to the heroic poet Chénier, the Spanish tenor's vocal artistry held us spellbound throughout,' wrote the *Daily Telegraph*. The critic of *The Times* remarked that 'Carreras sang the role with greatest distinction' and added that 'Chénier is a hero as well as a poet and Carreras provides heroic notes, which comes as no surprise to those who followed his career closely over the past year . . . He set alight the opening act, which at times only smoulders, with a ringing timbre and notes hit plumb centre. He is the most honest of tenors: he fudges nothing. And as his recent Rodolfos proved, the lyricism remains for Chénier's final aria, "Come un bel dì di Maggio" which, like the first act "Improvviso", the librettist based on the verses of the real Chénier.'

Why then, in spite of so much glowing praise and evidence to the contrary, does Carreras insist that this role stretches him to his vocal limits?

'Because I am essentially a lyric tenor and Chénier is a *spinto* role with quite a low, "central" *tessitura*. And like all *verismo* roles, it requires the sort of voice that can cut through and ride over a considerably dense orchestration. In the past, it was sung by people like Mario del Monaco and Franco Corelli, who vocally are light years ahead of me. Yet I must confess that I have always shied away from too "gladiatorial" a Chénier, for the simple reason that, although extremely brave – enough to tell the aristocracy the truth even before the Revolution and to defend himself in court against all odds – the man is not a gladiator but an artist, a poet, a sensitive, idealistic soul and a politically committed man. He is also a man in love, but this is not the most interesting thing about him because, even before he met Maddalena, he was in love with love. He carries inside him an image of his ideal woman and then happens to meet someone who seems like its embodiment. But he is more interesting and sensitive than either Cavaradossi, who is also a politically committed artist in love, or Don José, who is awakened by a specific woman with a particular body and pair of legs.

'So, for all these reasons, plus the fact that I am not six foot tall, a gladiatorial approach was out. Then I asked myself a question all singers should ask themselves when confronted by a new role: "What can I, with my particular human and artistic personality, contribute to this role?

Because if I can't match what others can do on the vocal plane, I have to beat them in other ways – beat them in the sense of succeeding in bringing out the character." And I consider that my best qualities as a singer are my flair for expression and my good declamation, both of which are needed for this role. So, obviously, where I score is in the intimate moments where sensitivity is required.' An interesting yet, in view of his performance, an overmodest assessment according to most critics; 'spanned it with consistently beautiful tone the fullest range from lyric to heroic', as the *Guardian* critic perceptively and accurately observed after the Covent Garden premiere.

Yet Carreras explains that Chénier's four big arias are all so difficult that they do stretch him to his vocal limit: the first act 'Improvviso', 'Un dì all' azzurro spazio', has a very high *tessitura* and comes right at the beginning before the tenor has had a chance to warm up his voice – something *all* singers, male and female, find especially hard; the second act aria, 'Credo in una possanza arcana', requires a very big, heroic sound that takes Carreras to his vocal limits. Vocally, the easiest of the four arias is 'Si fui soldato' in the courtroom scene of Act III, because although from the dramatic point of view it is the most heroic, its *tessitura* is more central and baritonal. But the problem is that it is followed, in the last act, by the most lyrical of all Chénier's arias, the romanza 'Come un bel dì di Maggio'. Having to sing such an aria and lighten the voice after a long evening's hard sing when the voice is tired from giving out so much volume, and especially after the more 'central' *tessitura* of the aria that preceded it, is extremely hard, as all tenors testify.

'If', explains Carreras, 'you are having one of those evenings when the voice seems to function as if by itself, fine. But this sort of evening happens very, very seldom. Only in ten out of a hundred performances do you get the feeling that you can do anything you like with your voice. Most evenings, say seventy out of a hundred, you have to take care, wait and see, heave a sigh of relief when a difficult note comes out sounding all right and hope you'll manage to cope with the next tricky spot. Then there are those performances, not more than twenty out of a hundred thank God, when you are completely on the defensive, and your only concern is whether and how you'll make it to the end!'

One of those rare, magical, evenings when everyone, himself included, surpassed themselves, was a concert performance of *Tosca* under Karajan at the Berlin Philharmonie in February 1982 with Katia Ricciarelli in the title role and Ruggero Raimondi as Scarpia. In fact Carreras says that he went through the whole evening in a sort of a trance and can remember nothing about his own singing, except that it was hard to have to sing the third act right after Act II without an interval or the chance to have a glass of water, 'so spellbound and out of myself did I feel'. (Normally in the theatre there are forty minutes between Act II and the tenor's big aria, 'E lucevan le stelle', in Act III.) And this despite the fact that Cavaradossi is not one of his favourite roles even though, from the vocal point of view, it is one of the easiest in his repertoire: quite short and allowing plenty of time between the tenor's two big arias – in the first and last acts – 'which everyone is waiting for'. Yet from the human point of view, he finds the character 'unchanging and not complex enough, a bit of a James Bond who can resist torture and indulge in all manner of heroics like singing "Vittoria, vittoria" at a most ill-advised moment'. (For a completely different view of Cavaradossi, see the chapter on Placido Domingo.) 'Of course, he, too, is an artist, politically committed and in love. But he is less sensitive and romantic than Chénier and less human than Don José, who happens to be another of my favourite roles and provides endless possibilities for discovering new things at every performance.'

Taking on Don José in *Carmen*, one of the most dramatic roles in the tenor repertoire, was another Carreras gamble. Yet he is quick to point out that, unlike the Italian *spinto* roles mentioned above, this role requires something more than the ability to add dark colours and the right accents to his voice. 'For Don José you need a certain "pulp", a certain volume, especially for the strongly dramatic third act, which I now have but which I didn't have five years ago.' He first tackled the role in Madrid early in 1982 and again in Zurich during the latter half of the same year, before bringing it to Covent Garden in 1983, by which time his interpretation had changed considerably. For, in the intervening months, he had recorded the role with Karajan (with Agnes Baltsa in the title role), 'and once you have sung any role with Karajan, you have a basis for your interpretation, eighty per cent of which remains even when you perform it with other conductors and producers'– which is why he found himself disagreeing with Ponnelle's view of Don José in Zurich, because it was more violent than his own conception of the character. 'Although I'm fascinated by his intensity and although he has already killed a man in a fight in his native Navarra before the action begins, I don't see him as a natural killer or butcher, but as a man who becomes violent through a series of circumstances – a typical Spanish trait. Essentially a man at the mercy, and not in command, of his destiny, yet a subtler character than he is often portrayed to be.

'Of course, the real clues for one's interpretation of any character are contained in the music and, through the music, Karajan helped me develop a view of José as a young, rather naive and over-optimistic boy who, right up to the last minute, believes that things will turn out well. In the first act, he is a simple and uncomplicated man who for the first time in his life discovers what it means to feel an overwhelming passion for a woman. Carmen bewitches him to such an extent that everything else becomes secondary and for her he is ready to betray his honour as a soldier. In the second act, he is a man head over heels in love. When he first appears, he has no intention of deserting the army, but being an impulsive and jealous man – and she gives him every reason to be – he reacts to circumstances in an immature way and is forced to join the smugglers. Karajan never indulges in verbal explanations of a character's psychological make up but conveys his feelings about the role through his way of conducting and phrasing. And, just by following Bizet's indications meticulously, he made me understand José more deeply through this recording than I would have even if I had sung the role on stage a hundred times.

'For example, he wanted the Flower Song sung more softly and intimately than usual, because although José begins it in anger, as he remembers his experiences and thoughts of Carmen in jail, he gradually softens up and more and more so as he approaches that high B flat in "Et j'étais une chose à *toi*" which, he insisted, showed a man no longer capable of restraining himself and should therefore be sung *pianissimo*, as Bizet marked it, because it is a very, very intimate moment, immediately followed by a declaration of love, "Carmen, je t'aime".' (Critics were quick to notice this truly wonderful piece of characterization: John Higgins wrote in *The Times* that 'Carreras's Don José is summed up in the Flower Song: sensuous, with some quite exceptional head notes for the penultimate phrase, "Et j' étais une chose a toi" '; Alan Blyth commented in *Gramophone* that 'Carreras's Flower Song, ending with a marvellous *pianissimo* high B flat, is a thing of light and shade, finely shaped, not quite idiomatically French either in verbal ['my French definitely smacks of the Midi,' grins Carreras] or tonal accent, but very appealing'.)

'In the last act,' continues Carreras, 'most tenors have the tendency to portray José as either excessively violent or oversentimental. And both these extremes are wrong. Because when José enters the arena and answers "C'est moi", he mustn't sound already defeated but hopeful and confident of convincing Carmen to take him back. He must beg, but not too much. And Karajan helped me find just the right colours with which to convey this impression.' (Again, the critic from *The Times* noticed this point of characterization and wrote that 'only in the final moments does José's obsession with Carmen truly emerge as the coaxing changes to an impassioned plea before the ultimate stabbing'.) 'But then the man is a genius with a sensitivity so incredible that, when transmitted to us, it unleashes hitherto untapped reserves inside us and makes us give one hundred per cent of ourselves and *really* sing. And one of his cleverest tricks is his knack of making you feel he is accompanying you, whereas, without realizing it, *you* are accompanying *him*. He has you at his mercy but appears to be following you like a carriage behind the horse and whenever you sing a beautiful phrase, he smiles and blows you a kiss, so of course you would cut the fingers of your right hand off for such a man! A lesson for many, or should I say most, conductors who tend to think of us, singers, as underdeveloped peasants and believe that, even in opera, everything depends on them alone! What these cretins fail to realize, but Karajan, being smart and cunning, understands fully, is that if the stage is not functioning properly, *they* won't be credited with any success, either.' (Karajan's own comment on singers is 'My singers are prepared in a way that makes them think they are free, and the moment they think they are free, they will sing well.')

Perhaps Carreras's instinctive affinity with Karajan explains why the latter has often succeeded in persuading him to undertake some roles he would otherwise never have thought of singing. ('Karajan is so persuasive that I sometimes think that if he asked me to sing Micaela I probably would,' admits Carreras with a broad grin.) Usually to good effect, but with a notable exception: Radames in *Aida*, a role outside Carreras's vocal capacity and which *could* have damaged his voice despite the fact that Karajan, who wanted a lyrical approach emphasizing the lover rather than the warrior, scaled down the orchestra so Carreras would have no trouble being heard. Although it was a respectable try which improved significantly in the second year of its run (1980), ultimately the role appeared to defeat him. It *is* one of the most arduous roles in the tenor repertoire, nerve-racking even for those with voices much bigger than Carreras's, chiefly because of its consistently high *tessitura* (no less than thirty-two B flats!) and the even more tiring fact that when the tenor is not having to sing high notes, he is having to sing in the *passaggio* most of the time. And this, as all tenors including Domingo, Aragall and Carreras himself point out, is one of the hardest and most taxing things to have to do. This mammoth role basically requires three different types of tenor: a *lirico-spinto* for Act I; a *spinto* for the Nile scene; a dramatic tenor for the trial scene; and a lyric voice for the last scene in the tomb, 'which requires a beautiful, long and soft lyrical line' and was obviously the easiest for Carreras's voice. And while he didn't actually say so, it is unlikely that he should ever wish to sing this role again.

The Karajan – Carreras collaboration started back in 1976 with a happier performance of the Verdi *Requiem* at the Salzburg Easter Festival and a recording followed by a stage production of *Don Carlos*, which was revived and filmed for Karajan's new film company *Telemondial* in 1986 (this in fact was Carreras's last performance of this role). Vocally, Carreras considers Don Carlos one of the hardest roles in his repertoire – especially in the five-act version – because of its length, intensity, very high *tessitura* and the stamina it demands; for although it contains only one aria, there are so many duets and trios that require the tenor to be on stage most of the time, constantly singing and at this very high *tessitura*. 'It's a role to sing, to play, to feel, much more interesting than either Radames or Cavaradossi, even though he has no arias like "E lucevan le stelle". Of course, I knew all about the historical personage from Spanish history. The real Don Carlos was a sexual maniac, an epileptic and a paranoiac, but you cannot portray such a character when singing music by Verdi.

'Verdi's Carlos emerges as a weak, nebulous character, full of doubts and at the mercy of external circumstances. Like the real Carlos, he is very young, immature, incredibly intense and tortured, seeking to escape from his despair through the idealism of Posa's beliefs, without being totally convinced by them, because he is too immature to make his own critical choices. But because of his disappointed love for his step-mother, he lets himself be used by Posa. In fact all his actions are motivated by a desire to attract her attention (and perhaps, even to blackmail her emotionally) and get back at his father as his behaviour at the *Auto da fé* scene indicates.'

Carreras's portrayal of Don Carlos was a great success from the beginning. After the Salzburg performance in 1976 John Higgins wrote in *Opera*: 'Carreras strikes me as being the most improved tenor of the year. The acting is still wanting, but when he opened his lungs, the rewards came. The voice is now large enough for the Festspielhaus, the tones have a new heroic ring. This was a rightly cheered theatre debut at Salzburg.' But by the time he came to sing it at Covent Garden, his acting had improved so dramatically that Alan Blyth commented in the same magazine that 'Carreras was a distraught, romantic figure of a Carlos. He phrased in that consistently eloquent manner of his and only once or twice was there a hint that the part is perhaps a degree too heavy for him.' Having sung several Verdi lyric and *spinto* roles, Carreras agrees with the prevailing opinion that a singer who can sing Verdi can sing anything in the Italian repertoire, because 'the Verdi style is very pure and requires both the ability to sing on the breath demanded by *bel canto* and the intensity of *verismo*'.

As he had recently added the role of Roméo to his French repertoire, which already included Don José and Werther, I asked him to define the essence of that most elusive of singing styles, the French style. 'It is a very clean and "classic" style – in the abstract, not the chronological, sense – which has to be sung in a "belcantistic" way, that is, avoiding *portamenti* that would instantly turn it into Italian *verismo*, and with attention to musical precison, technical perfection and, of course, diction.' I had particularly enjoyed his performances of Werther at Covent Garden in early 1980, which seemed to bring out the endemic melancholy of the character and to reveal a different facet of Carreras as an artist, hinting at hitherto unsuspected depths. I was therefore eager to explore his inner journey into this role, so different, after all, from all the Italian parts he had performed over the years.

'Massenet's Werther is quite different, more introverted, more passionate and less tortured than Goethe's, but still weak, fragile, indecisive and an emotional blackmailer trying to force Charlotte's hand by threatening suicide. Vocally, it is an extremely wearing role, with a *tessitura* lying mostly in the tenor's *passaggio*, which explains why it is usually sung by light lyric tenors like Alfredo Kraus who have a certain facility in this register. But *lirico-spinto* tenors like me have difficulties fighting this "tessitura di gallo", especially in the second act, which Kraus sings superbly but which both Domingo and I find taxing.

'Difficulties involving *tessitura* don't always have to do with high notes. It's often a question of what precedes those high notes. Sometimes an A natural preceded by passages written on the *passaggio* can be more difficult than a high C preceded by comfortable phrases. In *Aida*, for example, Radames has to sing thirty-two B flats; but the single B flat that poses a real problem – the one we all sweat over – is the one in "Celeste Aida", because by the time you climb up to this B flat you are already tired, short of breath and without the degree of support you would like. And this is the real difficulty. [Bergonzi agrees.] The other thirty-one B flats are no problem and none of us lose any sleep over any of them.

'Werther is similarly difficult in the sense that it taxes both light-lyric and *lirico-spinto* tenors at different moments. The second act, an apotheosis of lyricism, is easier for light-lyric voices like Kraus's – or of any tenor who specializes in singing *Manon*, *La favorita*, *La traviata*, *Rigoletto* and *Lucia di Lammermoor* – but difficult for us who also sing *Carmen*, *La forza del destino*, *Il trovatore* and *Andrea Chénier*. But we score in the strongly dramatic third act, for which light-lyric tenors lack the necessary intensity – something relevant to the very essence of the role which, despite its moments of intimacy and lyricism, *must* also have a big, virile sound. After all, Werther was first sung by Ernest van Dyck, one of the great Siegfrieds of his day.'

Carreras's other recent French role, Roméo in *Roméo et Juliette*, is much easier and vocally more comfortable than Werther, indeed almost ideally suited to his voice and written in a way that gives him time to breathe and to phrase. In fact, from the purely vocal point of view he could have sung it much, much earlier in his career. The reason why it came so late (in 1983) is that he considers it one of those roles that should only be sung in new productions, with plenty of time to prepare and get into the spirit of the thing properly. And as we touched on the subject of the preparation of roles, I asked him about his method of preparation and whether he is a quick or a slow learner.

'A quick one!' he beamed. 'Basically, all roles need the same kind of preparation: after conceiving the character's psychological make-up comes the moment we professionals call "putting the role in the voice", that is, singing it through in full voice from beginning to end, with a coach at the piano, to discover how it lies for your voice. In fact almost ninety per cent of your interpretation gels at this stage, after which (and I admit it shamelessly) I listen to the recordings of great colleagues, past and present, for ideas about solutions to specific problems and for further inspiration.

'Yet the decisive moment that will determine the remaining ten per cent of your interpretation comes when you first sing the role on stage with the orchestra in the pit, for this is when you find out whether you should change something in the breath support or in the way you climb up to the top notes, or whether to sing certain passages more closed or more open. Sometimes ideas that sounded fantastic in a small rehearsal room don't work in a large auditorium; and in music, detail is everything, in a sense. While you must, of course, have a broad, overall conception of how you'll sing a role, there are always myriad little things to discover. If you change the colour of a certain word by as little as half a semichroma [a quarter shade of colour] this may alter the expression of the whole phrase, so subtle is the process of colouring and phrasing. But this sort of insight comes only with maturing performances and with singing a role again and again until you are rid of technical problems and free to concentrate on this refining process. Yes, I know I am a gambler who delights in learning a new role each year (and who enjoys the challenge of singing for difficult, dangerous audiences like La Scala's even though I suffer badly from nerves). But I do also relish this process of perfecting my interpretations which begins after I have a role under my skin, because if you are a serious artist for whom your profession is more than just a "career" you crave this kind of self-taught maturity.'

Carreras's career began in his native Barcelona when he was only twenty-two. Chance would have it that Carlos Caballé, the impresario brother of the famous soprano, went to hear one of Carreras's teacher's other pupils. But as, 'for the first and last time in his life', he arrived early, he heard a bit of Carreras's lesson as well. He was impressed and told the young tenor to get in touch with him whenever he felt ready, and when, a few months later, Carreras did so Caballé started the ball rolling by organizing his debut – as Ismaele in *Nabucco* at the Teatro Liceo. A year later he was cast as Gennaro opposite Montserrat Caballé in *Lucrezia Borgia*. This was followed by his Italian debut as Rodolfo at Parma in 1971.

After his triumphant American debut as Pinkerton in 1972, the New York City Opera offered him a contract for three seasons, which proved to be a happy, fruitful and artistically fulfilling time: he sang all the lyric roles that became the staples of his repertoire for many years and, in the 1972-3 season, learnt eleven new roles in sixteen months! ('Goodness knows how I did it. I certainly couldn't do it now!') During those seasons he also made his San Francisco and Buenos Aires debuts; in 1974, a milestone year in his career, he sang Cavaradossi at the Metropolitan Opera, the Duke of Mantua at the Vienna State Opera and Alfredo at Covent Garden. Next season came his debut at La Scala as Riccardo in *Un ballo in maschera* opposite Caballé, by which time Karajan had already booked him for *Don Carlos* and the Verdi *Requiem*.

Like Domingo, Carreras is largely self-taught. The teacher at the Barcelona Conservatoire, whom he still visits for advice and career direction, is Francisco Puig, a man of considerable understanding who also taught Giacomo Aragall. Carreras recognizes the importance of finding the right kind of teacher, 'who understands your voice and is intelligent and sensitive enough to guide you without ruining your best qualities. Most of all, he should be aware that technique is at the service of interpretation, not an end in itself. But as I said before, the rest is up to the singer himself and can only be learnt through constant self-appraisal and refinement. One of the most useful times for a singer to learn is after a performance, when you are lying sleepless in bed – because naturally after a performance good, bad or indifferent, you cannot sleep – and have all the time in the world to examine and go over every detail of your performance, without any possibility of running away from the truth. And by self-examination I don't mean bemoaning the fact that you didn't hit a certain note straight or didn't sustain a high note long enough, but much more fundamental things to do with basic artistic truth, like: were you honest with yourself; did you sing for yourself or indulge in cheap histrionics to please others; how much of your basic conception of the character came through in this evening's performance? If you succeed in answering these sorts of questions truthfully, you open yourself up to a unending process of self-improvement.'

The road leading to a career as an opera singer began when Carreras went to see *The Great Caruso* at the age of seven and fell so under the spell of the operatic world that he went home and from that day on never stopped singing. He sang virtually all his waking hours, while playing, dressing or going about his daily tasks. His parents were not musical. His father had been a teacher with Republican sympathies and, because after the end of the Civil War he could not get a job in teaching, he became a traffic policeman. His mother was 'a dynamic and marvellous woman full of vitality' who pampered José, the youngest of three sons, in a typically Mediterranean fashion. Both she and her husband felt that, as the child had taken to singing in such a big way, he might as well be taught properly, and enrolled him in the local Conservatoire where he first studied the piano, as well as singing and *solfège*. When he was only eleven he sang the role of the boy narrator in De Falla's *El retablo de Maese Pedro* at the Liceo, which thrilled him because he was paid, like a true professional. But apart from his musical studies he was, he says, a healthy, uncomplicated, sports-loving, rather un-intellectual youth with an aptitude for science. In fact when, at the age of eighteen, it became obvious that he had a good tenor voice, he also enrolled simultaneously in the chemistry department of the local university as an insurance against the vagaries of artistic life.

One of the greatest shocks of his young life was his mother's death, which happened when he was eighteen and only at the beginning of both his musical and university studies. The sudden loss of such a loving and stimulating presence and the desire to fill the void by some sort of substitute was a decisive reason, he feels, why he sought to get married at the age of twenty-four. His wife, who is not connected to the music world, and he now have two children: a very musical boy who is studying the piano and who, despite an 'atrocious, grossly out-of-tune' voice, loves singing and can memorize any role he hears his father sing,

and a younger girl. But Carreras − a charming, open and natural man*
with a delightful sense of humour and plenty of sex-appeal − is honest
about the difficulties of combining an international career with a family
life, the dangers of alienation and of forming new ties. And although he
telephones his children every single day, sometimes twice a day, and
knows exactly what they are doing all the time, he actually sees so little
of them that he has come to regard them 'as a hobby rather than an
everyday reality'. He admits that, although of course he loves going home,
if he's there longer than a fortnight he gets bored. 'I miss, I need, the
intensity and constant movement of operatic life.'

However, he is not sure he will miss it when he eventually retires, or
whether he will choose to remain a part of it in some other capacity.
Although he certainly won't become a conductor or a stage director or
the general administrator of an opera house, he might enjoy being artistic
director of a recording company or putting himself in some position from
where he could help young singers. Sometimes, though, he feels it would
be best to leave the operatic world behind and explore 'other possibilities
within me'.

Until such time, however, there are still several roles he would like to
sing: notably Des Grieux in *Manon Lescaut*, 'a marvellous but *bestially*
difficult role, very intense and dramatic, and because of this and its high
tessitura, especially in the last act, uncomfortable for any tenor'. After that,
in about five years, he would like to explore Wagner, but not until he
has learnt German or until his voice has finished growing. Before then it
would be dangerous for a voice like his to be exposed to Wagnerian
singing, 'because the orchestrations are so big and dense, and the *tessitura*
of many of his tenor parts is quite baritonal, which could make me lose
the elasticity I need for the *bel canto* repertoire. But if, in five years' time,
I were to lose the role of Edgardo in *Lucia* which I will have sung over a
hundred times by then, it won't be such a tragedy. I would hate to lose
La Bohème, though, I would hate to leave Rodolfo.' (Strangely enough,
Placido Domingo made exactly the same remark when discussing the
effects that singing Tristan might have on his voice.)

Lohengrin is the first Wagner role he feels able to tackle and he agrees
with Domingo, who has already sung it and who feels that the greatest
difficulty of this role, which doesn't take the tenor voice any higher than
an A, lies in the fact that virtually all of it is written on the *passaggio*. This,

---

* Indeed he abhors any kind of 'airs and graces'. As he said in an interview with an American journalist,
'Today the idea of being a *divo* is old hat. Today's greatest artists are people *first*. Their artistry and
temperament are reserved strictly for the stage.'

especially in the last act, inclines the singer to enlarge his voice and make a bigger sound, because this is how the role is written, and if the artist is sensitive he will automatically respond. 'So it could well be an elixir of ruination.' Sir John Tooley does not share this pessimistic view and feels Carreras has a very good chance of success in this part, with the risk of losing only his *bel canto* roles. 'There is no reason why the German repertoire should be denied to singers who have specialized in the Italian repertoire. I think the notion that because you are an Italian singer the quality of your sound suits you only to Italian roles is nonsense. For a start, there are many Italian roles unsuitable for many Italian singers either because they are to heavy or too light, while some of the German roles may be quite suitable. In any case it's useless and wrong to try and classify singers into neat pigeon holes.' Carreras adds that *if* he does ever sing Lohengrin, he will never allow himself more than eight performances a year. If that proves successful, he may later take on Walther in *Die Meistersinger von Nürnberg*. 'And a really crazy thing that would thrill me beyond words would be one day to sing Siegmund. Just to feel the joy of actually singing the first act of *Die Walküre* myself, rather than just listening to others doing so, would be worth the risk of losing my voice!'

Then does the sound of his own voice, of all those high notes spinning out of his throat, exhilarate and electrify him, too, at the time?

'Oh no, I'm scared stiff in case they don't come out! But if and after they do, then yes, the pleasure, the satisfaction of having risen to the challenge, is quite unimaginable. . . . '

PLACIDO DOMINGO

'To be a tenor today, one must be a combination of things: one must have musical intelligence, a good physical appearance and, hopefully, a charismatic stage presence. Above all, one must be an expressive singer and actor. In a way, the voice need not even be the most important thing. Of course, the voice counts for a lot, but to conjure up a vivid characterization – *that's* what's vital! That's much more important than coming on stage as Mr X. When *all* these qualities are wedded to a great voice, then one is in the presence of a great artist. And, for me, Placido Domingo represents this ideal' remarked José Carreras to an American magazine some years ago. (This, despite the fact that, as anyone connected with the operatic world knows, singers in general and tenors in particular are not exactly famous for their generosity towards one another!)

His feelings – echoed by most singers who have worked with Domingo, whom Leontyne Price calls 'a tenor in a class of his own' and Ileana Cotrubas considers 'the most complete artist I have ever worked with' – admirably sum up both today's consensus on the art of operatic singing and the artistry of Placido Domingo: the consummate musician and actor who, at his best, delivers some of the greatest operatic performances to be experienced anywhere, and whose interpretations achieve total musical and dramatic unity and have extended the Callas/Visconti/Wieland Wagner revolution to the domain of the tenor.

According to Sir John Tooley, General Director of the Royal Opera House, Covent Garden, Domingo's contribution to the development of opera, and particularly of the tenor in opera – who is usually seen to be half-witted, totally indifferent to what's going on around, the wrong shape and the wrong everything, voice apart – can hardly be overestimated. 'For here's a fine-looking man with a beautiful vocal instrument, an extraordinary musicality – and I mean a *really extraordinary* musicality – and the ability to use his voice to dramatic ends in a way not matched by *anybody*. And when he's really on form, one can hear him shaping the phrases, not always in the same way from performance to performance (especially when working with a conductor like Kleiber), and the results are incomparable. He probes the characters deeply and recreates them in terms of a singer-actor in a most remarkable, imaginative and indeed compelling way.'

Domingo, whose lustrous, highly individual voice has been aptly described as dark, sensuous and velvety, with the resonance of a cello, is passionately committed to the operatic revolution begun in the fifties and considers it the main reason why opera is still thriving in an age dominated by films and television and essentially cinematic criteria of dramatic credibility. 'Opera, when done in the right way – a great production with great singing actors and a great conductor – is the most exciting artistic experience imaginable. But when badly conducted, or acted in an old-fashioned way, nothing could be worse! I mean, one would walk out after five minutes! Whenever I go and see such a performance I feel so offended and embarrassed as to be almost ashamed of being an opera singer, too, and belonging to the same profession. For nowadays all of us are so spoilt by films and television that we demand that opera be believable theatre.

'And most of the time, even when the libretti are somewhat primitive, we are dealing with masterpieces so profound that to get to the heart of characters like Otello, Hoffmann, Des Grieux, Canio or Cavaradossi and recreate them in a way that does justice to the composers' imagination, we almost have to go a stage further than the composers themselves: we have to make all those characters inhabiting different centuries and civilizations relevant to *today*; we have to find a way of conveying the *feeling* of their period, while interpeting them with the insights of the 1980s. This is one of the most difficult things about operatic acting. For when singing Cavaradossi, for instance, you shouldn't walk as we do today because everything about him – the costume, the boots, the posture – is different and instantly conveys a different "feel". Similarly, when singing Roméo you have to walk the way they did in the Renaissance: on your toes and sort of floating. And in *Otello* you have to move like a panther, with strong yet gliding steps ... Another important detail is the way you move your hands. Verdi always said "il gesto è la pronuncia del corpo" [gestures are the pronunciation of the body], and in the old days operatic acting consisted almost entirely of hand movements: the hands accompanied, as if to underline, the musical phrases whereas today the less you move your hands the better. But when you do, it should have the impact of a whiplash!

'All this is part of the effort to make opera valid by contemporary standards so that people can identify with and believe in the characters we portray. The gist of the problem facing us, contemporary opera singers, is how to help the young generation acquire a feel and an ear for opera. Established opera-goers do not present us with quite the same challenge. Even though they, too, infinitely prefer great singing to go hand in hand with great acting, they already have a taste for opera and are more tolerant of any shortcomings. The people we have to conquer are the young, who don't yet have any experience of opera. And I use the word "conquer" because, despite the fact that opera houses all over the world are full, from the social point of view opera is still a somewhat "elitist" art form. What we must do, what I'm *trying* to do, is reach many, many more people than the two thousand or so who fill each of the world's opera houses nightly, and bring today's social revolution to opera. To succeed, though, we must strive for the same level of dramatic credibility they are used to in the rest of the media.'

Acting is only part of operatic interpretation. The musical side is even more complex and difficult, and presents singers with a colossal challenge: the choice of being merely 'canaries', mouthing the words and producing hopefully beautiful sounds, or real interpreters, clarifying and illuminating the feelings and spirit behind the notes through the skill of their phrasing, the sensitivity and subtlety with which they colour their voices, the dramatic intensity they manage to inject into the recitatives. This is why, in Domingo's opinion, 'being a singer is not enough! In order to serve the composers properly, you have to be a musician as well. Because to *really* sing, you have to delve into a score deeply and meticulously and seek to unravel all the secrets it contains, all the little things behind the notes and between the lines. For example, whenever there is a change of key, usually there is also a change of mood – from bliss to wistfulness or whatever – and you should modulate your voice accordingly, even though the audience may often be unaware of you doing it.

'Another vital point is to colour your voice according to the instrumentation. Being a tenor doesn't mean you have to sing with the same voice all the time. Although your voice is one, its colour can, and indeed should, vary tremendously according to the character and style of the music, but especially according to the orchestration which, in opera, is everything! Because the geniuses who created the masterpieces we are trying to interpret, and who worked so intensely on the story, the background and feelings of each character, set the mood and atmosphere of each scene principally through the choice of a particular kind of instrumentation. [This is why Domingo feels 'kind of naked' when he sings to a piano accompaniment, which he finds ultimately frustrating, though enjoyable, because to '*really* feel the mood of what I'm singing, I *need* the orchestra!'] They do this so effectively that all we singers have to do is carry the mood a stage further, with our voice. For instance, after the celli solo before the love duet at the end of Act I of *Otello* the atmosphere is set for us so perfectly that we *have* to colour our voices like a cello, the perfect instrument for expressing a long, flowing, seamless *legato* line. If we fail to do this and come out with a slightly "white" voice, we would instantly dissolve and ruin the rapturous mood that should prevail throughout the duet.' (Anyone familiar with Domingo's portrayal of this role on stage or disc will have noticed that, at this point, his voice acquires a noticeably deeper, darker colour.)

At the beginning of a singer's career, this vocal response to instrumentation has to be conscious. But, given time and experience, it becomes almost automatic and 'an immensely creative and rewarding part of our craft'. (Baritone Thomas Allen, also a great singing-actor, makes the same point about vocal colours in his chapter.) Domingo has found that this colouring process is easier when he is working on a new production, when adequate time and careful day-to-day preparation give him a chance of refining his palette of colours to the extent that, by the opening night, he feels 'free to fly'. Although a singer of his experience and sophistication can still manage to produce a variety of vocal colours, even when he steps into a performance at the last minute, he only feels in complete command of his palette of vocal nuances after a long period of rehearsing and rehearsing and rehearsing.

And so it was with the role of Otello, rightly considered one of his two greatest portrayals (the other is the title role in *Les Contes d'Hoffmann*): one hundred and fifty rehearsal hours before he first sang it at the Hamburg State Opera in 1975, aged thirty-four – which, the pundits shrieked, was far too young for such a heavy and demanding role and sure to ruin his voice or, at the very least, destroy its lustre and capacity for singing lyrical roles like Rodolfo in *La Bohème*. Fortunately they were proved wrong. The opening night was a triumph, with fifty-eight curtain calls and unanimously enthusiastic reviews. Since then Domingo has become the greatest living interpreter of this role, which he has already committed to film under the direction of Franco Zeffirelli, who also directed him in productions of this work at La Scala and the Metropolitan Opera.

Domingo says that his immensely moving portrayal of Otello is based largely on Zeffirelli's ideas, which had, in turn, been influenced by

Lord Olivier's monumental yet controversial, 'African' rather than 'Moorish', interpretation of the role in Shakespeare's play at the Old Vic. (Olivier returned the compliment when he saw a video of the completed film and commented 'By God, not only does he act it as well as I do, but the bastard *sings* it as well!') 'I think of Otello as a man deeply rooted in his African origins, despite his great military career and the universal respect he enjoys in Venice. And the more rejected he feels by what he loves most in the world, the more he retreats into those roots, the only thing left for him to cling to. Scenically, the most poignant and effective way of communicating this retreat is to have Otello appear in Act IV dressed in completely different, African, clothes including an earring, which I don't use in the first three acts, where he wears Venetian costume. And his native clothes symbolize his return to the rituals and religious beliefs of his race. Because from the moment he enters Desdemona's bed-chamber, his every utterance has something to do with religion. His first question is whether she has said her prayers. He wants her prepared for death, which he sees as a ritual punishment for the terrible wrong he thinks she has committed. . . . But with the underlying hope that after killing himself, too, they might meet in another life where, perhaps, everything will be better. And, for me, the saddest thing in the whole opera is that he kills himself far from Desdemona's body, at least far enough for him not to be able to reach her. He tries, he crawls towards her, thinking about the love duet "Un bacio, un bacio, ancora un bacio", but he doesn't make it, he doesn't kiss her again. . . . And I find this devastating. For Verdi has written not only tremendous pathos into this scene, but also an incredible, plastic sort of beauty, if one can talk about beauty in death. . . .'

Domingo explains that another key factor to bear in mind when interpreting this role is Otello's relationship with Iago. He finds it difficult to imagine how anyone would believe a man like Iago, which is why, throughout the opera, he never looks him in the eye. If he did, he would be tempted to react in the way he would himself in such a situation and challenge Iago to stop insinuating things and come out with the whole truth – something Otello doesn't do. 'So I avoid Iago's eyes and let his voice do it all, like the sirens who beguiled Ulysses with their voices. And, like theirs, Iago's voice should have a very special kind of sound: a caressing, almost hypnotic quality that makes you dizzy so you cannot react in a fully rational way but only hear what you *want* to hear, what comes out of your own subconscious fears and self-doubts. After performing Otello many times, I have come to the conclusion that for reasons of pacing – because in Verdi's opera everything happens faster than in Shakespeare's play – it is better to delay the outburst by ignoring Iago's insinuations and treating them as unimportant for as long as possible.' (This slight change of pacing from his previous performances in 1980 was noticeable when he came to perform the role in Covent Garden in 1983.)

Domingo stresses that, from the vocal point of view, Otello is one of the most challenging roles in the tenor repertoire, largely because of the enormously demanding second act, which he considers 'almost an opera in itself, the equivalent of *Pagliacci* – tremendously intense. You start off with the tense and vocally demanding scene with Iago; this is followed by what I consider the most difficult section of the entire opera: the quartet, which has a hideously taxing *tessitura* with a top line of B flats, requires a "covering" kind of sound, never a *forte*, and has an almost *a cappella* ending. I can assure you that without this quartet, *Otello* would be a much, much, easier opera to sing! At the end of it, you have the exclamation "tu fuggi, m' hai levato alla croce", and from that moment on until the end of Act II you are constantly involved without any chance to rest: first Otello's intensely moving aria "Ora e per sempre addio" and then the highly dramatic duet with Iago, "Si, pel ciel".' Domingo considers Otello *the* most demanding of all his Verdi roles, along with Arrigo in *I vespri siciliani*, which he first sang in Paris in 1974 and which has a 'murderous *tessitura*' stretching up to a high D.

He has an intense love for Verdi, whom he considers 'a giant whose creative output spans almost the entire nineteenth-century'. 'He starts off rooted in the *bel canto* school of Bellini and, to a lesser extent, of Donizetti, and by the time he composed *Don Carlos* he was almost ushering in the birth of *verismo*. But he had begun conceiving a new kind of opera as early as the time when he composed *Luisa Miller* (1849) and *Rigoletto* (1851), where he already discarded the established pattern of recitative-aria-cabaletta. In fact the seeds of his future development are contained even in his earliest works, like *Nabucco* and *Ernani*, composed in 1842 and 1844 respectively: a new identity is immediately apparent in the dramatic power of his terse, virile, muscular style. His development reaches its apogee in *Otello* and *Falstaff*, where Verdi achieves complete fulfilment of his creative genius.'

From the technical point of view Domingo considers Verdi the most difficult of all Italian, and, after Mozart, of *all* operatic composers. He explains that young singers at the onset of their operatic careers can probably get through Puccini and other *verismo* composers without possessing a good technique. 'But they could never get through Verdi! It would show up at once, just as it would in Mozart. Because it's not true that Mozart cannot harm a young voice. On the contrary: singers singing Mozart without a good technique would soon strangle themselves. But if they *do* have a good technique, then Mozart and Verdi are healthier for the voice than many other composers, especially those of the *verismo* school. Puccini, for example, could be harmful on occasion, because his heavy orchestrations make it necessary for singers to push their voice to the limit. So, although one could get by singing Puccini without a good technique at the beginning, *continuing* to do so would be extremely dangerous.'

Domingo acquired his own impressive technique during a two-and-a-half-year period as a full-time member of the Tel Aviv Opera (1962–5), where he sang a great variety of roles, including Mozart roles like Ottavio and Ferrando which he has since given up. (He would, however, be interested in singing Ferrando again 'in a king-size production of *Così fan tutte* with Sherrill Milnes as Guglielmo, Agnes Baltsa as Dorabella and Margaret Price as Fiordiligi'.) Domingo arrived in Tel Aviv from Mexico, where his parents had moved in 1949, when he was eight years old. They were Zarzuela (a kind of Spanish operetta) singers and owned their own performing company. Thus Domingo grew up with theatre in his blood and sang many children's roles in his parents' productions, while at the same time taking piano and harmony lessons at the Conservatoire and nursing a secret dream to become a bullfighter. After his voice changed, he made his debut as one of the drunks in the chorus of *My Fair Lady* at the age of sixteen, and spent the next two years singing baritone roles – always the juiciest in Zarzuela – as well as operettas and musical comedies. But even though the baritone roles in Zarzuela are written for a high baritone and stretch up to A flat, Domingo soon began to notice a wobble in his voice, which worried him enough to consider giving up singing altogether. To help pay the bills – for he had married meanwhile and had a baby son – he started playing the piano at various nightclubs. A singer friend rescued him by suggesting that instead of wasting his time on such trifles, he should audition for the local opera house.

Domingo decided to try and chose for his audition two famous baritone arias: the prologue from *Pagliacci* and 'Nemico della patria' from *Andrea Chénier*. The auditioning panel liked his voice but pointed out that, in their opinion, he was a tenor and asked for a tenor aria instead. Domingo didn't know any, but he sight-read 'Amor ti vieta' from *Fedora*, where he promptly cracked on the A natural. But the panel confirmed he was a tenor and offered him a financially decent contract which involved his singing mainly *comprimario* parts and helping in the coaching of singers. He made his debut in 1959, as Borsa in *Rigoletto*, and stayed with the Mexico Opera for nearly three years. During this time, 1961, he made his American debut in Dallas singing Arturo in *I puritani* opposite Joan Sutherland and also sang Edgardo in *Lucia di Lammermoor* in Fort Worth opposite Lily Pons.

In autumn 1962 he left for Tel Aviv with his second wife, the soprano Marta Ornelas, one of the most astute, formidable musicians around and now the mother of his two teenage sons. (Marta Domingo's ear is proverbial: she doesn't miss the tiniest, slightest mistake in his, or anybody else's, performances and spots even the most imperceptible deviation from tempo, or a marginally delayed attack, in his conducting rehearsals.) In Tel Aviv Domingo began developing his voice in earnest. He worked at enlarging it in size and colour as well as on its direction and projection. But the first priority was to acquire the top notes no tenor wants to be without: the B flat, the B natural and the high C. Gradually he found these notes but they were too thin, too wobbly and tended to crack too easily – for instance, the first time he sang the title role in *Faust*, he cracked on the high C in 'Salut demeure'. He realized that the reason was his failure to support the voice properly, from the diaphragm. So, with the help of his wife and a baritone friend, Franco Iglesias, he set about learning the secrets of correct breath control, positioning himself against a piano in the process and pushing the thorax out during high notes. His voice gradually grew in size and security and began to project through the orchestra more effectively. (His thorax also grew in the process, for, as the distinguished coach and accompanist Nina Walker points out, 'the voice is a purely anatomical thing, it's part of the body, it grows with it and is affected by anything that happens to it'.)

In 1966, after nearly three years in Tel Aviv, Domingo joined New York City Opera, where he made his debut in the title role of Ginastera's little-known opera *Don Rodrigo*. A string of international debuts followed: the Hamburg and the Vienna State Opera in 1967, the Metropolitan Opera in 1968, La Scala in 1969-70, Covent Garden in 1972. (He had already made his British debut in 1969, in an unforgettable performance of the Verdi *Requiem* under Giulini at the Royal Festival Hall, at which I was lucky enough to be present. His singing of the 'Hostias' made it instantly obvious that he was to be one of the great tenors of the century.) Since then, Domingo has become one of the most prolific tenors in operatic history, with a repertoire exceeding eighty roles that span the entire tenor range: from the light-lyric (Nemorino), to the lyric (Alfredo,

Rodolfo, Cavaradossi), the *spinto* (Alvaro, Riccardo, Radames, Chénier, Calaf) and the dramatic (Otello, Hoffmann, Samson, Aeneas, Don José). Domingo also has a substantial French repertoire, has already embarked on the Wagnerian *Fach* with Lohengrin, his first Wagnerian role on stage, and has sung almost the entire Italian tenor repertoire, thus surpassing even the legendary Caruso who died without fulfilling his dream of singing Otello.

One of Domingo's outstanding interpretations in the *verismo* repertoire – and it is hard indeed to single out one of so many, including Des Grieux in *Manon Lescaut*, Dick Johnson in *La fanciulla del West*, Rodolfo in *La Bohème*, Calaf in *Turandot*, Enzo in *La gioconda* and the title role in *Andrea Chénier* – is his intensely felt portrayal of Cavaradossi in *Tosca*, about which he has strong views. 'Cavaradossi is usually portrayed as "Mr Tosca", just a pretty boy, "com' è bello il mio Mario", as Tosca sings. But this is utterly wrong in my opinion. The fact that Tosca commits the very brave act of murdering Scarpia doesn't mean Cavaradossi is a weak character. On the contrary: it is *he*, a committed revolutionary with Voltairian ideals and living on the dangerous edge of things, who is involved in politics and thus instantly reacts to the mention of Angelotti's name. Most of the time he has to humour Tosca and treat her like a child, with her jealousies and the dream world of her art.

'The man who first made me understand Cavaradossi was Götz Friedrich, who directed me in a production of *Tosca* in Berlin. He put me on the right path by pointing out that everything in this opera happens within one day and that Cavaradossi begins this day with an odd sort of premonition. Without knowing why at the time, he begins this day – from the moment he arrives at the church to resume his painting – feeling this is going to be a strange, funny sort of day, and one should try to put across this vague sense of malaise. Then, after Angelotti bursts in and asks him for shelter, he realizes why he has had this odd premonition. Therefore it almost disturbs him that Tosca, who, of course, knows nothing as yet, should choose a time like this to throw a jealous fit. For he knows himself to be in danger and he gets impatient with her. In Act III, in the Castel Sant'Angelo, he knows perfectly well he is going to die, that this will be no mock execution, but goes through the motions of believing it for Tosca's sake. So, his behaviour throughout the opera makes it clear that he is the stronger character of the two, unlike *Turandot*, where both the hero and the heroine are equally strong.' (For an opposite view of Cavaradossi see José Carreras's chapter.)

In the autumn of 1984 Domingo sang for the first time on stage a role longer than any of his Italian parts and longer even than the title role in *Les Contes d'Hoffmann:* Wagner's Lohengrin, at the Metropolitan Opera. So far, his only German roles had been Huon in Weber's *Oberon* and Walther von Stolzing in *Die Meistersinger von Nürnberg* on record. At the time of our first conversation he was greatly excited by the prospect because he loves the role intensely: 'Lohengrin is one of those marvellous, dream characters who stand for something great. He is a symbol and as such he is not so much an acting as a singing role, with some superb musical moments, like his duet with Elsa. [This view of Lohengrin is shared by René Kollo.] But from the textual point of view it is extremely difficult, because I shall be singing a very complex text and dialogue in a language I don't really possess in the way I do Italian or French.' He was working extra hard on the language and did so even more before he came to sing the role at the Vienna Opera in January 1985 because, as he never tires of stressing, 'a great proportion of my singing is based on the interpretation of what I'm saying. As Verdi never tired of saying, "la parola regna suprema" [the words reign supreme], because the composers wrote their music to the text. Therefore *what* we are singing should determine *how* we sing it.'

I was not present at Domingo's performances of Lohengrin at the Metropolitan Opera, but I heard him sing the role twice in Vienna. These performances were an unqualified triumph and were followed by seemingly unending standing ovations. I must confess that, despite my immense admiration for Domingo, I had not dared hope for what I was to witness: one of the most romantic and profoundly musical performances of this Heldentenor role in which beauty of sound is so often sacrificed to sheer volume. But Domingo produced beautiful, exquisitely modulated lyrical sound that emphasized the dreamlike, unearthly dimension of the role and delivered the text in surprisingly idiomatic German. Domingo now looks forward to singing the role again – notably at Covent Garden in 1987 – and to developing it further. 'I never feel I really "possess" a role until I have sung it at least twenty times. For although, in our profession, one can score a "success" the first time one attempts a role, *really* worthwhile results are achieved only through a process of constantly maturing performances.'

Domingo had attempted to sing Lohengrin once before, at the Hamburg State Opera, in 1968, while still in his twenties, and the experience had been highly traumatic. After working for days and days with a coach, his voice simply collapsed. He would attack a note, think it was secure and then the voice would go 'click' and the sound would break even in the middle of an F. Clearly, the strain of Wagner's vocal writing was too much for a young tenor under thirty; for although Wagner doesn't take the tenor voice any higher than an A – with the exception of the young Siegfried, who has to sing a high C shortly after his first entry – the overall *tessitura* of most of his roles is written largely on the *passaggio*. 'This means that by the time one climbs up to that A natural one is so exhausted that the A feels like an extreme high note and one really has to *push* the voice. Siegmund's A natural, for instance, feels like a B natural or even a high C and so does Walther von Stolzing's. This constant use of the middle voice and the *passaggio* notes which force one to push the voice is the main reason why Wagner is considered so dangerous for the voice, and especially a young voice.'

The eminent Wagnerian conductor Sir Reginald Goodall agrees and stresses that, as the approach to top notes is so different in Wagner from the Italian repertoire, singers should take care not to mix those styles; while laryngologist Dr Ardeshir Khambatta advises young or essentially lyric tenors not to have a go at the 'heroic, trumpeting voice of a Radames or a Wagner hero', because the results can be catastrophic. 'They can range from haemorrhage in the vocal cords to the sound suddenly fragmenting and collapsing with a sudden pain in the larynx, just below the Adam's apple' (exactly as happened to Domingo). Dr Khambatta explains that this can be cured by a long rest. But if the singer persists he may develop a fibroid nodule in his vocal cords, as did Caruso on two separate occasions (and Pavarotti, too, shortly before his professional debut, as he describes in his chapter). This is curable, either through an operation, as in Caruso's case, or by a long period of silence, as in Pavarotti's and Domingo's.

But for a mature tenor in his forties – Domingo was forty-five when he sang the role again at the Met and in Vienna – the dangers in singing Wagner are considerably reduced. They no longer lie in the voice cracking up, but in the possible loss of some of his lyric roles. This is the reason why Domingo has been so cautious about taking on Heldentenor roles, despite the fact that two are within immediate reach: Parsifal right away, and Siegmund within a year or so. Naturally, one day he would also like to sing Tristan, but every time he looks at the score he asks himself 'if it's really worthwhile sacrificing so much of my lyric repertoire just for the joy of singing Tristan. It's a very hard question to answer, because it would certainly mean losing Alfredo in *La traviata*, the Duke in *Rigoletto* and Rodolfo in *La Bohème*, and while I wouldn't mind losing Alfredo and the Duke, I would, ideally, like to be able to sing Rodolfo all my life. I am, in any case, one of the very few tenors in operatic history to sing Rodolfo after singing Otello. But it couldn't happen after singing Tristan – at least, it would be a miracle if it did. Yet unless I start planning for it now, it might never happen.' Domingo's two best roles, Otello and Hoffmann, would not be affected by any possible post-Wagnerian damage, because they are dramatic rather than lyric roles.

Hoffmann is one of Domingo's many French parts, which include the title roles in *Le Cid, Werther, Faust, Samson et Dalila,* Aeneas in *Les Troyens,* Vasco da Gama in *L'Africaine* and Don José in *Carmen,* which he has also sung on film. He has a strong affection for the French repertoire but admits that it took him a long time to discover and master some of the intricacies and subtleties of the French style and also to pinpoint the ways in which it differs from the Italian. This he did with the help of his wife, who said that one of the main differences is the way to sing *legato* phrases: 'In Italian singing *legato* means cutting neither the musical line nor separating the words, while French singing requires that one marginally separates the words while retaining the continuity of the musical line. If one fails to do this, one immediately sounds un-French. Yet singing French roles *too* correctly and *too* perfectly, with absolute tonal beauty and an impeccable accent, can make them lose some of their dramatic impact. So, one should compromise a little and strive to have as perfect an accent as possible while letting the voice go a bit. Otherwise French singing can sound bloodless and over-rarefied.'

Despite his beautifully sung, manly, yet heartbreakingly moving portrayal of the agony of Aeneas in *Les Troyens,* his intensely human and stoic Samson, and his individual view of Don José in *Carmen,* centring on the latter's typically Latin bond with his mother, Domingo's best French role is undoubtedly his incomparable interpretation of the title role in Offenbach's *Les Contes d'Hoffmann,* which he first sang in the Offenbach Centenary in 1980 at the Cologne Opera, the Salzburg Festival and Covent Garden (and is currently committing to film) and which caused the editor of *Opera* to name him 'the finest singing-actor in the tenor repertory of the present day'.

Domingo says he finds it infinitely more rewarding to portray, and easier to express himself through, characters who suffer a great deal. Indeed, the more a character suffers, the deeper he seems to immerse himself into the role and the better he sings. He doesn't quite know how to explain this, but thinks it may have something to do with the way the music for such roles is written, which compels a sensitive interpreter to plumb the depths of the character's emotions and communicate them to the audience, who must feel them too. 'Because in opera we are dealing with very melodramatic situations and extreme emotions most of the time. This kind and intensity of love is usually accompanied by sadness, suffering and tragedy. The drama is so strong that inevitably there is a combination of love and pain. This makes it easier for me to let go and try to reach the innermost core of the characters in question.'

At the beginning, he explained to Max Loppert in *Opera* magazine, he found Hoffmann an 'ungrateful' role to portray. He found it helpful to compare him a little, in his mind, to Beethoven who, despite his towering genius, also had an unpleasant, self-destructive side to his character and was difficult to live with and 'not easy to love. Yet people always sought him out, because of his music. The same is true of Hoffmann, who also has a strong self-destructive streak. Yet people are always encouraging him to tell his stories, because he tells them so very well.' Having found this and other insights into the character of Hoffmann, the role became increasingly interesting and is now a firm favourite of his. In a sense it is an unusual role because it gives the interpreter greater creative freedom than most operatic parts, which tend to be more precisely mapped.

In the case of Hoffmann, because of the different editions of the work – the Oeser and the older Choudens – and the fact that Offenbach never established a definitive ending, Domingo feels that he has the added advantage of a character not as definitely drawn as most operatic heroes, 'and this sets your imagination free to dream and work him out for yourself', thus providing the interpreter with an opportunity to bring something very personal to his portrayal. And now, having sung the role in productions of both the existing versions of the work, he still cannot decide which is *the* right one because, apart from considering it *essential* to include the epilogue, he thinks both have merits and demerits. But in both editions Hoffmann is a role 'difficult to act and to sing, with a high and uneven *tessitura* which demands different kinds of vocal colour, ranging from light singing in the Olympia Act, a pure lyrical sound for the Antonia Act, a rich, passionate voice for Giulietta and dramatic yet kind of destroyed tones for the prologue and epilogue.

'And the tremendous scope, not only for vocal but also for emotional and even physical development, provided by this role is what makes Hoffmann so very challenging and rewarding to portray. Unlike many operatic characters, like Cavaradossi, to whom everything happens within a single day, or Otello, where it takes a few weeks, or Werther, where it stretches to a few months, Hoffmann spans almost an entire lifetime. In the prologue and epilogue, I see him as a man of fifty. Then in the first flashback to his youth – the Olympia Act – he is a young and immature man in his early twenties. When we meet him again in the Antonia Act which, both for vocal and dramatic reasons – because it's the closest he ever comes to real love – should *always* be placed before the Giulietta Act, he is a man of about thirty-five. And in the Giulietta Act he is around forty-five and already beginning to feel cynical about love and disenchanted with this kind of life. The Giulietta Act, by the way, is the most difficult from the vocal point of view because it requires the richest voice towards the end of a long, hard evening's sing, and this leaves you vocally charged for the epilogue: exhausted, finished, just as the ending requires. So, you have to be one man at four very different stages in his life. And each stage requires not only a different vocal colour but also a different dramatic approach.

'Yet it is important not to forget the fact that all the characters in the different Acts are really one man and that the common denominator is the dissolution of love, with Hoffmann emerging as the loser throughout. For all his love affairs – and I believe that, although he must have had many more, these three represent crucial phases in his development – are unbalanced. He never manages to combine the ideal with the passionate, carnal aspects of love. The Olympia Act, with this foolish, illusory love, is barely credible. Hoffmann is the only person capable of falling in love with this puppet while everyone around him is laughing and having a ball at his expense. But he believes in it, and this shows the rather naive and idealistic side of his character which later develops into this very romantic, almost platonic love for Antonia, the love that never really happens, because of her sickness. It is not a complete, fulfilled love, however, only a romantic, platonic version of it, because the only thing those two ever made together is music. Through music they lived this strong, absolutely incredible love story. And Antonia's death is yet another step towards the dissolution of love, a process completed by Giulietta, the courtesan in whom Hoffmann foolishly hopes to find love again. By the end, he arrives at that certain cynical dimension characteristic of a man who, although completely defeated by love, yet pretends to be a great lover. But he is not, and his failure to find love is largely due to the presence of the devil inside him – not a real devil, of course, but Hoffmann's own self-destructive streak – who possesses him almost completely.'

Does this point about the presence of a self-destructive streak in Hoffmann, which Domingo obviously identifies with strongly, mean that he has a devil inside *him* too?

'Oh, yes! I do. All of us do. All of us have both God and devil, both good and bad, in us. But you have to negotiate with this devil, find out which way he is trying to lead you and decide on which occasions you may agree to go along with him, to some extent. For in many cases you make a sort of pact with this devil within you, because you see some things in him which you may like or feel you can use creatively, while certain other traits may be too much and lead to chaos. Every human being experiences this sort of conflict because the devil is always right there inside you, telling you "do this, do that", and some of his exhortations you accept while others you reject. The secret is to find the very delicate dividing line between the creative and the destructive side of the devil's influence. In Hoffmann's case, the devil is pushing him in all the wrong directions, without his ever realizing it, so anxious and desperate is he to find love, real love. But in the end he is saved by his muse. His love of writing is so strong that, when offered another drink, he refuses.' Nowhere was this made more clear than in John Schlesinger's Covent Garden production – televised live and now available on video – which Domingo considers one of the best he has sung in. In Schlesinger's words, the opera is seen 'as a story about a man, a poet, an anti-hero who is basically very unhappy both with the world and with himself and who has a terrible alcoholic problem. And this is how we portrayed him in the prologue and epilogue, where his talent finally proves strong enough and com-pels him to refuse another drink.' Domingo feels that this 'positive, yet not positively happy, ending' should be used in productions of this work.

Like all stage directors who have worked with Domingo, Schlesinger was impressed by his artistic integrity, his flexibility and his readiness to put all of himself into the production with total disregard for the effort involved. 'His flexibility and readiness to try new, sometimes scenically difficult, things, amazed me,' says Schlesinger. 'I suppose I had this old-fashioned idea in my mind of a *divo* who says "give me a handkerchief, put me at the centre of the stage and I'll be happy!". Well, as *you* know but I didn't at the time, Placido is the diametrical opposite of such a creature and often refused to do things the easy way because, he said, they *looked* easy and were therefore less effective dramatically. "Let me sing lying on that plank there," he would say, "it will have more impact." ' Piero Faggioni, who has collaborated with Domingo on numerous productions, finds his total, no-holds-barred generosity and capacity to give all of himself to a work 'mysterious'. 'I have never encountered it in another singer. He plunges into a work like a bull thrusting himself into the corrida, and at every performance he seems to go into a sort of trance, a process of liberation through singing. I never have the feeling that singing tires him, in any way. Nor am I aware of any physical exertion whatsoever. Just a liberation, an explosion of energies from within which can, I feel, be freed *only* through singing, like a volcano which can free itself only by erupting.'

Domingo's memory and capacity for learning roles and absorbing scenic details and instructions almost instantaneously are as proverbial and impressive as his vocal technique and willingness to immerse himself totally in his roles. Schlesinger remembers feeling 'staggered' when, the day after an overnight flight from Los Angeles, Domingo arrived at rehearsals at Covent Garden and within four hours absorbed and later remembered every detail of his instructions. Piero Faggioni was equally impressed when, after arriving late for rehearsals of *Otello* at Bregenz because of his wife's illness, Domingo still managed to absorb the whole staging and delivered a magnificent performance. James Levine, Music Director of the Metropolitan Opera, thinks Domingo nearly always manages to 'deliver the goods' because 'performing costs him less; phrasing, breathing and concentrating come to him more easily and there isn't the wear and tear and strain other singers experience'.

Domingo's reaction to this comment is that his ability to shut everything out and concentrate on his roles is the result of a great deal of conscious effort over the years. He is, like all singers, acutely aware of his voice as an independent organism with a life of its own, yet totally dependent on, and affected by, anything that happens to him: 'For worthwhile results to happen on stage, both of us, my voice and me, must be in good condition. Yet the merest hint of a chill, an upset stomach, pollen in the air (which affects the sinuses, thus blocking the resonating cavities), too much phlegm as a result of humidity or the opposite, a dry throat, all affect the voice adversely. Worst of all, your psychological situation, all the worries in your head. Sometimes you have so many worries that you doubt you can do it, produce the goods, at all. But in order to concentrate on your role you must forget yourself completely and, for the duration of the performance at least, throw off all those worries. This doesn't come naturally. You have to *learn* to do it and train this head of yours that never stops ticking to switch off.'

Domingo, a warm, humane man and a loyal and considerate friend greatly loved by those close to him, has learnt self-mastery to an extent that enables him to do just that, and to convince onlookers that his customary serenity and courteous behaviour in public and in private are innate. Only very seldom do those who know him well glimpse a crack in the panoply, which helps them imagine the toll extracted from the man within and from his nervous system by the demands of a career such as his.

It was surprising to learn that this great and dedicated singing-actor had no real ambition to become an opera singer. In fact, he had no great personal ambition or drive at all, but sort of stumbled into a singing career because people told him he could do it. 'I have many, many more dreams and fantasies now than I did as an adolescent. I never dreamt of becoming an opera singer at the beginning. Then I realized I could sing, so I began singing and was perfectly happy doing what I was doing in my parents' company. Then people began telling me I could do more. If they hadn't, I might have gone on singing Zarzuelas for life, perfectly contentedly. I had no ambitions beyond that level. But as I began discovering the world of opera, my ambitions grew. Now, the older I grow, the more dreams and fantasies and ambitions I have! First and foremost, my conducting career, and also more films, the foundation of a singing school, perhaps even serving my country in some official cultural capacity one day.'

Besides being a deeply and increasingly patriotic man and every inch a Spaniard, Domingo is also a 'non-fanatic believer' with a strong moral fibre which, together with his enthusiasms, helps sustain him through the constant, incessant pressures and aggravations of his international career. He is also a man with high ideals about the role of music within the overall context of human life. At the time of the Falklands crisis, which found him at the Teatro Colón in Buenos Aires, he said: 'Although I believe in the seriousness and importance of art, I also feel that it is a performer's responsibility to distract people from their daily problems and at the same time make them feel better about their own existence. I have always believed this strongly, because this way performing ceases to be just an end in itself but is taken a stage further, into a human dimension. I feel that, at times like this, people *need* art and music even more. And it would be profoundly rewarding one day to be able to play some role in the choice, distribution and accessibility of artistic events in my own country. Because I feel that easy access to great art has a strong impact on the quality of life in general.'

His response to the Mexican earthquake, in which he lost some close relatives, is well known. He gave up operatic performances for six months and only sang a few charity concerts in aid of the victims. Having himself taken part in the digging for survivors, this is no 'symbolic gesture' of goodwill but the response of a man who abandoned an important premiere of *Otello* at the Chicago Lyric Opera to rush and search for his relatives.

He still bears the scars of the shock of finding them dead. He was recently shown on television personally handing over the proceeds of six months' charity concerts in aid of Mexico to families of the victims. True admirers of Domingo won't have been surprised by this gesture, for the heart has always been the motor behind his art, his quest for understanding and his identification with the characters he plays and the composers he serves with such tireless devotion. Despite his great intelligence Domingo has been, and always will be, ruled by the heart. Caruso felt this 'something in the heart' to be one of the most important, *sine qua non* ingredients of a great singer. . . .

The only accusation hurled at Domingo from time to time is that he simply does too much, flying from performance to performance, role to role, film to television show to benefit concert and so on, seemingly unable to relax and take time off to replenish the well. 'His career has been marked by an insatiable appetite, almost a gluttony, for more roles, more performances, new places to sing,' wrote the *New York Times Magazine* in a comprehensive profile of Domingo. His riposte is that 'no one knows my voice as well as I do, and to no one is it as important' (the *Observer*). Dr Khambatta explains that there are no hard and fast rules about how often performers should sing. 'It depends entirely on the singer and on how comfortable he or she feels. There are singers who seek to appear on stage almost on alternate nights and who dislike taking long holiday breaks, because singing does a great deal for their ego, in every sense of the word. And if the ego works, the voice works. Eventually, I suppose, it will give way. But it all depends on what you want: ten years of glory or twenty years of mediocrity, or, at any rate, a situation where you are operating at half-steam for your particular temperament.'

These perceptive remarks and Piero Faggioni's observation about the sense of liberation experienced by Domingo during performances – perhaps the only time he feels completely, one hundred per cent alive, with all his energies engaged – go a long way to explain Domingo's *need* to do what, to others, seems too much. He is not bothered by the prospect of his voice lasting, perhaps, less long than it could if he were to spare it a little because 'as far as I·am concerned, my singing has been done – over 1,800 performances of eighty roles. I would, to be sure, *like* to go on singing for another decade. But if it proves impossible I would be sad, of course, but also serene in the knowledge that I have had *exactly* the sort of career I wanted – and become a full-time conductor!'

Domingo's increasing pre-occupation with conducting has been a major feature of his career in recent years: some see it as one of the two major dangers to his singing. The other peril is his recent expansion into popular music. Domingo, having started off quite successfully with the John Denver record (*Perhaps Love*, which sold over half a million copies in the United States alone, 'mainly to over-twenty-fives and women', according to Robert Campbell, Vice President of the Masterworks Division of CBS Records), feels quite obsessional about drawing a wider public to opera and thinks that singing this kind of song helps. Perhaps it does. And apart from overloading an already busy schedule, one cannot imagine that singing these simple songs in a *recording studio* could conceivably constitute a danger to Domingo's vocal health.

Conducting, which fascinates and intrigues him perhaps even more than anything else at present, is a different story. As he already explained, he plans to become a full-time conductor after his eventual retirement. To date, he has conducted *Die Fledermaus* at Covent Garden, the Bavarian and the Vienna State Opera and *La Bohème* at the Metropolitan Opera, to reviews ranging from polite to extremely encouraging. 'Like any instrument, the orchestra must be practised. Mr Domingo clearly has the potential to be a fine conductor; but it will take time for him to develop into a maestro', wrote *The New York Times*. The *New York Daily News* was enthusiastic: 'The success of the performance could come as no surprise to anyone who has kept up with Domingo's career. He is already a practised conductor in the chief opera houses of Europe and anyone who can get rave reviews conducting *Die Fledermaus* in Vienna *has* to be pretty good!'

Despite protestations from a fellow-tenor that 'Domingo wants to be the Leonardo da Vinci of opera' – and the answer to that is, as long as he has the necessary talents, why not? – the general feeling among professional musicians is that, although technically he still has a long way to go, Domingo certainly possesses the innate qualities required for conducting. He defines those qualities as 'a deep feeling for the music and the ability to communicate this feeling effectively to the orchestra. The rest you can learn and, as in singing, one is learning all the time, especially technical things to do with the *craft* behind the art.' (Herbert von Karajan named these two qualities as *the* essential attributes for a conductor when discussing the art of conducting in *Maestro*.) 'But', continues Domingo, 'conducting is far more intriguing than singing because your feelings about the music must be expressed through a hundred people. It is therefore crucial that your stick technique be clear enough for them to follow. I'm trying to improve mine all the time. But the most important quality in a conductor is not technique but the feeling for the music that forms the basis for his interpretation.

'The least attractive quality is the need for an almost aggressive streak in one's character, and this is very hard for me to acquire. Because so far, as a singer, I've been involved on the right side, the nice side, of music-making where others tell *you* what to do. And, as I'm usually quite well prepared, I've never had quarrels or problems with conductors, directors or colleagues because everything has tended to happen as a result of friendly teamwork. But conducting is not about teamwork – although in good conducting orchestra and conductor should ideally merge into one – but about authority, the transmission of your ideas about the music to the orchestra. And if one is faced with an undisciplined orchestra with which one still has to make music, then one's character must change!'

In this respect he has discovered that being a singer himself can be both an advantage and a disadvantage in operatic conducting, for it predisposes him towards being too flexible and too kind, sometimes to the extent of sacrificing his own ideas about the music in the process. 'I can sense intuitively when singers need more time to breathe and when it's better to keep going because the pulse of the tempo itself will help them. The disadvantage is that I cannot wholly disassociate myself from being a singer and helping too much even when I would actually prefer to impose my own view of the music and my own tempo. Maybe this will cease after I retire and distance myself from singing, with time.'

Ideally, one day Domingo would like to conduct the entire operatic repertoire he sang as a tenor. One of his most cherished dreams is to conduct the Verdi *Requiem* in a church, although the prospect of having to cope with the 'Sanctus' which, despite its double choir, still has to sound transparent, fills him with terror. Other tricky spots are 'the repeat of the "Dies Irae" at the end which, after all that has gone on, should sound different, stronger, than the first time round. And, of course, the beginning where, no matter who is conducting, the chorus is usually asked to sing *so* softly that one cannot really hear the notes but merely a whisper – Re-qui-em – almost without music. Even the celli sound far too muted and Verdi's instruction *piano* is so exaggerated as to become unrealistic. One *does* want to hear the notes! My ambition is to make them *sing* softly, not whisper! And the wonderful thing is that as we shall be in a church, there can be no applause!

'This brings me to something you asked me earlier on: what fulfils me most, singing or conducting. It's very hard to say. Both are very fulfilling. But there is a difference: after singing, no matter how exhausted I am, I *need* applause; after conducting, I don't. The music itself does it all for me ... And if, after two or three hours' total concentration, my conscience tells me it's been well done, then I could leave the theatre and go home perfectly happily without even taking a bow. I feel so absolutely happy inside I just don't *need* applause.'

NICOLAI GEDDA

'When I was young, I admired and loved what was going on on the stage and saw great singers, great artists, great performances. Now, I am often disappointed,' says Nicolai Gedda, honoured with the 1976 Nobel Gold Medal and labelled 'a paragon of extraordinary and unusual artistry'. Both the Medal and the accolade are richly deserved, for Gedda is a great stylist, a great linguist who sings with perfect diction in six languages and one of the most prolific and versatile tenors on the operatic stage, with a repertoire of over seventy roles encompassing all the different styles of singing at all of which he excels.

Gedda is now sixty and although he has gradually given up many of his roles, he is still active and his recitals and performances are a lesson in stylistic perfection. He attributes his sense of style largely to his expertise as a linguist and his vocal longevity to his excellent technique, which – unlike many of today's younger generation of singers, who feel that, after their debut, they can safely leave their years of study behind – he has never ceased to work at throughout his thirty-four-year-old career, which began in 1952. He stresses that it is technique, more than anything else, that determines a singer's lasting power and level of artistic excellence. 'The human voice is like a diamond – in need of constant polish, without which it becomes abused. First, there are signs of tiredness and wear and tear, then the high notes disappear, and so on.'

Technique becomes even more important with the years because, as Gedda explained in an interview in *Gramophone*, 'after a certain age muscles tend to stiffen so you cannot absolutely rely on the voice. That's why, if you want a long career, it's vital to have a good technique. In a sense, you can teach all the technique there is in fifteen minutes. It's putting it into practice that takes time. And nowadays young singers don't seem to have the time. I wish they did! With the result that one often hears of a new tenor or soprano being discovered only to disappear from the scene a couple of years later because they failed to develop. So, the great performances today are coming mostly from the old-timers – those who kept their voices and careers alive through study and constant work at their technique.'

Reasons for short-lived careers are manifold and range from illness to incorrect use of the voice. But, according to Gedda, the most common cause is insufficient study and the singers' failure to look after themselves and make the necessary sacrifices: refraining from smoking, excessive drinking, too much social and night life, and even from an excessively active sex life. He himself has tried to lead a moderate, normal life. 'I haven't lived like a monk or a hermit, but I've always been conscious, at the back of my mind, of the need to exercise care. Fortunately, I never smoked or cared for strong alcoholic drinks. I enjoy beer and red wine but never developed a taste for spirits or night clubs or late-night parties. I have also been very disciplined with myself when it came to choice of repertoire and only sang roles I personally felt happy with.'

His seventy-plus roles range from the Russian repertoire – Dimitri in Mussorgsky's *Boris Godunov*, Lensky in Tchaikovsky's *Eugene Onegin* and Hermann in *The Queen of Spades*, of which he is the foremost exponent among tenors – to French roles like the title roles in Gounod's *Faust*, Berlioz's *Benvenuto Cellini* and Offenbach's *Les Contes d'Hoffmann*; Italian light-lyric, lyric and *spinto* roles like Nemorino in *L'elisir d' amore*, the Duke of Mantua in *Rigoletto*, Arrigo in *I vespri siciliani* and Riccardo in *Un ballo in maschera*; Mozart roles like Don Ottavio in *Don Giovanni*, Tamino in *Die Zauberflöte* and Belmonte in *Die Entführung aus dem Serail*; other German roles like the title role in Wagner's *Lohengrin*, Flamand in Richard Strauss's *Capriccio*, Huon in Weber's *Oberon* and Adolar in *Euryanthe*; baroque roles like Admetus in Gluck's *Alceste* and Orfeo in *Orfeo ed Euridice* and Rénaud in Lully's *L'Armide*; the tenor leads in many operettas including *Der Zigeunerbaron*, *Die lustige Witwe*, *Das Land des Lächelns*, *Wiener Blut*, *Fra Diavolo*, *Eine Nacht in Venedig*, *Die Fledermaus*; contemporary roles like Anatol in Samuel Barber's *Vanessa*, Kodanda in Gian-Carlo Menotti's *The Last Savage*, Paris in Orff's *Il trionfo d'Afrodite*, and the tenor in Rolf Liebermann's *School for Wives*. As Gedda points out with justifiable pride, he has 'never been too lazy to study something new, and my knowledge of language has, of course, helped'.

Yet the roles Gedda did sing were only part of the repertoire he was actually offered – because, as Janine Reiss, the distinguished coach and accompanist (who as a teacher of the French style in particular has no equal in the music world) points out, 'you can be sure that, with his linguistic expertise and practically infinite *tessitura*, Gedda, who is per-fection in every style of singing, was offered practically *everything*'.

As an interpreter, Gedda is an involved, wholly convincing singing-actor with a commanding stage presence, charm, finesse, lightness of touch and a lyric voice with a lustrous, shiny patina, 'a glorious sheen', as Geoffrey Parsons puts it, 'plus a marvellous capacity for *legato*. You feel one note developing into the next all the time, as you do with Kraus, whereas with the more specifically Italianate tenors you get one note sort of *urging* itself onto the next, which is not *quite* such a natural process. It can be exciting, of course, which is not to say Nicolai isn't exciting. He is very, very exciting and totally musical: apart from the sheen so characteristic of his sound, there is the subtle refinement of his *legato* line and his phrasing, plus a range of colours so wide that it seems as if he were using a whole collection of different vocal instruments.' Another major characteristic of Gedda's interpretations is the superb diction and verbal clarity stemming from his fluency in so many languages, to which he largely attributes his mastery of so many different styles.

'A thorough knowledge of the language of every opera we sing is essential, not only in order to understand what we are singing, but mainly because the musical style of composition has a great deal to do with the characteristics of the language involved, and the right pronunciation helps solve at least half the musical problems. In Russian opera, for instance, however good a musician and noble a singer one might be, if one doesn't know the language and sings with a foreign accent, it won't sound "right" and the result can never be wholly satisfactory. This is why I always urge young singers to learn, but *really* learn, the language so they *can* get it right. Getting rid of an accent is easier in singing than in speaking: you have to work at every vowel, every consonant, every syllable and try to pronounce it as perfectly as possible. This kind of perfection, this "right-ness", is part and parcel of the style of every opera.'

The foundations for Gedda's own polyglot brilliance were laid by life itself. He was born in Stockholm in 1925 to a Swedish mother and a Russian father. He was adopted by his aunt, whose Russian husband, Mikhail Ustinov, was a member of the Don Cossack Choir, and he thus grew up in a bilingual home. (Gedda is his mother's maiden name.) In 1929, aged four, he accompanied his parents to Leipzig where his father became cantor and choirmaster of the Russian Orthodox Church. This meant that little Nicolai now added German to his two native tongues. When he was five his father taught him to read music, and as soon as it was discovered that he had a good soprano voice he began singing in a boys' quartet in the Russian church, as well as accompanying his father at parties, weddings and other private functions where they played the balalaika and sang Russian folk songs. Singing in the *a cappella* choir helped develop his pitch, for he says that, unfortunately, he is not one of the lucky few singers born with perfect pitch. 'Sometimes I can be a little flat. I cannot hear it myself but someone usually points it out and I then adjust my pitch technically. People with perfect pitch, like Elisabeth Söderström, *cannot* sing anything flat, which is both wonderful and awful because they suffer agonies whenever they hear anything out of tune!' After the advent of Hitler the family moved back to Sweden, in 1934, and Gedda, aged nine, went first to secondary school and then to the prestigious old Södra Grammar School, where he added English, French and Latin – from which he would later easily learn Italian – to his languages.

His voice break came late, at sixteen, and two years later he developed a good tenor voice. He dreamt of becoming an opera singer and, in view of his great height, a Heldentenor. But the family's reduced circumstances compelled him to seek regular employment as a clerk in a bank, after completing his year-long military service. During the next five years Gedda won prizes in many singing competitions, and this encouraged his confidence in the feasibility of an operatic career. He confided his dream to a client of his bank who was an instrumentalist in the orchestra of the Stockholm Opera and he recommended that Gedda audition for Karl-Martin Oehmann, a distinguished Swedish former dramatic tenor who had had a distinguished career and sung in the Berlin Städtische Oper under Furtwängler, Walter and Klemperer in the twenties, and who was now a singing teacher. Gedda sang Nemorino's aria 'Una furtiva lagrima' from *L'elisir d' amore* for his audition and Oehmann immediately agreed to take him on as a pupil.

Musician that he was, Oehmann realized straight away that Gedda was not a *tenorino* but a full-blooded lyric tenor. 'Because, although I didn't have huge volume, I had a dark colour that enabled me to sing both lyric and *spinto* roles. Oehmann taught me all the essentials of tenor singing, which I knew nothing about: breath support, the need to "cover" the *passaggio* notes and all those parts of the voice where you cannot sing in a normal way, plus the use of the chest. He was immensely musical and played the piano beautifully: everything he explained I caught very quickly and I made rapid progress with him.' After only two months as Oehmann's pupil, Gedda won the Christine Nilsson Scholarship and this enabled him to dispense with his work at the bank and enrol as a full-time student in the Opera School of the Stockholm Conservatoire. He was immediately singled out as a pupil of exceptional promise and his progress was so rapid that after two years, in 1952, the Administration of the Stockholm Opera decided to mount a production of Adolphe Adam's seldom-seen operetta, *Le Postillon de Longjumeau* – which has a leading role, Chapelou, written for a very high tenor – as a vehicle for him.

But an even more significant event for Gedda's future occurred before the opening night: the late Walter Legge, Head of Classical Artists & Repertoire Department at EMI, had planned a recording of *Boris Godunov* that was to feature Boris Christoff not only in the title role but also in the roles of Pimen and Varlaam, and had chosen Issay Dobrowen to conduct it. Dobrowen was in Stockholm at the time, and, as his stay coincided with a recital there by Elisabeth Schwarzkopf, Legge's wife, the latter decided to accompany her to the Swedish capital and discuss the recording with Dobrowen at the same time. He was met at the airport by the press, who asked if, while in Stockholm, he was planning to audition any Swedish singers. He replied he would be willing to, little realizing that, by next morning, he would be faced with a list of eighty names. In the circumstances, he asked the Director of the Opera for a room in which to hold the auditions.

Among the earliest applicants was a thin young man, over six feet tall. Legge asked what he would like to sing and he replied: ' "The Flower Song from *Carmen*". And he sang it with such astonishing beauty of sound, all except the last note, which was too loud [in the phrase 'Carmen je t'aime', which starts *pianissimo* then proceeds to swell and then ends softly]. I explained what I wanted him to do, the swell followed by a *diminuendo*, and asked him to do it again. Again, he sang it beautifully and did the ending exactly as I'd suggested. My next question was whether he sang any Mozart and he replied that he knew both of Don Ottavio's arias from *Don Giovanni*. And he sang both those arias more beautifully than I had ever heard them except by Richard Tauber and, on record, by John McCormack. I asked him to return later on that day, as I wanted my wife to hear him. She was equally bowled over. That same evening I sent two cables, one to von Karajan and one to Antonio Ghiringhelli, the Intendant of La Scala. They read: "Just heard the greatest Mozart singer in my life: his name is Nicolai Gedda." Of course, as his Russian was excellent too, I also signed him to sing Dimitri in the recording of *Boris Godunov*.'

Legge's faith proved justified on every count; the recording released in 1953 remains one of the greatest of our era and features Gedda's voice 'at virtually its purest, sweet yet incisive, fully formed but floating on a stream of air that never seems to require replenishment and adroitly inflected to the Russian text which Gedda pronounces better, perhaps, than anyone else in the cast', wrote an eminent music critic.

As a result of Legge's recommendations, Gedda sang the tenor lead in von Karajan's recording of the Bach B Minor Mass and made his debut at La Scala singing Don Ottavio. At the same time, his voice and knowledge of French secured him a three-year contract with the Paris Opéra, where he made his debut in 1954 as Huon in Weber's *Oberon*. Later on in the 1954-5 season, he made his Covent Garden debut as the Duke of Mantua. Thus, in the two years since his debut in Stockholm, Gedda had embarked on a fully fledged international career. He made his Salzburg Festival debut, as Belmonte, in 1957, followed in the autumn of the same year by his American debut, as Faust, in Pittsburgh and, a month later, by a triumphant debut, in the same role, at the Metropolitan Opera. Three months later, in January 1958, he also sang the tenor lead, Anatol, in the world premiere of Samuel Barber's *Vanessa* and Don Ottavio in several performances of *Don Giovanni*. His impact on Metropolitan Opera audiences was such that he was invited back several times every season for the next twenty years.

As soon as his international career made it impossible for him to study with Oehmann any longer on a regular basis, one of Gedda's primary concerns was to find a new teacher. 'For a while I felt a bit lost and soon realized I would have to find somebody else so that I could continue studying.' As he was now going to spend a good part of every season in New York, this seemed like the best place to look. The conductor Igor Markevitch suggested Madame Paola Novikova, who had been a pupil of the great Italian baritone Mattia Battistini and who was Irmgard Seefried's and George London's teacher. As Gedda knew London, who had sung Mephistopheles to his Faust in Pittsburgh, he asked him for an introduction to her. They seemed to click and she became Gedda's teacher for a decade, until her death in 1967. He thinks her having been a pupil of Battistini's was significant because 'when you hear Battistini – who sang well into his seventies with his unique A natural still intact, as my father, who heard him in recital, testifies – on record and when I think of Novikova's method, which I use and which works perfectly well, I hear *the* good old Italian school, the school of Caruso, Gigli and all the Italian greats'.

Gedda admits that no teacher, however great, is good for everybody, not least because they are often misunderstood by their pupils. As far as Madame Novikova was concerned, Gedda and London were her most illustrious pupils and best understood her method. Gedda thinks this could be because, being a Russian Jewess, she taught them in Russian. Although she spoke excellent Italian, her English was not so good, which may explain why none of her younger pupils made it in a big way. 'But if you hear London, whose parents were also Russian Jews but who didn't speak Russian, singing Boris, his singing and pronunciation are so perfect that they fooled even the Russians into believing he was Russian. And he got it all from Paola Novikova. That's the kind of perfectionist she was.'

Gedda feels that the timing of their meeting was crucial for his future development as a singer. 'It was the right time for me to find someone like her, because she gave me everything I needed at the time and helped me get rid of the bad habits I had begun to acquire – certain tensions, incorrect use of some of the resonating cavities, traces of forcing the voice – which would have proved fatal had they been allowed to continue.' As soon as those had been corrected, Gedda began to improve and develop again. Madame Novikova also noticed that, as a result of a childhood accident, he had a blocked nose and needed an operation. (While playing at school and standing on his head, the boy who was supposed to hold his legs failed to do so, and Gedda landed on his face. His nose, though not broken, was badly damaged, and the cartilage began to grow inside, blocking the nasal passages and inhibiting his breathing capacity.) She arranged for him to have it done by Dr Zimmermann in the outskirts of Munich. This cleared his nose completely. He had been warned that, as this would result in new acoustic sensations which he had to get used to, he should allow things time to settle and take about two months off work. This was in the early part of 1957. Then he gradually started studying again before going on to make his Salzburg and Metropolitan Opera debuts.

Throughout the next decade, Gedda had lessons with Paola Novikova three times a week, in the evenings, between rehearsals and performances at the Metropolitan, and worked with her on everything. 'We prepared every song and every role in my repertoire, which proved extremely worthwhile. Unfortunately there are very few people like her left today. I have the impression that knowledge of all the details that make up what we call vocal technique is dying out. And I'm very worried about it. Students and young singers are in a quandary over mistaken and often conflicting advice and cannot find anyone who is a link with the true tradition of the art of singing. The only person I know of who seems capable of helping some people is Vera Rosza in London.'

Gedda thinks that the best way for young singers to acquire stylistic sensitivity and refinement is by singing Mozart. 'Mozart does not demand volume or stamina, but does demand musicality and a sense of style. There are definite musical rules to be followed when singing Mozart: absence of *portamenti*, precision of intonation, purity of line and volume control. Of course those things are important in *all* music, but even more so in Mozart, where singers cannot get away with any of the things they could resort to when singing Puccini and, to a lesser extent, Verdi. There is a seriousness, an exactitude, a strictness, almost, that has to to be practised when singing or teaching Mozart, if you are to sing his music correctly and learn from it.'

After his eventual retirement, Gedda plans to devote all his time to teaching, which he regards as a 'personal mission'. He already did some part-time coaching in September 1984, at the request of the Director of the Stockholm Opera, who asked him to help coach the cast for a forthcoming production of *Eugene Onegin* in Swedish. Gedda agreed but insisted that his part in the preparation of the three principals should never be publicly disclosed. He felt deeply gratified when – after having set to work in a small chamber theatre with lovely acoustics in the old Conservatoire building – the result prompted the critics to write that 'at last, we have a genuinely *Russian* production of *Eugene Onegin* even though it's sung in Swedish!'. This obviously meant that the three young principals had got the style right.

This had been Gedda's aim in accepting the challenge. Right from the start he pointed out that, as his present career commitments made it impossible for him to work with them over a lengthy period, he wouldn't attempt to change anything radical in their singing techniques. This might have proved confusing and, in view of their current professional engagements, dangerous. 'But I agreed to explain *some* technical things that could be absorbed in the limited time we had and would improve their technique without forcing them to re-think their entire way of singing. The boy singing Lensky, for instance, wasn't concentrating enough on the correct functioning of all the different parts of his vocal instrument. The vocal instrument isn't just the cords and the throat, but also the chest, the diaphragm, the ribcage, the muscles you have to use, the tensions you have to relax, the resonators of head and chest. The chest itself is like the body of a cello, it's all resonance and it should be controlled and made full use of on stage, where it should *always* be kept high, *especially* when climbing down the scale to the lower notes. Otherwise, if you dropped it you would lose most of its use as a resonator. I also showed them the correct use of the resonating cavities of the head, the correct use of their teeth, plus the way to loosen the jaw, because many singers get into difficulties because of their stiff jaw. This sort of technical thing could be safely pointed out because, once aware of it, they could work on correcting it themselves, without it affecting their basic singing technique adversely. On the contrary.'

As far as the interpretation of Lensky, one of Gedda's most famous roles, is concerned, he explained to the young tenor that he sees Lensky, 'this poet, this romantic man with a typically Russian soul, melancholic yet fiery, temperamental and easily excitable', as Pushkin himself. 'Like him, Lensky is given to exaggerated jealousy and easy misunderstandings. He blows up the importance of a trivial incident by choosing to interpret as an insult Onegin's harmless little flirtation with his fiancée, Olga, at Tatyana's birthday party. The same thing happened to Pushkin himself, although in his case the entire incident might have been deliberately arranged by court circles who envied and hated him, in order to provoke him into an outburst of jealousy of his beautiful young wife. Then, in the duel scene, there is typically Russian resignation, a sense of the inescapability of death ... Again, exactly as in Pushkin's own case.'

After analysing his dramatic interpretation, Gedda proceeded to show the young tenor all the stylistic elements that make up the Russian style in general, and Tchaikovsky's in particular. The conductor, Yuri Ahronovitch, who pronounced himself delighted with the results, didn't speak Swedish – he communicated with the orchestra in German – and, as Gedda rightly points out, these stylistic points are things that 'someone *must* tell' the singers. 'So, I showed him how to sing a *diminuendo* because, even though the role was sung in Swedish, the phrasing is the same, it's Tchaikovsky phrasing, which always hinges on *rubato*. You cannot sing Tchaikovsky academically. You have to know what kind of things you can allow yourself – where to breathe and where *not* to breathe in those long, *legato* phrases. And the young Swedish boy naturally didn't. Because there are certain things youngsters *always* do when confronted by long phrases: they *push* certain syllables that they shouldn't because that syllable is part of the phrasing, part of the long, Russian *legato* line. When singing Lensky in Swedish, you still have to put the accents on the same syllables that you would in speaking. And when, as is sometimes the case, composers write a high note on a syllable that isn't accentuated, then you *shouldn't* accentuate it, but sing it lightly. Of course, I also drew his attention to some matters of nuance and dynamic. But the most important thing to know about Russian singing is how to handle the *rubato*, which is the essence of the Russian style.'

Gedda is also one of the two foremost exponents of the French style, along with Alfredo Kraus. According to Janine Reiss he possesses the ideal French voice, which, as she explains in the chapter on Kraus, should have 'a timbre sufficiently warm and rounded to make it a beautiful voice, but in comparison to an Italian voice like, for example, Bergonzi's it should be a little less sunny, and consequently a little less warm. The timbre of a typically "French" voice should instantly evoke, like the late Georges Thill's used to, a landscape of the Isle de France. Among living tenors, there is no doubt in my mind that the ideal singer for the French repertoire is Gedda.'

Gedda and Reiss both stress that French opera cannot be sung in the same way as Verdi or Puccini. The French style is cleaner, permits no *portamenti* but should, all the same, 'not be sung *too* academically, as this would turn it into Mozart' (Domingo makes the same remark when discussing French singing in his chapter). 'But half the difficulty of the French style lies in the language, which is difficult to master and which few foreign, especially Anglo–Saxon, singers, with the exception of the British baritone Thomas Allen, succeed in doing. This is why, even though some of them sing beautifully, the end result comes across as painful! The French, bless their hearts, tend to be quite indulgent about this, even though they shouldn't. There is no reason why foreigners cannot master French. Listen to Caruso's singing of the French repertoire. It's perfection, and he was a Neapolitan! But unlike Gigli, whose French was far from perfect, Caruso must have worked at it. It's the only way. *All* stylistic details and nuances boil down to a question of willingness to work, work and work. You have to see yourself as the composer's servant and work until you have grasped all the intricacies of his style.'

Gedda owes his perfect French partly to the fact that French was his one failed subject at school: thus he was forced to work at it, especially at his pronunciation, until he got it right. In the process he developed such strong 'respect and affection' for the language that when he first went to Paris in 1952 to make the recording of *Boris Godunov*, he was 'almost too nervous to speak in case I made errors!'. Little by little he became bolder and now speaks French with a fluency that has caused critics to write that when singing French his pronunciation is better than that of most French singers!

Gedda has sung virtually the entire French tenor repertoire: roles ranging from light-lyric like Nadir in *Les Pêcheurs de perles*, Gérald in *Lakmé*, Vincent in *Mireille* and Des Grieux in *Manon*, to lyric like the title roles in *Werther* and *Faust* to dramatic like Don José in *Carmen* and the title role in *Les Contes d'Hoffmann*. He has also sung, and still sings, Faust in

Berlioz's *La Damnation de Faust*. But one of his favourite French roles is Cellini in Berlioz's rarely staged opera *Benvenuto Cellini*, which he first sang at the Holland Festival in 1961, then in Geneva in 1964 and in the famous new production at Covent Garden in 1966, which was subsequently revived in 1969 and taken to La Scala for its bicentenary celebrations in 1976.

Ever since he began his research into this character before the 1961 Holland Festival – visiting Florence to see the original manuscript of Cellini's autobiography, as well as his sculptures – Gedda confided to *Opera* that he became thoroughly absorbed in the sixteenth-century Italian sculptor and goldsmith, and intrigued by the extremes of his 'Renaissance man's' character, which encompassed a capacity for tender love as well as brutal murder. He was also impressed by the fact that Cellini's autobiography was considered important enough to be translated into German by no less a man than Goethe. Yet absorbing and interesting though the character is, the opera as a whole isn't, in his opinion, well enough balanced dramatically, especially in the first act, with which Berlioz himself was far from satisfied. 'His musical intentions don't quite work, from the dramatic point of view. You have intrigue, with Cellini coming to the Balducci household in secret to visit his beloved, Teresa, and finding his rival, Fieramosca, hiding behind a screen. The first time I sang it, in Holland, was in a heavily cut Choudens edition. In London Colin Davis's wise decision to open up certain cuts produced a much better balanced result.'

From the vocal point of view Gedda finds the role 'beautifully balanced and beautifully written for a high tenor, and continuously developing until the climax of the final scene, when Cellini comes face to face with the Pope: first there is a meditation, and then the very dramatic unveiling of the statue of Perseus. Stylistically, Berlioz is a very Italianate composer who loved Italian opera and whose vocal writing gives you all the effects of the Italian style, from long, *legato* lines to arias culminating in high notes, often high Cs. So, from the vocal point of view, it is a wonderful tenor role.'

Cellini is considered so difficult vocally that, apart from Gedda, there is virtually no tenor alive who can sing it, which is why there have been no productions of this work since 1976. Gedda found it a comfortable part because, in the words of Luciano Pavarotti, himself a high-note-tenor, 'there is no tenor alive with a greater ease in the upper register than Gedda'. Janine Reiss disagrees with Gedda's description of this role as 'beautifully written' and states that Berlioz's works are generally not well written for the voice, and that this is as true of *La Damnation de Faust* as it is of *Benvenuto Cellini*. 'In fact the only way anyone can put either of those works on is by getting Gedda, whose style and control are such as to enable him to handle their murderous *tessitura* with ease.' (It's true that many of the performances of *La Damnation de Faust* that I have seen in the last few years – in Boston and New York in the winter of 1983 and Paris in the autumn of 1984 – all featured Gedda as Faust.) Gedda finds these works have a great deal in common, although the latter is 'neither as exposed nor as brilliantly written as *Benvenuto Cellini*. But it is well-spaced and much easier. Which is why I can still sing it!'

Another of Gedda's favourite French roles, and one for which he is justly famous, is the title role of Gounod's *Faust*. He says he is always drawn to 'interesting, psychologically complicated' characters and his brilliant, totally convincing portrayal caused him to be dubbed 'The Faust of Fausts'. Vocally, Gedda possesses both the sensuous, lustrous timbre necessary for the young Faust and the vocal weight required for the old Faust's more baritonal *tessitura* in the prologue, which poses some problems for Kraus, as he himself explains in his chapter. From the dramatic standpoint, Gedda thinks that Gounod's *Faust* has little to do with Goethe's. 'It's condensed, concentrated on certain scenes and very simple. Everything, all the content, lies in the music, Gounod's beautiful music, his arias and duets. Vocally, it is not a difficult role. There is that rather exposed high C at the end of the aria, "Salut demeure" but if the tenor has a high C – and if he hasn't he shouldn't be singing Faust or else he should be transposing it – that should pose no problems.'

Gedda is not as dogmatic about transpositions as Alfredo Kraus, to whom they are anathema. With a top like his, Gedda has hardly ever had to transpose anything – the single exception that springs to mind is the uncut Italian version of Rossini's *Guillaume Tell* in Florence, which no present-day tenor has ever sung on stage in its original *tessitura* – but his readiness to be flexible on this question stems from the time he heard Jussi Bjoerling sing Faust for his comeback at the Metropolitan Opera. 'He was getting on by then and transposed the role down a semitone. But if one were to sing it as beautifully as he did on that occasion, so what! The Paris Opéra, though, allows no transpositions and wouldn't allow him to do this when they contracted him to sing Faust there. So he got more and more nervous and more and more drunk with the result that he never sang Faust in Paris. The Parisians were definitely the losers!' Alfredo Kraus also agrees that exceptional performers who have sung roles in their original *tessitura* all their lives, but who can no longer do so because of age, should be allowed to transpose them down. 'In their case one can, and perhaps one should, make an exception', he concedes.

One of the few roles that even Gedda finds vocally difficult is the title role in *Les Contes d'Hoffmann*. From the dramatic point of view he is strongly drawn to this character, whom he considers as complex as Dimitri in *Boris Godunov* and Faust, and agrees with Domingo that the whole opera is about a process of degradation. The reasons why it is so difficult vocally, even though it is well-spaced, are: first, the fact that the tenor has to be on stage virtually all the time and use a different vocal colour for each of the three acts and for the prologue and epilogue; second, because he has to plunge into the difficult Kleinzach ballad immediately after his first entry, without a chance to warm up; and third, because the Giulietta Act, which is the most difficult vocally (and which, he again agrees with Domingo, should always be placed last, *after* the Antonia Act), requires the richest voice at the end of a long evening, when the tenor is tired.

The warm, sensuous timbre of Gedda's voice, his impeccable diction and capacity for spinning long, *legato* lines – admirably displayed in his singing of Russian roles – also render him an excellent interpreter of Italian opera: *bel canto* (Edgardo, Nemorino), Verdi (Alfredo, the Duke of Mantua, Arrigo and Riccardo), and *verismo* (Pinkerton, Rodolfo). The most outstanding among these are his interpretations of Nemorino and the Duke of Mantua, the latter being considered vocally, stylistically and dramatically outstanding even in decades that could boast of Dukes as exemplary as Carlo Bergonzi and Alfredo Kraus. Alas, I have not seen Gedda perform this role, but living in an age with so few tenors capable of singing it (Pavarotti doesn't seem to any more, Domingo hasn't done so for some time either, although he would love to, granted the right production, and Araiza has only just added it to his repertoire, successfully according to the Zurich critics), one can only envy those who grew up in those blessed decades.

Gedda's Nemorino, which I saw him perform at Covent Garden in 1982, was indeed a lesson in *bel canto* singing. His rendering of 'Una furtiva lagrima' made one understand why, during recording sessions in Rome in the summer of 1966, the distinguished baritones Renato Capecchi and Mario Sereni, who were singing Dulcamara and Belcore, tapped him on the shoulder at the end of this aria and said 'Nicolai, primo tenore', and a member of the orchestra exclaimed that 'nobody since Gigli had sung this aria in such a way'. Gedda comments that Nemorino is a typical *bel canto* role, something he always enjoys singing because it's 'pure honey for the voice, although anyone singing it without a good technique would probably strangle themselves, because it is written largely on the *passaggio* zone. His duet with Dulcamara, for instance, is all in F, F sharp and G, which means that one should close the throat a little. I remember Cesare Valletti – a good stylist with a lovely voice, a great Almaviva and an excellent Nemorino – coming to grief at the Metropolitan Opera because he sang everything open and found, in the middle of a performance of this role, that he couldn't continue. Unfortunately, he never really recovered from this blow and never returned to the Met. This should be a lesson for young singers who should learn *always* to "cover" the *passaggio* notes by closing the throat.' (All tenors I have spoken to agree about this basic technical point.)

From the dramatic point of view, Gedda feels Nemorino should be put across as 'very naive and a little bit dumb. But if you allow yourself to clown too much, it will be hard for the audience to believe Adina will fall for him; if, on the other hand, he has never had a drink in his life, as he proves in his scene with Dulcamara, then he must be a bit dumb! Perhaps I have occasionally exaggerated this element a little in my interpretation. But the part *was* written for laughs. It shouldn't be dull, it should be fun!'

Gedda considers Italian the ideal language for singing, because it has many open vowel sounds and few consonants at the end of syllables. French comes close, despite the complication of the 'nasalized' syllables. English, like German and his native Swedish, is not a very comfortable language to sing. Yet Gedda is considered to be as great a singer of English as he is of Russian, French, Italian and German. Ever since he sang Anatol in Samuel Barber's *Vanessa* at the Metropolitan Opera in 1958, it was noticed that his English was clearer, more perfectly enunciated and more intelligible than that of any of the American singers who made up the rest of the cast. He explained in an interview in *The New York Times* that this may be because English-speaking singers think that speaking English must mean they can also sing it, which is not necessarily so (Thomas Allen agrees). 'One should work at it exactly as one would at one's enunciation in any other language, work at those disagreeable diphthongs, mixtures of two or more vowel sounds, emphasize the vowel formations without forgetting the final consonants.' In the case of the bothersome 'R' sound, Gedda opts for trilling it 'firmly and forcibly' because the objective is to be clearly understood, not produce a result comparable to spoken English.

No discussion of Gedda as a singing-artist would be complete without mention of a genre at which there is no living tenor – and among the dead greats only Richard Tauber – to beat him: operetta. A string of

superb EMI recordings, under the supervision of the late Walter Legge –
including *Die Fledermaus, Der Zigeunerbaron, Eine Nacht in Venedig, Das
Land des Lächelns, Die lustige Witwe* – which have come to be considered
gramophone classics, bear witness to his excellence in this field. All were
recorded shortly after Gedda's professional debut at the Stockholm Opera,
between the years 1952 and 1954, when he was about twenty-seven, and
being given this oportunity at such an early stage in his career seemed
'like a dream come true'. Within those two years, according to Walter
Legge, 'Gedda had become a master of this literature', and the recordings
all won great critical acclaim. His interpretation of Prince Sou Chong in
Das Land des Lächelns in particular was described as being 'not only
impeccably well-sung but possessed of a patina, a lustre, a mixture of
charm and sparkle rarely encountered in any performance, least of all in
the recording studio'.

Gedda explains, with obviously deeply felt gratitude, that he owes his
mastery of the style entirely to Walter Legge, who taught him that, to
sing operetta, you need 'imagination, the right phrasing, the ability to
play with words and colours. All this I learnt from him', he told *Opera
News* after Legge's death, in 1980. 'He was not only a great recording
producer but a great musician as well, with enormous insight into phrasing
and vocal technique. He used to correct me here and there by suggesting
I put more *legato* into a phrase, or emphasize some tiny inflection there.
Everything he told me was constructive. He supervised the entire preparation and rehearsals of all his recordings, working on every phrase and
detail of our interpretations. With him I always did my best and was open
to suggestions, and, unlike most young singers today, never came back
with my own arguments. I was young and knew very little and everything
he told me I absorbed and followed. And I have never regretted doing
so! Nowadays this kind of in-depth musical preparation is virtually
unheard of, especially at recordings where the conductor and many of the
singers often sight-read. [This is true indeed, and only a few conductors –
like Karajan and Kleiber – forbid it.] In a way it is understandable that
one cannot work as one used to, what with rising costs, singers' schedules,
lack of time, the pressure conductors work under. But I fear that, as a
result, something has gone out of recordings – as it has from live performances most of the time.'

Gedda feels that Maria Callas was the last truly great singing-actress
and he is, as has been mentioned, disappointed with most of what he sees
on stage today. Apart from inadequately prepared singers performing the
wrong repertoire he considers that another major factor contributing to

the decay of vocal standards is today's producers, whom he calls 'a real scourge; un-musical and, even worse, anti-musical!'. He concedes there are some notable exceptions, but points out that in recent years he has had to put up with some productions 'the likes of which you wouldn't believe', staged by producers who completely ignored the composer's instructions in the score. He often found himself on the point of walking out in protest and it was only sheer professionalism and concern about the trouble and expense to which this would put the theatre in question that restrained him. Now, he demands approval of the producer and his main view of the work in question, as well as of the sets and costumes *before* signing any contracts: 'it's the only way'.

Today Gedda spends more of his working time on recitals and concerts than in the opera house. An immensely cultured and well-read man, expert in painting and sculpture, he has plenty of spare-time interests, the most pleasurable of which is, as he confided to *Opera*, visiting zoos. 'Animals are what I like best. I would like to have a complete menagerie in my home. But unfortunately I am not at home [home is a large house in the outskirts of Stockholm where he lives with his second wife, Greek-American born Anastasia] often enough to look after them properly. I'm a real homebody, a Cancer whose greatest pleasure is to stay home and curl up in front of the television and I look forward to the time when I can be at home more.'

He looks back to his long and successful career with satisfaction. 'I realize that being a singer and being able to give your best to the public is a great responsibility. You have to be in good physical shape and very disciplined. I always wanted a long career. Not a short, glittering, Callas-type thing, but a long, solid, fine career and the gratification of knowing that the people who come to my performances now still go away feeling satisfied and enriched. That has always been my ideal. So, I took care of myself and sacrificed certain things. You have to, if you want to last!'

RENÉ KOLLO

René Kollo is one of the most successful, and certainly the most engaging and interesting, among the few contemporary tenors specializing in the Wagnerian Heldentenor roles. According to Elijah Moshinsky, who directed him in a brilliant production of *Lohengrin* at Covent Garden, Kollo is unusual because 'unlike most Wagnerian singers, who tend to be rather thick-skinned, he is an enormously sensitive and intelligent man'. Kollo is unusual also because be began his career as a singer of operettas and *Schlager* in his native Berlin and because, although he has delivered some of the most memorable performances of Helden roles – Tristan, Lohengrin and the young Siegfried – to be seen anywhere today, he is, nevertheless, not considered an authentic Heldentenor. His beautiful, melodious, shimmery voice, which is capable of bringing subtlety of tone and colour to a repertoire often sung with relentless, monochromatic volume, is essentially lyric and lighter than a typical Heldentenor's. Alan Blyth remarked in his *Gramophone* review of the recording of *Tristan und Isolde* under Carlos Kleiber that 'Kollo is a Wagnerian tenor in the modern manner, less heroic, more refined'.

The ideal Heldentenor voice was defined by the eminent Wagnerian conductor Sir Reginald Goodall in the *Observer* as 'a combination of beautiful sound with considerable body of voice', i.e. the baritonal under-tones required by many of the Helden parts, which are: the title roles in *Lohengrin*, *Tannhäuser*, *Parsifal*, *Siegfried* and *Tristan und Isolde*, Siegmund in *Die Walküre*, Siegfried in *Götterdämmerung* and Walther von Stolzing in *Die Meistersinger von Nürnberg*.

In Kollo's opinion, no tenor is a Heldentenor from the beginning. The necessary vocal qualities and physical stamina have to develop gradually. 'Hans Beirer started off by singing operettas and even the legendary Dane, Lauritz Melchior – who, along with Max Lorenz, was maybe the only *natural* Heldentenor – began singing the Wagnerian repertoire in his late thirties and reached his peak well into his forties. So, at the beginning,

Heldentenors are simply tenors like all others. When, gradually and despite orchestras that have become increasingly loud and soupy and conductors who don't give a damn about the singers on stage, a tenor singing Wagner roles succeeds in getting himself heard, he is a Heldentenor', he told *Opéra International*. Kurt Moll and Bernd Weikl make the same point in their chapters, and so does Graziella Sciutti, now an eminent teacher, who confirms that 'Heldentenors are not *born* Heldentenors. The Heldentenor may have in him the *seed* for singing these Wagnerian roles; but he starts off as a lyric tenor. Then, if he doesn't push or misuse his voice, if he really has the seed, he will gradually develop into a Heldentenor. Nobody is a Heldentenor at twenty! Nor are there any great Wagnerian sopranos at that age. In her twenties even Kirsten Flagstad sang Italian *coloratura* roles like Amina in *La sonnambula*!'.

Heldentenors in the Melchior mould are now an extinct breed. (The last authentic Heldentenor was the late Wolfgang Windgassen, who concentrated mostly on the Wagnerian repertoire.) In Kollo's opinion, three main factors are responsible for the virtual disappearance of Wagnerian voices, which includes sopranos and Heldenbaritones as well: first, conductors who, with few exceptions like Karajan, Boulez and Kleiber, ignore Wagner's dynamic markings and fail to draw transparent playing from their orchestras. Therefore singers are compelled to shout, push and force their voices, not only sacrificing subtleties of tone, colour and dynamic range, but actually endangering their voices in the process. Second, stage directors and designers who ignore acoustic considerations when designing their sets or placing the singers. Kollo stresses that sets can and should be built of materials which, instead of absorbing sound, help it to resonate, and singers should be positioned in spots that help their voices to do the same. 'Only the late Wieland Wagner and, among contemporaries, Patrice Chéreau and Elijah Moshinsky have understood this.'

Yet the single most important reason for today's lack of Heldentenors is the inescapable truth that nowadays singers sing too much and plunge into strenuous roles long before they are vocally, physically or emotionally ready for them. This is especially dangerous for Wagnerian singers, who have to cope with exceptionally taxing and demanding roles and who, in Sir Reginald Goodall's opinion, 'should look after themselves like athletes. Diet, not speak before performances, and so on. They could sing other roles but not mix styles because the approach to top notes is different in the Italian repertoire. Needless to say, they shouldn't sing too much. But all of them do.'

Kollo is one of the few who don't. Acutely conscious of the fact that the parts he sings are 'no pushovers', he limits his performances to thirty a year, and has always guided his career with intelligence and discrimination. Apart from Wagnerian roles, his repertoire also includes Max in Weber's *Der Freischütz*, Bacchus in Strauss's *Ariadne auf Naxos*, the Emperor in *Die Frau ohne Schatten*, Hermann in Tchaikovsky's *Pique Dame*, the title role in Stravinsky's *Oedipus Rex* and, 'from time to time', some Italian roles like Calaf in *Turandot*, Cavaradossi in *Tosca* and Riccardo in *Un ballo in maschera*. He is thinking of taking on Otello in about two years' time, if he feels ready for it. He has long been a major television celebrity in his native Germany, with his own highly popular show called *Ich lade gern mir Gäste ein*, and appeared in several films of opera including *Arabella*, *Ariadne auf Naxos*, *Lohengrin* and *Die Meistersinger von Nürnberg*. In recent years he also began exploring the *Lieder* repertoire and has already given several recitals of Schubert, Strauss and Wagner songs. In March 1986 he directed his first opera, *Parsifal*, in Darmstadt, because he has 'a great deal to say about this immortal work'. At the same time, he said that, if the venture proves successful, he may consider a career as a stage director after his eventual retirement from the stage.

Yet Kollo's earliest musical ambition was to become a conductor; he even passed his entry exams at the Hochschule für Musik. But family circumstances which he would rather not discuss prevented him from beginning the course. He was born in Berlin in 1937. His father was the author and composer Willi Kollo and his grandfather, Walter Kollo, was a composer of operettas. Both his parents were in show business and the atmosphere at home was, he recalls, not conducive to serious musical studies. When his family discouraged his aspirations to become a conductor, he decided to become a singer instead. With the money he earned from appearing in various musicals, he started taking singing lessons with Elsa Varena and continued to do so for seven years. In 1965, aged twenty-eight, he was engaged by the Brunswick State Theatre, where he remained for two years. Then he moved to the Deutsche Oper am Rhein in Düsseldorf, where he was to become the leading lyric tenor in the company during the next four years (1967–71), with a repertoire that included Pinkerton in *Madama Butterfly*, Laca in *Jenůfa* and the title role in *La clemenza di Tito*.

He made his Bayreuth debut in 1969 as the Steuermann in *Der fliegende Holländer* and returned the following year as Erik in the same opera and Froh in *Das Rheingold*. This was followed by invitations to sing Eisenstein in *Die Fledermaus* at the Bavarian State Opera, Matteo in *Arabella* at La

Scala under Sawallisch and, also in 1971, his first two Helden roles: *Parsifal* in Venice and at the Vienna State Opera and *Lohengrin* at the Bayreuth Festival.

It is no coincidence that Parsifal should be not only his first Helden role, but also the first opera with which to test his ability as a stage director when he comes to stage it. '*Parsifal* is greatly influenced by Buddhism, which was having a profound effect on nineteenth-century religious, metaphysical and philosophical thought. Advanced thinkers were turning away from stagnant, orthodox Christianity, the sterility of official Church teaching and the dry, humanistic logic of the Age of the Enlightenment, and beginning to feel drawn to the more universal, mystical view of life embodied in Buddhism. Wagner was no exception. The result of his spiritual quest was a sort of mystical Christianity, encompassing a great deal of basically Buddhist ideas, which lies at the crux of *Parsifal*. It would therefore be wholly wrong to view this work as conventionally Christian. Of course, it is virtually impossible to "portray" ideas in scenic terms. They should nevertheless – as Wagner himself points out when discussing *Parsifal* and *Tannhäuser*, which is also profoundly influenced by Buddhism, in his diary, *The Brown Book* – underlie any staging of *Parsifal*.' From the vocal point of view, Parsifal lies well for his voice and he does not consider it as one of the most difficult Wagnerian roles. 'It's more difficult for high tenors. My voice has become slightly lower with the years so that, at the moment, I don't find it difficult. Naturally it was more problematic in 1971.'

Kollo's second Heldentenor role, Lohengrin, which he first sang at Bayreuth in 1971, has remained one of his most successful portrayals (he also sang it for his Metropolitan Opera debut in 1976, and at Covent Garden, Hamburg, Vienna and Munich). He brings a very special dimension to this role, which poses no vocal problems yet demands great vocal subtlety. 'Lohengrin is not an "actor's role". For he is not a flesh-and-blood character, but the human incarnation of a god in the ancient Greek sense of a god who assumes human form in order to intervene in human affairs but who, according to the Law of Hades, may not be questioned about his origins, or else he will again dissolve out of matter. And this inner dimension – half-mystical, half-real – cannot be transmitted through "acting" but projected through your presence and aura and through the voice, which should have a special, faraway, unearthly quality at all times.' Kollo succeeded in finding just the right shimmery tone and gossamer texture with which to convey Lohengrin's dual dimension when he sang the role in Elijah Moshinsky's production at Covent Garden in 1977, conducted equally sensitively by Bernard Haitink. Harold Rosenthal wrote in *Opera* that 'René Kollo at last gave a London performance worthy of his reputation. I have never heard him sing so well before, either at Bayreuth or Salzburg; his entrance was electrifying and his singing in the first and last acts had a real heroic ring to it as well as much beauty of tone.'

Moshinsky points out that the whole production was conceived along those lines and he considers his collaboration with Kollo one of the most rewarding he has ever had with a singer. 'Kollo is an artist with whom you can paint very subtle lines. So, our idea of Lohengrin as a two-dimensional character worked very well because he could pull himself out of the music and *think*. So he could play sub-text. He could also use his voice creatively, which is rare in Wagnerian singers, who tend to lack the subtlety and shading of vocal colour one gets in Italian singers and are usually vocally bombastic and dramatically primitive, barely skimming the surface of the roles and works they interpret.' (A notable exception was Hans Hotter, a master of vocal colours – the reason why his Wotan was so memorable.)

'Kollo has a wide palette of vocal colours, too, and is so sensitive on stage that he automatically makes other people sensitive and this instantly creates a special atmosphere – in this case a marvellous, floating, ethereal atmosphere. There is a soft touch about him which is especially good for Lohengrin, a role that often seems just long, bombastic and one-dimensional. But he could draw on his own problematic side – for he can be withdrawn, diffident and a little detached and has a reputation for not turning up at rehearsals willingly – and this suits Lohengrin, who is a nebulous and problematic character. I think he was interested, and invested a lot of himself, in this production. Unlike some Wagnerian singers I could name who think stage direction is about domination and submission, Kollo detests dictatorial direction and thrives on a creative exchange of ideas. He was most co-operative and never pulled rank – for as you know, he is a very big television star indeed in Germany. He and the rest of the cast were there right from the beginning of rehearsals and we could, for once, rehearse in sequence: this showed in the cohesion of the result, whereas when I heard him sing the role at the Met, the subtle, magical dual dimension was entirely missing from his interpretation. He was playing it all upfront … I would love to direct him in *Tannhäuser* one day.'

Kollo is indeed capable of occasional evenings when he seems sunk into a sort of apathy, apparently disinterested in what's going on around him.

This happens when productions fail to stimulate him intellectually or draw an emotional response. In the case of Wagner operas such detachment is catastrophic, because Wagnerian singing is about giving all or giving nothing. There is no possibility of partial involvement. If the singer is not totally steeped in his role, giving it all his physical, emotional and nervous energy, he is in fact giving nothing. (Wolfgang Windgassen had off-evenings like this, too.) Wagner himself states in *The Brown Book* when discussing Ludwig Schnorr von Carolsfeld, his first Tristan – who, incidentally, died shortly after the premiere – that if a singer cannot immerse himself into the spiritual content of his works to an extent where he automatically forgets to spare himself and unleashes all his resources, then all is lost. There is nothing worse than a Wagnerian performance from which such commitment is missing.

As Moshinsky explains, 'Wagner demands complete submission from his singers, who have to surrender themselves, almost masochistically, to a tremendously complex and usually negative series of emotions. He pulls people in and he also pulls them down. He is so demanding and so neurotic that depression is quite a frequent symptom among Wagnerian singers. Unless they have a particular desire to battle with these heavy roles or unless they are thick-skinned – which Kollo certainly isn't – they end up feeling they are victims to their roles instead of having the sensation of creating them. And this can be a problem.' It is therefore up to the director, when confronted with sensitive artists like Kollo, Behrens or Thomas Allen, to find a way of stimulating and enabling them to invest their resources *creatively* in their roles instead of merely surrendering to the obvious passion and emotion of Wagner's music.

This is easier to do in some operas than in others. In *Siegfried* or *Lohengrin*, for instance, one is dealing with what Moshinsky calls 'cardboard characters', heroes or symbols of something, rather than human beings, and these are the most difficult to infuse with the right qualities. Tristan, on the other hand, is wholly human and consequently much more interesting, according to Kollo, 'because it's always more interesting to portray a human being. But to do Tristan justice dramatically and vocally – for, apart from everything else, you have to sing against the vibrations of a highly dramatic soprano, which is always difficult – and express everything inside him, you must throw yourself into the role with every fibre of your being.'

Kollo first sang Tristan in 1981 in a production, conducted by Daniel Barenboim and directed by Jean-Pierre Ponnelle at Bayreuth, where he was rightly hailed as 'the sensation of the evening' (*Hamburg Abendblatt*), and he has also recorded this role for Deutsche Grammophon with Margaret Price as Isolde and Carlos Kleiber conducting. He has strong views about the role and the opera as a whole, which he regards not as a conventional love story but as a deeply philosophical and disturbing piece about decadence, permeated by a *fin-de-siècle* atmosphere of apathy, malaise, indifference, *laissez-faire* and the renouncement of traditional values – an exact parallel to our own times, and what he sees as the end of our art and our Judaeo–Christian civilization. 'Consequently this opera is almost always wrongly staged, too beautifully and too romantically, because directors fall into the trap of staging it as a mere love story. In doing so they are staging only the music, which is indeed incredibly erotic and sensual, but fail to consider the libretto, which is quite different. The score is an erotic, symphonic piece and the libretto is a story about decadence. Of course, if one interprets the music as psychology at its deepest level, then the score and the libretto match completely.

'Then *Tristan und Isolde* emerges as much more than a love story. For a start, it isn't about carnal love or its fulfilment, which never actually happens, but about love in its most idealized, sublimated, discarnate form, a love that happens only on the inner planes and transcends time and place. Even the so-called love-duet in Act II is in fact a philosophical dialogue about escape from this earth – away from King, Honour, Duty and all the other values Tristan, the greatest hero and bravest warrior, has hitherto lived and fought for – into space, an interstellar universe without end and without limits.

'In order to express its true meaning, this opera requires a perfect production, with a minimum of movement and a minimum of action: for it is not about action, but about life on the inner planes. The only moments of action occur in Act II, where King Marke, prompted by Melot, surprises the lovers and for a few brief seconds a great deal goes on. This is the day intruding on the night and thus precipitating the end. Everything else about the staging should be slow and static, and have a grey, heavy, melancholy feel that depicts the lack of faith in ourselves as human beings that results whenever we renounce faith and traditional moral values. There should be a sense of ... paralysis, almost. Even in the love-duet, Tristan and Isolde shouldn't move or even look at each other, but just gaze into space, sunk into a state of rapture through their contemplation of this ideal love without end. The only person who understood this was Wieland Wagner, the greatest stage director of all time, and the only one to understand his grandfather's work. To my deep and lasting regret, I never worked with him.'

From the vocal point of view, Kollo considers Tristan one of the three most strenuous and taxing Wagnerian roles – the others are Tannhäuser and the young Siegfried – because of its length and the size and volume of the orchestra. 'Acts II and III, in particular, are extremely difficult. Act II has a very high *tessitura*, higher than Act III which, from this point of view, is very well written. But the problem here is the length, which is immense, and the fact that one is already tired from coping with the demands of Act II.' 'Kollo towered over a mediocre ensemble, a glowing Tristan with a flexible, predominantly lyric-coloured, elastic voice, and captivated [the audience] through intensity, dramatic accents, a wide range of shades and half-tones. His powerful tenorial raving in the third act showed astonishing staying power', wrote *Opernwelt*.

The title role in *Siegfried* is equally demanding vocally, yet in dramatic terms it presents no problems to someone like Kollo, whose physique renders the concept of a young innocent hero credible. It is an uncomplicated, one-dimensional role, for the young Siegfried is a symbol rather than a real person: 'a half-symbolic, half-mystical figure, a hero placed into the world by God, by Wotan, for a purpose he knows nothing about. He is primal innocence personified, having been told or taught nothing about himself or the world. And this state of fearless innocence can only be projected through vocal means and through a sort of "aura" if you like. Vocally it is *the* longest Wagnerian role and very arduous indeed. Act I has an extremely high *tessitura*, with a top C at Siegfried's first entry. You can relax a little in Act II, when Siegfried is roaming in the forest, but there is still plenty of singing to be done in Act III, before and after Brünnhilde awakes.'

In contrast to the young Siegfried, which is a vocally taxing but dramatically simplistic role, the *Götterdämmerung* Siegfried presents no vocal problems. It amounts to about half an hour's singing, but dramatically it is more interesting: 'For here Siegfried finally loses his innocence and acquires knowledge. He sees himself and everything becomes clear to him. He understands the purpose of his incarnation and place in the general scheme of things. And so he has to die.... It's a wonderful scene, with the chorus all around him.' Kollo thinks it essential for singers to understand the philosophical meaning behind these works before taking on the Helden roles and his own intelligence, perception and considerable culture are a crucial factor contributing to the effectiveness of his performances.

Kollo first sang the young Siegfried in 1976 in the Bayreuth Festival Centenary production of *Der Ring des Nibelungen*, conducted by Pierre Boulez and directed by Patrice Chéreau, to well-deserved critical praise. For he succeeded in bringing both beauty of sound and an aura of radiant innocence to a character often depicted as little more than a brainless, ridiculous oaf. It is therefore a sad shame that a disagreement with Wolfgang Wagner prevented Kollo from singing the role in Brian Large's television film of this production. Kollo has since sung the young Siegfried in Berlin and San Francisco, where he also sang the *Götterdämmerung* Siegfried, the latter for the first time. Both performances drew critical praise. When Kollo sang Siegfried at the Deutsche Oper in Berlin, *Opera* remarked that 'in the title role René Kollo delivered what must have been the performance of his career so far: extraordinary staying power and subtle articulation through every range of passion, tenderness and child-like innocence as the now petulant, now curious adolescent in home-made overalls, longing to break away from "parental" restrictions and start the business of living.' 'René Kollo's Siegfried, new to me, was beautifully sung and acted with what seemed a rare intelligence: the strange tension in his expression as Mime revealed what was truly on his mind was nothing less than riveting,' wrote the San Francisco critic of *Opera*.

At the time of writing, Kollo had not yet tackled the third sacred monster among Heldentenor roles, Tannhäuser. He was supposed to sing it at the 1985 Bayreuth Festival but withdrew from the production and was poised to sing it for the first time in May 1986, at the Geneva Opera. As he already stated in his analysis of *Parsifal*, *Tannhäuser* is also permeated by the Buddhist metaphysical concepts that Wagner was so preoccupied with at the time. But these are not as clearly, deeply or convincingly worked out in *Tannhäuser* as they were later to be in *Parsifal*, probably due to Wagner's youth and relative spiritual immaturity. 'This makes Tannhäuser *the* most difficult role to interpret from the dramatic point of view. Here you are dealing not with a symbol or a hero or a demi-God, but with a man and a man's aspirations to the highest ideals as well as his knowledge that he is bound to fall short of them again and again. For Tannhäuser and Wolfram are really one man, just as Parsifal and Amfortas are one, symbolizing the Good and the Evil in us. Putting this across is extremely difficult, because you are basically trying to convey abstract concepts. And in this case, you cannot just rely on your voice. You have to act and use your dramatic skills, too. At the same time, you have to sing excruciatingly difficult music – especially in Act II, which is very high indeed. In fact, all of Wagner's earlier tenor roles are too high, again probably due to inexperience. Once you get to Tristan and Walther, the *tessitura* gets considerably more comfortable.'

Walther von Stolzing – which Kollo first sang with great success at the 1973 Bayreuth Festival and later at the Salzburg Easter Festival under Karajan – is a role for which he has a special affection because 'he is not a hero or a mystic or a symbol but simply a dashing young man, a young aristocrat, cheeky and not too profound, which is fun once in a while!'. Vocally it is not easy – no Wagnerian role is – but it is not as demanding as some of the other Wagner roles in Kollo's repertoire. Despite an eventual disagreement, he relished the experience of singing Walther under Karajan, 'the only conductor who when he wants or feels like it can produce really transparent sound in Wagner. And when you work with a conductor like him, you can do much more with Wagnerian roles: you can bring more colour and subtlety and sing transparently, too, instead of bellowing and fighting a losing battle against the orchestra, which is what most conductors reduce us to.' 'René Kollo had all the handsome, youthful good looks for Walther and, in the helpful acoustic of the Festspielhaus, his voice rang out with clarity and pride, seeming more mature than before', commented *Opera*.

Kollo stresses that, conductors apart, another reason for the virtual disappearance of Wagnerian voices is the poor calibre of most of the people in charge of operatic institutions, the recording industry and musical life in general. 'And this on top of directors who know and care little about singers and symphonic conductors who know nothing about opera or the intricacies of voice production. This is the real problem. It's not true to say there are no voices around. There are, and there always will be, voices. But they will never come to fruition because, instead of being built up, nowadays singers are simply used up! As long as they can hit the notes, they are offered huge parts right away, sing them for a couple of years, and then burn themselves out. This is simply catastrophic for the future of opera. [Carlo Bergonzi makes precisely the same point in his chapter.] One cannot pull Tristans, Brünnhildes and Turandots out of a drawer. One has to build them up, gradually, carefully and, dare I say it, lovingly, for the future. Unless we make this kind of concerted effort at long-term planning, opera will soon disappear as an art form. I fear that this has begun to happen already, and this may be one of the reasons for its unprecedented popularity. People sense it may be on its way out, and are rushing to savour as much as they can. For, unlike the paintings of one's choice which can be admired in a museum, one's favourite operas can only be staged and enjoyed if the right voices are available. One believes, one hopes, that opera will go on forever. But if there are no singers, this won't be possible.'

ALFREDO KRAUS

'Alfredo Kraus is one of the few great stylists on the operatic stage', declares Nina Walker, the distinguished coach, accompanist and former Assistant Chorus Master at the Royal Opera House, Covent Garden. 'Every performance of his is a lesson in the art of singing. He concentrates on a small, specialized repertoire which he sings marvellously well, with total ease, great charm and impeccable style. This is what operatic singing is all about! But the breed of Kraus, Bergonzi and Gedda has nearly vanished and excessive travel is largely to blame. Yet I can't understand why singers feel they *must* do this and jet from place to place, performance to performance and rehearsal to recording session and get so exhausted.'

Kraus doesn't, although he admits that, had he been born into today's younger generation of tenors, his mentality might be different. A slim, elegant man in his late fifties who cuts a dashing figure on stage and sounds younger than many a tenor half his age, Kraus, whose beautifully modulated lyric voice has a remarkable upper extension stretching effortlessly up to high D natural, is the antithesis of today's tenor as we have come to know him. For he seems perfectly content with a reputation resting on artistic achievement alone and built entirely without the aid of public relations and para-musical gimmicks. This might explain why, although Kraus is one of the most expensive tenors in the world – until the rise of Pavarotti, Domingo and, more recently, Carreras, reputedly *the* most expensive – he has never been, in the widest sense of the word, the most popular.

His respect towards the works he interprets and towards the public has never allowed him to prostitute himself by agreeing to sing the wrong roles or to debase his standards by transposing the *tessitura* of roles he might *like* to sing, but for which he does not possess the necessary vocal resources. Although he admits that, in theory, he would have greatly enjoyed singing Radames, Calaf and the title roles in *Lohengrin* and *Tannhäuser*, he realized that in practice this would have proved both dangerous for his voice and unfair to the music. He therefore decided to concentrate on the light-lyric repertoire of a classic *tenore di grazia* (an eighteenth-century term used to describe a tenor closely resembling what we now call a *tenore leggiero* – light-lyric), plus some lyric roles from the Italian and French repertoires that require an easy top. But in enlarging it to include the latter, he never modified its main direction by venturing into other categories (i.e. *spinto*, or dramatic).

In its entirety, Kraus's repertoire consists of about twenty roles: Italian roles like Elvino in *La sonnambula* and Arturo in *I puritani*; Ernesto in *Don Pasquale*, Nemorino in *L'elisir d' amore*, Edgardo in *Lucia di Lammermoor*, Tonio in *La Fille du régiment*, Fernando in *La favorita* and Gennaro in *Lucrezia Borgia*; Almaviva in Rossini's *Il barbiere di Siviglia*; Faust in Boito's *Mefistofele*; Alfredo in *La traviata*, the Duke of Mantua in *Rigoletto* and Fenton in *Falstaff*; and French roles like Nadir in *Les Pêcheurs de perles*, Des Grieux in *Manon*, Gérald in *Lakmé*, Roméo in *Roméo et Juliette*, and the title roles in *Faust*, *Werther* and *Les Contes d'Hoffmann*.

The rightness of Kraus's choice of repertoire and unusually realistic appraisal of his vocal potential were soon confirmed by Giacomo Lauri-Volpi, the famous 'high-note-tenor' of the past who vividly recalls being visited by the young Kraus, accompanied by a Spanish musicologist: 'I was greatly impressed by the voice of this personable young tenor and by its uncommonly easy upper extension, suppleness and finesse as well as by his line and spontaneity. "Here, at last, is a typical classic *tenore di grazia*", I exclaimed. What a change from the paltry, "short" voices, with their anaemic top and disproportionately heavy middle, that one is used to hearing today!'

Lauri-Volpi was talking during the fifties when, as the eminent Italian musicologist and writer Rodolfo Celletti points out in *Opera* magazine, stylists had all but disappeared from the operatic stage. 'For this very reason, the appearance on the scene of a singer like Alfredo Kraus was of the greatest importance, for he could be considered, along with Carlo Bergonzi, as the only tenor in the last thirty years capable of giving performances of Bellini, Donizetti and certain Verdi operas, founded on a true professional competence and a precise stylistic vision of the romantic musical theatre of the period 1830–60.'

Apart from a few admitted mistakes at the beginning of his career – two performances, in 1956, of Cavaradossi in *Tosca*, one of Pinkerton in *Madama Butterfly* and two, in 1960, as Rodolfo in *La Bohème* – Kraus has never sung *verismo* roles. His light, highly musical but slightly 'dry' voice with its clear, controlled timbre does not possess the necessary weight, roundness and lusciousness of tone for such roles and attempting to force it would certainly have ruined his top and damaged his agility. *Verismo* operas are responsible for prematurely ruining many voices, mainly because their dense orchestrations incline singers to push their voice and feel they can dispense with a sound technique, style and purity of line and make do with sheer volume – a passport to disaster, as all tenors in this book testify. Kraus rightly believes that *verismo* can and should be sung 'belcantistically', with good taste, purity of line, without excesses. (His model is Aureliano Pertile, Toscanini's favourite tenor, who, despite his dramatic voice, managed to sing *verismo* in a pure way.) But he concedes that, for his own particular voice, *verismo*, even when sung as it should be, would still be dangerous. Therefore he turned his back on it.

The result is that he has preserved his voice almost intact into his late fifties; he has outlasted many of his celebrated contemporaries who, like Cesare Valletti and Giuseppe di Stefano burned themselves out prematurely; and, although he no longer sings Arturo with its series of D naturals, which, of course he refuses to transpose down, he can still deliver ringing high Cs, and did when he sang the title role in *Faust* at Covent Garden in June 1983. After he sang Werther in April 1984 at the Paris Opéra the magazine *Musique* made the following comments about his vocal longevity: 'It is no miracle that, at fifty-seven, Kraus remains one of the youngest tenors, with an amazingly fresh voice and clear timbre. ... For he has never been a tenor given to excesses, a fetishist of vocal power *per se*, a bellower of high notes or seeker-after-effects.' *Le Matin* added: 'His performances are a double lesson in the art of singing. First because they demonstrate, through good taste, how this much-abused music should be sung and second because they prove how an intelligent, perspicacious singer can enjoy a long career with a carefully chosen repertoire of a handful of romantic roles.

Kraus is convinced that the reason for his vocal longevity and excellence in his chosen field is his clear-sighted, realistic assessment of his voice. 'As in everything else in life, self-knowledge is the key to a successful singing career. In our case, this involves an accurate and thorough understanding of our voice, the instrument we have to manage. For it goes without saying that we couldn't begin to manage an instrument we only half-understand. Having assessed our vocal qualities and – most important – accepted our limitations, the next step is to choose a repertoire that suits us and takes these into account. After making our choice, we should dedicate all our resources to becoming a specialist in this field – just as we would in any other profession, from architecture and medicine to law –

and, if possible, the *number one* specialist!' (A diametrically opposite view to that of his young compatriot, José Carreras, who confides in his chapter that he 'couldn't bear a boring career consisting of going round the world, year after year, with a repertoire of a handful of roles, even if I were to sing them near-perfectly!'.)

Born in 1927 at Las Palmas, of an Austrian father and a Spanish mother (it is from *her* that he inherits his blond colouring), he learnt to play the piano as a child and sang first in the school choir and later in local churches. After school he trained as a property valuer while continuing his music studies – he is an accomplished pianist – singing on an amateur basis. A music-lover and connoisseur who heard him at a soirée in a friend's house persuaded him to consider singing as a professional career. With his family's blessing, he began taking singing lessons, first at Las Palmas, then in Valencia (where he also did his military service) with Professor Andres, Barcelona with Madame Markoff and eventually in Milan, where his teacher was the Spanish soprano Mercedes Llopart, who had been well known in Spain and Italy in the twenties and thirties and had sung at La Scala under Toscanini.

Apart from Mercedes Llopart, whose teaching was, he says, decisively important, his teachers had helped him to acquire a sound vocal technique but had generally been mistaken in their advice about repertoire, possibly because Kraus's voice has a substantial timbre which, in the sort of small rooms voice teachers usually work in, made it sound more dramatic than it really is. 'For a while, I tried following their advice and learning some dramatic roles, but without ever feeling really comfortable. I *could* sing them, but not without pushing, forcing and tiring my voice – a rather unhealthy state of affairs. I realized my voice needed strengthening, not forcing.' So he ignored their suggestions and concentrated on light-lyric roles like Elvino, Almaviva, Nadir (which, according to the Italian critic Giorgio Gualerzi, who heard him sing it in Turin in 1959, he sang better than anyone in living memory) and the Duke of Mantua in *Rigoletto*, with which he made his professional debut at the Cairo Opera in 1956, aged twenty-eight, after winning first prize at the Geneva international singing competition and successfully auditioning for an influential Milanese agent. Chance had it that the audition was attended by a representative from the Cairo Opera House, who offered him an engagement right away.

Kraus's Cairo debut was notably successful and the Duke of Mantua became one of his principal roles. Despite the fact that, from the dramatic point of view, he finds it unsatisfying, 'un-complex, easy to grasp and offering little scope for character development', the Duke remains a favourite, and Kraus still sings it today with the same ease with which he sang it thirty years ago – a rare achievement. 'As a character, the Duke of Mantua is a libertine and makes this obvious from the first words he utters, the aria "Questa o quella". His only poetic moment comes when he momentarily believes himself to be in love. But it's quickly over because he cannot help being what he is or leading the life he does. A cynic through and through, he is quick to take advantage of Gilda as soon as he discovers his courtiers have abducted her and brought her to his palace. Being head over heels in love with him, she concedes, and this spells the end of his infatuation. He is so used to his caprices that he ends up with a common whore who, by chance, and through Gilda's self-sacrifice, saves his life. At the end, we leave him exactly where we found him: singing "La donna è mobile". So, for him, nothing has happened, nothing has touched or changed him.

'As there is little character development in this role, the Duke's personality must be put across mainly through vocal interpretation and through a certain physical presence that exudes impudence, cynicism, boldness and superficial charm. Full stop. But I think all my colleagues would agree that from the vocal point of view, the Duke of Mantua is one of the most difficult roles in all Verdi, indeed in the whole tenor repertoire.' (Bergonzi, Pavarotti and Aragall do agree and make precisely the same point in their respective chapters.) 'Not because of "La donna è mobile" and its B natural – that, in a sense, is the stupidest moment in the whole opera – but because of the hidden difficulties lurking around every corner. The opening aria "Questa o quella", for instance, which is not an aria of the rabble-rousing kind and sounds deceptively easy, demands a lightness of touch and agility which are hard to achieve at the beginning of the evening, before you've warmed up.

'The second act contains an extremely difficult duet, and in the third act comes the aria "Parmi veder le lagrime", which is one of the most difficult in all Verdi from both the vocal and the stylistic points of view, because it has everything: recitative, drama, lyricism, poetry and you have to switch from one to the other and change your vocal colour almost instantaneously. My teacher, Mercedes Llopart, told me that tenors are always terrified of it. And as she sensed that the Duke of Mantua was an ideal role for my voice, she made me sing "Parmi veder le lagrime" at every lesson, three times a week.' No wonder that when Kraus auditioned for the Milanese agent, the latter was stunned by his exemplary rendition of this aria and asked how a young, inexperienced tenor could sing it so perfectly. 'Because I sing it almost every day,' he replied.

Kraus's successful Cairo debut was followed by invitations to sing Alfredo in *La traviata* in Venice, Turin, and Barcelona during 1957 and at the Stoll Theatre in London in 1958, where his partner was the then equally unknown young soprano Renata Scotto. But the highlight of 1958 was singing the role in Lisbon opposite Maria Callas, an occasion he recalls with gratitude and special satisfaction. Overawed by Callas's fame and reports of her difficult temperament off stage and on, he was understandably nervous. To his surprise, she proved an outstandingly supportive and sympathetic colleague whose stimulating presence was a contributing factor to his own success. 'Had I had a more ordinary partner, I would probably never have had the success I did. But Callas's presence spurred me on to sing better than I ever had before in my life.' (A live recording of this memorable occasion is available on disc.)

Kraus has always enjoyed singing Alfredo, 'a romantic, ingenuous, almost childish character', and considers it a good role for a young tenor. 'In dramatic terms, although he does develop in the course of the opera and is therefore less difficult to portray than the Duke of Mantua, he is nevertheless not easy to put across, because characters lacking "meat" are never easy.' He attributes the success he has always scored in this part to his effort to make something of a character usually portrayed as 'slightly stupid, weak and lacking "grit". But in Act II in the *cabaletta*, often omitted but in my view essential for its important insights into Alfredo's character, we see him develop an adult, manly determination. The *cabaletta* offers a glimpse of remorse, repentance and an unexpected outburst of temperament which would be lost if you sang only the aria. Therefore at least one verse of the *cabaletta* – which, because the music is simple, is enough – should always be included, not for applause-begging reasons but for what it says about Alfredo's character.'

A year after his appearance in Lisbon with Maria Callas, Kraus made his debuts in La Scala as Elvino and Covent Garden as Edgardo opposite Joan Sutherland. During the same year, 1959, he first sang a role that was to become among his most famous: Arturo in *I puritani*, also in Lisbon, under Tullio Serafin, the grand old man of operatic conducting. Kraus was understandably touched and proud when, after the performance, the old maestro went backstage, took his hand and said: 'Kraus, Bellini has written this opera just for you!' Kraus continued singing this fiendishly difficult role, with its impossible *tessitura* culminating in a series of D naturals, for twenty years without any transpositions. A unique achievement, because the very few tenors capable of handling this *tessitura* in the first place usually start transposing it down a semitone after a couple of years. Pavarotti, for instance, transposed the D naturals down to D flats when he sang *I puritani* at the Metropolitan Opera in 1976. (The reason is that through singing heavier, *spinto* roles tenors tend to lose some of their high notes and develop darker colours and heavier voices, with the notable exception of Kraus, who has stuck to a handful of roles.)

No wonder that in 1963, after seven years in the profession and aged only thirty-six, Kraus – along with his contemporaries Nicolai Gedda, Cesare Valletti, Luigi Alva and Léopold Simoneau – was included in Rodolfo Celletti's *Grandi voci*, which came to be regarded as the bible of the singing profession. Kraus stressed to Celletti that his fairly late start and relative maturity at the age of twenty-eight saved him from many of the errors often committed by young singers. First of all he was psychologically ready to adjust to, and cope with, the pressures and strain of singing in big theatres; and second, by then he had a solid cultural, musical and technical foundation. 'The stage forms the artist but ruins the singer. And I am a singer by profession. To be a singer you need a technical knowledge which you cannot have at twenty, twenty-two or twenty-five. Technique is the basis for everything. You cannot be a singer if you are not first a vocal technician and you cannot be a great artist unless you are also a good singer.'

During the sixties, Kraus also made his Metropolitan Opera debut as the Duke of Mantua (1965-6), and sang Don Ottavio at the 1968 Salzburg Festival under Karajan. Yet he has eschewed Mozart roles because, although he loves Mozart and enjoys hearing Mozart roles sung by colleagues, he finds them unrewarding to portray himself. By the seventies, he felt ready to tackle slightly heavier Italian lyric roles like Tonio in *La Fille du régiment* and Gennaro in *Lucrezia Borgia* and to begin exploring the French repertoire. He explains that as soon as he began to sing these roles, he experienced 'a conjunction of the singer and the actor', and his acting ability began to flower and bring another dimension to his artistry.

At the beginning of his career he was often accused of a certain coldness and 'stiffness' on stage and of making rather stylized movements, possibly because, as he explains, the dramatic scope of some of his early roles like Elvino and Nadir is not great. And as far as *bel canto* roles are concerned, the dramatic side is decidedly underdeveloped in favour of the vocal, musical, stylistic element, which is all-important. (Interestingly enough, José Carreras, an essentially lyric tenor, experienced the same flowering of his acting ability after expanding into *spinto* roles that Kraus did after branching into the purely lyric repertoire.)

Kraus's reasons for wishing to explore the French repertoire in particular as soon as he gleaned that his voice was ready for it were, first, his liking for challenges, and second, the realization that, if he proved successful in mastering this style, a substantial, exciting new repertoire would open up for him. Although, in essence, the French style came to him naturally – because his voice possesses the right colours for French opera – he worked extremely long and hard to polish and perfect it, because he knew how unique, elusive and different it is from the Italian style.

Janine Reiss, an unequalled coach and teacher of the French style, explains that 'the main characteristics of the French musical style, and of French style in all the arts, are clarity and measure. In French art, even romanticism is expressed with an element of measure. But in operatic singing, this is particularly hard to achieve, because great opera singers are artists who use their voice with voluptuousness, sensuality and even a dose of narcissism. These are all qualities I try to encourage in singers or even inculcate if they are not there to begin with, even though it's hard to inject sensuality in someone who hasn't got any. I do this because, up to a point, singers should be in love with their voice, and love themselves *through* their voice. Only then will they be able to supervise and master their instrument and communicate to the public the great joy and exhilaration they experience in using it, which is such a vital part of the excitement of singing! But there is a danger that, in experiencing this joy and exhilaration, they may lose the sense of measure so essential to French singing. So, one's main task is to help them achieve the right balance between the two and learn to express even the most unbridled passions within a certain frame.

'To come to specifics: in the operas of Massenet, Gounod, Bizet or Debussy, when a link between two sounds is desired by the composer, it is always indicated in the score. But for a singer who enjoys the sound of his own voice, a link nearly always means a *portamento*, which is a way of going from one sound to another by making a third sound, not contained in the score, between the two. The human vocal cords are like the cords of a violin, with which you can also express half-tones and quarter-tones, which is exactly what happens in both vocal and string *portamenti*. But in French singing *portamenti* are taboo! In French singing a *legato* should be a real *legato* without *ever* becoming a *portamento*! [This is also true of Mozartian singing.]

'Apart from clarity and measure, the French style also demands a total observance of rhythm. If singers respect the composer's rhythmic indications, they will find themselves supported by the music, as if they were leaning on it. The music will help them, because they will have the metre, the rhythm and the harmony of the orchestra on their side in the expression of their role. Another vital point they must learn is the absence of *coronas* – i.e. sounds on which you linger for no apparent reason and which render a certain word more important than another without the text demanding it – which simply don't exist in French singing. One should always remember that the point of departure for any given melody or opera is always a literary text, a poem, a play or groups of words. But opera tends to be a machine that devours the text because, through the voice, there is a tendency to forget this essential, primordial point and to be surrounded only by the sound that carries the words. Singers are so preoccupied with their instrument and the difficulty of producing, pacing and controlling the sound they make that they often forget *what* they are singing. So, working on the text is a specific work that has to be done separately.'

Janine Reiss also points out that, just as there are naturally Italianate voices, there are also singers like Gedda and Kraus whose vocal timbre and colour are particularly suited to French opera. Voices like Domingo's or Carreras's, on the other hand, are a little bit too rich and too lusciously sensual for French singing. 'One feels like pruning them a bit, exactly the way you would a rose bush. The ideal French voice is one whose timbre is sufficiently warm and rounded to make it a beautiful voice but which, when compared to an Italian voice like, for example, Bergonzi's, is a little less sunny and consequently a little less warm. If one were to draw a parallel with colours and wines, a French voice would be almond rather than emerald green, and a Bordeaux rather than a Burgundy.'

Alfredo Kraus thoroughly agrees with Janine Reiss's analysis of the French style and adds that it is the most refined of all styles. 'It demands good taste, subtlety, finesse, sensitivity and control. Continuity is very important, and those long *legato* phrases and long breaths require tremendous breath control. Outwardly nothing much happens but inwardly a great deal goes on. You have this appearance of nothing on the surface, but with great depth inside, inside the phrases and inside the words, which are all-important. And to Italian and Spanish voices, the French language sometimes seems anti-musical, anti-singing, because it seems to go against the natural musical and vocal line.★ This always displeases the French, although they, themselves, are the first to admit it.'

Kraus confides that secretly he has always enjoyed this challenge, this struggle, against the French language, the fact that he *has* to succeed in controlling everything despite the language being against him, that he *has*

★ For an interesting technical point about French singing, see also the chapter on Placido Domingo.

to win! Because he believes that, provided a singer possesses the necessary vocal resources and provided he is prepared to work hard enough, there is always a solution for every vocal or stylistic problem. 'Ultimately the human voice is capable of achieving everything.' Callas believed this, too, and was a great fighter who worked tirelessly until she found a solution to all problems and who enjoyed the exhilaration of winning against all odds. Kraus shares this view and says that 'the very knowledge that the French language was against me was enough to make me determined to conquer it'.

He succeeded so well that, after his debut at the Paris Opéra as Werther, the French magazine *Opéra International* wrote that 'the opening night was a miracle and established Alfredo Kraus as the greatest French singer of the post-war era. What seduces and impresses most is the quality of his French diction, delivered with unprecedented clarity and finesse. In his mouth, every word has a precise sonority and each word accompanies each note without ever hiding behind it.' Incredibly enough, this performance of Werther in April 1984 was Kraus's debut at the Paris Opéra! Throughout his long career, this great French stylist had never sung any of his French roles in Paris. '*No* theatre is indispensable to *anybody*', says Kraus, 'when you consider that Enrico Caruso, the greatest tenor of all time, never sang at La Scala!'

Ever since Kraus first sang Werther in Rome in 1970 (and subsequently in Chicago in 1971, La Scala in 1976, Florence in 1978 and Covent Garden in 1979), he was hailed as an outstanding interpreter of this role. He agrees that this 'is the most complete portrayal I do on stage', and understands why a friend is always telling him he has Werther, and also Des Grieux, under his skin. 'I felt this from the beginning. But with experience and the constant polishing, re-examining, pruning and perfecting that are part of the maturing process of a role, I now feel that when I walk on stage to sing Werther and Des Grieux, I don't simply portray them. I *am* them.' ('From the moment he walks on stage, we feel ourselves in Werther's, not Kraus's presence,' wrote *Opéra International*.)

Kraus's Werther is 'a highly complex, morbid, sick character with an inborn death wish who sees in everything a cause for crying. Everything, even a beautiful landscape, is seen through a negative prism. When, in his first entrance, he sings a hymn to nature, he is sad and melancholy inside, as if he feels excluded from this joy and certain he will die young. Death is always present in his mind, in fact he carries it inside him. But this is very difficult to convey, because Werther is an introvert.' (José Van Dam makes exactly the same point about the difficulty of putting across introverted characters on stage in his discussion of the Flying Dutchman.) 'So, I don't see him as a healthy, full-blooded man. But he isn't a complete romantic, either, because of this intense inner drama he is going through all the time, but a romantic with a brooding, dramatic dimension.'

Kraus explains that in earlier years his interpretation only took account of the character of Werther himself, whereas now it also takes into account Charlotte and *her* mentality and psychology and also Albert and the whole stiflingly middle-class atmosphere of the small provincial town. And he has come to the conclusion that Werther is not only sick but also a little mad, with an almost sadistic streak in his make-up. 'To begin with, he presses his suit when he knows Charlotte is not free; then he seems almost to rejoice in his suffering and finds a way of expressing it poetically. But it's more than mere masochism because he doesn't only want to suffer and punish *himself* but also to punish *her* and make *her* suffer.'

The greatest technical difficulty in this role is not purely vocal in the sense that it doesn't have to do with *tessitura* or difficult notes, but with the problem of finding a way to express the character's morbid state of mind *through* the voice. 'Because, as Werther is an introvert, you cannot put this across solely through your physical presence. It has to come out in your expression, your phrasing, your vocal colour. Phrases should do more than express the meaning of the words. They should also communicate the character's chronic malaise, his morbid melancholy and death wish. This is very, very hard to achieve, and even more so on record.'

Kraus is not enamoured of recordings and dislikes having to reproduce a work piecemeal, disjointedly and without the aid of its natural setting in the theatre. 'How can you communicate the inner workings of a character this way?' In the case of *Werther* he was particularly apprehensive and his principal fear was that this malaise, expressed through the voice, might not come through on record. But he admits that this time, possibly because Tatiana Troyanos and he had often performed this work together on stage, they succeeded, and he was gratified that the critics noticed and commented on his 'sick sound'. 'This was important to me.'

When asked to explain how he creates this sick sound he replied that the selection of the right vocal colours is the result of a long process of thinking about and living with this character over the years, i.e. of maturing his interpretation. This doesn't happen automatically. 'It comes from thinking about what you are singing at every moment, which requires tremendous concentration. Every note, every word, every inflection and stage movement are thought about and balanced within the entire context of the role and the work as a whole, and this involves a terrifying amount of physical and mental work. It's not just a question of a note not coming out as it should or of a high note cracking, but of everything being perfectly related to everything else and continuously sustained. The control and concentration are such that by the end of the evening I am exhausted, and more so after singing Werther than any other role in my repertoire. All I can do is go home, have something to eat and collapse for a few hours in front of the television with my wife and perhaps a couple of very close friends. And during the night I sleep badly because I'm still tense and steamed up. Only by the second half of the next day do I begin to recover. Singing is very stressful, you know.... This is why I cannot understand how most of my colleagues can manage to fly off to another performance or rehearsal the morning after.'

Kraus needs at least a week at the end of a run of performances before he feels ready to tackle another role: not necessarily to rest his voice, but to prepare himself and gradually come out of a certain world, a certain style, before immersing himself in another. This gap is even more important before singing recitals which involve about twenty pieces of music of different styles, all of which must be perfect, whereas in an opera there are some moments like trios or parts of certain duets where he can relax briefly. 'This is my way of doing things. I couldn't do them differently. I couldn't do this *métier* frivolously. I give my all to every performance and, unlike colleagues who manage to do their work and be constantly on the move, I cannot.'

Kraus's unhectic, leisurely approach makes him 'sheer joy to work with', according to Nina Walker. 'He is never on edge, but always in complete control of himself and of the music. At rehearsals he never "marks" [i.e. mouths the words] but, unlike other singers, he is rested enough to be able to sing out. Nowadays most singers arrive so exhausted that they *have* to mark and consequently they get into trouble because they lose the positions. But being able to sing out your role at rehearsal is very important, especially for the conductor. In this as in so many other things, Kraus is the exception.'

Unfortunately I have never seen Kraus perform Des Grieux, Roméo or Hoffmann on stage – although I greatly prize his recordings of the former two, both of which won universal critical acclaim – and so had to refrain from discussing them with him in detail. But I saw him sing the title role in Gounod's *Faust* at Covent Garden in June 1977 and June 1983 and, like his portrayal of Werther, these performances demonstrated what French singing is all about. He likes this opera (which he considers both very beautiful and representative of the French style of its period, 1859) more than he does the role of Faust, which is beset with vocal difficulties and basically requires two tenors: a dramatic tenor for the old Faust and a lyric voice for the young Faust. 'A French theatre did once mount a production with two tenors but nowadays who could afford to pay two tenors?'

Kraus explains that Faust is *just* within the limits of his vocal possibilities. 'If it were a *tiny* bit more dramatic, I couldn't sing it. Because apart from the "Salut demeure" with its famous high C, the overall *tessitura* of the role is low, especially in the prologue which, for me, is the most difficult section of the whole opera. First, because you have to convey the impression of an old man through your voice: second, because trying to do this while singing at this low *tessitura* can pose problems of intonation: you risk giving the impression that your voice is wrongly placed.'

After Faust is transformed into a young man, the *tessitura* becomes easier for Kraus's voice and, from the dramatic point of view, the character is more interesting. 'Faust is a pure young man in love until the devil intervenes in the person of Mephistopheles and tempts him into becoming a carnal sensualist. This is the beginning of his misfortunes: first he kills Marguerite's brother and then indirectly causes her death. He realizes his guilt, repents and his frustration at his own impotence comes out as anger at the devil. But there is nothing he can do about it, for he has made his pact with him. All in all, not a very rewarding character to portray. Everything hinges on style, which is all that matters in this opera.'

According to Kraus, style in general, as opposed to the French style in particular, is a distillation of many other qualities: intelligence, sensitivity, finesse, a cultivated spirit and, above all, imagination – and is consequently very hard to define, let alone acquire. 'Through good teaching and personal effort, you can acquire a good vocal technique. But without a generous dose of the qualities mentioned above, you can never acquire a sense of style. To begin with, we singers have to work with an instrument which, although the most perfect musical instrument in the world, is nevertheless also the most incomplete because it can be neither seen nor touched. And because it is half-inside and half-outside our body, we cannot even hear it the way others do. That's why all of us are so surprised when we first hear the sound of our own voice on tape. So, it takes a lot of imagination to regulate and balance those two sounds. But if we aspire to being stylists as well, then to our fantasy and other natural sensibilities must be added all the qualities I just mentioned.'

Kraus is as renowned an exponent of the *bel canto* style as he is of the

French style and considers both Bellini and Donizetti to be 'the most complete composers as far as pure singing is concerned'. He stresses that *bel canto* demands the same perfection, good taste and stylistic refinement as the German *Lied*, but with the additional element of drama and resultant moments of vocal abandon that accompany the dramatic climaxes, which don't exist in *Lied*. (Like Hermann Prey and Simon Estes, he recommends *Lieder*, however, as an excellent school for style.) Another basic characteristic of the *bel canto* style is the importance of the recitatives, which are as vital and demand as great a perfection of phrasing as the recitatives in Mozart. 'Recitatives are often the most beautiful, and difficult, moments and contain the key to the whole drama. Unfortunately they are often merely skirted over by singers who don't understand Italian and whose only concern is to rush forward to the aria. I remember being impressed when, during rehearsals for his Salzburg production of *Don Giovanni*, Karajan spent most of his rehearsal time on the recitatives and hardly bothered with the arias which, he said, would take care of themselves. Unlike so many Germanic conductors or many of today's younger generation of conductors who think they can conduct opera without knowing much about the genre, Karajan understood this, probably because he did all his basic training in the theatre [seven years in Ulm and five at the Aachen State Theatre].'

Kraus rightly feels that one of the main problems besetting opera today is the disappearance of the old breed of experienced operatic conductor who understood the voice, the mechanics of vocal production and the art of accompanying singers and who had the patience, insight and wisdom to nurture young voices and to spend time on what used to be called *la concertazione*: the meticulous, step-by-step preparation, with the conductor himself at the piano, of every phrase, every recitative, every detail until the final product emerged perfect and seemingly spontaneous. 'Nowadays most conductors tend to use the orchestra as a display vehicle for themselves and don't understand the simple fact that if the stage is functioning properly, they, too, will be credited with success, while the opposite is not always true. Most of them are symphonic conductors of great merit to be sure, but have little training or experience in opera, and even less humility.

'Consequently they fail to adapt their conception and technique to the forces at hand and to realize that ultimately the conductor's job is the fusion of the qualities of the various individuals – singers and chorus – into a successful whole. For this he needs flexibility and elasticity: first of all because each singer is an artist with something to say: second, because each voice should be accompanied differently – a dramatic tenor should not be accompanied in the same way as a lyric voice with an easy top, for instance – and *tempi* should be adjusted to the breathing capacity of individual singers.' Interestingly enough, conductors like the late Karl Böhm, Sir Georg Solti, Carlo Maria Giulini, all of whom, like Karajan, were trained in opera houses, agree with Kraus completely and make precisely this point whenever discussing operatic conducting. So does James Levine who, in his capacity as Music Director of the Metropolitan Opera for the past ten years, has had to deal with singers all the time: 'I try to support, encourage and merge with the assets of each artist. The composers were looking for artists who are empathetic with their creations, and you don't help achieve this by putting square plugs into round holes or by working in a high-handed, dictatorial way.' But he and the few conductors mentioned above are exceptions.

Kraus was lucky enough to begin his career at the time when there were operatic conductors like Serafin, Votto and Gui, men who, in the words of Janine Reiss, 'understood the voice and the way it should be used, who had ideas about interpretation, and to whom singers could go with their score and emerge the richer. Because although they weren't great stars of the podium, they were people who had had time to reflect about the interpretation of each operatic role and to bring to it a mellowness that today is very, very rare. Which is why you find me doing the work I'm doing. In those days, there would have been no need for me because the conductor himself would have had both the ability and the time to prepare his singers.' Kraus remembers with gratitude his work with men like Serafin and his breed, from whom he and the singers of his generation learnt a great deal.

'I remember once auditioning for the role of Fenton in *Falstaff*. At the end of the audition, the conductor said: "Yes, I'll take you, but I would like you to come to my home every day so I can really teach you this role." I did and, thanks to his patience – he pointed out the significance of every note and every pause, went through all the phrases and the general style of the piece – and through this musical study, the character of Fenton matured inside me. Many years later, when the Rome Opera was preparing a production of *Falstaff* in honour of the Queen of England, the conductor beckoned to me and said: "Kraus, you and I must study this aria together." And he drove me crazy, but the result was worth it. And, unlike many of today's arrogant young conductors, these men were not dictatorial. They never said: "This is how it should be." Instead, their way was always "Kraus, come, let's work on this together and let me show you how this should be done". This way of teaching and passing on knowledge and the tradition of the art of operatic singing is a kind of mission. Unless they *are* passed on, one of the links in the chain will be shattered and the chain will remain broken first in one, then in two, then in more places until nothing remains.'

Today's generation of singers are not so lucky. No such help is forthcoming to them, desperately though they need it. The dearth of genuine operatic conductors is matched by an equally dangerous dearth of good teachers, and young singers embark on a professional career insufficiently well prepared. Then, after their debut, there is usually no one at hand who, like Serafin, can teach them how to phrase, or how to sing *piano*. Kraus cannot really fathom why this should be so but suspects it may have something to do with the debasement of vocal and stylistic standards that resulted from the proliferation of *verismo* opera. For reasons he has already explained, *verismo* resulted in many singers feeling they could embark on lucrative careers with no vocal technique to speak of, and after very short periods of study: often no more than two years, unlike Kraus or Bergonzi or Pavarotti, all of whom studied for seven years before their professional debuts. 'This led to the disappearance of good, serious voice teachers and thus began a chain reaction of unsound technique and inadequate preparation – with the result that good teaching and good techniques are now amost extinct, except in very few, isolated cases, where, by some act of God, some teacher has preserved the knowledge and tradition of our art.'

To help remedy this calamity, Kraus gives an annual course of masterclasses, lasting about ten days. Each course is followed by practical sessions where he first demonstrates the application of the theories he has just expounded and then proceeds to correct each singer who in turn sings an aria. 'This way, I hope to help them clarify their ideas.' He has already given classes at Madrid University at the instigation of the Spanish government, in New York, Chicago, Florence, Barcelona and the Canary Islands. But his aim is to be heard by voice teachers as much as by students, 'because it's really teachers rather than singers who are lacking today. If I can advise a single singing teacher, ten, maybe thirty, students will eventually benefit from my experience.'

Two main things Kraus would like to teach are respect for traditions and respect for the original *tessitura* of every role. He is *against* today's mania for complete, exaggerated textual fidelity and *for* the observance of orally transmitted traditions which, in his view, are almost always justified. 'If the composer saw fit to change or add something during rehearsals, after his score had been printed, it was usually for a good reason: either because he had had insufficient time or inspiration to finish the work as he would have wished or, more likely, certain details were purposely decided at the last minute when the specific vocal qualities of all the various singers involved could be taken into account. "Tradition" is what saved those corrections which eventually became law, and it is thanks to tradition that so much of the performing heritage of the past has survived. Therefore, if a singer *can* sing any high notes not contained in the score but traditionally always done, he should go ahead and sing them: first, because there is something very special about high notes that arouses great excitement in the public, and second, because if you remove them you create a situation where anyone, however mediocre a singer, can sing those roles, and those operas. But not everyone can sing those high notes and this makes all the difference, and contributes an extra special element to the grandeur of opera.'

The same thinking applies to his absolute insistence on respect for the original *tessitura* of every role. He was appalled when he sang Edgardo in *Lucia di Lammermoor* in Florence in 1983, alternating with two colleagues who both transposed the *tessitura* down a semitone. The fact was never even mentioned in the reviews, 'as if it made no difference! But singing the last act of *Lucia* the way Donizetti wrote it, rather than a semitone lower, *does* make all the difference and failing to notice this seems to me a very serious and important matter. Because I feel that critics and public alike are in the process of *un*learning what singing really is. They think that what they are used to hearing today is what the art of singing is about. But it's not true! This is *not* what the art of singing is about! This is *not* the way to sing, or, at least, not the way one *should* sing! But neither the public nor today's generation of singers know this, because the dearth of good teachers has deprived the latter (and the lack of good singers deprives the former) of a living link with the true tradition of our art.'

Kraus explains that it is a singer's job to educate the public, even if this means being less 'popular' at a mass level. The way for singers to do this is by constantly striving to improve and surpass themselves, thus helping the public surpass *them*selves too, and arrive at a deeper understanding of opera and the art of singing. 'It would be simple for us to deliver our voice such as it is, without particular excellence of style and without purity of line. The public would accept this all too easily: no one can pretend that one hundred per cent of the public who come to our performances really understand what we are trying to do. But the artist has a duty to be a teacher, an educator, beyond popular tastes and fashions. Instead of "singing to the gallery" we should sing for that section of the public – be it fifty, twenty, ten or even one per cent – who *really* understand. I deeply believe in elitist standards, not from the "snobbish" social aspect but from the point of view of quality and excellence. In singing for this minority of the public capable of truly appreciating what we do, we also help raise the level of understanding of the majority who have now heard and will know the difference between excellence and mediocrity – maybe not today, but certainly tomorrow or the day after. What does it matter if one is temporarily antagonized? I give my art. It is the public who should come to me, not vice versa. This is the way of bequeathing something valid and worthwhile to the future of our art.'

No one who understands and cares about the art of singing would dispute the noble and significant contribution made to both its present and its future by this exacting, dedicated and uncompromising gentleman among singers.

LUCIANO PAVAROTTI

Luciano Pavarotti, whose sensuous, honeyed lyric voice with its pro-digiously easy, silvery top has aptly been described as combining the *pastosa* (soft, elastic) quality of Gigli's with the high notes of Lauri-Volpi's, is one of the most popular tenors in operatic history and one of the very few to break through the undefined but real dividing line between purely operatic fame and mass appeal: the first to understand, manipulate and exploit, aided by an expert, well-oiled publicity machine, the American yen for 'hype'; to begin giving recitals in stadiums, parks and other such mass-audience venues far removed from the conventional opera house and concert hall; to make best-selling records of popular tunes that broke all sales records for a classical artist; to appear on television chat shows, lead the New York Columbus Day parade on horseback and do many of the things normally expected of film and pop stars; also the first to demand, and get, fees originally of 20,000 and eventually of 50,000-plus dollars per solo appearance, a figure apt to swell to 200,000 dollars for a recital in mass-audience venues like Madison Square Garden or Central Park. For, as Herbert Breslin, the astute New York-based agent who masterminded Pavarotti's transition to superstardom puts it, 'no one ever loses money on Luciano Pavarotti!'. His recitals are always sold out, jam-packed and invariably end with his hordes of cheering fans being driven to delirium.

These occasions represent Pavarotti at his best. White handkerchief in hand and unhampered by the need to act – for he is no singing-actor – he gives audiences everything he's best at: hushed *pianissimi* and exquisite singing in the *mezza voce* plus a display of ringing high notes that inspired his recording company to label him 'The King of the High Cs'. 'When singing high notes, I feel like a show jumper before a two-metres-plus bar,' he beams. 'Stretched to my limits. Excited and happy, but with a strong undercurrent of fear. The moment I actually hit the note, I almost lose consciousness. A physical, animal sensation seizes me. Then after it has been successfully negotiated, I regain control.' Doubtless, the frisson produced in the audience by its participation in both the tenor's exultation in his own voice and his fear of failure – which lie at the roots of tenor-worship – is a major contributing factor to the success of those evenings.

On stage, on the other hand, Pavarotti's inability to act is a drawback. It is due partly to his physique (his weight, estimated at between three hundred and fifty and four hundred pounds, but never disclosed, fluctuates) and partly to his conviction that, for an opera singer, singing supremely well is enough. 'It is not necessary to be a Laurence Olivier,' he snapped at a *Newsweek* reporter who commented on this important gap in his artistic make-up and accused him of always strolling around the stage in a variety of loose smocks designed to disguise his weight, 'in a lavish Hollywood musical called *The Great Pavarotti*'. But even he had to admit that the soundtrack is usually magnificent.

The reasons for Pavarotti's immense popularity lie in both the unusual beauty of his voice and in his attractive, larger-than-life personality, which exudes charm, bonhomie, a quick, sharp Emilian wit and an equally larger-than-life appetite for the good things of life – food, wine, girls, fame and applause – and combines simplicity with shrewd, earthy, tough-minded attitudes towards himself, his voice, his artistry, life in general and money in particular.

Pavarotti's own assessment of his artistic and human qualities, and of the reasons for the extent of his popularity, is characteristically short and to the point: 'I'm a *real* singer – very professional. Ergo, I am an eternal student, which is possibly my greatest quality. I also have a natural flair for phrasing that can be neither bought nor acquired. As a human being, I have goodwill for people which must, I suppose, be counted as a quality because they, in turn, are full of goodwill towards me. It boils down to a mutual exchange of love. They also remember that I was the *first* to sing for mass audiences and that I continue to do so.'

Pavarotti stresses that his greatest musical joy is not hitting high notes but singing the *bel canto* repertoire, which he considers 'the essence of music and musical expression'. Top notes are satisfying only because they prove his voice is in good shape and he deplores their excessive glorification, which he considers ridiculous. 'Top notes are like the goals in football. If you can do them, fine. If not, no matter. You can still be a great tenor without the high C. Caruso didn't have it. [He did, however, learn to manufacture it.] Neither did Tito Schipa. Schipa didn't even have a particularly beautiful voice. But he was a great singer. His musicality was so great that it enabled him to override every handicap. Listening to his records, you can hear him guiding his voice along, like a skipper steering his ship through all kinds of treacherous waters in an exemplary way that should be a lesson to us all. He had something far more important, twenty times more important, than high notes: a great line.'

Line, or phrasing, is the way a singer shapes the music within the beat given by the conductor. And, as Pavarotti explains in his autobiography, *My Own Story*, there are several things a singer can do to create excitement within a musical phrase, like, for instance, coming in a fraction of a second ahead of the orchestral beat or hitting a note a split second after it. A natural flair for phrasing is possibly the greatest gift a singer can have. As Pavarotti explained, it cannot be taught but constitutes a vital part of a singer's innate musicality. It can also compensate both for the absence of high notes, as in Schipa's case, or for the lack of a sophisticated musical education, as in Pavarotti's.

All voice coaches who have worked closely with Pavarotti point out that he can barely read music and learns his roles mostly by ear. (Until recently, this was not so unusual, especially among Italian singers.) But they also stress that, although not an especially good musician, Pavarotti is, nevertheless, 'super-super-musical'. Leone Magiera, the distinguished Italian voice coach and accompanist, often finds himself surprised by instances of Pavarotti's spontaneous musical sensitivity: 'He comes up with interpretative ideas that I, for one, may never have thought of. He has this incredible ear and instinctively *knows* how a phrase should be sung. He just *feels* it. And he is almost invariably right.'

After innate musicality, Pavarotti considers the next two most important qualities a singer must have are 'a tremendous personality and, most important, the ability to communicate and make contact with the public, otherwise he might as well stay at home and sing in the bath!'. This communicative gift, which the legendary Caruso possessed to a remarkable degree and which, in the words of the late Rosa Ponselle, 'makes its way across the footlights and sometimes even through the electric circuits of a recording machine', is, in Pavarotti's opinion, even more important today, the age of television and videodisc, than it was in the days of Caruso, when opera singers were judged by much smaller audiences and solely on the basis of what they did in the theatre. Now they are judged by millions, some of whom may never even set foot in an opera house. Therefore, being popular today means 'that you are liked and that you strike a chord both as an artist and as a human being'.

Yet a career as important as Pavarotti's requires more than just charisma and vocal beauty: immense dedication and years of hard work – in Pavarotti's case, seven years of study in his native Modena and neighbouring Mantua. Luckily, although poor, his parents were musical. His father, a baker by profession, was an opera buff with a good enough tenor voice to sing in various church choirs and the local opera chorus. (The rest of the household amounted to what Pavarotti calls 'a nest of women': his mother, sister and adored grandmother, who lived in the same block.) Fernando Pavarotti owned a substantial collection of recordings of all the great tenors of the past and of his day and could instantly pick the best performance of any given aria in the tenor repertoire. (To this day, he coaxes his son by comparing his performances to those of Caruso, Gigli, Schipa or Tagliavini.) But despite his respectable tenor voice he never wanted to, and according to his son he never could have, become a professional singer because he was shy. 'Mind you, all of us are shy at the beginning. But if we aspire to a career in the performing arts, we must not remain shy. We must conquer our nerves and shyness and anything else that might make us feel insecure and thus inhibit our power to communicate. My father's shyness was partly attributable to his total lack of musical education and vocal technique. I was luckier.'

As soon as Fernando Pavarotti discovered his son also had a good voice, he introduced him to all the local choirs he was involved in. One of them, the Rossini Chorus of Modena, won first prize at the International Choirs' Festival at Llangollen, Wales, in 1955, when Luciano Pavarotti was twenty. He remembers the day as 'the proudest in my life' and states it was this experience that made him decide to become a professional singer. At the beginning his father, who was fully conscious of the immense difficulties and hardships involved in forging a successful career in opera, was against the idea. But his mother was all for it, and 'with my father saying "no" and my mother saying "yes", the answer was naturally "yes"'!

The first step was to arrange for some elementary music lessons with the wife of a local Conservatoire professor. Next, Fernando Pavarotti wanted an expert professional assessment of his son's vocal potential and took him to a well-known local tenor and singing teacher, Arrigo Pola. The latter was so enthusiastic about what he heard that, knowing the Pavarottis were badly off, he offered to teach Luciano free. He says he never doubted his pupil would one day become a great tenor and was determined to teach him the basics of vocal technique – correct breathing and placement of the voice, which underlie all good singing – and of tenor-singing right from the start.

For the first few months they did nothing but vocalize and work on vowels, that is, as Pavarotti explains in his book, doing elaborate exercises designed to open up the jaws, enlarge the voice and perfect his enunciation, 'making the clear, exaggerated pronunciation of vowels automatic'. He stresses that the importance of good, clear enunciation in operatic singing cannot be overstressed, for without it a lot of the poetry and dramatic impact are lost. 'This is why it should be worked on and worked on, slaved over really, until it becomes so automatic that you don't have to think about it any longer. And unless this is done early, it is difficult to master later on.' Geoffrey Parsons, the eminent accompanist who has worked with most of today's great singers, remembers first hearing the young Pavarotti in his Glyndebourne debut as Idamante in 1963, and thinking he'd 'never before heard anyone singing Italian like that. The quality of the *sound* of his Italian made it sound like music itself.' (Indeed both Pavarotti and his fellow Emilian, Carlo Bergonzi, enunciate the language and declaim the texts superbly.)

After completing their exercises with vowels, Pola and Pavarotti vocalized, 'hour after hour, day after day, not music, just scales and exercises'. To good effect; for after six months of this rigorous and monotonous regimen, Pavarotti's voice began to feel much more secure, and he was ready to begin work on some scores: Rodolfo in *La Bohème*, the Duke in *Rigoletto* and a few other major roles. Pavarotti points out that he obeyed and followed his teacher's advice blindly, without ever questioning anything and that throughout his career, he has *always* followed the counsel of teachers and colleagues, 'unlike today's young singers who are always doubting, questioning and wanting to discuss every minor point'.

A vital lesson Pavarotti – who is blessed with perfect pitch – learnt from Pola was how to avoid bad *portamenti*, which he considers anathema to good singing. Many singers allow themselves to indulge in such *portamenti*, i.e. the habit of sliding into a note rather than hitting it directly. Pola insisted that every note should be hit spot on, with an almost Mozartian exactitude, rather than through the back door, as he put it, by jumping to any note in its vicinity and then sliding the voice into correct pitch.

After a year's work with Pola, Pavarotti had two octaves of his total range in good shape. Then, suddenly, he stopped improving and seemed permanently stuck at the same level, against some block he could neither understand nor identify. Pola, who was due to leave for an extended stay in Japan, introduced him to the best teacher in the area, Ettore Campogalliani, who had previously taught singing at the Boito Conservatoire in Parma where his pupils had included Bergonzi, Tebaldi and Scotto. One of his current pupils in Mantua was Mirella Freni, with whom Pavarotti made the thrice-weekly train journey from Modena. But during his first two years with Campogalliani, Pavarotti had still not found a way of surmounting the invisible block that barred his way to further progress. On the contrary, he seemed to be *re*gressing. 'Then, all of a sudden, I saw the light! I realized that being a singer requires a lot more than just a good voice and sound vocal technique, and that things like musicality, interpretation, the ability to relax the diaphragm also form a vital part of the art of singing. I also understood that the voice *itself* consists of more than mere vocal sound: it consists also of breathing and colour – or rather, a variety of colours. This discovery was a giant leap forward for me and opened the way to an endless process of self-improvement.'

From that moment on, he made consistent progress and says that during his remaining years with Campogalliani – with whom he continued to study until after the onset of his professional career in 1961 – he learnt to blend and make the transition between the three different voice registers (lower, middle and upper), seamlessly, without any noticeable change of gear. This is an essential part of good singing, yet young or inexperienced singers are seldom able to achieve it. For, as Campogalliani pointed out, it requires mastery of the *passaggio* zone, a dangerous area where it is easy for the sound to break or assume an unpleasant quality. But if those *passaggio* notes are handled in the right way and sung with a 'closed throat' (which, as laryngologist Dr Ardeshir Khambatta explains, means allowing the larynx to float downwards rather than upwards) then they can not only be successfully negotiated, but also open up the top effectively, thus making it easier to hit the high notes accurately and with full volume. All the tenors in this book agree that the *passaggio* notes should always be 'covered' (the term often used for singing with a 'closed' throat), and point out that this has a great deal to do with ensuring vocal longevity.

Pavarotti made his professional debut in April 1961, as a result of winning first prize at the Achille Peri competition for singers from all over Emilia. The prize consisted of the chance to sing Rodolfo in a production of *La Bohème* at Reggio, Emilia. Until then, he had spent his last two years as a student of Campogalliani's in a state of acute depression, because of the lack of professional openings. He had been studying for six years and living at home, because this was the only way he could afford his lessons. A part-time job as an assistant schoolmaster – which he hated and which yielded only eight dollars a month and was soon replaced by a more pleasurable one as an insurance salesman – provided some pocket money. In the circumstances, it was impossible even to contemplate marriage to his fiancée, Adua Veroni, who did later become his wife and mother of his three, now grown up, daughters.

This anxiety about his future as a singer brought on a form of vocal disease: after a disastrous unpaid recital in a neighbouring village the doctor diagnosed a nodule in his voice. (A fibroid nodule can, as Dr Khambatta explains, either be cured by a period of complete rest and silence or, as in Caruso's case, removed surgically.) In despair, Pavarotti decided that if his next recital proved equally disastrous, he would abandon his ambition to be a singer and return to selling insurance. But total silence for a fortnight did the trick and the recital surpassed anything he had done previously. As a result, someone suggested he should enter the Achille Peri Competition. The prize, with its chance to perform in a theatre, at last, was a turning point in Pavarotti's life and he threw himself into the rehearsal work like a maniac.

Chance had it that Pavarotti's first public performance, as Rodolfo, was heard by Alessandro Ziliani, formerly a tenor himself and by then an influential Milan-based agent who had travelled to Reggio to hear Nabokov's son, who was also in the cast. After the performance he was interested in signing on only Pavarotti whenever the latter felt ready for a full-time professional career. The prospect of some steady work at last boosted Pavarotti's morale so much that, five months after his debut at Reggio, in September 1962, he married Adua. Ziliani was soon in a position to offer him engagements both in provincial Italian cities – the most important of which was a chance to sing the Duke of Mantua in *Rigoletto* under Tullio Serafin at the Teatro Massimo di Palermo in spring 1963 – and abroad, in Amsterdam and Dublin.

Dublin proved to be the second important turning-point in Pavarotti's career, for a performance there was attended by Joan Ingpen, then Artistic Administrator of the Royal Opera, Covent Garden, who was searching for a young Italian tenor to cover Giuseppe di Stefano – who at the time had a history of last-minute cancellations – for some forthcoming performances of *La Bohème*. 'There was this large young man, not as big as he is today but big, and at the time very inept on stage, singing a bit to the gallery and holding on to his top notes, but my God, what vocal material!' she remembers. She immediately approached him with an invitation to sing the last performance of *La Bohème* at Covent Garden if, in return, he agreed to cover di Stefano for the rest. Pavarotti, still unknown, was delighted to accept. In the event he was lucky, because di Stefano cancelled all but the premiere and the first half of the second performance and the young unknown scored an enormous success in the rest.

Pavarotti explains that he has always been lucky with Rodolfo, one of his two favourite roles and *the* role in which he was also to make his La la (1965), San Francisco (1967), Metropolitan Opera (1968) and Paris Opéra (1974) debuts. 'Right from the beginning this was a good role for me, a beautiful young role which strikes a universal chord and with which I could immediately identify. Also, a very subtle role through which you can project great feeling. Like me, Rodolfo is a romantic. He speaks a universal lovers' language as true of yesterday as of today and tomorrow and which can be understood even on the moon! The words are great and if you follow the composer's instructions, you cannot make a big mistake. Technically, it is not very difficult. As in most *verismo* roles, you are cushioned by the orchestra and far less exposed than in Verdi or *bel canto*. But his first act aria, "Che gelida manina", contains a monster of a high C!'

While at Covent Garden, Pavarotti also replaced di Stefano in the popular Sunday peak-hour television show *Sunday Night at the London Palladium,* where his charm, wit and ingenuity were as much appreciated as his singing. He was instantly invited back whenever he next happened to be in London. As Pavarotti's agent rightly points out, no amount of skilful publicity can substitute for this knack for instant witty retorts, some of which have become journalistic legends, like his reply to a pretty American television interviewer, Pia Lindstrom, who asked if it was true that God had kissed Pavarotti's vocal cords: ' 'e kissed *you* all hover!', he grinned, displaying his colourful English, in which aitches are always removed from their rightful places and inserted in the wrong ones.

Pavarotti's success at Covent Garden marked the beginning of his international career, with two immediate and important results: first, an invitation to sing the tenor version of Idamante in *Idomeneo* at the Glyndebourne Festival. The renowned coach Jani Strasser made this a particularly good place for young singers to polish their singing and interpretational technique. Many years later, Pavarotti confided to an interviewer that it was here, under Strasser's guidance, that he learnt to sing *piano* – a quality that was to become one of Pavarotti's main gifts as a singer, along with his famous high notes.

Despite the fact that this was the first time he was singing Mozart, 'his style sounded authentically Mozartian', according to Geoffrey Parsons, who was also working at Glyndebourne at the time; and his eagerness to absorb, learn and improve everything from his singing and the Mozartian style to the English language impressed everyone concerned, and contributed to his popularity in the company. Although Pavarotti considers Idamante, originally written for a mezzo soprano, too high for even a high–note tenor like himself, both Geoffrey Parsons and soprano Judith Raskin remember him tackling this *tessitura* with ease 'and of course, there was this glorious voice! I'd never heard anything like it before in my life. A really astonishing, silvery, yet full-bodied sound that possessed a wonderful, sweet quality', says Parsons. Raskin remembers members of the *Idomeneo* cast rushing to her own rehearsals and urging her to come and listen to the 'fabulous young Italian'.

The second important result of Pavarotti's successful Covent Garden appearance was his encounter with Joan Sutherland, with whom he has since sung countless performances and made dozens of recordings. Again, it was Joan Ingpen who engineered the meeting by urging Sutherland and her husband Richard Bonynge to audition Pavarotti who, she thought, could sing Sutherland's repertoire and also had the advantage of being tall (for, as another tall soprano, Beverly Sills, confided to *Time*, 'it's a relief to be able to put your head on a tenor's shoulder!'). Sutherland and Bonynge recall being amazed by 'that phenomenal voice, with its fabulous resonance, shading, range and security, the kind of natural voice that comes along once a century!'. They immediately asked Pavarotti to join their touring company, which was to embark on a fourteen-week tour of Australia in 1965, and sing Nemorino in *L'elisir d' amore*, Edgardo in *Lucia di Lammermoor*, Elvino in *La sonnambula* and Alfredo in *La traviata*, opposite Sutherland – an excellent and healthy choice of roles not only for Pavarotti's particular voice, but for any young tenor at the beginning of his career. In the event, Sutherland and Pavarotti first sang together *before* this tour, when she asked him to replace Renato Cioni as Edgardo, in Miami, in April 1965 – this, Pavarotti's American debut, proved so successful that he remained a faithful visitor to the Miami Opera's annual winter season.

The Australian tour proved not only successful but crucial from the point of view of self-improvement. Riveted by Sutherland's ability to sing the most difficult music written for her range night after night without ever wavering in the level of her singing – something he himself had not yet achieved – Pavarotti explains in his book that he set about learning the secret of her technique: breath support, which, in his words and in the opinion of virtually every singer in this book, 'amounts to eighty per cent of the art of singing because leaning on the diaphragm, a large and, if developed correctly, a strong and highly elastic muscle, removes the strain from the vocal cords and ensures the sound will come out as it should'. (This is the reason why babies can cry all night without any signs of fatigue: if they relied on their throats, they would stop much sooner!) Supporting the voice from the diaphragm means greater vocal longevity, both in an evening and a whole lifetime.

After his return from the Australian tour, Pavarotti – whose vocal cords were, according to his doctor, in excellent condition as a result of his newly learnt breathing technique – was ready for the string of important international engagements that lay ahead: La Scala, where he sang Rodolfo in Zeffirelli's now famous production of *La Bohème* under Karajan in 1965; the Vienna State Opera during the same year; further appearances at Covent Garden with Sutherland in *La traviata* and *La sonnambula* and at La Scala as Tebaldo in the tenor version of *I Capuleti e i Montecchi* under Abbado; his San Francisco debut in 1967 and, a year later, his Metropolitan Opera debut, both as Rodolfo; plus a historic performance of the Verdi *Requiem* at La Scala in 1967, under Karajan, to commemorate the tenth anniversary of Toscanini's death.

Throughout his career, Pavarotti has displayed remarkable intelligence and unusual caution in his choice of repertoire and the management of his voice. During the first decade, the sixties, he made his name as a high-note tenor by concentrating almost entirely on the light-lyric repertoire: *bel canto* roles like Elvino in *La sonnambula*, Arturo in *I puritani*, Fernando in *La favorita*, Nemorino in *L'elisir d' amore*, Tonio in *La Fille du régiment*, and some of the lighter Verdi and Puccini roles like Alfredo in *La traviata*, the Duke of Mantua in *Rigoletto*, Pinkerton in *Madama Butterfly* and, of course, Rodolfo in *La Bohème*. He solidly refused to contemplate singing anything that might damage his voice, even at a time when he badly needed the money. When shortly after his debut at La Scala, the administration offered him the Italian version of Rossini's *Guillaume Tell* ('an impossible role even Gedda – and there is no tenor with a greater facility in the top register than Gedda – had to transpose down'), he flatly refused. Two years later, in 1967, he also refused Cavaradossi in *Tosca*, on Giuseppe di Stefano's advice, because the dense orchestration of this opera would have compelled him to push and force his voice to a then dangerous degree. Whenever asked which is his favourite composer, he replies 'I like Verdi best, but my voice likes Donizetti!'.

In fact he considers *bel canto* 'the best medicine for the voice, because of the discipline and the combination of qualities it requires: agility, elasticity, a smooth, even flow of liquid, well-focussed sound, uniformity of colour, the ability to spin long, expressive *legato* lines without recourse to *portamenti* and, most important, without ever overdoing anything or giving the impression that you are over-exerting yourself, something you can do in *verismo*. Every singer needs *all* of those qualities as part of their technical equipment. And if they are interested in having a long career, they should impose on themselves the task of mastering the *bel canto* style like a religious duty! Because they could never acquire those qualities by singing Rodolfo or Cavaradossi or any other *verismo* roles, which, from the technical point of view, are not all that difficult.' (Carlo Bergonzi, Alfredo Kraus, Placido Domingo and José Carreras all make precisely the same point and also stress that *verismo* operas are partly responsible for the disappearance of good stylists from the operatic stage.) 'But, alas, now-adays very few singers are prepared to try this solution and most prefer to plunge into the meatier repertoire right away – a guarantee for their never fulfilling any early promise they might show.'

Pavarotti's favourite role from his earlier repertoire – and one which he has continued to sing to this day, long after his gradual expansion into the *spinto* repertoire which began in the late sixties and seventies – is Nemorino which, along with Rodolfo, he hopes to go on singing to the end of his career, and considers 'an exultation of the singer in the role', and the most complete portrayal he gives on stage.

In *My Own Story* Pavarotti analyses the role of Nemorino admirably, both vocally and dramatically, and explains that one of the reasons he is so especially attached to it is that Nemorino is 'a very definite and clear character, half-comic, half-sad, like life: a simple country boy, yet not stupid. He figures a way around all obstacles and gets what he is after. I like to think of myself this way, too!' From the vocal point of view, he starts off in Act I, with a lovely aria, 'Quanto e bella quanto e cara', his declaration of love for Adina, which is not without its dangers, especially for the tenor who has not had a chance to warm up.

But Nemorino's big moment comes in Act II, when all the cast leave the stage and the tenor is left alone to sing one of the greatest and best-known tenor arias, 'Una furtiva lagrima', which Pavarotti considers not only exceptionally beautiful, but also a curious aria, because 'up to that moment, all the music in this opera has been lively and lighthearted; brilliant, to be sure, but always within the confines of the *opera buffa* idiom. Suddenly everything stops and there is a total change of mood. This aria of unsurpassed loveliness and seriousness, as though Donizetti were saying "we've been having fun this evening but just in case you've forgotten, here is a reminder that I'm a very good composer and you are listening to very good singers". This aria is also curious in another way. Most great tenor arias in Italian opera end with a *bravura* high note that, if all goes well, sends the audience into a frenzy. "Una furtiva lagrima" has no such surefire crowd activator – only excruciatingly beautiful music that can show up every flaw in a badly trained voice. It is the most restrained of Italian tenor arias and, from the point of view of getting through it, not an especially difficult one. But from the point of view of eliciting the enormous emotional potential from the music, one of *the* most difficult.'

The most technically difficult *bel canto* roles in Pavarotti's repertoire are Arturo in *I puritani* and Elvino in *La sonnambula*. The former, which consists of the tenor singing full-volume in the upper register throughout, he describes as 'pure tightrope walking'. In Arturo's last act duet with Elvira, after the lines 'Ah, l'ira fremate', there are two Ds and a top F and, immediately after his first entry, the tenor has to sing an aria, 'A te, o cara', which contains a D flat. Pavarotti is one of the very few tenors alive able to do that – the others are Kraus and Gedda – but even Gedda transposed the F and the two D naturals into D flats when he sang Arturo at the Metropolitan Opera in 1976. (Kraus, on the other hand, sings this role without transpositions.) Yet Pavarotti maintains that a tenor with an easy top doesn't have to be an incredible singer in order to sing an incredible performance of *I puritani*. 'But if he wants to sing Elvino really well, he has to be a very good singer indeed, because this role requires great phrasing in the *mezza voce* as well as an easy top and is *the* most difficult of all *bel canto* roles'. (Alfredo Kraus agrees.) 'When I first sang this role with Sutherland in London, I knew that if I succeeded in making a success of Elvino, I would have mastered *bel canto*.' He did score a great success.

The role that helped Pavarotti's transitions to superstardom and paved the way to his becoming a household name is Tonio in *La Fille du régiment*, which he first sang with Sutherland in 1966 at Covent Garden and then in 1971 at the Metropolitan Opera. The reason why this is a high-note tenor's opera *par excellence* is one of its arias, 'Ah, mes amis, quel jour de fête', which contains no less than nine high Cs within a single line. Pavarotti remembers that when Sutherland and Bonynge first suggested that he try singing it without any transpositions, he thought they were mad. But as they were good friends, he agreed to try it at rehearsal, with the proviso that if the nine high Cs didn't come, and he was sure they wouldn't, they would be transposed to B naturals. Yet this proved the only occasion in his career when Pavarotti was surprised by his own voice, for to his utter astonishment the voice was there, complete with all nine high Cs, which caused the entire orchestra to rise from the pit and applaud him. Now that he has sung Tonio many times, he doesn't consider its most difficult moments to be those high Cs, 'but all those little cries Tonio has to utter, which have to be sung in tune'.

After singing this role at the Metropolitan Pavarotti came to be regarded as a major vocal phenomenon. Joan Ingpen remembers the sheer thrill of sitting back, night after night, and *knowing* those high Cs would never fail to come out, loud and ringing. Tickets for those performances became very hard to get and lucrative offers began pouring in. Incidentally, this was when Herbert Breslin became Pavarotti's press agent; subsequently, he also took over as his manager.

Although Arturo and Tonio are so taxing, and for that reason rarely heard, the yardstick by which Pavarotti judges both himself and other tenors is the Duke of Mantua in *Rigoletto*, *the* most difficult role in the light-lyric, or indeed, the entire tenor, repertoire, as Bergonzi, Kraus and Aragall also stress. 'The tenor who can manage to cope with *all* the problems in this role and acquit himself well is truly a great tenor,' he says reiterating the point made by Bergonzi. 'From the dramatic point of view it is easy, because the Duke is so loathsome and *antipatico* that he is easy to portray. He is not grey, he is wholly black and therefore easier than grey characters, who are always more problematic. But from the vocal point of view, although well-written, it is a real monster and allows the tenor no respite. He has to sing very difficult music throughout, in every act. In Act I you start off with the deceptively easy-sounding aria "Questa o quella", immediately followed by the Duke's *duettino* with the Countess of Ceprano, "Partite crudele", which contains some of the most difficult music for the tenor, written entirely on the *passaggio* and which must, nevertheless, be sung rather softly, thus posing some embarrassing problems of intonation.' Interestingly enough, Pavarotti is the only tenor who, in discussing this role, singles out this *duettino* as one of the main difficulties in the role. (Yet his point about singing *mezza voce* – or indeed *piano* – in the *passaggio* zone being extremely difficult is confirmed by Bergonzi, who knows how to do this almost effortlessly, as he demonstrates in every role he sings, by observing all the composer's markings of *piano* and *mezza voce* in the *passaggio* zone.)

During the seventies Pavarotti began a gradual expansion into *spinto* roles, some of which he started to try in the late sixties. As always, his major consideration was that they should be right for his voice, that he could sing them without damage to his vocal cords, and that they should be interesting dramatically. Being a high-note tenor he had to be especially careful, because if he chose roles that were *too* heavy or dramatic he would risk losing some of his top notes or impairing their quality. As he explains in his book, he was 'blessed with a lyric voice, not too heavy, with an easy top, well-suited to a large repertoire, primarily the *bel canto* works of Bellini and Donizetti. Yet I have also been able to sing some of the Verdi and Puccini roles without much strain. But certain dramatic roles like

Otello and Chénier, for instance, will always remain beyond my reach .... ' (He did sing Chénier on record.)

As tenors grow older there is (as Carreras also points out) a tendency for the voice to darken and acquire a more 'baritonal' quality. This doesn't mean that the tenor will necessarily lose his top, just that his voice will acquire a natural darker colour (Pavarotti emphasizes that this should be natural as opposed to forced). It usually occurs around the age of forty, so he waited until then (1974) before tackling Rodolfo in *Luisa Miller*, 'which has a last act as heavy as *Otello!*'; until 1975 before singing Manrico in *Il trovatore*; and until the age of forty-four before taking on Enzo in *La gioconda* in San Francisco in 1979, which, because of its heavy *verismo* orchestration, requires even greater weight of voice. So far, with the possible exception of Manrico – which has the lowest *tessitura* of any Verdi tenor role and yet contains an aria, 'Di quella pira', with a high C preceded by a very difficult approach before shooting down again to a low *tessitura* – Pavarotti has not put a foot wrong in his choice of roles. An example many a young singer would be wise to follow.

Pavarotti's first, and favourite, *spinto* role, the one which, he confides in his book, he would choose if he could sing only one role for the rest of his life, is Riccardo in Verdi's *Un ballo in maschera*, which he first sang in 1969 in San Francisco. He felt his voice had darkened enough by then and although it wasn't easy – no operatic role ever is – it felt comfortable and he scored a great public and critical success. As anyone who saw the live telecast from the Metropolitan Opera would agree, it remains one of Pavarotti's most vocally thrilling interpretations.

He explains in *My Own Story* that he loves Riccardo so particularly because 'the whole opera belongs to the tenor and the fantastic music Verdi wrote for him provides opportunities to display many different types of tenor-singing. In scene two of Act I, for instance – the fortune-teller Ulrica's hut – he has three stretches of music plus a difficult trio, all in different musical styles, and each requiring a different sound, phrasing and dramatic mood. And the love duet in Act II is incredible! The only love duet I can think of that can match it in intensity is the one in *Tristan und Isolde*. The love duet at the end of Act I of *Otello* is a masterpiece, too, but a different kind of love is being expressed there. For direct, immediate passion I know of nothing in Italian opera that can match this one in *Ballo*. It ends with a high C. Generally, when I approach a high C, I can think of little else. But in this duet the music is so sensuous and exciting that I get carried away and forget about the high C until just before I sing it. Maybe Verdi thought about this, because in the music he gives the tenor and the soprano a few seconds in which to collect themselves before sending them up to that final note.'

By the time Pavarotti tackled his second *spinto* role, Rodolfo in *Luisa Miller*, in 1974, his voice had grown even bigger and more secure, which made him suspect it was probably getting ready for Radames, which he sang seven years later, in 1981, at the San Francisco Opera. He explains that because of his perhaps excessive caution, his voice has remained the voice of a lyric tenor, 'a little *spinto*, perhaps, but essentially lyric. I can sing Calaf now, but I can also still sing Nemorino!' – no mean achievement for a great tenor in his fiftieth year. Pavarotti considers that, unlike Manrico, Radames is a well-written role, probably because of Verdi's greater maturity at the time. He agrees with Bergonzi and Carreras that, out of the thirty-two B flats contained in this role, the one to worry about is the one at the end of 'Celeste Aida' ('un trono vicino al *sol*'), 'because you cannot push up to it the way you normally would to a B flat. The overall *tessitura* of the aria, which allows few places to breathe, is low so you cannot push. And in the circumstances, it is very difficult to sustain an even, flowing line.'

Pavarotti agrees with the prevailing opinion that a singer who can sing Verdi can sing anything, because Verdi is *the* most difficult of all Italian – and after Mozart, of all – composers to sing. While Bellini and Donizetti also write in a very pure vocal style that leaves little room for bluffing, Verdi demands all of this *plus* a voice capable of sustaining very difficult music. 'Verdi's style of composition is powerful, substantial, virile. Even when he marks an orchestral attack *pianissimo*, for instance, it is always a *pianissimo* with substance, with balls, if I may use the word. The same sort of substance is injected into his recitatives, which are always important and should never be neglected or glossed over.' (Conductor Riccardo Muti makes precisely the same point about Verdi recitatives and says that one of his criteria in judging singers is the power and drama they manage to inject into Verdi recitatives.) 'Another main characteristic of Verdi's is the fact that he leaves singers very little room for conjecture and manoeuvre. Everything is written down in the score and only very tiny things – a nuance here or there – can be changed according to the singer's taste and inclination. 'Otherwise, all details to do with expression are actually written down in the score and if you tried doing anything differently from the way indicated you might get away with it for a week or two. But if you are really musical, after a fortnight at most of doing your own thing, you will invariably find yourself doing what Verdi actually wrote, because it's always right!'

Verdi is Pavarotti's favourite operatic composer but his favourite classical composer of all is Mozart, 'because as an overall musician Mozart is the best, the greatest, the most immense genius of them all'. His tremendous love for this composer prompted him to choose the title role of *Idomeneo* – Mozart's most forward-looking opera, which paved the way for what future composers like Verdi were to do – for the opening of the 1982-3 season at the Metropolitan Opera. (He also sang it at the 1983 Salzburg Festival.) This was something of a sacrifice he undertook for his 'personal pleasure and satisfaction' and also in order to prove even to his most ardent fans that he could stretch himself and deliver 'more than they had come to expect of me'.

Vocally, this role is written for a baritone with a good top. Its highest note is a mere G – with an optional A and an A flat in one aria – and Pavarotti's voice is at its best above G. Keeping his voice down to this *tessitura* was therefore a sacrifice and, in view of his great love for this role, a worthwhile and infinitely rewarding effort, because of the 'upliftment I experienced, especially at that terrible moment when the chorus appears and you can almost *feel* the presence of death. At that moment you feel yourself lifted so high, that the whole performance becomes a spiritual, mystical experience.'

Basically, the Mozart style of singing is fairly similar to *bel canto* and demands the same discipline, exactitude and purity of line. Yet Idomeneo is not a typical Mozart role; because unlike most Mozart operas, where the situation is contained within an acceptable form reflected in the poise and discipline of the singing, in *Idomeneo* the drama is so strong that it takes the tenor to his limits. 'It's such a deeply tragic work that at certain moments it's difficult to control yourself. The recognition scene, for instance, is so terribly moving, especially for those who have children of their own, that in this case you can, I feel, allow yourself a little cry here or there, even if it's not actually contained in the score. It's terribly difficult to control yourself at such moments ... I remember that when, years before, I sang Idamante at Glyndebourne, Richard Lewis who sang Idomeneo often cried and, because crying on stage is contagious, I had to fight hard to keep back my own tears. But I confess that when I came to sing Idomeneo myself, I found it very hard not to cry, not to think of my own daughters. ...' This is probably the reason why this was one of the most moving and effective dramatic portrayals in Pavarotti's career, obviously deeply felt, and beautifully, if not always one hundred per cent idiomatically, sung. Along with his interpretation of Nemorino, it remains in one's memory as his most complete dramatic achievement.

Sir John Tooley, General Director of the Royal Opera House, Covent Garden, thinks that, with *Idomeneo*, Pavarotti regained his true form. This followed a bad patch of about two years during which his popular appeal had reached its apogee and the para-musical activities that made him a household name – apart from the activities referred to earlier, these included appearing on television commercials for American Express and magazine advertisements for Blackglama mink – occupied a great deal of his time, and had caused a slightly supercilious, not to say contemptuous, attitude towards him in certain musical circles. This was partly motivated by envy, because by now Pavarotti was becoming a very rich man indeed; but as he himself admits, it was also partly deserved, because these activities began to affect the quality of his voice. But with this performance of *Idomeneo* he re-established himself as a serious singer.

For, luckily, by that time Pavarotti had begun to realize the dangers to which all those activities were exposing his voice and, in the words of Giuseppe di Stefano, the strain that this kind of explosion of exaggerated publicity and popularity was placing on him as an artist. 'We, opera singers, cannot be imposed on the public through publicity and marketing techniques like cigarettes or Coca Cola,' said di Stefano at the time. 'Because singing before the public is hard enough when you are considered a great opera singer. But when people start calling you "the greatest since Caruso", or "the greatest tenor of the century", the burden on your shoulders becomes unbearable because you simply cannot – nobody can – be at your best at every performance. The public, on the other hand, have been encouraged to expect miracles every time you open your mouth. I'm sure Callas's problems began when she started demanding 10,000 dollars a night, a colossal sum in those days. But I think Luciano will eventually see the light and awaken to the dangers of this situation. He is very realistic, he never has lost his head and never will.'

In the event, di Stefano was proved right. In recent years Pavarotti has eschewed most of his para-musical gimmicks and concentrated on operatic performances, recordings and recitals. Although many musicians and music lovers bemoan his wasting time with popular recordings, this, as in Domingo's case, cannot really harm his voice. But giving frequent recitals in mass-audience venues where he has to sing loudly all the time and display a constant succession of his famous high notes *can*, as Geoffrey Parsons explains, be endangering some of the exquisite subtlety he used to bring to *pianissimo* or *mezza voce* passages. Still, his voice remains in remarkable condition and, on a good evening, one would never suspect he is fifty years old.

Like all Pavarotti ventures, his expansion into recitals began slowly and cautiously because, as he explained to *Newsweek*, he is 'not a man who risks wildly but who likes to prepare every step'. He points out that concerts and recitals require even greater concentration than operatic performances because, unless he himself believes in what he's doing, the public will get bored. Right from the very first recitals – in Minneapolis, Dallas, Washington, Chicago and finally Carnegie Hall in New York – the response was 'jubilant applause bordering on hysteria', to quote a Chicago critic. After so much acclamation, Pavarotti's agent felt it was time to try something even bigger: a nationally televised solo recital live from the Metropolitan Opera and relayed at the peak time of four o'clock on a Sunday afternoon. High stakes indeed, and Pavarotti was understandably terrified. An assistant conductor, Gildo di Nunzio, confided to *Time* that after visiting Pavarotti in his dressing-room before the telecast he felt so sorry for him that he wouldn't have liked to be in his shoes for anything. 'He didn't think he could do it and wished he could cancel.' Pavarotti himself admits in his book that this was the single most nerve-racking occasion of his career.

'When you give a performance before a thousand people, you are, of course, terrified of singing badly, but there are ways you can lessen the nervousness. Because if you sing below par one night, you can sing enough good performances later to erase this memory. But if you sing on national television and your voice cracks on a high C, you then have a terrible amount of statistics to overcome. My manager and others are always telling me how wonderful television is for the career and how quickly and efficiently it gets across to vast numbers of people the good news about Luciano Pavarotti. They don't always remember that, on certain days, the news may not be so good! And all that efficiency and mass-audience aspect of television can work just as strongly against you. Sometimes I feel I am the only one to realize things can go wrong. I don't think I am the type who worries too much. I am just realistic and know what can happen. As the moment approaches for this kind of recital to begin, the worry and anxiety take over and crowd all other thoughts from my mind. I remember sitting in my dressing-room and asking the time every five minutes on that day. One friend told me I was crazy to worry, that the audience out there loved me. He didn't understand a very simple fact: maybe they do *now*. But that doesn't mean they will still love me when it's over.'

Pavarotti's usual remedy against this kind of stage fright is being surrounded by a lot of people before a performance. I remember feeling astonished when, a few years ago, I went to interview him for a British newspaper and he suggested that we begin our interview in his dressing-room forty-five minutes before a performance of *La Bohème* while he was being made up and fitted with his costume. But he explained that 'talking takes me out of myself and, provided it's not too loud, also helps warm up the voice'. Intermissions are another no-man's land, when 'you are out of battle for a brief spell without the war being over!'. Although he has now relaxed his former rule of receiving no one except his wife during intervals, he is by no means the social animal he becomes after the performance, when he receives almost anyone wishing to see him and, being an outrageous (but on the whole harmless) flirt, kisses every woman in sight on the lips, signs countless autographs without demur, and generally revels in the afterglow of applause and the palpable affection – 'the oxygen I breathe' – with which he is enveloped by the public.

In earlier years, his ideal way of unwinding after a performance was to take a lazy, luxurious, hour-long bath followed by dinner, preferably in his own or a friend's flat – where, being an excellent cook, he often does the cooking himself – rather than in restaurants. Nowadays, the size of the queue outside his dressing-room dictates that he eschew the bath and just make do with a gargantuan meal after he has signed the last autograph (the time spent signing autographs is never long enough!), unless he is on his famous diet consisting of zucchini, rice, and about half a pound of meat or fish cooked in a few drops of oil. Perhaps over-eating is his reaction to the tremendous strain of his singing career. Whatever the reasons, he considers 'this inability to push away the dining table' to be his biggest and ('because I'm usually strong-minded and a very determined person') his unique weakness. 'I could tell you all sorts of fanciful stories about my glands making me fat. But I would be lying. It's the food!'

Pavarotti's main relaxation is his month-long annual August holiday at his large seaside villa at Pesaro on the Adriatic coast, where he gathers his entire family, parents, sisters, in-laws, nephews and nieces. He also owns an office block and a record store in Modena, plus a spacious seventeenth-century mansion set in twelve acres of land which he is converting into a house for himself, with separate apartments for his entire family. 'We're all going to live there – *everybody*! I want to prove that families can stay together even in this day!'

Looking back on his life, his long, successful career and phenomenal popularity, is there anything this obviously contented, shrewd, sunny-natured Libran would like to change?

'Just my size,' he sighed.

THE BARITONE

The term derives from the Greek word 'baritonos', generally used to designate the normal male speaking voice. Applied to the male singing voice, it denotes the register between the tenor and the bass, with a range from A below the stave to F and G above. A baryton-martin is a French term denoting a light type of baritone voice.

THOMAS ALLEN

Thomas Allen, whom Harold Rosenthal saluted in *Opera* as 'certainly the best British baritone since the war and the equal of most singing anywhere', is the epitome of what a contemporary opera singer should be: first and foremost, the possessor of one of the most beautiful, manly, richly coloured lyric baritone voices of our day and a superb stylist equally at home in Mozart and Verdi, in the French and Russian repertoires, and the Wagnerian idiom, as well as operetta and twentieth-century works. Secondly, he is a profoundly convincing singing-actor who combines dramatic intensity with finesse and invariably succeeds in making real flesh and blood characters of all his operatic roles. In addition, he has star quality – that indefinable something that comes pouring over the pit and the floodlights and grips the audience by its scruff – animal magnetism and charm, the equally indefinable quality that goes straight to the heart and instantly puts the audience on the side of whatever characters he portrays.

The compelling dramatic power of most of Allen's interpretations is partly due to the wholehearted, quasi-obsessional way he experiences and identifies with his roles – a trait that became immediately apparent in our conversations, when he discussed the various operatic characters in his repertoire with the mixture of affectionate familiarity and intimate, perceptive detail with which one would discuss mutual friends. 'I have never forgotten a remark of Tyrone Guthrie's, who once said to Laurence Olivier during rehearsals for a role the latter was having difficulty with: 'You don't love this man, do you?' and Olivier had to admit he didn't. And this is the secret. You *have* to love the people you portray, otherwise the audience won't, either. You have to find something in them that you can take and identify with, and *then* you have a basis for work.'

Allen's exceptional vocal and dramatic gifts have propelled him to the pinnacle of the operatic profession: from the Welsh National Opera – where he went straight from the Royal College of Music – to Covent Garden, La Scala, the Vienna, the Hamburg and the Bavarian State Opera, the Salzburg Festival and the Metropolitan Opera. He says that he has never had a specific plan either for his voice or his career and that he is not an overly ambitious man. 'But I *am* aware of something in myself which needs to be fulfilled and which I have to feed. Like all artists, I feel myself driven by this element I have never wholly understood. Not being especially ambitious, I have tried and failed to account for the fact that I have wanted to sing at the Met or La Scala not because I, myself, particularly *wanted* to, but because these were the right goals and opportunities for fulfilling this something within. I suppose that anyone with a specific talent is inherently directional and programmed in a certain way.'

Allen, a highly intelligent, articulate, friendly and warm-hearted man with abundant energy and a sharp, probing curiosity about a wealth of subjects, had neither wanted nor planned a career in music until after he left school in his native Seaham in County Durham. Until then, his predilection was for science – chemistry, physics and biology – and his aim was to become an eye surgeon, 'because I have always been fascinated by the eye, its mechanism and the way it functions: it's a microcosm – and I have always been interested in things in miniature – a wonderful piece of machinery and, in human terms, what holds one to people'. He displayed no great dramatic aptitude either, despite an appearance in a school production of Shaw's *The Devil's Disciple*, mainly because in this rough part of the world it was considered 'sissy' for boys to have any artistic leanings.

He was first introduced to music by his father, a salesman in the local store and a keen amateur musician who ran his own glee club and dance band, accompanied a male choir and collected musical instruments. As well as a piano, a violin and a guitar, the family also possessed a nine-foot-high two-manual pipe organ built by Tom's grandfather who, unlike most of the family who had been miners, was a metal-worker. When Tom was eight, he asked his father to teach him how to play both the piano and the organ and confesses that, to this day, 'the sound of an organ absolutely fascinates me and makes me itch to get my fingers on it'. He also possessed a reasonably good treble and sang in various church choirs. His voice broke early, at thirteen, and by the age of sixteen it had settled into a firm baritone, good enough for him to sing solos in the Robert Richardson Grammar School choir and give a few concerts at various local Women's Institutes. The men responsible for recognizing the exceptional quality of his voice and for encouraging him to enter local competitions and festivals were the physics master at school, a former BBC singer who began giving him singing lessons in the lunch hour, and also the music master, who taught him the organ for a while, plus some basic harmony, and 'probably made me appreciate what high standards in music were all about'.

Music soon became his consuming passion and he was beginning to wonder whether it might be possible for him to earn a decent living as a singer. After auditioning for Arthur Hutchings, Professor of Music at Durham University, the latter was impressed enough to help set up an audition at the Royal College of Music in London. It went well, Allen was accepted, and he moved to London for the 1964-5 scholastic year with the intention of becoming a *Lieder* and oratorio singer because, at that stage, he had never even *seen* an opera as there were no opera houses near his home town. His first three months in the capital were spent in dingy lodgings in Stockwell where, miserably homesick for his happy family life up north, he cried himself to sleep every night. (Allen is an only child who has 'tremendous love' for, and has remained extremely close to, his parents, and is in turn very close to his own teenage son, 'more like brothers, really'.) Fortunately, life at the Royal College soon became interesting enough to absorb his energies and, after moving to less depressing lodgings, things began to look up.

His professor of singing throughout the four-year course was Hervey Alan, to whom he is grateful for assessing and placing his voice correctly, guiding his vocal development but, most of all, for leaving a natural voice alone and not disturbing what was already there, 'something fairly rare among contemporary teachers'. The main task was to brighten up what was, in his words, a rather 'plummy' voice that was going through a stage of singing 'too prettily'. But what helped brighten it up, more than anything, was his involvement in opera, which was also instrumental in making him 'a bigger performer than I would ever have been, had I stuck to *Lieder* and oratorio'. His involvement with opera began during his last year at college, when he was asked to replace an ailing student in an opera-school production of Arthur Benjamin's *The Prima Donna*. He has never forgotten the exhilaration of this first contact with the theatre, which was to prove decisive for his future. After the performance the director declared that if Allen didn't take up opera, he'd be a bloody fool! Allen decided to heed his advice.

At the end of the last year at the RCM he won the coveted Queen's Prize, part of which consisted of coaching lessons with James Lockhart, then on the music staff at Covent Garden, but who had just been named Music Director-elect of Welsh National Opera. Lockhart was impressed enough to suggest that Allen audition for the Welsh National, where he was immediately offered a place as a full-time member of the company as from 1969. He accepted and, with the help of a £800 grant from the Gulbenkian Foundation, spread over two years, began his professional career. Before moving to Cardiff, however, he spent a pleasant summer in the chorus of Glyndebourne Festival Opera, where he also understudied the role of Albert in Massenet's *Werther* and was awarded the Christie Prize, which he couldn't accept as he had already 'thrown in his lot with the Welsh National Opera'.

Allen's five years (1969–74) with Welsh National Opera were crucial for his future development, under the ever watchful eye of James Lockhart, who 'gave me the benefit of his musical experience, his experience with languages and helped give me confidence to overcome my self doubts and natural fears. Whenever I protested that I was not capable of singing any of the roles he suggested – like Figaro in Rossini's *Il barbiere di Siviglia* or the title role in Britten's *Billy Budd* – he would calmly reply: "I wouldn't give them to you if you weren't capable!"' Allen's debut with WNO in 1969 as Figaro proved Lockhart's judgement right. 'In his first major role, Thomas Allen, the Figaro, suggested a talent to watch. Sharp articulation . . . a rich voice and the kind of personality that seems to take production naturally added up to a blend of real promise,' wrote *Opera*.

The Rossini Figaro was followed by Paolo in Verdi's *Simon Boccanegra* and four Mozart roles: Guglielmo in *Così fan tutte* in 1970, Figaro, and eventually Count Almaviva in *Le nozze di Figaro*, also in 1970, and Papageno in *Die Zauberflöte* in 1971. This is where, under Lockhart's tutelage, he laid the foundations for his mastery of Mozartian style, and surely it can be no coincidence that two of the greatest Mozart singers of our day – Allen and Margaret Price – began singing Mozart at Cardiff under Lockhart. Since leaving college, Allen has never had a singing-teacher, preferring to be his own 'singing doctor', and declares that his *real* teacher was Mozart.

'I learnt my Italian through Da Ponte and my singing through Mozart, because in Mozart you cannot get away with anything. He demands good intonation, utmost precision and terrific discipline – the opposite of sloppy singing! You observe note values and rhythmic patterns, you cannot indulge in *portamenti* and, of course, there is the eternal argument about whether to use *appoggiaturas* or not. I tend not to use too many but this, too, is something that has to be learnt, it's part of the schooling. To this day, Mozart remains the yardstick by which I judge the condition of my voice: if, after undertaking a big new Italian or French role I can return to my Mozart parts with ease, then everything is all right.'

Allen was reluctant to undertake Figaro in *Le nozze di Figaro* because the *tessitura* is a bit too low for him. Still, he was glad to have yielded to Lockhart's persuasion, because from the dramatic point of view he has a special affection for this role. 'I love its vital spark, the sharpness of touch and the alertness it requires, plus the undercurrent of something bordering on the dangerous. It also has a kind of political "meat" which is totally missing from Rossini's Figaro (for although both Rossini's and Mozart's operas are based on Beaumarchais, the former has more sunshine and makes for a more ebullient, fun evening-for-all), but which one must guard against overstating. Like all Mozart operas, it demands finesse, a sense of measure and a certain restraint, as John Moody, a great connoisseur of eighteenth-century style, taught me. As well as showing me the right way to hold a coat or fold a sleeve, he explained all sorts of important points like the fact that Figaro, being a servant, should never touch the Count or the Countess and that a certain decorum should prevail even in the most dramatic moments, because the conventions of the day required this to be so.

'These considerations are crucial and must be observed at all times in *Le nozze di Figaro*, an opera in which everybody knows their place. The key to Figaro is a lightness of touch which should be even greater than the Count's and which should, at certain moments, make the latter look like an absolute donkey! Figaro just has that edge over him. The Count would be considered a very clever man in most societies. But he is up against a man like Figaro, who has been involved in, and manipulated, his life for years and thus knows more about him than is healthy. This lightness of touch should prevail in all Figaro's reactions to the Count: even the phrase "io non impugno mai quel che non so", which Figaro sings in Act III, should be flung at the Count very lightly, totally innocently, with a smile, and never even for a second suggest a confrontation. Some people try to turn it into a slanging match, eyeball to eyeball, but I don't see it this way at all. Figaro's subtlety and lightness of touch should leave it hanging in the air.... For, having said this terrible thing, in the next breath he sings "ecco la marcia" and is immediately off on another track. A wonderful role to play and to sing because, apart from the low *tessitura*, his tunes are much easier than the Count's.'

Allen first sang Count Almaviva, also with Welsh National Opera, in 1970, and eventually it was to prove *the* role that propelled him into a fully fledged international career. In 1977, he was invited to sing it at Covent Garden in a star-studded production – with Teresa Stratas as Susanna, Agnes Baltsa as Cherubino and Hermann Prey as Figaro – under the late Karl Böhm, who considered Allen one of the best interpreters of this role he had come across in his long, distinguished career. This came only months after Allen's triumph as Don Giovanni with the Glynde-bourne Festival Opera. As well as being vocally and stylistically impec-cable, both portrayals are also dramatically riveting in their mixture of arrogance, manly allure and suggested potency. 'Thomas Allen's Count is less ferocious but no less fascinatingly composed than his Don Giovanni – of steel, quick wits, unlikeable cruelty, a line of purring seductiveness and a voice lithe, firm and superbly fitted to the music,' wrote Max Loppert in the *Financial Times*. Michael Geliot, who saw Allen's first Count in John Moody's production at the WNO, and who was a considerable influence on him at the time, was quick to perceive and exploit this potency: 'There is a demon in Tom and his Count was a man who has something in common with Don Giovanni.'

Allen himself states that this sort of suggested visceral potency – 'balls in the voice', as a colleague puts it – is something people tend not to talk about. 'Yet it's what makes the Count and many other roles work. Very few voices have it. But unless you sense this kind of potency in the Count or Don Giovanni, the roles would simply not work because no one would believe these men could behave the way they do. Eugene Onegin should have it, too, but in a more understated way and projected through still-ness, because it stems from his past rather than his present actions in the drama.'

From both the vocal and the dramatic points of view, the Count is the most difficult of all Mozart baritone roles because, as Allen points out, 'it is a classical role and he is a classical character, so you have to stand up there and be a model of Mozartian singing all the time. It requires a refinement of voice and elegance of body, gesture, movement and every-thing else. One should also be aware of, and take into account, many things, like the paintings of Watteau, Fragonard and those Figaro-type pictures of Goya's, as well as the points about eighteenth-century etiquette that I learnt from John Moody. The role also makes considerable vocal demands: you have to maintain some of the agility in your voice for the singing of it – the Count's big Act III aria, "Vedro mentr'io sospiro", for instance, has an enormously florid section at the end – as well as that lightness of touch for the recitatives and the playing of it. The Count is always being caught in embarrassing tussles with girls – Susanna in Act I and Barbarina in Act III – so this sort of situation is bouncing off him all the time and he has not merely to act, but to *react*, which is very important. But the marvellous confrontation with his wife in Act II and some of the more aggressive moments in Acts III and IV demand some of the heaviness of a Don Giovanni.'

Despite its multiple vocal and stylistic demands, the Count is the most comfortable Mozart role for Allen's voice, along with Don Giovanni, which he first sang in 1977 with the Glyndebourne Festival Opera in a fascinating production by Sir Peter Hall. The production was dominated by the latter's view of Don Giovanni as a man constantly in search of a deity, constantly challenging and asking the question, 'Is there anybody up there listening to me?' As Peter Hall explains, 'What makes *Don Giovanni* so exceptionally interesting among Mozart's works is that, musically, it looks forward to the nineteenth century. The very beginning of that overture takes one right through Beethoven to Verdi and beyond, almost to Mahler, in fact. But dramatically the opera looks back to the Middle Ages and is in some respects a morality play. I believe the whole thing is based on the premise that if there is a God and if we are punished for our sins, then Don Giovanni is very much a man of the Enlightenment who would like to believe, would like to have faith, but does not and who in a sense waves his penis in the air to see if God will respond. He becomes more and more awful to see if anything will happen to him and finally something does. And this, I feel, is mirrored in the score, especially at the end of Act I.' At this point Don Giovanni was made to exit with a cheeky bow, one of the most lightheartedly mocking, provocative gestures in any staging of this work, executed by Allen with superb finesse and aplomb. 'I came to that conclusion by working on the piece and by having in Tom someone who has a wonderfully harsh tenderness.... It's a real paradox: he can play an intellectual, he can play an outsider, he can play an aristocrat and I thought his portrayal was wonderful, really wonderful.'

Peter Hall usually settles on his final interpretation during rehearsals, when, confronted by his cast, he can assess the qualities they can bring to the work and to their roles. The only conscious decision he made before beginning rehearsals was to set the production a bit after the date of composition of *Don Giovanni*, 'only to get to that moment when the Enlightenment broke up and turned into the Romantic Age, because that moment *is* in Mozart. There are two geniuses who, to my mind, were extremely lucky in their time of birth: one is Shakespeare, who inherited an absolutely regular form of English poetry which he could make irregular, make breathe, and the other is Mozart, who inherited a century of classicism which he could modulate into sudden romantic anguish [as he does in *Idomeneo*, for instance]. Both were geniuses who made their own rules, *the* supreme geniuses.... So, having decided to set the production a bit later but still very close to Mozart's time, I set out to try and find the piece, with the singers, because working with the cast is the only creative way to work. It drives some singers mad because some of them, the lazy ones, like to be given the moves and told what to do and just do it, which is very boring and dead. But singers like Tom are highly intelligent performers who enjoy exploration. This is what directing a piece is all about. Before beginning rehearsals I only know the *piece*, or so I hope. I then begin to think on my feet, take what the singers do and what I do and edit what we all discover. That is when all sorts of crucial details are decided.'

The result was one of the most complex and intriguing portrayals of the title role in living memory. As well as the fascinating dimension of his challenge to God, Giovanni emerged as an electrifying mixture of exquisite social grace and a potency that encompassed both naked desire and a subtle ·sadistic streak: 'A Giovanni both repulsive and attractive, leeringly vicious and masterfully fascinating, a Giovanni in whom cruelty and courage are both surfaces of the same coin, a Giovanni who holds the stage by right, not by accident' wrote the *Financial Times*. Rodney Milnes's verdict in *Opera* was that 'in the title role, Thomas Allen has taken a giant leap forward in a career whose potential now seems boundless', and Allen himself considers this production one of the most gratifying experiences of his career. 'I hope you understand how marvellous and how important it was for me to have made a success of it. For when it was first mentioned at Glyndebourne that I would be doing it, many people shook their heads and voiced doubts about whether it would work, because I was too nice a guy and so on. But I knew I had something different inside me which I could bring to the role and this, I think, is what helped with it.'

Since then Allen has also sung Don Giovanni at Covent Garden in 1984, Houston, the Bavarian State Opera in 1986 and will do again at La Scala under Riccardo Muti in 1987 and in Japan. He feels that this is a role he can go on developing forever. Each production may provide a different key to the character which, in turn, could change the vocal emphasis in certain passages or the approach to the recitatives, where something always varies slightly even from performance to performance. 'This is something I find particularly wonderful, and one of the reasons why I love opera: because in the dialogue and the recitatives you come closest to being a straight actor. You can afford a little extra time, a second or so longer for dramatic moments, you have that leeway, whereas in arias you have the conductor putting down beats and cannot take such liberties. But in recitatives and dialogue you make your own timing. This is why they are the moments I treasure most. As far as the rest of the music is concerned, although, especially in Mozart, all the answers lie in his score, I have occasionally felt the need for another second or so before saying a certain word than I was being allowed, either because the chemistry was not yet right or because a colleague did something slightly differently at this particular performance which in turn needed a slightly different reaction from me.'

The intense electricity Allen exudes during performances of *Don Giovanni* means he never sleeps well after singing it. 'The problem with a role like this is that it never allows you a moment's respite. It's climbing forever onward. It starts off in quite a rumbustious way and proceeds to climb on a crescendo of tension all evening until the final moment, when you have to produce the heavy artillery. So you just have to keep going on and on. If you allow the tension to relax even for a second, you might as well not bother to continue with the performance at all, because everything will have been lost. Because there is this manic drive, almost like a death wish, hurtling Giovanni on to his destiny, and you have to ensure that the thread of mounting tension runs right through the piece. I know one ought to be able to communicate tension without actually experiencing any oneself, but I haven't yet learnt how. I still tense up, I have to, it's the way I work and the way some roles work. The kind of tension and animal strength Giovanni has to have all the time does affect me, physically and mentally. Even now, as we're discussing the role and I'm preparing to sing it again, at Covent Garden, it begins to stir me up. I feel impulses running through my arms and legs, I can sense them tensing up. And this tension won't cease until the end of the present run of performances. This is why I need several days between performances and prefer not to have to sing it more than twice a week. The only other role that is even worse in this respect, and drains me even more, is Eugene Onegin.'

Allen first sang Tchaikovsky's alluring and complicated hero for Welsh National Opera in 1980, and subsequently at Ottawa in 1983 and Covent Garden in June 1986. All three productions were in English but he is looking forward to singing the role in Russian for the first time at the San Francisco Opera at the end of 1986. He considers it one of the most fascinating roles in his repertoire and musically full of wonderful things. Despite the stylistic differences between the two operas, he finds this role somewhat similar to Don Giovanni in the sense that both demand ever-increasing tension, a sense of potency that alone explains the fascination the characters hold for their heroines and both have endings that drain every drop of his energy. This work in particular is so intense that, in sheer self-defence, he has to stand apart a little, 'otherwise, if you let them get higher than the chest, the emotions involved in the final scene would tear you apart'.

'Onegin haunts me in the same way that *Jane Eyre* does, whose relationship to Rochester has always fascinated me.' (He named this as the one book, apart from the Bible, that he would take to a desert island with him in the late Roy Plomley's popular BBC radio programme *Desert Island Discs*.) 'It's the sort of relationship that, I feel, Tatyana could have enjoyed with Onegin, had he not resisted it. . . . Yet resisted relationships have an identity of their own, as if the resistance is part of the meat the relationship is made of. And, like all relationships that contain an element of struggle, they seem to count more, somehow.' From the dramatic point of view, *Eugene Onegin* is an extremely interesting opera. Although the libretto is based on Pushkin's poem, he finds a very Chekhovian element in it, and the more Chekhovian the production, the better he likes it. Being a great lover of Chekhov, he felt especially fortunate that both the WNO and Covent Garden productions had sets which, in Act I, opened on to a very spacious stage with a Russian dacha at one corner and 'a wonderful, warm, country feeling with trees on the horizon and agricultural life all around'.

He also believes in a somewhat Chekhovian approach to the character of Onegin himself. 'The opera begins very quietly, with people sizing each other up and Onegin prowling about in a predatory manner, circling around Tatyana pretty flagrantly, in a particularly odious way. You have the feeling of those two being strongly aware of each other, and you also have some wonderful, quiet sections where nothing much happens – exactly like the moments one comes across in Russian literature and drama, like Act II of *The Cherry Orchard*, for example. Onegin himself I see as a jaded, blasé, rather slimy figure with a stiff, negative, grey presence, a white face and a deeply disdainful attitude towards the country and country gentry, a man who so far has had everything he wanted out of life.

'I always try to bear in mind two vital questions: what happened to him before the beginning of the opera? We know he has inherited a lot of money from a rich uncle and one therefore imagines he has led a rather cool sort of life. The second question is what happens to him between Acts III – where he kills his friend Lensky in a duel – and IV, where he comes across Tatyana again? Obviously, he has not found peace. Like so many people, oneself included, he has been a restless soul for years. He now comes to the crucial realization that he, too, loves Tatyana, too late.

For he had failed to recognize the potential for change in people and to foresee the possibilities in a situation – always a tragic error in life, in those days as much as in our own. It is ironic that she, who was so much younger and less experienced than he, recognized this potential in him, while he failed to perceive it in her. It's true, of course, that her obvious enthusiasm for him and inability to conceal or control her feelings, which culminates in her letter to him in Act I, must have been embarrassing to him, in a sense. For how could he be expected to cope with a girl who thinks she sees in him the incarnation of all the characters in the romantic novels she is forever buried in? In no way could he . . . .

'But when confronted by the woman this naive, sentimental girl has grown into, in Act IV, he is overwhelmed. The floodgates open and he experiences this manic passion to see her again, to tell her he has resolved all the conflicts and the stubbornness in himself, that he loves her and wants to have her. And she, now married to a rich, loving but elderly prince, rejects him, despite the fact that she still loves him. She puts doors between them and closes them and he is left out there, in the snow, alone and rejected in the cold, a terrible place to be. I find this scene quite shattering to perform. The happiness that was once so close, and he simply threw it away. . . . Terrible. He says the only thing left for him now is death. . . . The only other ending I know in opera that is as draining as this is the finale of *Don Giovanni*, where you are dragged to hell.'

Vocally the role is a 'one off'. It bears no similarity to any of the other roles in his repertoire even though it could, in a sense, be labelled 'Italian' because of its long, flowing lines. The *tessitura* of the role has always been comfortable for him, and experience makes it easier for his voice to project through the heavy Tchaikovsky orchestration. By the time he sang it, for the second time, in Ottawa in 1983, he found he could take more risks because he knew exactly where the vocal problems were: early on in the opera, where Onegin emotes so little, and in the Gremin Palace in Act IV, before the piece starts gathering momentum. 'They are in those lyrical passages where, after you have allowed yourself to burst forth, you suddenly have to rein your voice in, so that you don't start a downhill descent from which you can never come back. You have to express Onegin's feelings but also bear in mind that you still have to climb up another mountain and down another hill.' (José Van Dam makes the same point apropos his discussion of *Der fliegende Holländer*.)

Despite a certain nervousness about his ability to communicate to the audience what Onegin is saying in the first three acts, where he emotes so little and seems 'like a negative, black hole in many ways', Allen is, as already mentioned, immensely excited at the prospect of singing the opera in Russian for the first time. He has already listened to it in Russian, 'a wonderfully poetic language', and to his ears the right vocal colours are automatically there, emerging out of the text and out of those consonants which – in Russian more than in any other language – will change the way he'll colour his voice. 'Vocal colours are an integral part of the stylistic demands of each role. You have to recognize them and use them for all they're worth. When I sang the role in Ottawa, my colleagues there said they understood things about the role that they never had before and would have done so even if I'd been singing in Chinese!

'The reason was that I had found the vocal colours that made them understand Tatyana's infatuation with a man who, to their eyes, had always seemed like a total bastard, full stop. In fact a television interviewer asked me if I found it difficult to portray cads like Onegin and, alarming though this may sound, I had to say that I don't! Because roles like this allow you to open all the valves, draw out and reveal things in yourself that are normally contained and hidden deep inside. And while there should, naturally, be something striking and magnetic about Onegin's physical presence and about the way he moves and talks – all of which requires concentration to put across – the real work is done with vocal colours.

'No matter what he's saying to her, whether it's the most hurtful, unfeeling statement in the rejection of her letter, if you have the right colours in your voice, the reason for her fascination with him is made apparent. They can suggest this potency, this something in his shirt and trousers which must obviously spring from his past, which runs through his coolness, and which is what keeps her hooked to him. We never hear much about it, but Tatyana senses it, she knows. This standing back – which Onegin, who refuses to allow himself to get involved, does any- way – and thinking about the words and the right way to colour them helps bridge the gap between his aloofness and intriguing allure.'

The potential for Allen's rich palette of vocal colours was there, even in his college days, when he could imitate any sound, any voice 'like a parrot' and copy anybody's performance. When he went to Welsh National Opera, he soon discovered he could find a warmth, or a coolness, in his voice that not everybody else could manage. It was the beginning of his conscious development of an unusually rich and varied palette of colours that is now one of his greatest gifts as a singer. He explains that 'this is what renders each voice individual and instantly identifiable on disc or radio'. He can now take this palette for granted and seldom has to think about shades and nuances consciously. Ideas come to him out of the blue, any time, any place, in taxis, trains or during walks in the country. Unlike Gobbi, who, in his book, talks about using 'a dark blue or a yellow voice' for certain roles, Allen says he doesn't know how to analyse or describe vocal colours: 'They happen spontaneously and have a great deal to do with my emotional response to the character and the dramatic action. This is what determines whether there will be a shiver in the voice, whether it will come out cold, with an edge to it, or warm, with a bloom to it.'

The colours in the title role of Britten's *Billy Budd* – one of Allen's best roles, which he first sang at the Welsh National in 1971, at Covent Garden in 1979 and which he will also sing at the Metropolitan Opera in 1989 – are determined by the cold, white element of the moon. 'The warmest colours I use in this role come in the phrase "Christ, I dreamed I was under the sea", which Billy sings as he lies asleep in his hammock. This is one of the moments that you wait for consciously, because you just *have* to put the voice in the right place in the body. And if you do, I feel you should be able to melt everybody with it, because this was Britten's intention.' Michael Geliot, who directed the Welsh National production of this opera, remembers that 'Tom used a beautiful *mezza voce* in this scene, which perfectly expressed the half-dreaming quality of those lines. And although I put his hammock at the back of the stage, he never complained – unlike most singers, who cant that if they have to sing softly they need to be up front – but just did it. The concentration was such that he would have been heard even if he whispered, because he can simply *compel* concentration.'

From the dramatic point of view, the real challenge in this role was putting across Billy's total goodness in a way that made it convincing without being 'goody-goody'. Geliot continues: 'Billy Budd is about whatever one calls "goodness" against whatever one calls "evil", with the two principles personified by Billy and Claggart respectively. So, Billy could all too easily become a "too-good-to-be-true" character, too much like the boy in *Death in Venice*. But Tom, being very agile, witty and manly, used the shanty scene (where, like in army quarters, there is a lot of knocking and banging about) to suggest just the right measure of manliness, along with a great gentleness, which is also characteristic of Tom. Later on, when Billy is in chains and Dansker comes to tell him the crew are ready to mutiny and save his life, suddenly the music changes and the timbre of Tom's voice changed and he addressed his old friend "Dansker the Indomitable" in very formal terms that caused the latter to snap to attention. For he knows this to be the voice of authority, even though it comes from a man in chains. Whether he knew it or not, Tom was a great help to me in this production and is, to me, the epitome of Billy Budd.'

Allen explains that most of the clues for finding the right vocal colours are in the words and the use one makes of them. 'The music is absolutely crucial and you are there to do justice to it, but the words can give you so many clues as well, because the composer wrote his music *to* the words.' He agrees with Nicolai Gedda that English is not an easy language to sing, 'and it's a great mistake to think that, because it's your own language, you don't need to work at it. It needs to be worked at, like any other language. You have to pay attention to diction, and find the right colours and expression.'

Strangely enough, the easiest language for him to sing is French. He doesn't know why this should be, because he only studied it at school and didn't touch it again until he joined Covent Garden as a company member. Now he has taken to French and French opera in a big way. 'It seems to come naturally to me, possibly because the French style has certain affinities with Mozart's. There is an elegance, a sense of measure and a classical dimension about French singing which always reminds me of Mozart. Even the most extreme emotions have to be contained within the bounds of good taste. I like to feel that elegance is a key element in my work, too.'

Allen's first French role was Valentin in *Faust* at Covent Garden, and he has since sung the title role in *Hamlet* by Thomas on record and Oreste in Gluck's *Iphigénie en Tauride* (at the Paris Opéra in 1985) for which he has a special affection. 'It's the sort of classical role I can bring off. It has the right pedigree and is more austere than any Mozart part and even more to my liking because of those wonderful, high-arching French baritone phrases which I can sing with great ease, for no particular reason, because of the way the voice seems to have developed. I have never consciously "pushed" it in any specific direction.'

Allen's greatest achievement in the French repertoire is his portrayal of the title role in Debussy's *Pelléas et Mélisande*, which he first sang at Covent Garden in 1978, to universal critical acclaim. He is usually 'terrible about learning things' and tends to leave it too late and learn them very near the time, because he cannot do it slowly and steadily. He needs to be panicking. 'It's bad, but I'm afraid I cannot do it any other way. I study in all sorts of ways: listening to tapes, sitting in the tube with a score or writing out the parts, which is very helpful but a labour of love. I gave myself four

weeks to learn Don Giovanni and three for Ford in *Falstaff*. But Pelléas
was an exception. I knew it was a unique role in a musically unique work
and therefore gave myself longer: I learnt it slowly over a period of two
years because I was very worried about my capacity to cope with it.'

Pelléas makes different demands on the baritone from anything else he
has ever sung. 'It's written in a different, conversational style, almost like
plainsong – which is quite a challenge – and lies very high for the baritone
voice, which is why it is also often sung by tenors. But on the whole,
maybe because I'm prejudiced, I prefer to hear it sung by baritones because
they bring greater resonance to the spoken parts. Although fiendishly
difficult, the role is wonderfully structured for the voice and contains its
own warming-up apparatus. You step on stage and start singing a phrase
which develops and vanishes and then you go on to the next scene when
you sing another, slightly higher, phrase which then develops in its turn.
The whole thing is an exercise in itself and by the time you reach Pelléas's
big moments, the voice is warmed up and takes care of itself. But it's also
a frightening role, and it made me understand why tenors tend to get so
well-paid! Having to live with the knowledge that an A or a B natural,
to say nothing of a high C, awaits you can't be fun.'

The fact that *Pelléas et Mélisande*, 'an amazing work, both musically
and dramatically', enjoys rather limited popularity pleases him, because
'if it appealed to everyone, its value would be considerably less than it is.
In fact, it's so very special that it should be only for the initiated, only for
enlightened people. What Pelléas and Mélisande are saying to one another
is of such import and depth that it could never appeal to a wide audience.
Very few people can respond to it, which is why opera houses are seldom
full when they put this opera on. But we, singers, have the added privilege
of being involved in the music, of being part of the orchestra and the
fabric of it all, which is quite a unique feeling and unlike any other
experience I have had as a singer.'

The very fact that he is a baritone means that the character emerges as
'meatier' and more robust than it would if sung by a tenor. As he is not
a *baryton-martin* in the French tradition, he has to sing it with his normal
voice – plus the extra top the role demands – which means that Pelléas
ends up 'rather heroic'. This also has a lot to do with the way he conceives
and plays the character, however. 'One often comes across singers who
make it impossible to believe that Pelléas could ever make passionate love
to this woman! But the tensions in the piece are too high for it to be
played in too rarefied a way. I remember once auditioning for Karajan,
who asked, among other things, about the roles in my repertoire. When

I mentioned Pelléas, he exclaimed "You mean Golaud. You are a Golaud. You are too manly for Pelléas! When you walk onstage, one immediately senses the presence of a man. But Pelléas is a boy, not a man!" And I beg to disagree about that. I feel the music is too strong, too singeing for a boy. It's the music of a man desperately wanting a woman. It's all very well to say that Pelléas and Mélisande live in the woods or the bottom of a well or somewhere. Their music shows they have very strong feelings for one another. So, at certain moments, I always kiss Mélisande and thoroughly relish the experience because it's what the music is saying!'

He responds to eroticism in music strongly: 'I'm not telling you *how* strongly, but I'm very much aware of it and things like the love scene in Monteverdi's *L'incoronazione di Poppea*, which is mind-bogglingly erotic, do affect me a great deal. I saw it in Vienna the other day, and it literally took my breath away. This kind of thing is also what draws me to Wagner. Not only this of course, because there is deep emotion and spiritual content as well in Wagner's music. But there is also the sheer passion, the volume of the thing and the turgid nature of a great deal of the orchestral writing, which is amazing and unlike anything else. When I sang my first Wagner role – Melot in *Tristan und Isolde* at Covent Garden in 1973 – I found it fabulous just to stand there during Marke's monologue and listen to that sound rolling along. I literally wallow in it and have a strong feeling for Wagner. And I fear that once I embark on the Wagnerian repertoire, I might get seduced and hooked for life.'

In September 1984, shortly after that particular conversation, Allen sang Wolfram von Eschenbach in *Tannhäuser* at Covent Garden. Despite the fact that, like most colleagues, he finds *Tannhäuser* 'a problematic, un-fathomable work', he responded strongly to the emotion of the role. 'When I first saw the opera I was overwhelmed and couldn't believe how beautiful that ending was – absolutely heart-rending. So I thought that when I came to sing the role I should consciously try to get myself under some sort of control because obviously one cannot allow oneself to get into this sort of state without one's performance going vocally haywire. [As all the great singing-actors in this book, like Domingo, Raimondi and Ghiaurov, also point out.] But at the finale of *Tannhäuser* there is no substitute for sheer mental and physical commitment to it because this is the only way the thing can work; it's enormously passionate and enormously demanding and I found myself being totally carried away by it, as if by a huge tidal wave that one had to go along with. And, in this sense, it was wonderful just to let oneself go, take the bull by the horns and just let it all pour out.'

But mastering the vocal demands of the role – which include a kind of sustained singing different from anything he was used to at a *tessitura* a third of a semitone lower than the music he usually has to sing in a sustained way – successfully took a lot of conscious mental preparation and 'a slower body rhythm. It may sound crazy, but this meant getting hold of myself and consciously slowing everything down, learning to think more ponderously and keeping my metabolism low-key – the polar opposite of Don Giovanni, for which I have to get myself hyped-up! Here, I found myself having to cool down, and this made me very nervous.' No trace of nerves was discernible in his performance: moving, convincing and permeated by his empathy for the character's idealism and nobility. There was little doubt in my mind that this was sure to prove one of the great Wolframs of the future and the critics seemed to agree: 'Thomas Allen was an excellent, wholly persuasive Wolfram. It was clear by the end of the evening that this was the hero's part', wrote Harold Rosenthal in *Opera*. His verdict was echoed by *The Times* with the comment that 'Thomas Allen offers the finest singing of the evening in a performance of great nobility, affectionateness and intelligence'.

Allen is convinced he was right to begin his serious involvement with Wagner in this role, just as he was also right to begin his exploration of the Verdi repertoire with Rodrigo, Marquis of Posa in *Don Carlos*, because 'as you rightly say, both are very noble, idealistic characters ready to sacrifice themselves for their friends – the kind of thing I can do well! And they are the kind of roles that allow me to do what both Sir Geraint Evans and James Lockhart always urged me to: use that certain nobility in my voice and carriage for all it's worth and try and sing as if through a velvet glove. They drummed into me that never was I to try and do what Gobbi did, which was to cut through the orchestra like a laser beam!'

When Allen first sang Posa at Covent Garden in 1984, he was hailed by *Opera* as 'the finest to be heard anywhere in the world' and he was equally successful with his portrayal of Ford in *Falstaff*, which he sang both at Covent Garden in 1984 and the Vienna State Opera in 1985, again to general critical praise. He greatly enjoyed both experiences and loves each role for different reasons: Posa for the nobility he already referred to and Ford 'because it fits me like a glove and because of that wonderful jealousy scene, that sudden statement when you see the real man, which is like an oasis within the rest of the work, when he seems to be at the beck and call of Alice all the time'. Allen's only other forays into the Verdi repertoire were Marullo in *Rigoletto* at Covent Garden in autumn 1972, a role that in Max Loppert's words, in an admirable profile of Allen in *Opera*, 'one had seldom seen and heard projected with such incisiveness', Paolo in *Simon Boccanegra* at Covent Garden in 1973, and Germont in *La traviata* at the Welsh National Opera in 1981 and subsequently at the Vienna State Opera.

Allen doesn't see himself essentially as a Verdi baritone because 'nowadays the fashion is to sing Verdi with a big, dark voice, quite unlike the kind of voice De Luca used. The man responsible for this change of style was the late Leonard Warren [the American baritone who died on stage at the Metropolitan Opera in 1961, after singing Carlo's aria 'Urna fatale del mio destino' in Verdi's *La forza del destino*], a great favourite of the recording industry and, in vocal terms, a real sledgehammer! Until then, most great baritones like Battistini and De Luca sang Verdi in a more elegant, belcantistic way. And I am all for that. If this old style of singing Verdi were to become fashionable again then, yes, the natural progression would be from Posa, Ford and Germont to some of the bigger roles but never to Rigoletto. Meanwhile, my natural guardedness prevents me from accepting offers to sing Macbeth, Miller and the Conte di Luna in *Il trovatore*. In twenty years' time I might, perhaps, become a Conte di Luna. But not yet. My voice doesn't lend itself to this kind of heavy singing on a regular basis. I am not a Cappuccilli or a Sherrill Milnes. I don't see myself in that category and don't want to push my voice in that direction, otherwise it would go in the direction of Amonasro – not at *all* the way I want it to go.'

Indeed, long ago someone told Allen never to sing anything Italian, but 'I suppose that, like myself, the voice has grown more experienced and more extrovert over the years, so that I can now take more risks than I used to'. His *bel canto* repertoire includes Belcore in Donizetti's *L'elisir d' amore* and Figaro in Rossini's *Il barbiere di Siviglia*. On the whole he tends to eschew *verismo* for the same reasons that he avoids the heavy Verdi roles, with a couple of exceptions, including one of the best Marcellos in *La Bohème* in living memory at Covent Garden in 1983 and Vienna in 1984 and a marginally less successful portrayal of Lescaut in *Manon Lescaut* at Covent Garden in 1983. There are no plans for further *verismo* roles in the near future, even though he recently looked at the score of Giordano's *Andrea Chénier* and got rather excited by the role of Gérard. 'But, alas, I don't have what it needs and to attempt it would result in a short career, whereas I would like to think I'll have a long career. Mind you, if I were pushed for work, I might be tempted to be less cautious. But as it is, I'm kept so busy with the things I do well and with relative ease, that I can afford to be careful! I don't think I do too much, but I always seem to be busy and tend to work fairly hard.'

Allen also greatly enjoys singing early music and needs 'the calm and sobriety of baroque music just as I need the energy and swell of romantic music'. In summer 1985 he made his debut at the Salzburg Festival in the title role in Monteverdi's *Il ritorno d'Ulisse in patria*, to excellent reviews in the world press: 'One should cite the splendid Ulisse of Thomas Allen, great, profound, and moving', wrote *Le Monde*, while *Il Corriere della sera* remarked that 'Thomas Allen was a vocally superb Ulisse and his scenic presence was of an exceptional level'. One of Allen's fondest wishes is to sing the Bach St Matthew Passion again, for the first time since his student days, because 'I like the musical discipline of the concert hall, which is far greater than that of the operatic stage, where one can get away with a relative degree of murder!' (This might, perhaps, be a reference to one of his own wicked hobbies of inventing spontaneous *bons mots*, definitely not to be found in the various libretti, and skilfully interpolating them into the text, much to the amusement of the quick-witted in the audience and of those in the know!) He is also an exceptionally gifted *Lieder* singer and a recitalist capable of forging an immediate rapport with his public.

In May 1986 Allen gave a towering performance of the title role in Busoni's *Doktor Faustus* at English National Opera. Other twentieth-century roles he has sung are Count Mario in Thea Musgrave's *The Voice of Ariadne* at the 1984 Aldeburgh Festival, Ned Keene in Britten's *Peter Grimes* at Covent Garden in 1975 and a stupendous portrayal of Prince Andrei in Prokofiev's *War and Peace* at English National Opera in autumn 1982, an experience he looks back to with particular pleasure: 'It was a huge, enthralling, tremendous evening in the theatre and I was just desperate to take part in it, somehow.' He would also like to sing the title role in Alban Berg's *Wozzeck*, 'one day, crazy though this might seem. But I don't yet have what it requires.'

One of the things he has noticed over the years is that his portrayals have grown 'less active, because with experience, I have discovered the strength and power there is in keeping still. I remember Jon Vickers standing for a long time with his back to the audience during a per-formance of *Parsifal*, and the power of his concentration was such that his stillness was like a magnet! I'm trying to learn to do this myself.' This will be an additional quality to an already formidable list at the disposal of this amiable, attractive and exceptionally sensitive man, whose stage presence instantly commands attention. When pushed, he had to admit that he is indeed 'aware of something in myself, a switch, an aggression, some kind of electrical force I can turn on and grab hold of people with. I don't know if it's a physical thing or a mental thing, but I'm aware of its being there.' He also admits to knowing he has 'a vital spark – for the moment, anyway!', and he is dead right.

Left: GIACOMO ARAGALL as Cavaradossi in *Tosca*, one of his favourite roles because 'it's wonderful for a singer to portray a painter and a revolutionary to boot'.

Right: FRANCISCO ARAIZA as Ferrando in *Così fan tutte*, the longest and one of the most difficult of all Mozart tenor roles because it requires 'two kinds of tenor voices: a lyric and a dramatic', and a role instrumental in establishing Araiza's reputation as one of the best Mozart tenors around.

JOSÉ CARRERAS as Don José in *Carmen*, one of his best roles: 'essentially a man at the mercy rather than in command of his destiny', at the finale of Act IV, after he has stabbed Carmen to death.

JOSÉ CARRERAS as Andrea Chénier, 'an artist, a poet, a sensitive, idealistic soul and a politically committed man'.

Left: CARLO BERGONZI, one of the greatest Verdi tenors in operatic history, in a lighthearted *bel canto* role: Nemorino in *L'elisir d'amore*, for which 'the timbre of the voice should be lighter and clearer than in Verdi roles'.

Right: PLACIDO DOMINGO in the title role in *Les Contes d'Hoffmann*, 'a character not as clearly drawn as most operatic heroes, and this sets your imagination free to dream and work him out for yourself'.

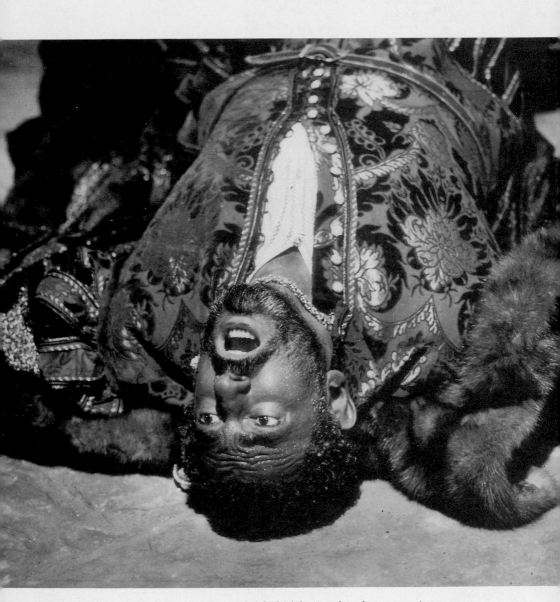

PLACIDO DOMINGO as Otello, a role of which he is, today, the supreme interpreter: according to Piero Faggioni, 'a soul in the process of liberating itself through singing'; according to Lord Olivier, 'not only does he act it as well as I do, but the bastard *sings* it as well!'

Left: NICOLAI GEDDA as Lensky in *Eugene Onegin*, 'this poet, this romantic man with a typically Russian soul, melancholic yet fiery and, like Pushkin himself, temperamental and easily excitable'.

Below: RENÉ KOLLO as Lohengrin, 'whose half-real, half-mystical dimension cannot be acted but only projected through your aura and through a vocal sound with a special, unearthly, faraway quality'.

Above: LUCIANO PAVAROTTI in disguise for a party but very much his own beaming, jovial self!

Left: ALFREDO KRAUS as Werther, 'a highly complex, morbid, sick character with an inborn death wish, who sees in everything a cause for crying and whose all-pervasive melancholy must be reflected in your voice and communicated right from his first entry'.

Below: LUCIANO PAVAROTTI as Rodolfo in *La Bohème:* 'right from the beginning this was a good role for me, a beautiful young role that strikes a universal chord, speaks a universal lovers' language as true of yesterday as of today and tomorrow and which can be understood even on the moon!'

THOMAS ALLEN as a Don Giovanni 'both repulsive and attractive, leeringly vicious and masterfully fascinating, a Giovanni in whom cruelty and courage are both surfaces of the same coin, a Giovanni who holds the stage by right, not by accident!'.

THOMAS ALLEN as Eugene Onegin, the role that drains him more than any other, 'a jaded, blasé, rather slimy figure with a stiff, grey, negative presence'.

THOMAS ALLEN at rehearsal for the 1977 Covent Garden production of *Le nozze di Figaro* under the late Karl Böhm that triggered his international career. (Left, Teresa Stratas as Susanna; right, Agnes Baltsa as Cherubino.)

RENATO BRUSON as Macbeth, 'a man who knows fear, who is aware of powers greater than himself and conscious of the role played by the supernatural in human affairs'.

RENATO BRUSON as Simon Boccanegra, 'a noble, mellow, poised but intensely lonely man who is motivated by his great love for his daughter and altruism towards his fellow men, all of which should be reflected in his singing, which should also be poised and noble'.

Above: SHERRILL MILNES as Macbeth: 'from the dramatic point of view, it is essential to bring out the very definite sexual attraction between Lady Macbeth and Mister'.

Left: PIERO CAPPUCCILLI as Iago, a role 'which would become monotonous and infinitely less intriguing if the baritone didn't use a wide and subtle palette of shades of vocal colour with which to mirror his moods and dramatic situations'.

SHERRILL MILNES as Rigoletto, 'a *very* hard role full of traps, the biggest of which is the twisted, bending posture you have to adopt in order to give the impression of a hunchback and which is not a good singing position because it inhibits breath support'.

Above: BERND WEIKL as Hans Sachs, 'a mixture of sensitive poet and earthy, village philosopher ... a good and warm-hearted man, but also a tricky and egocentric one'.

Above right: HERMANN PREY as Papageno, 'the man I and everybody else would like to be: simple, with an earthy, peasant philosophy, fond of food, drink and a girl from time to time'.

Right: HERMANN PREY as Eisenstein. 'The lighter the music, the more difficult it is to sing. It's important for operetta to have swing and lightness of touch but *never* to go over the top, otherwise the whole thing would become indigestible.'

Left: SIMON ESTES as the Flying Dutchman, 'a very complex figure who on the one hand wants salvation but on the other hand doesn't, who wants to find a woman who'll be true to him but on the other hand doesn't'.

Below: RUGGERO RAIMONDI as Don Quichotte, a role which, according to Piero Faggioni, resembles him a little 'because despite his intelligence and sophistication, Ruggero has remained a rather naive and idealistic man who carries out his profession for love rather than for reasons of glory'.

RUGGERO RAIMONDI as Don Giovanni, his most famous role, which he considers 'a great hole, a mythical character who exists only by reflection, through other people's reactions and desires' and for which a singer needs 'a spermatozoic voice'!

JOSÉ VAN DAM as Wozzeck, a character 'whose entire existence centres around Marie and their child, for whose sake he submits to a life of victimization and humiliation at the hands of his superiors . . . and despite the tragic ending, the sheer strength and intensity of this man's love makes *Wozzeck* one of the most beautiful love stories in opera'.

JOSÉ VAN DAM as the Flying Dutchman, 'a very tense, very dramatic yet introverted character who feels almost like an extra-terrestrial, so withdrawn and uncommunicative has he become after all those years at sea'.

Below: PAATA BURCHULADZE (left) as Ramfis in *Aida*, the role that launched his international career when he sang it at Covent Garden, and with which he dominated a cast of major stars, 'because Ramfis *is* dominant, important and omnipotent, the power behind the throne and the man who controls everything in Egypt'.

Right: NICOLAI GHIAUROV in the Coronation scene in *Boris Godunov*, where Boris 'begins to think aloud. He prays to God to bless and protect his reign but is overcome by a sad premonition that he and his people will be overtaken by disaster.'

Below: NICOLAI GHIAUROV as Mephistopheles in Gounod's *Faust*. 'The rapid, galloping orchestral bars that herald Mephisto's first entry outline all the elegance and cavalier fashion with which the character is viewed, through French eyes.'

Left: KURT MOLL as Baron
Ochs in *Der Rosenkavalier*,
a portrayal renowned for its
charm, lightness of touch
and subtle Austrian
inflections, which he learnt,
'phrase by phrase', from
Herbert von Karajan.

Below: KURT MOLL as
Gurnemanz in *Parsifal*, 'a
role that contains some
lyrical *legato* passages so
beautiful that it is easy to
lose oneself in the music and
forget to pay attention to
certain crucial technical
points'.

SAMUEL RAMEY as Mephistopheles in Gounod's *Faust*, 'not really the devil but the devil in disguise, out to amuse himself . . . it's important to establish the character's Gallic lightness of touch from the beginning, without hamming or being too demonic'.

RENATO BRUSON

Renato Bruson, the distinguished Verdi baritone, began his singing career in 1961 and soon made a name for himself as a *bel canto* specialist. His rise to national, and later international, prominence coincided with the major Donizetti revival of the sixties and early seventies and, having discovered that *bel canto* was ideally suited to his voice and artistic temperament, Bruson set about the task of mastering the vocal and stylistic requirements of this demanding style with great enthusiasm and conscientious application. He sang the principal baritone roles both in famous Bellini and Donizetti operas like *I puritani* and *Lucia di Lammermoor* and in less well-known and rarely performed Donizetti works like *Il Duca d'Alba*, *Poliuto*, *Caterina Cornaro*, *Roberto Devereux*, *Linda di Chamounix*, *Fausta*, *Belisario*, *Maria di Rohan* and *Gemma di Vergy*. Indeed, Bruson is probably the only living baritone to have sung the principal baritone roles in seventeen Donizetti operas.

He attributes his great love of *bel canto* in general and Donizetti in particular to his singing teacher at the Padua Conservatoire, Elena Fava Ceriati, who was steeped in the tradition, 'and there is no greater master of *bel canto* than Donizetti'. Bruson's own complete mastery of this singing style caused the French magazine *Opéra International* to hail him as the supreme exponent among today's baritones of the traditional Italian bel-cantistic school, the heir to such illustrious predecessors as Battistini, Galeffi, De Luca and Stracciari. In reply, Bruson pointed out that any success of his in carrying on this tradition, rooted in the nineteenth and continued into the twentieth century by these great artists, is due not to any conscious or unconscious effort at emulation, but to sheer and constant hard work – 'the only way!'.

The reason for this statement is that Bruson did not have a chance to familiarize himself with the traditional Italian school of singing or indeed with the operatic world itself until after he enrolled at the Padua Conservatoire. He was born in 1936 in the Veneto into a very poor peasant family who did not have the means either to pay visits to opera houses or to own classical recordings. His mother, though, loved singing and, as soon as she discovered her son had a good voice, she sent him to the local church choir where he sang throughout his school years. After school, someone suggested he audition for the Conservatoire. Having no specific alternative plans, he agreed to try, and was immediately offered a scholarship for the five-year course that included classes in piano, harmony, poetic and dramatic literature as well as *solfège* and singing.

Bruson heartily agrees with the general feeling that there is no better training for a young voice than *bel canto*, 'because *bel canto* demands and develops certain qualities that underlie *all* good singing and are therefore essential for every singer: clear enunciation, a noble declamatory style, uniformity of colour and the ability to sing long, even *legato* lines on the breath. And, because the orchestration in *bel canto* operas is thin, indeed sometimes almost non-existent, the singer is very exposed, with nothing to hide behind and nothing to help him set the atmosphere of a scene and create the "feel" of a character. Everything, therefore, hinges on the quality of one's singing, which should be as near-perfect as possible; and this requires great technique, discipline and concentration. [Pavarotti stresses the same points.]

'This is why a voice that has mastered the exigencies of *bel canto* is sure to develop naturally into a voice capable of singing the Verdi and perhaps also the veristic repertoire. For time is as crucial for vocal development as a sound technique. Even at my age, my voice is still developing. You rightly pointed out that there seem to be no Verdi voices coming up at present; but there are plenty of Donizetti voices around which, if allowed time to develop *naturally*, will certainly grow into Verdi voices within a few years. The problem is that nowadays everyone wants to be a Verdi singer *right away*! And this is impossible! In my own case, there are several major Verdi roles – like Iago, Macbeth or Falstaff – which I now sing with ease but could never have coped with at the beginning of my career.'

After graduating from the Conservatoire, Bruson concentrated largely on *bel canto* and also worked hard at gradually mastering the Verdi baritone repertoire and on acquiring the vocal inflections and nuances demanded by Verdi's style of composition. He made his professional debut at the 1961 Spoleto Festival as the Conte di Luna in *Il trovatore*, which he also sang for his Metropolitan Opera debut in 1968–9. In 1970 he sang Renato in *Un ballo in maschera* at the Maggio Musicale Fiorentino and also made his Chicago Lyric Opera (1973) and Covent Garden (1975–6) debuts in the same role. He had meanwhile made his British debut at the

1972 Edinburgh Festival as Ezio in *Attila* and was soon singing at all the major international opera houses, including the Vienna, the Bavarian and the Hamburg State Opera, the Deutsche Oper and the Teatro Colón.

Indeed, Bruson has sung most Verdi baritone roles, including – apart from the three already mentioned – Francesco Foscari in *I due Foscari*, Francesco in *I masnadieri*, Germont in *La traviata*, Don Carlos in *Ernani*, the title roles in *Macbeth*, *Nabucco*, *Rigoletto* and *Simon Boccanegra*, Miller in *Luisa Miller*, Guy de Montfort in *I vespri siciliani*, Carlo in *La forza del destino*, Amonasro in *Aida*, the Marquis of Posa in *Don Carlos*, Iago in *Otello* and the title role in *Falstaff*. He stresses that Verdi's music requires a different approach from that of the *bel canto* school of Rossini, Bellini and Donizetti, in whose operas the vocal element is far more important than the dramatic content, whereas in Verdi both are crucial and every note emerges out of the words and of dramatic necessity.

'Verdi is very sanguine and his music should be sung in a vigorous, incisive way. There is a "spring", a virility, in his phrasing which is absolutely typical of him and which does not exist, to the same degree, in any other composer's music. For while there is also a certain virility in Donizetti's style of composition, it is never as powerful or all–permeating as in Verdi's. This incisiveness is also typical of the dramatic essence of his operatic characters, whose range of emotional extremes is wider than that of characters in *bel canto* operas. The anger of a Verdi character, for instance, is more pronounced, more intense and more dangerous than that of a Donizetti character.

'Another main feature of Verdi's style is the absolute clarity characteristic of his phrasing and the crucial importance of the words, which are inseparable from the music and part and parcel of the effort to achieve a clear delineation of the personality of every character. Verdi never tired of stressing that "la parola regna suprema" [i.e. the word reigns supreme], and is known to have made the life of his various librettists a misery until *the* right words had been found that perfectly conveyed the "feel" and inner world of each of his characters.'

Surprisingly enough, Renato Bruson does not agree with the prevailing opinion among singers, who tend to consider Verdi an extremely difficult composer to sing, because although Verdi is very demanding, he writes well for the voice and does not make unnatural vocal demands, unlike the composers of the veristic school, which Bruson has eschewed almost entirely throughout his career. "In *verismo* operas I come across vocal problems of a kind never encountered in *bel canto* or in Verdi or in any nineteenth-century work. But at the turn of the century, with the advent of *verismo*, composers began to make unnaturally strenuous vocal demands in the shape of sudden springs to high or low notes, while their loud and dense orchestrations, albeit helpful in creating the atmosphere of a character and of a scene, nevertheless force singers to push their voices.' After singing Scarpia in *Tosca*, Escamillo in *Carmen*, Alfio in *Cavalleria rusticana* and Gérard in *Andrea Chénier* a few times at the beginning of his career, Bruson decided that *verismo* roles suit neither his vocal nor his temperamental make-up. Indeed, he lacks some of the extrovert vocal and dramatic qualities – like the particular kind of bravura and confident animal magnetism – required for many *verismo* roles, and excels at the portrayal of calmer, more poised and noble characters like the Marquis of Posa and Simon Boccanegra, which suit him perfectly, as do many Verdi baritone roles. Off-stage Bruson, with his horn-rimmed spectacles, looks like a lawyer, a professional man. On stage, though, he takes on the character of whatever role he is singing.

'Vocally, Verdi roles don't present the kind of problems encountered in *verismo* and dramatically they are infinitely more interesting than *bel canto*. The reason why I claim – and I hope this doesn't sound like some kind of boast – that vocally they are not difficult is that they are so well written for the voice that if one adheres to Verdi's scores and ignores the exigencies of so-called 'tradition', which often amounts to little more than the accumulated bad habits of past performers, one shouldn't come across any real problems. The kind of difficulties one does encounter in the tougher Verdi roles usually arise either out of dramatic necessity – like Rigoletto being a hunchback or Falstaff being enormously fat – or out of "traditional" changes or additions to his scores.'

Bruson cites Rigoletto, rightly considered one of the most difficult roles in the entire baritone repertoire, as a good example of what he means. For if one were to sing Rigoletto exactly as Verdi wrote it, it would automatically become much easier, as he discovered when he sang it in the original, authentic version of this opera at the Vienna State Opera in 1982 under Riccardo Muti. He admits that, although he has always been in favour of absolute textual fidelity, he felt somewhat dubious and apprehensive about singing the unadorned version of such a well-known and well-loved role in a house as conservative and traditionalist as the Vienna State Opera. Therefore he was doubly gratified at his own success in communicating the tension of this character and at the team's success in putting across the tragedy of this work without recourse to any of the vocal gimmicks, pseudo-effects or additions demanded by tradition.*

Examples of such changes and additions are the phrase 'ah, è follia', at the end of Rigoletto's big aria, 'Pari siamo', which is usually sung higher than Verdi wrote it; the A flat which most baritones sing at the end of 'vendetta, vendetta, tremenda vendetta', along with the soprano and which, again, is not written in Verdi's score; the phrase 'a l'onda, a l'onda' in Act IV where baritones usually sing the second 'a l'onda' higher than the first despite the fact that both are written exactly the same; and Rigoletto's last phrase at the finale of Act IV, 'ah, la maledizione', is written in a more restrained and dramatically more effective way than the strangled cry culminating in either B natural or A flat that one is almost always treated to.

Bruson explains that, apart from such latter-day additions and alterations to the score, the other main difficulty in Rigoletto is the character's physical deformity – 'that damned hump, never to be forgotten', as Tito Gobbi exclaimed in his book *My World of Italian Opera* – and that when he sings Rigoletto standing up straight, as in the recording studio, instead of in the hunchback position he is forced to adopt on stage, the role becomes considerably easier.

The same is true of Falstaff, whose enormous bulk means that the baritone has to wear heavy padding and thus lose 'two or three litres of water in sweat at every performance. If one were to sing it in ordinary clothes, it wouldn't be a particularly demanding role. But on stage it's physically exhausting, like running a race and *then* having to sing!' Tito Gobbi, one of the greatest interpreters of this role, confirms that 'having to sing all his so-called philosophy in the Honour scene and describe all his rascally plans while moving his great bulk is no easy matter. Nevertheless his bulk is Sir John Falstaff's visiting card and he must play it for all it's worth.' Vocally, Bruson does not consider it a difficult role. 'The only vocal difficulty in *Falstaff* is the need to master Verdi's new, "modern" style of composition, with its very advanced orchestral chords and new kind of recitative, the "*canto recitato*", a kind of continuous musical prose so different from the normal "*recitativo cantato*" we encounter in his earlier

* Muti's experiment was, in fact, greeted with a mixed reception by the first-night audience, who clearly missed the familiar, traditional version. But it won high critical acclaim and Bruson's performance was praised by critics and public alike: *Opéra International*, whose critic was wholeheartedly *for* Muti's cleaned-up version, wrote: 'Thanks to Renato Bruson – who revealed all the pain, suffering and impotence of this character, so severely hit by destiny and whose singing was characterized by a nobility and rare melodic vigour – Rigoletto was divested of any veristic tendencies and firmly restored to an almost *belcantistic* elegance.'

works. One first comes across this "*canto recitato*" in Verdi's penultimate opera, *Otello*, but it reaches its complete realization in *Falstaff*.'

Bruson recorded and later sang Falstaff on stage in Los Angeles and at Covent Garden under Carlo Maria Giulini. His vocally impeccable performance lacked some of the charm, bonhomie and *joie de vivre* that permeated Gobbi's and, more recently, Giuseppe Taddei's interpretations, possibly because the entire production, imbued by Giulini's view of this work as 'a very serious opera', lacked sparkle. The critic of *The Times* remarked that 'Mr Bruson's Falstaff is not the Falstaff we are used to. Unlike other Falstaffs, he is for the most part sober and shrewd.... His performance also departs from convention in being beautifully sung throughout: nothing is forced, the line is pure and natural and delivered with conversational ease.' After the production's transfer to Covent Garden, the same newspaper wrote that 'in Bruson, who has taken on Falstaff at a time when his voice is at its peak, unlike most baritones who prefer to leave it until later ... a world short of Falstaffs has acquired a new one of strength, stature and high intelligence'. Bruson adds that he started off by thinking he might be, at forty-six, too young for the role (Taddei, who sang it in von Karajan's Salzburg production, for instance, was sixty-four at the time), but decided he wasn't. Despite the fact that he is a master of *legato* singing, he told *The Times* that 'the cheering thing about Falstaff is that there is no *legato* required. If you are going to perform Iago, then the voice must be in perfect condition: but with Falstaff, you can speak a little.'

Iago is, according to Bruson, one of the most difficult Verdi baritone roles. Bruson first sang it in 1980, at the Maggio Musicale Fiorentino, and again the guidelines for his interpretation are textual fidelity and an abhorrence for cheap vocal and scenic histrionics. It is vocally difficult, both because it contains different vocal demands from Verdi's earlier baritone roles and because in *Otello* one first encounters Verdi's new and more advanced style of composition, discussed above, which, as Bruson explains, 'definitely has to be worked at'. There are some other vocal difficulties as well, of a kind never encountered in earlier Verdi operas, which is why he states that the voice should be in peak condition before tackling this role: 'There are passages where, after singing at a relatively high *tessitura*, you suddenly have to dive down to extremely low notes. This occurs at the end of the "Credo", at the end of the quartet in Act II, and in Act III, at the arrival of the Venetian ambassadors, where he suddenly has to sing a B natural, a note low enough for a bass who alone could effectively project it through this loud an orchestration. And this

B natural *feels* even lower because it follows a relatively high passage.' (It is interesting to hear that baritones experience the same vocal problems with low notes that tenors encounter with high notes: i.e. that their relative difficulty depends largely on the passages preceding them.)

From the dramatic point of view, although 'evil through and through and perfidious to the nth degree, Iago is a fascinating character to portray, especially if one aspires to bring out all the subtleties with which Verdi and his librettist, Arrigo Boito – a great poet in his own right who also wrote the libretto for *Falstaff* – invested him. Verdi wrote to Boito that he imagined Iago as tall, thin, dressed in black and very handsome. To the painter Morelli he also stressed that Iago should have "a gentlemanly countenance". The evil should be only inside, hidden away from everyone, otherwise it would be obvious for all to see. The only baritone in my experience who really understood this was Tito Gobbi [who wrote in his book that 'the most serious mistake anyone can make is to represent Iago as a sort of demonic creature with a satanic sneer and devilish glance'], whereas most of the time we are confronted with portrayals that proclaim Iago's villainy from the first scene in Act I!' *Opera* reviewed his Florence performance as follows: 'Heavens be praised, the baritone singing his first ever Iago was Renato Bruson, refined in both voice and acting, subtle in both, musicianly, and capable of imposing a definite personal stamp on the role.'

Bruson goes on to explain that this is another role often abused because of practices attributed to so-called 'tradition'. It is, for example, considered 'traditional' for the baritone to burst into a bout of satanic-sounding laughter at the end of the 'Credo', even though Verdi wrote no such thing in his score. Therefore, true to his passionate belief in adhering as closely as possible to the composer's wishes, note values and written indications, and in refraining from any conscious deviations from the score, Bruson omitted it from his performance. 'I did just what Verdi wrote, and had twice as much success! For in our world of opera, there are two kinds of singers: those content merely to sing, full stop, who often feel they have to rely on gimmicks and pseudo-effects for their success, and singing-actors and actresses whose aim is to reveal the full dramatic content of the roles they interpret. Since the days of Callas and the operatic revolution she pioneered, the former breed – for whom opera consists only of the big arias, whereupon they place themselves centre-stage, or even at the proscenium, and deliver their piece, often indulging in self-invented pyrotechnics – is on the decline. Today the operatic stage can boast of artists who are willing to use themselves as vehicles for the realization of the works they interpret instead of using the works as vehicles for themselves.'

Bruson is definitely an interpreter in the contemporary mould whose most memorable interpretations have been of noble characters like Simon Boccanegra and the Marquis of Posa in *Don Carlos*, in which he has always scored major successes. He finds Posa ideally suited to his temperament, interesting and rewarding to portray 'because his is a noble, deeply loving nature full of comprehension and compassion for everybody and this is reflected in his music, which presents no vocal problems whatsoever and consists of beautiful, noble singing along flowing, melodic lines. His love for his friend, the Infante Don Carlos, is so great that it could almost be misinterpreted as a homosexual passion. But I feel it is love in its purest form, motivated by his desire to imbue the future King of Spain with some of his own ideals about freedom. And he is ready to sacrifice himself both for those ideals and for his friend.

Verdi himself thought Posa too idealistic, as he confided to Italo Pizzi, who reports in the fascinating volume *Interviews and Encounters with Verdi* by Marcello Conati that Schiller was too good, too naive and too idealistic and therefore fails to penetrate and analyse the human mind as much or as profoundly as Shakespeare. Many of his characters are thus idealized and unreal. Just such a character – one of the most lovable and attractive – is the Marquis of Posa in *Don Carlos*. The character is, in Verdi's words, 'an anachronism who finds himself professing humanitarian ideals in the most modern sense of the word – and that at the time of Philip the Second!'. In fact Verdi was so convinced of the incongruity of this character that he wanted to omit it and told Pizzi that 'although I have set this character to music, I am quite aware of how he holds up the drama, and I had already intended cutting him entirely, when my friends [he did not say who] discouraged me, and I retained him'. Bruson experiences a sense of deep personal exultation and fulfilment when singing this role.

The same is true of Simon Boccanegra, Bruson's number one favourite among his roles and one which 'takes a lot out of me because I experience this man very deeply. I live and weep with him all along.' He first sang Boccanegra in 1967 and sees him as an introspective character who does not express his feelings in a brazenly extroverted manner and who, far from being a man of power, is, on the contrary, motivated by altruistic and humanitarian impulses. 'Unlike Macbeth, Boccanegra never sought power but had it thrust upon him by the people, spurred by Paolo Albani. He accepts the office of Doge of Genoa not out of personal ambition but for the good of all and also because of his desire to regain his lost love,

Maria Fiesco. So, it is obvious from the start that he is a very warm, human and humane man. Although we know he has been a corsair fighting the Saracens off Genoese waters, he must have been a very special kind of corsair. After he becomes the Doge he develops and mellows even more, especially after he finds Amelia, his daughter by the now dead Maria Fiesco. He begins to feel the burden and the loneliness of power and his essentially loving nature deepens and acquires a new dimension through paternity. And all of this should be reflected in his singing, which should also be noble, mellow and poised, even in his big scene, the Invocation to the Council. Because although this is impassioned indeed, it is not the rhetoric of a demagogue advocating action, but a plea for peace, brotherhood and goodwill.'

Some critics have complained that Bruson sings this aria in too restrained a manner. Yet he stresses that he will always continue to sing it the way Verdi, 'who was not stupid and who knew exactly what he was driving at, marked it: *piano* or *pianissimo*'. Indeed Verdi made precisely those points about the character of Boccanegra when, in 1880, he complained in a letter to his publisher, Giulio Ricordi, that the baritone engaged to sing the role at La Scala, the later famous Maurel, was too young and therefore 'certain to lack the quiet composure, the visual authority, so important for the role of Simon . . . a passionate, ardent, fiery soul with outward dignified calm – so difficult to achieve – that is what is required for Boccanegra'. Bruson's view of the role, therefore, exactly coincides with Verdi's and this is obviously the reason why his interpretation of it is rightly considered among the best.

After Bruson's 1986 Covent Garden performances, John Higgins wrote in *The Times*: 'At the helm is Renato Bruson, who for some time has been challenging Cappuccilli for supremacy in the title role. Bruson now paces himself with great artistry throughout the part, saving his vocal resources first for the Council Chamber Scene, which has him perched high above the warring factions of Genoa, and then for the final death by poisoning, which has him gazing out into the Mediterranean that brought him both fame and fortune. There is more than a touch of Boris Godunov now about Bruson's introspective Boccanegra. It is not merely the histrionics of the death agonies but the feeling of isolation that he stresses so artfully. During the action of *Simon Boccanegra*, Simon has really only two relationships: first with his rediscovered daughter Amelia and finally with his adversary Fiesco.'

Another role in which Bruson is particularly successful and which he sings very often is the title role in *Macbeth*, a character diametrically opposite to the noble, altruistic, humane and personally unambitious Boccanegra. 'Although Macbeth is not wholly evil but a weak man who, left to his own devices, would never have thought of committing the atrocities he did, he was nevertheless an ambitious, power-thirsty soul who, spurred by his wife – who is evil personified – did find inside himself reservoirs of ruthlessness that made him capable of committing them. Yet Macbeth is also a man who knows fear, who is aware of powers greater than himself, and conscious of the role of the supernatural in human affairs. I am fascinated by his complexity and by his curious interplay of ruthless strength and weakness.'

Bruson's absorption in this character, which he sang for the first time in 1968, explains why he has scored great successes worldwide – at Covent Garden in 1981 in a spectacular new production conducted by Riccardo Muti and directed by Elijah Moshinsky, at the Paris Opéra in the autumn of 1984 and in most major international opera houses. After the London premiere the critic of the *Financial Times* wrote: 'Bruson showed himself a born Macbeth – in lean, haunted visage, in the restrained intensity of his stage movements, above all in the long-lined eloquence of his singing. He excels at unobtrusively finding the sense of those markings – *sotto voce, cupo, soffocato, con dolore* – out of which Verdi made an entirely new kind of baritone villain-hero; and his aria, at the end of the evening, filled with sound and fury signifying rather too little, was the only truly Verdian moment in the production.'

Bruson explains that Macbeth's music reflects the fundamental differences between him and Boccanegra: for in order to express all the inner complexities in Macbeth's character, Verdi gave him some very anguished, febrile, fragmented passages – in 'fatal mia donna' and in the banquet scene, for instance – where the melodic line is permeated by a sense of infinite anxiety. There are also moments where you can hear evil in his music, unlike Boccanegra's in which there isn't a trace of hate, evil or lust for power. 'Therefore, one's singing in *Macbeth* must needs be more emphatic, more impulsive and straightforwardly dramatic than in *Boccanegra*, except at the very end where, yielding to a moment of weakness, Macbeth sings the aria "pieta, rispetto, amore", although I must say I find it hard to imagine how, after all he has done, he can even *think* of pity, respect and love. . . .'

In comparing the vocal aspects of those roles Bruson points out that Boccanegra, with his noble, even, poised singing, is almost entirely *bel canto* while Macbeth is almost *verismo*. 'Vocally both roles are extremely comfortable for me. On balance, though, I would say that Boccanegra is marginally harder because vocally it is more exposed: the voice should always be absolutely clean and perfectly poised. In Macbeth, on the other hand, you can occasionally hide behind the louder, stronger orchestration – that reflects the nature of his character – and camouflage the odd vocal fault. In Boccanegra you cannot camouflage anything, which is why, although he has only one big aria and Macbeth has several, it is on the whole more difficult.' Interestingly enough Verdi himself considered Boccanegra one of the most difficult baritone roles he ever wrote, even more difficult than Rigoletto, as he pointed out in the letter to Giulio Ricordi quoted above: 'It is a role as tiring as Rigoletto but a thousand times more difficult. In Rigoletto the role is already there, and with the requisite amount of voice and feeling one can get away with it quite well. In Boccanegra voice and feeling are not enough. The role lacks the theatricality and has to be *made*. So great actors above all.'

Yet, according to Bruson, *the* most difficult Verdi baritone roles are neither Boccanegra nor Rigoletto, nor even Iago, but some of the roles in his early operas and especially the Conte di Luna in *Il trovatore*, with which he made his professional debut. He thinks most baritones would agree about this, 'first, because the role is extremely high. In the trio, for instance, the Count has to accompany the tenor and the soprano, *in the tenor's octave*. Secondly, because the orchestration is thin throughout and this leaves you very exposed. In the Count's big aria, "Il balen del suo sorriso", for instance, the accompaniment is virtually non-existent – just a harp and a clarinet – which means that not only are you singing at a very high *tessitura*, but from a totally exposed position as well. From the dramatic point of view, on the other hand, it is an uninteresting role that amounts to very little. Like Renato in *Un ballo in maschera*, it never gave me much satisfaction and I abandoned both those roles some time ago.'

Although it is true that the Conte di Luna is not particularly well-suited to Bruson's artistic temperament, it can, in the right hands, be an extremely exciting role in an opera which, in the words of von Karajan (who has a very special affection for it, despite its rudimentary and somewhat incomprehensible plot), 'encapsulates the whole gamut of primitive human emotions: love, hate, jealousy, possessiveness, vindictiveness. Indeed, after conducting it I feel a deep sense of satisfaction, like having eaten a T-bone steak or a huge hamburger – very wholesome.' The truth is that to do this role justice a performer needs a different, more visceral kind of dramatic presence, and a slightly more wide-ranging voice than Bruson's relatively 'short' baritone, which, as he himself points out, would certainly run into difficulties with the high *tessitura* of this role.

At the time of our meetings Bruson – who dislikes pigeonholes and who, despite his reputation as a Verdi baritone and *bel canto* specialist is constantly seeking new suitable roles (he has sung Athanael in Massenet's *Thaïs* and Bénédict in Berlioz's *Béatrice et Bénédict*, for instance) – was looking forward to singing the 'role all baritones dream of', for the first time: the title role in *Don Giovanni* at the Rhenische Oper in Bonn. He was already deep into the score and immensely excited by the challenge of mastering a completely new style of singing, the Mozartian style, so different from the Italian, and felt fascinated by this character, whom he was greatly looking forward to portraying on stage. As well as the performances in Bonn, he was scheduled to sing Don Giovanni again in Washington under Daniel Barenboim.

'No matter how "successfully" I might be said to have tackled a role the first time I sing it, I always look forward to doing it better next time . . . and the one after. It is only through a process of constantly maturing performances that one can achieve some sort of artistic result.'

PIERO CAPPUCCILLI

Piero Cappuccilli belongs to that rare, nearly extinct, breed of baritones capable of excelling in virtually all the major Verdi roles, ranging from those in his early operas – like Ezio in *Attila*, Don Carlos in *Ernani* and the title roles in *Nabucco* and *Macbeth* – to the great warhorses of his middle and late periods like Rigoletto, Simon Boccanegra, Amonasro and Iago. 'I adore Verdi,' he confirms. 'He just suits my voice and I never encounter any difficulties when singing his roles which, although extremely demanding, are nevertheless well written for the voice.' Cappuccilli's robust, sonorous, resonant baritone has a compass of two and a half octaves, is produced seemingly without the least exertion and sustained by a breathing technique legendary in the operatic world. (It has aroused the outspoken admiration of many colleagues, including Domingo and Pavarotti, who acknowledge they learnt a great deal from observing Cappuccilli at work.)

The most essential attribute of a good Verdi baritone, according to Cappuccilli, is a voice that stretches to at least two octaves. Otherwise he won't be able to cope with the *tessituras* of some of the big roles which require him to plunge down to a G or an A below the stave – the domain of the bass – or climb up to A flat and A natural, i.e. the tenor register. 'But the trouble is that nowadays voices tend to be "short" at either end and this immediately puts certain roles like the Conte di Luna in *Il trovatore* beyond them. They also lack some of the substance, intensity and resilience that one associates with the true Verdi baritone sound, which I always liken to that of a piano, the most complete of musical instruments, because it contains not only notes, but harmonics as well. Think of an "arpeggio", for instance: it contains a cluster of notes and harmonics. Great voices should be like that, too, and sing not just on the note but also on the harmonic. This was certainly true of Tagliabue, Galeffi and Stracciari. But alas, Italy doesn't seem to produce voices like that anymore.'

Today's lack of Verdi baritones – or indeed Verdi mezzos, Heldentenors or dramatic sopranos, that is, all the heavier voices that are more difficult to sustain – is due to a variety of causes. In Cappuccilli's opinion, one of them may have something to do with ecological factors like atmospheric pollution, urban smog and so on, conditions that were virtually unknown until the mid sixties. Since then, they have been recognized as harmful to the human breathing apparatus, and are therefore bound to affect the vocal cords, too. 'If you think about it, there were still plenty of great voices around in the fifties and up to the mid or late sixties. Then, all of a sudden, they apparently ceased to emerge. Most of the voices that have come up since are of inferior quality.' (Peter Katona, Artistic Administrator of the Royal Opera, agrees and observes that each new generation of singers is slightly, yet consistently, inferior to the one immediately preceding it.)

But infinitely more serious than ecological factors is the dearth of good teachers and of coaches experienced and caring enough to nurture young voices, help them acquire a good technique and offer them valuable insights into interpretation. This means that young singers usually embark on professional careers 'without really knowing how to sing, let alone sing Verdi, the most difficult of all Italian composers'. On top of which, because of the way musical life is organized – with the proliferation of opera houses and an over-active recording industry, both avid for enough voices to service their needs – singers are often asked, and agree, to sing too much and to perform roles for which they are neither suited nor technically equipped. The combined effect of these three major factors on the art of singing has been, as Cappuccilli vehemently and rightly points out, 'catastrophic'.

In his opinion this sad state of affairs – 'short' voices and inadequate technical preparation – also accounts for the prevalent fashion for performing original, 'so-called authentic', editions of some of the standard repertoire. Cappuccilli is deeply suspicious of the motives behind this vogue and is far from convinced by protestations of 'purism' and 'fidelity to the composer's intentions'. He points out that in most – albeit not all – cases composers produced second versions of their works because they were dissatisfied with the original. 'Therefore the *real* reason behind the trend is often lack of singers capable of tackling the *tessitura*, or coping with the high notes in the traditional versions, i.e. of *real* singers who know what singing is all about. This is why we find ourselves in a situation where any *comprimarios* with neat enough little voices are built up to be what they are not and made to sing parts to which they cannot begin to do justice. And they sing, or rather, butcher them for a year or two and in the process burn themselves out.' (Alfredo Kraus makes similar points about the declining standards of singing and the fashion for 'authentic' versions.)

Inadequate vocal resources also explain why singers who label themselves specialists in this or that area of the repertoire are reluctant to take on the most demanding roles in the field they are supposed to excel in: 'Why do baritones shy away from singing the Conte di Luna in *Il trovatore*, for instance? In the old days no one would *dare* call themselves a Verdi baritone without having this, and most other major Verdi roles, under their belt. Di Luna is a difficult role, to be sure, but not all *that* difficult, provided of course that one knows how to sing and cope with tricky *tessituras*. In this case the *tessitura* is quite high and one also has to sing *a mezza voce* in the *passaggio* zone. This is where they all come apart.' As Carlo Bergonzi (a master of this, as of all, aspects of the art of singing and an exemplary Verdi stylist from whom Cappuccilli himself learnt a great deal) explains at length in his chapter, this is one of the most difficult technical problems to surmount and requires a perfect technique.

Cappuccilli possesses both a masterly technique and a naturally strong, vibrant and resilient voice. Yet as a youth, he had no plans, or ambition, to become a singer. He was – and this was to serve him in very good stead in the future – a keen and active sports fanatic who had a go at most games and also spent three invaluable years as a professional underwater diver. A more perfect exercise for developing the muscles that control breathing, i.e. the diaphragm – and for learning how to hold, meter and release the breath in a regulated way – would be hard to imagine. This hobby, plus a singing teacher capable of developing this capacity for breath control even further, lie at the crux of his now proverbial breathing technique.

Initially Cappuccilli, who was born in Trieste in 1929, had planned to become an architect, and displayed no interest whatsoever in opera or serious music. What voice he had, he used for singing Neapolitan songs and themes from popular films. But his grandfather and uncle were both opera fans and when the family moved back to Trieste from Bari, where they had spent the war years, the latter was impressed enough by his nephew's voice to suggest he seek professional advice. Cappuccilli, who was about to enrol at the University as a student of architecture, says he reacted to this idea with 'something bordering on disgust! I had not even seen an opera in my life and as for a singing career, well, nothing could have been further from even the wildest stretches of my imagination or ambition.'

Gradually, out of curiosity, he gave in to his uncle's promptings and agreed to audition at the local opera house. Sitting in at the audition at the suggestion of the Director was Luciano Donnaggio, a retired bass who had just returned to his native Trieste with the intention of becoming a singing-teacher. His verdict was that Cappuccilli had the makings of a 'stupendous' baritone voice and should therefore become his first pupil. Faced with such praise, Cappuccilli decided to give singing a try, parallel to his architectural studies. But after three months of unending sessions in *solfège* (both sung and spoken), he got fed up and simply did not turn up for further lessons. Finally, six months later, Donnaggio rang him up to enquire what had happened to him and he replied he had neither the time nor the appetite for a singing career. Furthermore, compared with architecture, which promised a secure future in a solid profession, singing seemed like a very uncertain prospect, with no guarantee that he would really 'make it' in a big way. And what was the point of sweating it out for years only to become a chorister or a *comprimario*? Besides, he had no money to spare for singing lessons.

Donnaggio's reply to this torrent of evasive remarks was that he was prepared to stake his reputation on the premise that Cappuccilli's vocal material was such as to *ensure* he would make it to the top, and to prove his faith in this reluctant pupil he was disposed to teach him without remuneration. This he did for five full years, during which Cappuccilli's vocal development began in earnest. They worked not on the size of his voice – his rare, two-and-a-half-octave stretch was there from the start – but on how to sing and recite on the note, how to develop his breath control further and how to master the technique of increasing and decreasing the volume within a single phrase seamlessly and effortlessly, i.e. singing an 'arc'. This involved an exercise called 'the fork': leaping from *pianissimo* to *forte* and back to *pianissimo* in quick succession. Working long and hard on the fork and on sustaining and metering his breath at will lies at the foundation of his ability to sing *a mezza voce* in any zone.

Like Bergonzi, whose breathing technique is also masterly enough to arouse the stupefaction of younger singers, Cappuccilli professes himself 'mystified' that this should be considered something to be marvelled at. 'I do nothing more than breathe normally,' he says, echoing Bergonzi's similar remark, 'but what I have learnt to do perhaps better than many, is to meter and release my breath and tailor it to the nature and requirements of each musical phrase: certain phrases I would sing on one long breath, while in others I might take as many as four short breaths.' His capacity to sustain long phrases on one breath is such that Placido Domingo confided to the *Observer* that 'you can tell when a conductor like Abbado has been rehearsing with Cappuccilli: he'll take the tenor/baritone duet from *Don Carlos* very slowly!' The distinguished coach and accompanist Nina Walker, who has worked with Cappuccilli on numerous occasions at Covent Garden, confirms that he can 'go on for pages and pages without breathing'. She was so impressed that she asked him how he did it. His reply was that, doing all the snorkelling and underwater diving during his teens, a time when the body was still growing and developing, meant that his lungs grew too. She adds that all singers should be advised to do some form of exercise, especially while they are developing: ideally swimming, which is 'such a healthy and un-neurotic thing to do'.

Luciano Donnaggio's one condition for taking Cappuccilli on as a pupil had been that, as soon as he pronounced him ready for it, the latter should go to Milan and audition for some people at La Scala. Towards the end of 1955, after five years' study, Cappuccilli duly presented himself to Maestros Confalonieri and Campogalliani (the expert who had taught Bergonzi, Pavarotti, Freni and Raimondi), who were coaches at the singing school of La Scala. Their reaction was enthusiastic – so much so that they asked Cappuccilli to present himself at their classes every evening and demonstrate to their other pupils 'what singing is all about'. At their suggestion, Cappuccilli entered and won first prize at the G.B. Viotti singing competition. He was immediately engaged to sing Tonio in *I pagliacci* at the Teatro Nuovo in Milan, where he made his professional debut in early 1957. This was followed by engagements in Emilia and invitations to sing Scarpia in *Tosca* at the Teatro La Pergola in Florence and the Conte di Luna in *Il trovatore* at the Athens State Opera. Four years later, in 1964, he made his La Scala debut as Enrico in *Lucia di Lammermoor* and two years later came his first appearance at the Arena di Verona as Rigoletto. In 1967 he made his British debut in the Visconti production of *La traviata* at Covent Garden, under Carlo Maria Giulini. This was followed by his American debut, in 1969, at the Chicago Lyric Opera as Francesco Foscari in *I due Foscari*.

Francesco Foscari is the first of several early Verdi roles Cappuccilli has sung with distinction throughout his career and he stresses that these roles are by no means easy. 'In early Verdi, the vocal element is far more important than the dramatic content. They are "singers'" rather than "singing-actors'" roles. Naturally, one should establish some sort of identity for the character but, with the exception of Nabucco and Macbeth, there are no hidden depths and complexities to unravel and bring out. Vocally, they are without exception extremely difficult: the orchestrations are "thin", and, while you are certainly accompanied, you are not supported and cushioned by the orchestra the way you are in *verismo*. Secondly, the *tessituras* of most of those roles are "ambiguous" and hover a great deal around the *passaggio*. Ezio in *Attila* and Don Carlos in *Ernani* – the latter also requires singing in the *passaggio a mezza voce* – are good examples of what I mean. Also very demanding is the title role in *Nabucco*, which hides nothing and is, dramatically, one of the more interesting early Verdi roles.'

Most demanding, and rewarding, of all early Verdi roles is the title role in *Macbeth*. Cappuccilli waited eighteen years before taking it on and agrees with both Milnes and Bruson that it is one of the most 'emotionally draining of all baritone roles because of the character's inner complexity and the variety of dramatic situations in which he finds himself, which in turn demand a wide variety of vocal colours and subtlety of interpretation'. Verdi himself pointed out the need to bring different shades and nuances of colour to the interpretation of this role in a letter to the baritone Felice Varesi recently published in *Opera*: 'I am sending an adagio in D flat major which you should colour "*cantabile*" and "*affettuoso*".'

Cappuccilli emphasizes that Macbeth experiences a multiplicity of moods and situations seldom encountered in other operatic roles: 'When we first come across him he is a powerful, assured, victorious warrior. Then, after allowing his wife to persuade him to commit the first murder, he loses his strength – loses himself, really – and becomes a pawn to her will. He doesn't know who he is or what he wants any more and returns to the witches to ask if he should take a step back or continue to yield to his wife's promptings. And this vast psychological leap from confident strength to inner turmoil and self-doubt must be indicated through a dramatic change in vocal colour. Nowhere more so than in the banquet scene, where – at the nadir of his powers, in the midst of hallucinations he cannot begin to understand – he has to sing a very difficult scene.

'His wife's death eventually frees him from this spell and enables him to regain some of his former strength and courage. He understands where he went wrong and, I believe, commits an "active suicide" in allowing himself to get killed. At this moment, *after two and a half hours on stage*, he has to sing an aria, "Mal per me" – which is often omitted but which I always include – the first part of which should be sung *a mezza voce*!' Although Verdi himself omitted this aria from the second, Paris, version of *Macbeth* and, bowing to prevalent French fashion, substituted a grand choral finale, the consensus among baritones who perform this role is that the aria should always be included as it helps put the whole character in context.

Cappuccilli feels more spent and exhausted after singing Macbeth than any other role in his repertoire: more worn than after Nabucco which, from the strictly vocal point of view, is equally demanding, or after Rigoletto, which is vocally heavier. What consumes and drains him is Macbeth's psychological complexity and tortured state of mind, which he has first to understand and then communicate to the audience. It is the only role that makes him lose weight. 'Normally I seldom sweat or wear myself out during performances. But when singing Macbeth I lose two kilos at every performance, not just because of the amount of running around I have to do, but because of the adrenalin I have to expend.'

It is rare for Cappuccilli to experience and react to roles with such intensity. For his cool, well-balanced, usually composed and unruffled character is as proverbial as his breathing technique and far removed from the usually highly strung artistic temperaments of the operatic world. He never displays any signs of nerves, stage fright or pre-performance tension, all of which he dismisses as insecurity. He believes singers should lead normal, sane lives and not 'overprotect' themselves. He professes himself 'puzzled by the paradox of colleagues who during the rehearsal period eat, drink and live normally in every respect, and sing extremely well, but who, come the performances, are transformed into nervous wrecks, lock themselves in, abstain from drinking and so on, and sing less well!

'This is a psychological problem I have never been able to explain. The only protection we singers should resort to is to acquire a sound technique at the beginning of our careers and then proceed a step at a time, never exceeding our vocal means. This is the only way to be free of insecurity, stage fright and suchlike, because we are then masters of our voice instead of the reverse. Then we can afford to relax because we *know* the voice is ready to respond to every exigency.' Cappuccilli learnt this serenity based on total vocal mastery from Carlo Bergonzi, from whom he also learnt a great deal about technique, 'because one can learn from a tenor and a bass as well as from a fellow baritone'.

Cappuccilli's own career direction has been exemplary. At the beginning he sang mostly *bel canto* and the lighter Verdi roles, like Germont. As he already stated, he waited eighteen years before first tackling Macbeth and twelve before singing his favourite Verdi role, Simon Boccanegra. As both Sherrill Milnes and Renato Bruson have also declared their special affection for this role, and Tito Gobbi wrote in his book *My World of Italian Opera* that he 'cannot describe the joy, the respect, the sheer love with which I have tried to serve this work', I asked Cappuccilli why

Boccanegra inspires such enthusiasm in its interpreters. 'Vocally it is a non-stop aria, pure *bel canto*', replied Cappuccilli, who first sang it at La Scala in 1969, 'and from the dramatic point of view immensely rewarding because one is portraying a character who, while being the epitome of goodness and altruism, is nevertheless complex, sophisticated and tormented enough to be interesting. There is also this interplay between the personal drama – embodied by his paternal dimension – and the context of power politics, the public man.'

This paternal element, which Verdi explores so profoundly and movingly in this role, caused Cappuccilli to reconsider his whole approach to Rigoletto, another of Verdi's famous fathers. After singing Boccanegra for the first time in Milan, Cappuccilli was due to sing a performance of Rigoletto in Venice – the 161st of this role in his career, to be precise. To his astonishment, he discovered that, as a result of having sung Boccanegra, his interpretation of Rigoletto had changed significantly: 'From the dramatic point of view it had become much easier because, through singing Boccanegra, I had explored the inner aspects and dimensions of paternity much more deeply. The result was the best performance of Rigoletto that I had sung to date.' He explains that Rigoletto is more difficult than Boccanegra; it is exceptionally long, with a great deal of singing which, in addition, has to be done from a hunchback position. This makes it considerably more difficult, as both Milnes and Bruson also stressed in their chapters. 'It also has a difficult *tessitura* demanding a wide palette of vocal colours – sometimes even lighter and darker shades of the same colour within a single phrase.'

Boccanegra and Rigoletto are two of a series of 'paternal' Verdi roles, which also includes Germont in *La traviata*, Miller in *Luisa Miller*, and Amonasro in *Aida*, and Verdi's continual preoccupation with the theme of paternity fascinates Cappuccilli. 'Verdi's fathers are invariably interesting and complex, unlike his female heroines, many of whom strike me as somewhat "cardboard" characters. All Verdi fathers experience a conflict between their paternal feelings and politics or social conventions, yet all are totally different: Miller is the most tender, Rigoletto the most tormented, Boccanegra has to act his paternal role within the context of power politics, Germont is torn between his son's or his daughter's happiness and Amonasro is, perhaps, the least sympathetic, possibly because of the urgency of his predicament. These differences in their characters are naturally reflected in the way the roles are written and should be sung.'

Verdi's greatness as a composer lies precisely in the fact that, despite the great vocal demands he makes on his singers, he nevertheless presents them with enormous expressive possibilities for exploring a great variety of human emotions and psychological situations, as Cappuccilli pointed out in an interview in *Opéra International*. 'Think of the contrasts between characters as widely different as Macbeth, Nabucco, Amonasro, Iago and Posa in *Don Carlos*, for instance. Posa is a less dramatic role than the others, but difficult all the same, because he has to sing constantly, both lyric and dramatic music: his duet with King Philip II is very dramatic, while his farewell to Don Carlos is a beautiful *bel canto* aria with a pure *legato* line and should – again at the end of a long evening's singing – be sung *a mezza voce*. But despite its difficulties it is, like most Verdi roles, very well written.'

Cappuccilli emphasizes that, to sing Verdi, a baritone needs more than the set of vocal qualities he named in the beginning of this chapter: he also needs a wide palette of vocal colours, plus a variety of shades of the same colour with which to mirror the diversity of moods and dramatic situations experienced by Verdi's characters – especially those like Iago, which would otherwise become monotonous and infinitely less intriguing. He stresses that the bigger the voice, the greater the danger of its becoming monotonous, if not shaded. 'This is why I have worked extremely hard at shading and colouring my voice. Through my architectural studies I developed a passion for paintings, especially for strongly coloured ones, which arouse instant joy in me, and I try to apply this passion for colour to my operatic singing.' Cappuccilli's voice is not naturally richly coloured, so it was interesting to discover that the need to shade it is something he is conscious of and works hard at. Indeed, the only criticism ever levelled at Cappuccilli – both by critics and people in the profession – is that he occasionally omits to do this and ends up sounding mono-chromatic, especially in productions that fail to arouse his interest or to involve him emotionally. The exceptional quality of his vocal material and his superb technique ensure that he never delivers a bad performance. However, he does sometimes produce less than moving or haunting portrayals, lacking in subtlety and in one hundred per cent dramatic commitment. But at his best, and especially when working with colleagues, conductors and producers he respects, he is second to none, and remains, at fifty-six, at the peak of an exemplary career.

Away from Verdi, one of Cappuccilli's best interpretations is Tonio in *I pagliacci*, the role with which he made his professional operatic debut nearly thirty years ago and which he has continued to sing regularly over the years. Other *verismo* roles in his repertoire include Alfio in *Cavalleria rusticana*, Barnaba in *La gioconda* and Gérard in *Andrea Chénier*. In earlier years it also included Scarpia, which he decided to shed at a certain moment, as 'part of the choice one has to make to preserve one's voice in peak form'. *Verismo* is in many ways easier to sing than either Verdi or *bel canto*, which require line and stylistic refinement as well. He agrees with Pavarotti that *bel canto* is particularly suited to young voices and included several *bel canto* roles in his early repertoire: Enrico in *Lucia di Lammermoor*, Riccardo in *I puritani*, Ernesto in *Il pirata*, the title role in *Guillaume Tell* and Figaro in *Il barbiere di Siviglia*. Every young voice, in his opinion, should give itself time to grow healthily by singing these as well as some of the lighter Verdi roles like Germont in *La traviata*, Ezio in *Attila* and eventually the Conte di Luna in *Il trovatore*, i.e. roles that bridge the passage from lyric to dramatic, and wait until the voice is ready for heavier stuff like Renato in *Un ballo in maschera* or Carlo in *La forza del destino*.

For agility and precision, he particularly recommends Figaro in *Barbiere*, to which he himself has kept returning, with great joy, over the years: 'I always have great fun in this role! After first singing it very early in my career, I left it alone for eight years and then sang it in 1968 at the Teatro di San Carlo in Naples, where I played the guitar in the serenade and generally enjoyed myself hugely, because it was a marvellous production conducted by Nino Sanzogno with a cast headed by Alfredo Kraus. Then I left it alone for another twelve years before singing it first at the Teatro Liceo in Barcelona and immediately afterwards in South Africa, with such ease that I thought it was time to do it again in Italy: so when I was asked to sing it in Parma I accepted, especially because I knew nobody thought I could still do it! But to their surprise, the voice was still intact with the necessary agility, precision and lustre.' The reviews were enthusiastic and this was one of the greatest satisfactions in Cappuccilli's career, because singing this role in his mid fifties proved that he had conducted his entire career along the right lines.

At the time of our encounter his cherished dream was one day to sing the title role in Wagner's *Der fliegende Holländer*, because he would like to add a Wagnerian role to his repertoire. The Dutchman would, he feels, be the ideal choice as the whole opera is closer to Verdi than Wagner's other works 'because it contains a strong element of *bel canto* and is also highly dramatic [José Van Dam, one of today's most distinguished interpreters of this role, also stresses both these points in his chapter], although, like all Wagnerian characters, he is a little bit abstract and nebulous'. Another ambition is to sing the title role in Thomas's *Hamlet* with Gruberova. Cappuccilli confided to *Opéra International* that he would like to continue singing as long as his voice remains intact. 'But I have no intention of dying still breathing the dust of the *palcoscènico*. As soon as my voice loses some of its quality, I hope I'll realize it and quit singing as soon as possible!'

SHERRILL MILNES

'Baritones are traditionally behind the sopranos and tenors in the popularity contest, but I guess I'm fortunate to be at a level at which I don't feel I have to race,' declared the American dramatic baritone Sherrill Milnes in an interview published in *Opera*. He is right about both points, for although the roles they portray are usually meatier, sexier, more interesting and multi-faceted than the stylized, one-dimensional tenor 'heroes', baritones don't often arouse the same adulatory excesses in audiences as tenors and some sopranos. The explanation probably lies in the fact that the baritone voice, being the natural extension of the normal speaking voice, involves less effort to produce and considerably less danger to sustain, than the tenor's. Ergo, it doesn't pander to the 'arena mentality' that constitutes an important part of an operatic audience's psychology.

It is also undoubtedly true that Milnes, one of the most popular baritones of our day and one of the very few to achieve star status, certainly doesn't have to race! The possessor of a big, powerful, dramatically expressive 'he-man' voice (as *High Fidelity* magazine graphically put it), and an equally manly, rousing stage presence that exudes drama and quickens the pulse, Milnes has been at the pinnacle of the operatic profession for over fifteen years. His international career began in 1970, after he made a triumphant debut as Macbeth at the Vienna State Opera under the late Karl Böhm. Since then he has sung an extensive repertoire – consisting of all the big Verdi roles, a good deal of *verismo*, Don Giovanni and a few rarities from the French repertoire like Hamlet by Thomas – in every major theatre in the world: the Hamburg and the Bavarian State Opera, the Deutsche Oper, Covent Garden, La Scala, the Paris Opéra, the San Francisco and the Chicago Lyric Operas and, of course, the Metropolitan Opera, his 'home base', where he made his debut as Valentin in *Faust* in 1965 and became an 'overnight sensation' in 1968 after singing Miller in *Luisa Miller*.

Milnes's rich, vibrant, expressive sound lends itself well to recording, and he is one of the most recorded baritones of recent years. His albums succeed in transmitting some of the dramatic power of his stage interpretations, and it was therefore not surprising to learn that 'when standing in front of a microphone, my metabolism gets higher than when I'm on stage because I know this is going to be for ever'.

Milnes is a cosmopolitan, widely read, sophisticated and, at the same time, quintessentially and refreshingly American 'farm boy', as he puts it. He was born in Downers Grove (a suburb of Chicago, Illinois), on a dairy farm. Both his parents were musical, especially his mother, who was a piano teacher and church choir director. So, while growing up in the fresh air and participating in farm chores – according to fellow baritone Piero Cappuccilli nothing is more propitious for the development of a potentially great voice than a healthy environment in its growing stages – Milnes learnt to play not only the piano, but also the violin, the viola, the double bass, the clarinet and the tuba, thus laying the foundations for his exceptionally accomplished musicianship, now renowned among singers. He received his BME and MME in musical education from Drake University. Later he sang in the Chicago Symphony Chorus under Margaret Hillis, with the intention of becoming a music teacher. To help pay for his tuition, he earned his living by playing string bass in a jazz band. As well as singing in churches, synagogues, at women's clubs, local opera groups, and in TV and radio commercials, he also entered many singing contests. In 1960, aged twenty-five, he auditioned for the Boris Goldovsky Opera Company, with which he then travelled most of America during the next five years – covering 100,000 miles by bus, singing over three hundred performances of a dozen or so roles – until his debut at the New York City Opera in 1964.

He considers his five years with the Goldovsky Company 'the luckiest possible beginnings for a career like mine. First, because all of Goldovsky's productions were in English which, of course, somewhat changes the feeling of opera roles but on the other hand *really* gives you a chance, in your native language, to refine character and discover things you would like to do when you eventually graduate to the original language. And this is wonderful. Although it amounts to knowing only part of the roles, it nevertheless constitutes a solid foundation on which to build later. Second, because Goldovsky used, and still uses, smaller sets with an acoustical ceiling and a small orchestra of twenty-five instruments. This meant that I could sing certain big roles, like Rigoletto, earlier than usual for a young baritone because on one hand I didn't have to cope with an orchestra that forced me to push the voice and on the other because I had a set that favoured the sound by helping project it forward.' (The crucial importance of acoustic considerations in the building of operatic stage sets has also been stressed by René Kollo.)

Of course, he stresses that this doesn't mean that those roles were easy to cope with from the vocal point of view. 'They were hard, because a role like Rigoletto is always hard! There is no such thing as an "easy" performance of Rigoletto, not at any stage in a baritone's career, and I am sure my colleagues will agree. [They all do.] If someone were to claim Rigoletto is easy for him then you can be sure there's something wrong with his performance. Because this role is full of traps: the biggest trap is, of course, the posture you have to adopt while singing it, i.e. the fact that you have to do a certain amount of bending over in order to give the impression of a hunchback, and this twisted posture is not a good singing position: it inhibits breath support, it makes it hard to tuck your chin in, in order to project the sound forward. So, you cannot adopt any of the usual "good" singing postures that contribute so much to sound projection. Secondly, the *tessitura* is generally high, especially in his duets with Gilda. Third, it is a very long role, much longer than Germont in *La traviata*, which is rightly considered a good "beginner's" role for Verdi baritones because, despite the anachronism of having the oldest character in the opera usually sung by the youngest member of the cast, it is shorter and less demanding, both vocally and dramatically.

'Therefore Germont does not tire the voice. The biggest challenge in this role is to succeed in not looking young. This cannot be done with the voice, because a *legato* line is a *legato* line, beautiful singing is beautiful singing and a young sound is a young sound. So, it has to be done with the body, with the way Germont stands and walks, which is why he is easier to sing on record than on stage, where he has to have a certain bearing. Because although he is old, he is an aristocrat and should move and stand like an aristocrat, even though he is weaker than his son Alfredo or other aristocratic characters like Rodrigo in *Don Carlos*. For many years when singing Germont I was always the youngest member of the cast. But when I next sing it, at the Met, I shall be the eldest!' (Milnes is now fifty-one).

Milnes stresses that age also helps in the interpretation of this role in the sense that, having lived a little and had children of his own, he now finds it easier to sympathize with Germont's problem, because, although many productions fail to indicate this, Germont does become sympathetic towards Violetta in the end. 'The music changes, and although he cannot change his position about his son's liaison with her being an obstacle to his daughter's marriage, he has understood the depth of her love and the magnitude of the sacrifice he is demanding.'

Age also helps the understanding of the father/daughter relationship in *Rigoletto*, because it would be a little hard to manufacture the feeling Rigoletto has for Gilda without having had children of one's own. This paternal dimension should be apparent in the quality of sound as well as in the dramatic interpetation: 'At court, Rigoletto is the opposite of the man he is at home, and this should be reflected by a corresponding difference in one's sound. He should have a brighter, nastier, more "snarly" sound at court, where his job is to make the Duke laugh. And if he doesn't, he gets fired, and if he gets fired he has no money and would be forced to leave town. It is historically true that in those days physically handicapped people were locked away somewhere. So the only possibility for making an honest living would be as a jester, and the easiest way to be funny is by being sarcastic and poking fun at other people. Then, the moment he is at home, he changes to a tender, over-solicitous father and one should find a warmer, mellower tone, but taking care not to screw up the technique: because whenever he has to sing with Gilda, his music is at its highest *tessitura*.'

In fact, he finds Rigoletto's first duet with Gilda, 'Figlia-mio padre' (Act I, Scene 2), even harder than the big Act II duet, 'Piangi, fanciulla', because by then the voice is warmer and because, generally speaking, voices tend to rise a little and get higher during the course of a performance. Milnes stresses that, although not everybody's voice responds in this way, most singers find this to be true and points out that basses, for instance, are usually in trouble when their lowest notes occur in the last act but cope with them far more easily near the beginning of an opera. 'So, I suppose that my voice isn't as ready in Act I to cope with this high *tessitura*, which sits on C-D-E flat-F-E flat-F. But by the time I reach Act II I have done a lot of singing, I have sung the big aria "Cortigiani, vil razza dannata", and the voice is at its peak of warmth and position, so that the second duet does not seem so hard. There is a point, of course, where you begin to get tired, but even so, the voice is lighter and finds it easier to maintain a high *tessitura*. Then, after you have sung "Vendetta, tremenda vendetta" at the finale of Act II – whether you sing the high A flat at the end or not – you are home and dry. The last act makes no great vocal demands on Rigoletto: it's mainly acting. In fact it's the only part of the role I really enjoy singing, because I know all the worries are behind! There are the top notes, the altered top notes at the finale [to which Renato Bruson refers, and objects, in his chapter], but, after all, it *is* the finale! And in the death scene, you can relate all the family feelings you have experienced as a human being – the death of your parents, your children's illnesses and so on – and put them into this moment. This is what acting is all about.'

Milnes was reminded of a story he heard about Laurence Olivier and Dustin Hoffman when the two were on the set of the movie *Marathon Man*. Hoffman was supposed to look utterly spent for a certain scene and, to achieve the desired effect, stayed out all night, didn't sleep for days, and walked the streets. When he arrived on the set looking terrible, Olivier commented on how sick he looked and Hoffman recounted what he had done. Horrified, Olivier was said to have exclaimed 'Dear boy, how perfectly ghastly, wouldn't it have been simpler to act?'

Milnes was quick to add, though, that had Hoffman been a singer rather than a straight actor he could never have got away with wearing himself out *and* delivering the goods, because the voice is a physical thing and, in operatic acting, the vocal, physical demands are paramount. 'This is the basic difference between singing and acting, between straight acting and operatic acting. Straight actors almost never play roles that stretch their actual physical skills right to the limits whereas in the big operatic roles singers are *constantly* being pushed to the limits of physical stamina. In addition, singing is made even more precarious by the fact that the voice is such a fragile thing and can be affected by factors like pollen, phlegm, dust in the theatre, the slightest health upset. You might be in great voice when suddenly a piece of phlegm just flicks into the sound and sometimes the audience hear it and sometimes they don't. But *we* hear it and we feel it and it is one of the factors contributing to the unpredictability of the instrument we have to work with.'

He explains that this is one of the reasons why singing is such a high-tension profession, especially when one is talking about the top twenty-five or so singers from whom audiences expect wonders all the time. This tension and constant awareness of 'the voice' is often reflected in what he calls silly little mannerisms like throat vibrations aimed at checking whether everything in there sounds all right. It isn't always possible to judge the condition of the voice first thing in the morning. There have been mornings when he got up thinking he might have to cancel that night's performance only to find that, after two hours, the body warmed up and the voice began to feel normal. The opposite has also happened on occasion and he considers this independence and unpredictability of an instrument that resides in his own body 'inexplicable and something akin to magic: for although you can tell whether the voice will be somewhere within the area of normal, you can't be sure of *exactly* how the sound will come out, until after it happens. It is an entity within ourselves, dependent yet also independent, and never wholly controllable. In fact it feels almost like a third person and I suppose this is why Caruso never referred to it as "my" voice but as "the" voice.'

To escape from the high-tension environment of performing life and relax the nervous system as much as the voice, he recommends adequate vacation time but adds that it is important to allow sufficient time at the end for the voice to be warmed up and got going again. After a two- or three-week break, for instance, it is advisable to spend at least a week vocalizing and exercising to get it back to full strength. His own voice is always in peak form a few weeks after his holiday.

Milnes's exceptional musicianship means he can learn and study roles by himself and the time he devotes to doing so varies according to the role. Once, having been rung up by Rudolf Bing, who was then General Manager of the Metropolitan Opera, and asked if he could sing Renato in *Un ballo in maschera* in a month, after looking at the score and noting the fact that this is not a long role, he agreed. But he points out that it is infinitely better if, instead of five weeks, one can take five to six months, which he considers 'a reasonable time to learn a role, get it into the throat (*ingolarlo*, as the Italians say), and mature with it a bit. In the case of *Un ballo in maschera*, though, I used every trick I could think of: wearing earphones and listening to tapes of it all the time, saying words in rhythm and so on. You can only sing hard two to three hours a day before the throat fatigues. But the mind doesn't fatigue and you can use the mind and the ear a great deal to help memorization.'

Certain roles, like Don Giovanni, for instance, which Milnes first sang at the Metropolitan Opera in 1974, take a lot longer to master. He took over a year to prepare it, and this despite the fact that he had already sung it in English with the Goldovsky company, and despite the fact that it presents no vocal difficulties. 'As a vocal exercise, Don Giovanni is easy. Unlike the tenor and all the soprano roles in this opera, it is not a vocal "tour de force" role. It's a "*pizzazz*" role, a sex appeal role, eye to eye, and a good change from all the hard, vocal-power parts I tend to sing most of the time. And, as such, it's physically hard and hard on the nerve endings. [Thomas Allen, who also excels in this role, makes precisely the same point.] Vocally it has a range of only an octave and a half from A below the stave to E above and no high notes, unlike Rigoletto, which contains difficult notes like Fs, F sharps, a G and a top A flat that sits on the power part of the voice which is constantly being stretched. This is why Giovanni can also be sung by a bass, as well as a baritone, provided the colour of his voice is right.'

Giovanni's only two arias, the Champagne aria and the Serenade, are short and not really challenging from the vocal point of view. Most of the time, throughout the recitatives and the dialogue, his potency and magnetism can only be conveyed by the tension and electricity the singer manages to exude through his physical presence. 'Vocally, the closest Giovanni comes to being a "tour de force" role is in the Supper scene, which I love doing but which, like the last act of *Rigoletto*, is mostly acting. You can make a lot of sound, of course, especially when the Commendatore walks in, but it's not singing a long *legato* line, it's exclaiming, gasping and so on. So Giovanni's *tessitura* poses no problems for baritones, at least. Basses may find it more problematic, of course, because they have to *work* to keep on top of the pitch.'

He stresses that the successful portrayal of Giovanni depends on a certain physical factor and on the right vocal colour, i.e. on the image that any one sound evokes in the audience. There are basses who could sing all Don Giovanni's notes but who would, nevertheless, be totally wrong for the part. 'The late Fernando Corena, one of the greatest Leporellos I ever worked with, could easily have sung all Giovanni's notes, but it would have been foolish for him to attempt this role and he knew it. Conversely, Cesare Siepi, one of the greatest Don Giovannis ever, could have sung all Leporello's notes, but what a sad waste that would have been! So, what I'm trying to say is that, to sing Giovanni, you need a specific vocal colour and you need sex appeal! It's a very physical part and the only one for which the late Tito Gobbi wasn't one hundred per cent right. The sound itself wasn't sexy enough. Maybe he just waited too long . . . for there has to be a certain balletic quality about Giovanni and a certain insouciance, physical and moral. The whole principle of the "droit de seigneur" was based on this and, for Giovanni, only two women in his life could be safe from him: his mother, whom we know nothing about, and the sister he didn't have! Every other woman it was not only his right, but his duty, his responsibility, to seduce!' After Milnes performed this role at the Salzburg Festival under Karl Böhm, *Opera* wrote that 'Sherrill Milnes is now the Don Giovanni of one's dreams. He begins with the advantage of the right voice for the part, a high baritone; apart from which he sounds and looks sexy and dangerous, a manic womanizer, a ruthless killer and compulsive liar. In addition to which he was in splendid voice, dominating stage, orchestra and cast with tones of steel and velvet by turns.'

Jonathan Miller, who directed *Don Giovanni* for the English National

Opera in 1985, views Giovanni as a man who is 'intoxicated by women and who has a chronic addiction to sexuality. To join eyes with a woman or glance at a pair of legs is instantly to be drawn into some sort of contact. He is so attractive to women because he is so attracted *by* them. Of course, his inability to form any attachment that outlasts lust leads to a trail of injury, especially at a time when the convention of the day had it that liaisons of this sort meant that women would be dishonoured and so on.' Milnes feels that this point is what makes the opera a morality contest between the forces of good and evil.

'I always think Giovanni has got to be mean, he's got to be dangerous, he's got to be tough. But there has to be something about him that people like. If he were a Mephistopheles pure and simple, or a Scarpia pure and simple, it wouldn't work. There has to be a Mephistophelian touch about him, but the charm has got to be there, too, so that when he goes to hell one can feel "what a pity" for a moment, before pulling oneself together and realizing that it's right, it has to be. But that slight regret has to be there. If, on the other hand, one were to overdo the charm and portray him as a hail-fellow-well-met, a womanizer pure and simple, this would also be wrong, because it would be too lightweight and miss the point about the moral clash between good and evil.'

Milnes stresses that another crucial point about the interpretation of Don Giovanni is the interplay with the other characters and especially with Leporello, whose personality can make a vital difference to his portrayal of Giovanni. Just how vital this difference can be is illustrated by Milnes's anger at the management of the Metropolitan Opera some years ago when they planned to change the singer who was to portray Leporello on tour without first notifying him and, more important, without allowing adequate rehearsal time for him to adjust to his performance. Originally it was going to be Walter Berry, with whom Milnes had performed the opera in Salzburg and who was a very good Leporello of a kind, a good servant who really subordinated his personality to Don Giovanni. But, as yet unbeknownst to Milnes, who only heard the rumours through the proverbial grapevine, Berry was to be replaced by Fernando Corena, with whom Milnes had also sung often but whose Leporello was vastly different, and indeed the polar opposite of Berry's, 'the cheeky, insubordinate kind'.

So Milnes called the management and, in his own words, hit the roof! He said they just couldn't do this because this whole opera hinges on the Giovanni-Leporello rapport and that changing one of those two characters therefore makes an enormous difference to the whole relationship and he couldn't be expected to make the necessary modifications to his own interpretation in one short rehearsal. As he explained, Corena 'who was a great Leporello, could make up words until tomorrow and sing recitatives until next week if one didn't interrupt him and come in on his lines. This is why he was so great in roles like Bartolo, where he could just rattle on. But in this opera Giovanni always has to be on top. So you had to step in on his lines and he expected you to. This needed adequate rehearsing and I did persuade the management to provide us with more time. Even so, I had to concentrate extra hard because I had to come in right *on* that last line of Fernando's all the time, because if your Leporello becomes stronger, then you, as Giovanni, must become even stronger in your ordering him about. If he gets very busy and gesture-y, then you dominate him in other ways, for instance by *not* looking at him when you order him about. It's constant give-and-take.'

Milnes explains that this kind of interplay between the two protagonists is also crucial in *La traviata*, where the interpretation of Germont can change a lot depending on who is singing Violetta, but doesn't apply as much to roles like the Conte di Luna in *Il trovatore* or Rodrigo in *Don Carlos*. But it does constitute a vital element in *Otello*, where the interpretation of Iago is enormously affected by the tenor singing Otello, because some Otellos are more difficult than others to dominate mentally.

'Jon Vickers's Otello, for example, is larger than life, pained but powerful and kind of balletic, choreographed, almost stylized. It would be wrong to try and dominate him too overtly, because if Iago were to overstep this boundary it would instantly be "off with his head" or "back home on the next ship out". You have to let Jon's Otello hang himself, work *himself* into a corner and go about it with a very soft touch. "Oh, I'm so sorry, Sir, I'd die for you, I wouldn't have told you about this dream of Cassio's if I'd known the effect it would have on you" sort of thing. Placido Domingo's Otello is much more vulnerable and you can afford to be a *little* more menacing and use some subtle threatening gestures, though not within his sight. You, as Iago, can safely assume that, if you overstepped the mark, the reaction of Jon's Otello would be physical, volatile and acute, whereas Placido's Otello might not react so violently, he might withdraw more into himself and suffer more inwardly. But every performance of this opera is different and their reaction to what you say is not necessarily the same from performance to performance.'

Vocally, Milnes does not consider Iago an especially difficult role. The range is from a low C to F sharp, which makes it a bit lower than Rigoletto, Carlo in *La forza del destino* or Don Carlos in *Ernani*. It is not an especially long role because, although Act II is relentless for Iago (as indeed it is for Otello), he fades away after Act III. The real challenge lies in the fact that the baritone has to use a wide and subtle range of vocal colours in order to bring out all the facets of the man, clear or implied. Milnes feels that from both vocal and dramatic points of view, Iago is not a young man's role, at least not if one is to get the maximum out of it and be able to 'bury' the sound and bring out the many faces of Iago in quick succession: the quick smile, the hidden menace, the fleeting glimpse of envy. But one should be careful not to fall into the trap of making Iago too multi-faceted, because the portrayal would then get confusing and end up communicating nothing. Franco Zeffirelli, who directed the first production of *Otello* Milnes sang in, at the Metropolitan Opera in the autumn of 1972 – and whom he considers a genius, 'a genius and a flair director as opposed to a homework director and definitely one of the top six in the world, along with Otto Schenk, Götz Friedrich, Giorgio Strehler, Jean-Pierre Ponnelle and the much underestimated Tito Capobianco' – pointed out to him that two layers are enough.

'In Act I, the smile should be very much in evidence: "Oh, I'm so sorry you're drinking so much, have a little more", and all very buddy-buddy. There are a couple of asides when he shows what he really is, but the rest of the time he should come across as a nice guy. There is always a question in my mind when I sing this role: has Iago done this sort of thing before or is it his first try? In Zeffirelli's Met production Iago was portrayed as being virtually possessed by an outside evil force that makes him do things he's not even always aware of. He sings the "Credo" as if listening to this other force dictating the words that come out of his mouth. And at the end of it, instead of the traditional laughter, he screams, because suddenly the *real* Iago is back and horrified at what he's just uttered, about there being no afterlife and so on. This view isn't necessarily correct and doesn't hold all the way through the opera but it was an interesting concept to fool around with . . . Iago is a great role with infinite possibilities, but it's really Otello's opera.'

Milnes's favourite Verdi part is the title role in *Simon Boccanegra*, which he first sang at the Chicago Lyric Opera in 1979 and again at Covent Garden in 1980. Piero Cappuccilli and Renato Bruson have also expressed a special affection for this role, and I wondered what particular aspects or qualities about it strike such a deep chord in its interpreters. He replied that 'Boccanegra is the greatest human being any composer ever wrote about in *any* vocal category including tenor, bass, soprano or mezzo. I'd defend him with my life! He doesn't just deal with personal affairs but timeless concepts appropriate to every age, like love, peace, brotherhood and getting along with one's fellow men, that we must live together in harmony and love. His one big aria, "Plebe, patrizzi", would be as relevant today in a discussion in international politics as it was in thirteenth-century Genoa.

'Secondly, Boccanegra has to cope with a great personal, human tragedy over his daughter, which Verdi wrote about *so* well, better than in any of his operas that focus on the father/daughter aspect. And, oddly enough, he does not have a single aria in which to express his feelings for his daughter, which is a unique situation in a Verdi opera. So, you have to indicate the depth of his feelings and of the bond between them intangibly, with the way you look and with your gestures. Again, I don't think this is a young man's role. You need a lot of life experience before you can do it justice and bring out the great leader and the passionate, loving father in him.'

All of this makes Boccanegra a taxing role, even though vocally speaking it is not especially difficult. The range presents no problems and the *tessitura* is not terribly high. What it does require, though, if one is to highlight the character's two dimensions as a leader and a father, is richness of sound right through. And although it isn't as long as *Rigoletto*, Milnes stresses that it *seems* long because all the operas in which he has to die at the end seem longer than they are: 'Boccanegra's death scene is wonderful. Death scenes are always satisfying to play because succeeding in making the audience weep is what our art is all about. In operas where I grow older on stage and die at the end, I have to go through a great many psychological and physical changes. This is true both of *Simon Boccanegra* and of *Macbeth*, although in the latter case it's not so much a question of living through a long span of years but of dissipation due to strain, fear and sleepless nights. In Simon's case it is the weariness of disappointment because he hasn't been able to bring his people together and therefore feels his life has been a failure. His disappointment is evident in his death scene where, until the end, he doesn't know that he has been poisoned. And because of all the emotional and physical changes you have experienced by then, the opera feels much longer than three hours, infinitely longer than, say, *Il trovatore* or *Il barbiere di Siviglia*.'

The same is true of *Macbeth*, with which Milnes made his triumphant Vienna State Opera debut in 1970 and has since sung in almost every major opera house. He points out that, as in all operas based on Shakespeare plays, the first premise to be cleared is whether one is interpreting Shakespeare's or Verdi's Macbeth, and the answer is that it should definitely be Verdi's.

In any case, he points out that Verdi and his librettist, Piave, worked out their libretto from an Italian translation of the play which, according to the eminent coach Ubaldo Gardini, already sounds different. So the *Macbeth* in question is three removed from Shakespeare. One of the main differences between the opera and the play is that in Verdi the role of Macbeth is shorter than in the play, while the opposite is true of Lady Macbeth.

Another vital premise to decide on is what version, or combination of versions, of this opera to use. Verdi was forced to revise his original editions of 1847 before the opera was to be performed at the Paris Opéra in 1865 and, in compliance with local fashion, insert things like big choruses and the mandatory ballet. This was the case with *Don Carlos* and *Les Vêpres siciliennes*, which were specially written for the Paris Opéra, or with any operas of his that were to be performed there. Milnes cannot believe that Verdi loved those ballets and thinks that one would be more justified in omitting them. On the other hand, he agrees with most Verdi scholars and specialists, including the conductor Riccardo Muti, a well-known purist in these matters, that the changes Verdi made to the vocal solo music are a distinct improvement on the original version because he was then eighteen years older and musically more mature. Therefore these changes should be observed. However, the most controversial of all the changes Verdi made for the Paris version was the ending, and Milnes, along with most baritones who sing Macbeth, is totally against the new ending: 'the original version ends with the aria "Mal per me", which is a summing-up of a lot of the things said in Shakespeare's play but omitted from the opera. This is followed by only eight bars of music, the usual solid dramatic salvo with which all Verdi operas of the early and middle period end, be it *Rigoletto*, *La traviata*, *Il trovatore*, *Ernani*, *Luisa Miller* or *La forza del destino*. But the Paris management decided they wanted a morality play about the clash between the forces of good and the forces of evil and persuaded Verdi to remove the aria "Mal per me" and again, in compliance with local fashion, substitute a grand choral finale, which is okay but certainly cannot be numbered among Verdi's great choruses. Therefore the ending I prefer is the one in the original version, which is far more effective, and I consider it mandatory to retain the "Mal per me" which restores some of the balance between Macbeth and Lady Macbeth in the opera, keeps the length of the role almost equal to that in the play and rounds off the opera in a logical way. Otherwise, both the audience and the interpreter feel frustrated.'

When Milnes found that it was to be omitted from Peter Hall's much criticized Metropolitan Opera production, he almost withdrew from it. Although he did not regret his decision to sing it, he did feel so angry and frustrated after the premiere that he 'literally felt like punching someone and it would have had to be the conductor, Jim Levine! When he came up to me after the opening I said: don't talk to me, don't be near me because I'm so frustrated I might punch you right in the mouth. And I wasn't "putting on a number", I was genuinely upset and it took over an hour for me to work through the frustration of performing *Macbeth* without this aria. It felt exactly like *coitus interruptus*, if you'll excuse the metaphor. At the moment of climax, one withdrew!' Sir Peter Hall disagrees: 'I don't believe Verdi meant that last aria to remain. I think that sudden, brutal extinction of Macbeth was his real dramatic intention. From the point of view of the singer and the audience and giving a certain classic rounding-off to the piece, I can understand why one might want to retain it. But I don't believe it's right, and neither did Jimmy Levine. *Macbeth* in my view is a nineteenth-century melodrama, it's Shakespeare seen through the eyes of the nineteenth century, whereas *Otello* and *Falstaff* are huge pieces which stand on their own and go *beyond* Shakespeare, to a genius called Verdi.'

'Vocally speaking,' says Milnes, '*Macbeth* is one of the more difficult Verdi roles, harder than Carlo in *La forza del destino*, for instance, which has beautiful singing, high notes and long *legato* lines. But it is not full of vocal effects like grunts, groans and anguished chokes, which are an essential part of Macbeth and which cost the vocal mechanism, and indeed the whole body, more and make you more tired at the end of the evening.' (All the baritones who sing Macbeth agree and Cappuccilli loses two kilos at every performance.)

From the dramatic point of view, one of the most essential points to bring out is 'the very definite love and sexual attraction between Lady Macbeth and Mister'. He does not think Macbeth was pushed to committing violent acts by her but sees the whole process as a two-way stream: she's more overtly aggressive while he takes a little longer. 'I think he would have killed Duncan anyway, but maybe not that night. She just pre-empts him, she's bolder and wants to grab the first opportunity, while he wants to take time to think about it. Being a great warrior, his morality is closer to the surface while hers is more hidden. But it's an interesting rout for the two of them: she starts off strong and very overt in her ideas and ambitions – the reason she appears so dominant – and slowly crumbles. The blood on her hands grinds inside her. He starts off more slowly then grabs hold of himself and grows in stature as the opera nears its end. Even when all the witches' prophecies, on which he has been counting, crumble away and work to his disadvantage, he tells himself, "so be it, I'll have a go and if I'm to die, I'll die fighting". This is another reason for retaining his aria "Mal per me", which sums him up and shows he was not just a bloodthirsty killer but an ambitious man who lived according to the mores of the eleventh and twelfth centuries; because, historically, in those days might made right and twenty of Duncan's predecessors were killed by their successors. So murder was not such an off-beat thing. Ambition and power were an integral part of the historical context. For all those reasons, provided one retains this aria, Macbeth is a wearing but immensely satisfying role.'

Milnes is also fascinated by another great Shakespearian hero, albeit this time by a French composer: Hamlet by Ambroise Thomas, a role which he *thinks* that Thomas Allen and himself are the only two living baritones to know and to have sung, and 'a wonderful role to play because you are the blond hero for a change, and usually baritones are never blond or heroes! It's a Shakespearian *Lohengrin* and this is wonderful because you don't have beards and heavy costumes and all the sort of thing we baritones usually have to contend with. Vocally the range is similar to a Verdi baritone's, although the *tessitura* is not as high as often, despite a G sharp and several Gs. It is written along flowing, long lines which are always a joy to sing.'

Milnes has sung the role both in English and in French, which, he says, is easier in terms of pure vocalism because the lines flow well. Yet in dramatic terms it feels like a French grand opera somewhat related to Shakespeare, whereas in English it feels quite different, more like the Shakespeare play. On the whole he prefers singing it in English, especially for English-speaking audiences, because 'there's that rub and so many things that *are* Shakespearian. From the dramatic point of view the opera has a better setting for Ophelia's mad scene, because in the opera the love between her and Hamlet is very clear, upfront, overt and fully expressed whereas in the play it is taken for granted but never spoken about. There is a ten-to-twelve-minute love duet between the two in the second scene – "I love you, I love you, too", all that sort of thing set to really gorgeous music – which ends in a big, prolonged kiss. Then Hamlet confronts his father's ghost and his whole psyche closes up and he pushes her out of it because his inner self is taken up with the matter of murder and with the whole Christian ethic versus his father's exhortations to avenge him. And, since in the opera their love and total dedication to one another is so overt, it makes sense that his withdrawal would cause her to feel so lost and slowly to close up within herself, too, and this is what makes me feel that the setting for the mad scene is better in the opera than in the play.' 'The brooding hero must be the challenge of a lifetime for any baritone, and Sherrill Milnes rose to it magnificently. He sang with breadth and splendour and fervour beyond even the highest expectations occasioned by his best work in the past. The tone is massive, the top wide-open, the dynamic scale enormous, the dramatic conviction disarming', wrote *Opera* after the San Diego premiere.

Milnes went on to explain that *Hamlet* is a problematic opera in the same sense that Verdi's *Macbeth* is problematic because the composer returned to his score and made some, in this case inadequate, changes. As Shakespeare was not as deified in France in the 1860s as he was later to become, Thomas and his librettists felt it was all right to fool around with the play and change the plot. 'Believe it or not, in the original edition, Hamlet lives!' It was only years after the premiere that Thomas was told by an English opera house that he had to be joking, that it was a sacrosanct Shakespeare play and Hamlet therefore *had* to die. So he rewrote the ending. But the problem is that, in order to insert a death scene, he only rewrote the last four pages and didn't change the lead-up to the death-ending; so the preceding twenty pages were written towards an ending that left Hamlet alive, and, in order to make the death-ending logical and meaningful, one has to make some cuts and revisions to those preceding twenty pages. 'This is what we did in the recording of this fascinating opera, which I would love a chance to perform in Europe, and preferably in England.'

Unfortunately, Milnes has not been singing as much in Europe during the past five or six years as before, when he used to maintain a ratio of five months in Europe to seven in the United States. In the 1980s he reduced the number of months spent in Europe to three and now does most of his work – which he limits to sixty-five performances a year – at the Metropolitan Opera and the Chicago Lyric and the San Francisco opera houses, plus recital tours, mostly in order to spend more time at home – a spacious, fourteen-room apartment on New York's Riverside Drive, equipped with a gym and all the accoutrements that bespeak a hi-fi freak – with his wife and teenage son.

A few years ago Milnes experienced some physical problems and had to cancel many months of engagements. Since then, he has looked after his voice even more diligently than before and is 'even tighter and more disciplined about my life-style than before. On the day before a performance I refrain even from a social drink.' (A view diametrically opposite to that of Piero Cappuccilli, who maintains singers should live completely normal lives. But as the voice is a totally individual instrument its needs vary from singer to singer, and ultimately there can be no hard and fast guidelines.) 'When you are in the world market of singers you are so fêted that if you are not careful you could go to a party every night and have glasses put into your hand every two minutes. So it's a discipline you've got to learn if you're to sing the kind of roles I do, for I don't sing Marcellos or Sharplesses etc., I sing all the heavy roles that push the body right to its limits. I know this sounds like an exaggeration, but it's nevertheless true that each of them amounts to an Olympic event.'

His future plans depend on how much darker and deeper his voice will get, because as singers grow older their voices tend to get lower, and Milnes's is darker now than it was ten years ago. When asked if his plans might include some Wagnerian baritone roles he replied that the Heldenbaritone parts demand much more than that. 'The *tessitura* is a major second, maybe even a minor third, lower than that of Verdi baritone roles, because despite the odd E and F their basic range is the C to C octave, and you have to sing all those notes with full, fat, resonant tone. Dramatically, those roles, those Wotans and Flying Dutchmen, are very different from Verdi roles, very "innisch", very introspective.' Although Milnes sang an unforgettable Donner in *Das Rheingold* in 1968 at the Metropolitan Opera under Karajan ('He sang his "Heda, Hedo" in a voice of such opulent beauty that one was galvanized', wrote *Opera*), he says that the only Wagnerian role he might be interested in, provided his voice darkens enough, is Wolfram von Eschenbach in *Tannhäuser*, 'an Italianate baritone role that happens to be in German', with which most baritones prefer to start exploring the Wagnerian *Fach*. The reason he has not attempted it so far is that it would take an enormous amount of time for him to 'make it my own', and he is not sure whether, in the end, it would prove a worthwhile exercise when there are so many other 'off-beat things, like Hamlet' that he would rather do.

Like Placido Domingo, a colleague whom he much admires and by whom he is also held in high esteem, Milnes's exceptional musicianship has led him to study conducting. He has already conducted many oratorios and symphonic pieces, as well as making a record on which he and Domingo conduct each other. He stresses that, to conduct opera in particular, 'every conductor should, at some point early on in their career, have sung – at whatever register and however awful their best sound might be – an entire opera, from memory. Then they would understand some things all singers know but which most conductors don't: that, for example, when a singer is singing *mezzoforte* or louder, by and large they cannot hear the orchestra because the very act of phonating makes a resonance which, above a certain volume, blocks the ears as a receiver of sound. Very, very few conductors know that – and anyway the pit is the worst spot from which to judge balance between orchestral versus vocal volume – and often come up with suggestions like "listen to the bassoon line!". But I could only do this if I were to stop singing because, although normally one hears everything from the outside, we singers hear as much from the inside out, with the resonance going through the bones. This is why we never sound the same to ourselves as we do to everybody else and why, when we sing, when we take those ink blobs in the score called music and put them into vibrations that assault the ears of the audience, we are, we become, someone else.'

HERMANN PREY

The main characteristic of Hermann Prey's long and distinguished career is versatility. He is one of the greatest *Lieder* singers of the century, a tireless champion, and almost peerless interpreter, of Schubert (with whose genius he feels a near-mystical identification), as well as an accomplished operatic singing-actor, a gifted comedian and a popular television personality in his native Germany. Prey views his profession as a *Gesamtkunstwerk*. And although he feels justifiably proud of achievements as important as the foundation of the Schubertiade at Hohenems and Vienna and the recording of an entire anthology of German *Lied*, the thing of which he feels proudest of all is his versatility! A prime example of this was the time in summer 1984, when he excelled in a Schumann *Lieder* recital in Munich on the evening after he sang Beckmesser in *Die Meistersinger von Nürnberg* at Bayreuth. He feels this was a vindication both of his yearning for a many-sided career and of the diligence with which he has preserved the expressive and dynamic subtlety of his highly individual lyric-baritone voice.

Prey's restless, mercurial, many-sided temperament (he is keenly interested in subjects as diverse as cosmology, metaphysics, jazz, architecture – to a degree that makes it possible for him to design his own houses – and everything to do with nature, including a precise, minutely detailed knowledge of every type of berry and mushroom growing in Germany) is quintessentially German and proud of being so, yet possesses a lightness of touch, gaiety and ebullience not usually associated with Germans, and needs this versatility in order to fulfil itself. So, when Prey gets tired of opera, he devotes several months to *Lied*; when he feels he has thought too much about *Lied* he will yearn for a change of mood and go off and sing operetta; after that he might, perhaps, make a film or television special; then he'll change gear again and plunge into a deadly serious course of masterclasses. It was therefore not surprising to hear that the pursuit of a many-sided career was a conscious goal of his right from the beginning.

'There was a time when the artist who sang Schubert, Schumann,

Brahms and Wolf was an entirely different animal from the one who sang *Il trovatore*,' he explains. 'Even the great Caruso's repertoire consisted of only one style: the Italian.* My aim, on the other hand, was to sing everything. I avoided narrow specializations like being a famous Bach or a famous Verdi baritone. The proof is that my repertoire stretches from Monteverdi, Telemann, Bach, Mozart and Rossini to Wagner, the lesser German romantics (Lortzing, Nessler, Marschner), to Alban Berg and contemporary works and from *Schlager* and operettas to virtually every known composer of *Lied*. I feel that, if possible, singers should strive to master all the various styles, but with one important proviso: never singing beyond one's *Fach*, i.e. one's natural vocal possibilities.'

Prey stresses that a repertoire as varied as his demands great stylistic sensitivity in the approach to phrasing, projection, colouring and shading and all such matters to do with expression, but not a different vocal technique, which is one and the same for all composers, styles and periods. 'Once a singer is properly vocally equipped and prepared they can sing anything, because *all* composers demand total *vocal* competence: in Brahms, for instance, one has to sing long lines but the same is true of Schubert, Schumann, Bach and Verdi.' He also points out that while dynamics stay the same regardless of the size of the concert halls he sings in, timings can vary according to the size of each hall: in London's intimate Wigmore Hall, for instance, he usually takes seventy-five minutes for Schubert's song cycle *Die Winterreise*, while in New York's much larger Carnegie Hall, where he has to reach more people sitting further away, he might stretch the time to eighty minutes. 'Naturally, such liberties are impossible in the opera house, where the tempi are set by the conductor. But they are a vital element in *Lieder* recitals and something about which I make up my mind on the spot, on the spur of the moment.'

Spontaneity and immediacy are as characteristic of Hermann Prey's artistry as is versatility. There is a freshness and unpredictability about his response, both to operatic roles and *Lieder*, which can vary noticeably from evening to evening and prevents his interpretations from ever lapsing into routine. Viennese-born Lies Askonas, a connoisseur and lover of music who has been Prey's British manager for many years, sums it up as follows: 'If one were to hear Schubert's *Die schöne Müllerin* sung by Dietrich Fischer-Dieskau, also a very great artist, several times, it would practically always be the same: at least, the *structure* would be the same, although he has modernized his interpretation, which has become more

* In fact Caruso also excelled in the French repertoire, which he sang with an impeccable accent, unlike Beniamino Gigli, whose French was strongly Italian-sounding.

and more interesting over the years. But Hermann's response to the songs depends very much on his own mood: sometimes they come out joyful and sometimes full of sorrow. He is impetuous, spontaneous and individualistic and this element of surprise is one of the most essential and, to me, most delightful aspects of his artistry.'

Prey explains that his spontaneous response – which has nothing to do with improvisation, which he detests, and is only made possible by years and years of immersion into the works and preparation at the deepest level – is conditioned not only by his own mood but also by the mood, quality and responsiveness of the audience, whose role is decisive in determining the quality of a *Lieder* recital. 'As long as I am in good shape and not suffering from any vocal or other health complaint, then I find that, arrogant though this may sound, my rapport with the pianist and, to a far greater extent, with the audience is what will determine whether this will be an ordinary or an extra-ordinary recital, where something special might happen. Needless to say, warm, responsive audiences ignite and inspire me to give performances that are a bit above the ordinary whereas an indifferent public acts like a wet blanket and pulls me down. I try to reach them, but they always manage to cramp me.'

In opera, of course, the capacity for spontaneity is conditioned by multiple factors like the mood of the orchestra, the conductor and his tempi, the state of health of his colleagues, the lighting, the sets – whether they help voice projection or not – and the quality of the orchestral sound which can, in some cases, be an inspiration in itself, 'like the wonderful Mozart sound of the Vienna Philharmonic', and a myriad imponderables. 'I cannot do it alone. Which is why *Lieder* recitals are more satisfying in many ways.'

Yet Prey enjoys his operatic work enormously and his performances exude high spirits, boisterous energy and the same gift for instant communication that is so typical of his recitals. His repertoire includes all the major Mozart baritone roles – Papageno in *Die Zauberflöte*, Guglielmo in *Così fan tutte*, both Figaro and Count Almaviva in *Le nozze di Figaro* and the title role in *Don Giovanni* – two Wagnerian roles – Wolfram von Eschenbach in *Tannhäuser* and Beckmesser in *Die Meistersinger von Nürnberg* – and five roles in operas by Richard Strauss: Harlequin and the Musikmeister in *Ariadne auf Naxos*, Storch in *Intermezzo* and both Olivier and the Count in *Capriccio*. His most famous role in operetta is Eisenstein in Johann Strauss's *Die Fledermaus* and, in Italian opera, Figaro in Rossini's *Il barbiere di Siviglia*. He sings a great many roles in German romantic operas, like Peter the Great in Lortzing's *Zar und Zimmermann;* and has also sung roles in contemporary works like, for example, the title role in Henze's *Der Prinz von Homburg*, which was written for him. As a young man he also sang, in German, some of the more difficult Verdi roles such as the Conte di Luna in *Il trovatore*, Don Carlos in *La forza del destino* and Posa in *Don Carlos*. But despite constant requests from management his only Italian role in the past fifteen years has been the Rossini Figaro, which he has performed all over the world, including the Salzburg Festival, Covent Garden, La Scala and the Metropolitan Opera.

Naturally, it would have been wonderful to sing Posa at La Scala, he admits; but he resisted doing so, just as he resisted singing Falstaff and all the big roles in operas with heavy orchestrations, 'because to do those justice you have to be a dramatic baritone like Gobbi or Taddei who can cut through the orchestra but who, on the other hand, don't sing *Lieder*. And, while I wanted my career to be as versatile as possible, I also wanted to conduct it along lines that would not make it impossible for me – a lyric baritone – to sing *Die Winterreise* the way I did last night. This could not happen if I had continued with the heavy dramatic roles because right from the beginning I noticed that they exacted a heavy toll from my voice. I had to push it and actually felt physically uncomfortable while singing them. So, with the exception of the odd 'peripheral' role like Germont in *La traviata* and the title role in *Eugene Onegin*, I dropped them. I also refused invitations to sing Jokanaan in *Salome*, a wonderful role, as well as Mandryka in *Arabella*, because think what they would have cost! By allowing myself to sing this loud – and I would have to, in order to ride over the Strauss orchestra – I would have lost all dynamic subtlety and would therefore no longer be capable of singing *Lieder*. But as it is I've retained my *mezzoforte*, *piano*, *pianissimo* and even *pianississimo*, plus every other imaginable half-tone with which I can reach the last row of halls as large as Carnegie Hall!'

Yet Prey admits that singers should occasionally stretch themselves a little in order to grow, provided they don't endanger their voices in doing so, and would himself one day like to 'crown' his career by singing the title role in Verdi's *Falstaff* and Hans Sachs in *Die Meistersinger von Nürnberg*. However, he has promised himself this wouldn't happen before his sixtieth birthday, still two years away at the time of printing. Then, he thinks he might be ready to try out Hans Sachs in a small theatre like Bayreuth where the acoustic is 'unique' and where he already sang Wolfram in 1965 and Beckmesser in 1981. Wolfram, which he originally sang at the Hamburg State Opera and with which he made a triumphant Metropolitan Opera debut in 1960, is the role closest to his heart because 'it is the incarnation of a *Lieder*-singer and the only Wagnerian role one hundred per cent suited to my voice.★ It is wonderfully lyrical and dramatically rewarding as well – in fact, a singing-actor's dream.'

After taking Wolfram into his repertoire, Prey felt sure that Beckmesser would also be a suitable role for him: essentially lyrical and with a high *tessitura* which lies very well for his voice. Yet he kept refusing invitations to sing it – from Karajan at the Salzburg Easter Festival and Everding at the Bavarian State Opera – first because he had never sung a 'character baritone' role before, second because the character is 'a loser', and third because he is usually portrayed, both vocally and dramatically, in an exceedingly cheap and vulgar fashion.

What changed his mind was a discussion he had with Wolfgang Wagner, who responded to these complaints by showing him a letter of his grandfather's in which Wagner expressed his profound dissatisfaction with the way Beckmesser had been portrayed at the premiere, and stressed that he should be played neither as a loser from the beginning nor as a clown. 'Wagner wrote to the conductor in charge of the second performance that Beckmesser should be as serious as the other masters and that he becomes ridiculous, or rather tragi-comic, only because of his unhappy, unrequited love for Eva. And although the audience knows he will be beaten by Walther von Stolzing, Beckmesser should begin his song at the contest, as though there were still hope of his winning. Instead, it turns out to be total disaster, and only then does he become tragi-comic.'

Prey also stressed that Beckmesser's music is extremely difficult to sing and requires technical perfection. Because the character himself is supposed to be extremely musically knowledgeable, know the *Tabulatur* better than all the other masters and be a fantastic singer, Wagner wrote some extremely difficult *coloraturas* for him, like the embellishments of his serenade to Eva, which require great skill and meticulous preparation. 'But unfortunately this role is often abused, both vocally and dramatically, by singers who try to cheat their way around its vocal difficulties by ignoring Wagner's score and reducing Beckmesser's music to a sort of *Sprechgesang* punctuated by half-cries, exclamations and clownish gestures that turn him into a character straight out of a Broadway musical!

'Needless to say, this is not what Wagner intended. If it were, he would have written the role for a straight actor who, of course, couldn't begin to sing those high notes! So I based my interpretation solely on Wagner's score, followed his instructions minutely and portrayed Beckmesser as a

★ Wagner based his character on the real Wolfram von Eschenbach (1170–1220), who was a Minnesinger at the Thuringian court of Landgrave Hermann.

gentleman, an intellectual, a respectable town clerk who ranked second only to the Mayor. This way, the tragedy of his obsession with Eva was brought out even more sharply.' Prey's interpretation, poles apart from the usual caricature, was also supremely musical. As Harold Rosenthal wrote in his review in *Opera*, 'this Beckmesser should have won the competition as the most accomplished vocalist around', so lyrical and mindful of the composer's dynamic marks was his rendition, which drew other rave reviews both in Germany and abroad. *Die Süddeutsche Zeitung* wrote that 'Prey sang Act I like an English gentleman, Act II like a German romantic – crystal clear, to boot – and Act III like an Italian Orpheus; i.e. he sang Beckmesser as a *bel canto* star, with no trace of the usual cries, shrieks and exclamations. The fact that Eva didn't choose him is proof of the eternal fickleness of women's hearts!' *Opernwelt* praised Prey's 'highly intelligent character study and the impressive vocal/musical refinement he brought to the role ... which he sang, as one would expect, with a *Lieder*-singer's crystal-clear enunciation, great style – beautiful, flowing, richly yet subtly coloured *bel canto* sound – but without this clarity ever interfering with the line. On the contrary, it enhanced it and the result was an intensely vivid characterization.' Indeed, Prey's interpretation came to be considered a milestone in the history of the role and he himself looks upon it as 'one of the two peak achievements of my career: the other is my portrayal of Papageno in *Die Zauberflöte*'.

His affection for Papageno is so strong that if he were told he could sing only one role for the rest of his life it would have to be Papageno, 'for I don't have to play Papageno. I *am* Papageno, or rather he is the man I, and everybody else, would like to be: simple, with an earthy, peasant philosophy, fond of food, drink and a girl from time to time. He suits the German mentality better than any of the roles I sing. The Rossini Figaro, for instance, I had to work extremely long and hard at, not just at the language because I already sang Mozart's Da Ponte roles in Italian, but at the whole atmosphere we call *Italianità*. But Papageno comes to me naturally, as do the roles in German romantic operas like Lortzing's *Zar und Zimmermann*, *Der Wildschutz*, *Der Waffenschmied*, Nessler's *Der Trompeter von Säckingen* or Marschner's *Hans Heiling*, which suit me in the same way that Wolfram does. The rest I do because it's my profession and I sing them well.'

Prey first sang Papageno at the Bavarian State Opera in 1964, and eventually at every major opera house in the world. He rightly considers it as greatly and as often abused a role as Beckmesser; but in this case, he points out that the man responsible for this 'tradition of abuse' was the creator of Papageno himself, the actor/manager Emmanuel Schikaneder, who wrote the libretto for *Die Zauberflöte*. 'Although he wrote in his text that Papageno is a being halfway between man and animal, like those Egyptian frescoes with animal heads, when he came to portray him on stage he bowed to prevalent Viennese fashion and played him as a Commedia dell' Arte figure, a harlequin or clown. Yet in Schikaneder's original text there are long passages subsequently deleted from the libretto in which he describes Papageno as a being from the realm of the Queen of the Night. There are, for example, long gaps in the dialogue that immediately follows Tamino's first meeting with Papageno and the deleted passages contain important clues to Papageno's background. When Tamino asks how come he doesn't know who his mother is, Papageno points in the direction of the fortress in which Sarastro and the Queen of the Night lived together before their separation and adds that he doesn't know whether she is still alive or what happened to her and that he was raised by a funny old man.

'So, Schikaneder didn't portray Papageno as the character he had himself conceived. I do. I play him as a sort of Peter Pan, a genie, a being who could almost fly but doesn't. This was also the conception behind Günther Rennert's Metropolitan Opera production, with sets and costumes by Marc Chagall, that marked the inauguration of the Met's new house at Lincoln Center in 1967. I think we succeeded in presenting Papageno as a being who doesn't just crash on to the stage, bang, out of nowhere, but who has some kind of background. And I remember Chagall, who was particularly thrilled with this production and conception of Papageno, coming up to me after the premiere, shaking my hand and saying: "Monsieur Prey, you are Mozart!".' When Prey sang Papageno in August Everding's naturalistic rococo production at Covent Garden in 1983, the reviews were enthusiastic: 'Hermann Prey left no doubt as to why his Papageno is much loved abroad: he is a completely natural comedian, puppyish and thoroughly engaging, and he sings all his music with a mastery that shows itself as spontaneous loveliness', wrote John Higgins in *The Times*. Prey would one day like to direct a production of *Die Zauberflöte* himself, because he thinks he has found a marvellous idea both for the production and the stage design, which he is naturally reluctant to discuss. But as he is booked at least until 1990, this is unlikely to happen before then.

Having sung all the major Mozart baritone roles he considers the most vital thing about the interpretation of Mozart operas to be the crucial importance of the ensembles and recitatives. 'One should be able to sing a melody so well that people can immediately distinguish which voice is singing what in the ensembles. And the recitatives are vital in Mozart: they are what "makes" the operas what they are, what sets the colour and atmosphere for every scene and where the characters' innermost thoughts are voiced. They should therefore always sound natural and unaffected and never, *never* be "declaimed" in a self-conscious, contrived manner. In *Don Giovanni*, for instance, the protagonist's character is established entirely through the recitatives: otherwise, he has only two arias, the Champagne aria and the Serenade.'

At the time of our conversations Prey had not sung Don Giovanni for about fifteen years or so, but was about to do so in Cape Town in 1985, and will do so again in Vienna in 1986. The reason why he abandoned this role for so long is that, although he is convinced it should be sung by baritone voices like his, in recent years the trend has been for it to be sung mostly by basses or heavier baritone voices. 'If you read the La Scala posters of a hundred years ago, they state quite clearly that the roles in *Don Giovanni* are as follows: Don Ottavio, *tenore*; Don Giovanni, *baryton-martin*, i.e. a light baritone; Masetto, *baritone*; Leporello, *basso-comico*; the Commendatore, *basso profondo*. But nowadays one can seldom distinguish one voice from another, because all four tend to be basses or bass-baritones, and the interpretation of Don Giovanni – which I feel should be elegant, very light of touch and very arrogant – often descends into the realms of the morbid. It all began in 1936, when Bruno Walter first conducted this work with a bass, Ezio Pinza, in the title role. It was thought to be very sexy, and it therefore became fashionable to use heavier voices.'

Prey has sung both Count Almaviva and Figaro in *Le nozze di Figaro*, as well as Figaro in Rossini's *Il barbiere di Siviglia*. Indeed, he once sang two performances of Mozart's and two of Rossini's Figaro within a single week at the Vienna State Opera, which was 'very interesting and apparently without precedent!'. He is therefore in an ideal position to define the differences between the two roles: 'The German tradition has always been to treat the Rossini work as a light opera and the Mozart opera as serious and almost holy. But I was fortunate enough to sing the former under Claudio Abbado – at the Salzburg Festival and La Scala – and musically it seems to me every bit as serious as Mozart's, especially when conducted with such flair and attention to detail. Naturally, the two roles have to be sung differently, because Rossini's Figaro is a high baritone while Mozart's is a bass-baritone.'

At the beginning of his career Prey used to sing Count Almaviva rather than Figaro, which has tended to be one of the mainstays of his repertoire

in recent years. But although he feels that vocally he is a better Count –
whom he sees as a debonair figure of about twenty-eight, about two years
younger than Figaro – because the high *tessitura* of this role is better suited
to his voice, he has won greater acclaim as Figaro, 'possibly because he is
a more engaging character'. Yet Figaro's recitatives are a bit too low for
him and so are the ensembles, where Figaro has to sing even lower than
Bartolo, a bass.

Prey agrees with the general opinion that singers who can sing Mozart
can sing anything, because the clarity, precision and special approach to
phrasing and the articulation of notes that Mozart demands require special
training which is an excellent foundation for singing all kinds of music.
It is therefore better for singers to begin their careers with Mozart rather
than come to him later, after singing Verdi, Puccini, Wagner or Leoncavallo, 'and even better if they come to him through *Lieder*-singing,
through Bach, Beethoven and Schubert, as I did'.

A classical education is also the best possible training for operetta, which,
as Prey rightly points out, has to be done extremely well or miss the boat
completely. If artists can sing Bach, Mozart, Schubert, Rossini, Beethoven
and Brahms then they can safely make an excursion into lighter stuff and
put all the finesse they have learnt from the classics into operetta, which
demands impeccable taste and an exact knowledge of what's going on in
the music. 'I don't know where it comes from, but I have a feeling for
this sort of Viennese music, which cannot be sung in too square or too
straight a fashion but has to have charm, wit and lightness of touch. Like
popular music, it has to be sung off the beat. Good popular singers like
Sinatra, for instance, or some of today's best pop singers are not consistently
on the beat, and sometimes the same should apply to the operettas by
Johann Strauss.'

Prey, who is a superb interpreter of Eisenstein in *Die Fledermaus* – which
he sang, among other places, at Covent Garden in a sparkling new
production conducted by Zubin Mehta on New Year's Eve in 1977–8,
which was relayed live on television throughout Europe and the United
States – continued to explain that if, for instance, one sang Eisenstein's Act
II aria 'Dieser Anstand, so mannierlich' dead on the beat, 'it would sound
dead wrong! It has to have swing, to come and go, it's essential to the style
of the thing. But it's important not to go too far and over the top,
otherwise the whole thing becomes indigestible. Not easy. In fact, the
lighter the music, the more difficult it is to sing and to conduct. I know
what I'm talking about, because as well as singing operetta, four years ago
I made a recording of popular music and it was one of the most difficult

things I've ever done: it had to sound relaxed, it had to be off the beat and debonair, all of which is extemely hard.'

It is sad, in a way, that Prey's 'excursions' into operetta occupy only one per cent of his artistic time, because his portrayal of Eisenstein was a gem and a lesson in the style of this genre: not only did he sing all the notes – the part is written for a tenor – but his acting of the role bubbled with seemingly spontaneous energy and high spirits. It was prepared with meticulous precision, like all Prey's interpretations, for, as he has explained, he hates 'improvisation' and feels that only after a painstaking technical and musical preparation can an artist be free to be spontaneous. 'And none of this could happen at all without a sound classical training.'

Prey's basic musical training took place in his native Berlin, where he was born in 1929 into a simple family. His father was a butcher and his mother, who had a good singing voice, encouraged her son's musical leanings, which manifested themselves early, unaided and unexpected, as poetic souls often do. He joined the Berlin Mozart Choir at the age of ten, as a high soprano. His voice dropped almost overnight – at Christmas 1944 he was still a high soprano and by Easter 1945 he was already a baritone – at the time of the Russian advance, when Berlin was being laid waste by Allied bombs. His high school, which had a good choir, was destroyed and he had to go to a different one, with a tradition for singing in chapel. After he graduated from school in 1947, his mother encouraged and supported his wish to study singing at the Hochschule für Musik and, to prepare for the entrance exams, he began taking singing lessons with Harry Gottschalk, who has remained his mentor and the only singing teacher he has had throughout his long career. In fact he still visits him whenever he happens to be in Berlin.

He continued to study with Gottschalk throughout his three years (1948–51) at the Hochschule für Musik, where he joined the conservatoire's singing class. He had no money, so to pay for his lessons he formed a jazz group – bass, guitar and piano or accordion, playing the latter two instruments himself and also composing songs for the group, the foundation of his lasting love for jazz, of which he possesses a large collection of records. At the time neither he or Gottschalk were certain exactly how to classify his voice – as a tenor or a baritone – but Gottschalk decided to go for baritone. He then proceeded to teach his pupil the basics of singing, such as breathing and supporting the breath, thus laying the foundations for his future development. But Prey, who left Berlin at the end of 1951, soon became his own teacher because, as he was lucky enough to begin recording as early as 1954, he could listen to, criticize and correct himself through his recordings, and he attributes most of his future development to this process of constant self-examination and improvement.

In any case, most people overestimate the importance of singing teachers, whereas, according to him, their contribution amounts to no more than ten to fifteen per cent of a singer's potential achievement. 'This is what I keep telling my students. One can certainly teach some technical, external things like how to breathe and sustain the breath. But the most important things, like how to *feel* the breath and how to locate the best spots for resonance, one can only find out for oneself. No teacher in the world could teach them to a pupil who has no instinct and no feel for them.' As well as teaching his son, Prey also regularly gives masterclasses and courses on singing Schubert, Schumann or Brahms. In most cases he tries to ensure that at the end of the course the pupils have a chance to record and listen to themselves on video, and in this respect he considers today's singers luckier than those of his own generation. He feels that this opportunity of self-improvement should be used as much as possible and could, perhaps, compensate for the sad lack of guidance facing most young singers today. Apart from this, he is, as he has already stated, sceptical about the number of things that can be taught.

'What can one teach? It's hard for me to tell because so much of what I do is done instinctively. I suppose that, because of my stage experience, I can indicate some of the things that have to do with the art, as opposed to the technique, of singing, so that the end result sounds natural rather than contrived. I can teach them how to handle dialogue, for example – always with a natural speaking voice! – and where to breathe, how to darken or lighten the voice, how to enunciate clearly, how not to be rigid or muffle the sound, and how best to project it. The rest comes with stage experience and with repetition. The more one sings each role or each song, the more profoundly artistic the result. One has an overall view of the work and, instead of singing each phrase at its face value, one is aware of its place within the whole and of how it links with another phrase two bars or two seconds later. One also knows where to let go and where to hold back without losing intensity. All those things, as well as a feel for acting, can only be learnt from experience.'

Prey says that his own voice has mellowed and become deeper with the years and that experience makes it easier for him to sing high notes *piano* and that he has more feeling for rhythms now than he did at the beginning of his career. Yet his voice was essentially the same at twenty-five, when he made his first recording, which he finds 'astonishing because it reveals that a great deal of what later came to be considered as "typically

Prey" was already there'. In those days Prey, possibly because of his keen interest in poetry, wanted to be a *Lieder* and oratorio singer and gave his first *Lieder* recital in Berlin in 1951, while still at the conservatoire. But he realized that to be a successful *Lieder* singer one had first to become well known in opera, otherwise the public would not attend his recitals, especially in those days. (Even now, although he can fill Carnegie Hall, he says that the public for *Lieder* remains small and very special. In Germany, for instance, despite his huge popularity and television fame, he finds it is not all that easy to fill the concert hall for a *Lieder* recital.) So, on his graduation from the Hochschule für Musik, he accepted the offer to join the Wiesbaden State Theatre, where he stayed for a few months, which were interrupted by a jaw infection that put him out of action for a while. On his recovery he enrolled in an American youth singing competition run by the occupying forces and won first prize, among 3,000 participants. The prize included some concerts and recitals in the United States, including one with the Philadelphia Orchestra under Eugene Ormandy.

On his return to Germany in 1953 Prey joined the Hamburg State Opera at the invitation of the late Günther Rennert, one of the most inspired stage directors and operatic managers of the post-war era, and remained there, under Rennert's eye and guidance – 'I still eat out of that cake and savour all he taught me'. In 1960 he laid the foundation for his distinguished operatic career, sang most of his roles for the first time, and shaped himself as an artist. At the same time he made a string of important international debuts: at the Vienna State Opera (as the Rossini Figaro) in 1957, the Salzburg Festival in 1959 and the Metropolitan Opera, as Wolfram, in 1960. Five years later, after leaving Hamburg in order to pursue the many-sided career that had become his goal and devote long periods entirely to *Lieder*, he made his debut at the Bayreuth Festival in 1965 as Wolfram, La Scala in 1969, the Chicago Lyric Opera in 1971 and Covent Garden in 1973. He has also enjoyed an extremely busy career in the recording studio.

He publicly acknowledges that the two proudest achievements of his career, 'my two fondest dreams come true', are his recording of *The Lied Edition Prey* for Phonogram and his foundation of the Schubertiade, originally at Hohenems, and subsequently at Vienna. *The Lied Edition Prey*, a chronological anthology of the German *Lied*, consists of twenty-seven records of four hundred and fifty-three songs, divided into four albums: *From Minnesang to Beethoven and Loewe* (five records), *Franz Schubert* (eight records), *The Romanticists from Schumann to Wolf* (eight records) and

From the Turn of the Century to the Present Time (six records). This monumental achievement, unique in the history of recording and the result of years of research and in-depth study, took five years to complete and was released in 1976. The same year saw the foundation of the Schubertiade at Hohenems: a festival – conceived and master-minded entirely by Prey, who was its Artistic Director until 1981 – dedicated entirely to Schubert. The festival was an enormous success from the beginning. Yet when the management proved reluctant to stick to Prey's original aim of performing Schubert's works in chronological order, he severed his connection with Hohenems and founded a new Schubertiade at Vienna in 1983, and will do so again in New York City in 1988.

The first Vienna Schubertiade was dedicated to Schubert's output up to 1815, his eighteenth birthday. Prey sang thirty songs, twenty of which were new to him because hitherto he had been less involved with Schubert's early works than with his later masterpieces. 'It was riveting to trace and experience the development of the young Schubert through so many songs, piano pieces, trios, quartets, octets etc., and to see how great his creative genius was right from the beginning, how much he developed with each work he wrote and how inexhaustible was the inner spring that fed him. Even as a young teenager he wrote breathtaking songs to Schiller ("Die Leichenfantasie") and Goethe ("Rastlose Liebe", "Meeres Stille", "Das Sängersehnsucht" and "Heidenröslein") texts.' The second Schubertiade, of 1984, started with the year 1815. Prey, who has unearthed numerous hitherto unknown songs and has spent hundreds of hours immersed in Schubert and his world, has created something unique in this festival.

Although this book is strictly about the discussion of operatic roles, it seemed a pity to conclude a conversation with Prey without asking some questions about the interpretation of Schubert songs and about the reasons for his total spiritual identification with this composer. He replied that, as far as the technical aspects of the interpretation of Schubert songs are concerned, the most vital thing to bear in mind is the crucial importance of rhythm. 'Tempo, and the way the various tempi relate to one another, is so crucial to Schubert that I feel one could write an entire book not on "Schubert and Melody", which might seem like the obvious thing, but "Schubert and Rhythm". It takes time, years of familiarity and awareness of the relationship between all the songs in each cycle, in order to discover this: that "slower" or "faster", for instance, doesn't mean "slow" or "fast", but slower or faster than what has gone on before. There is a world of difference between the two.'

When it comes to his spiritual identification with Schubert, Prey is less articulate. 'I cannot put into words exactly what it is that binds me to him so strongly. I'm not even sure I know. . . . ' Perhaps it is the tenderness in his music, which the eminent conductor Carlo Maria Giulini, himself deeply drawn to Schubert, pinpoints as the centre of this composer's spiritual world. 'The music of all great composers contains the whole gamut of human emotions – love, hate, passion, despair, jealousy, tragedy, yearning for redemption, joy, laughter, etc. But in Schubert you also find tenderness, this very, very intimate and special sentiment which you also find in some of Bruckner's music and which, in turn, requires great tenderness on the part of the performer. In our times, especially, we need Schubert very much. Perhaps this is why his greatness is finally recognized in the way it deserves.'

Perhaps it is this element in Schubert's music that strikes a chord in Prey, who has done more than almost anyone to revive interest in Schubert and who as an adolescent witnessed the devastation and the razing virtually to the ground of his native city. Schubert certainly afforded consolation and hope of spiritual regeneration to Richard Strauss; a letter written during those terrible days and quoted in Peter Adam's fascinating and deeply moving television documentary about the great composer, screened by BBC 2 in January 1984, reads: 'Now, I sit as a sad invalid among the ruins of Berlin, Dresden, Munich, Vienna. It is terrible. . . . The Munich Theatre where my father played the first horn in *Siegfried* and where I conducted my first opera in 1886, totally destroyed! I listened last night to the Schubert Octet. What does one care about the destruction of the so-called world? The German spirit is not in the Prussian Emperor, but in such works. They will remain until the crust of the earth has turned to ice.'

Prey suggested it might be better to ask other people to describe what he feels, and what happens, when he sings Schubert. Geoffrey Parsons, who has accompanied him in numerous recitals over the years, speaks of 'total immersion in the works, which have become so ingrained as to carry total conviction'. Lies Askonas vividly remembers the first time she ever heard Prey singing Schubert at the Salzburg Festival, long before she became professionally involved with him: 'I cried so much that I practically needed a boat to tow me home. I am Viennese – you know what a special feeling we Viennese have about Schubert – and I had never heard anybody sing Schubert like that before. As an interpreter of Schubert, he has almost no one to contest with. And although some purists may claim that his interpretation of *Die Winterreise* is not as intellectually, consciously worked out as some other artists', for me it is the deepest. While other people give you their thoughts about the songs, this man is a poet, he carries you with him. And you never walk out in total despair. He always gives you hope.' Edward Greenfield made precisely this point in his review of Prey's 1984 Wigmore Hall recital in the *Guardian*: 'The contrasts of tone-colour, often extreme but always kept within bounds, never forced, made this not the dark experience it can often seem.'

Prey, although unable, or reluctant, to sum up his special relationship with Schubert, admits that it amounts to something almost mystical. As a young man, for example, he always used to make the same mistakes – to do with rhythm, a changed word or a phrase wrongly sung – in certain spots of *Die Winterreise* and his pianists never tired of pointing them out to him. Many years later, after a Schubert recital in New York, the Director of the Morgan Library invited him to peruse the original manuscript of this song-cycle, which forms part of the library's collection. 'So I spent some riveting hours, milling over the manuscript and discovered, to my intense astonishment, that Schubert had originally written those passages the way I'd been singing them as a young man and only later did he erase and correct them. So my erstwhile mistakes coincided with his original intentions – such is the bond between us!'

It is all the more surprising, therefore, to hear that as a student Prey did not count Schubert among his favourite composers, who at the time tended to be the romantics: Schumann, Brahms and especially Hugo Wolf, who was very much in fashion in the late forties and the fifties. 'Schubert came later. Obviously he needed time. When I first sang *Die Winterreise*, aged twenty-two, I didn't find those songs particularly special. I only began to understand and immerse myself in them at the age of twenty-five.'

He says that his interpretations never become routine because they are constantly renewed by the new insights that come from continuously refining, polishing and delving deeper into the works. 'For instance, last week I was rehearsing *Die Winterreise* with Geoffrey Parsons, who has a facsimile of Schubert's original score and pointed out that, in the song "Irrlicht", a certain passage in the second line of the last verse – the words are "Ich wind' mich ruhig hinab" – is marked "major" in the standard edition we all use, while in Schubert's original it is marked "minor", which is much more beautiful. And I only found this out after singing this song for thirty years!', he beamed, leafing through his own much-used score which, he says, feels like an old friend one knows intimately but who still retains a certain mystery.

Prey, a tireless workaholic forever seeking further insights into his art, is obsessed with his profession, which, in his words, demands such a degree of concentration, absorption, passion and constant hard work that everything else suffers in the long run. Personal attachments, family life, friendship, all are allotted second place, 'that is, if you are going to devote yourself one hundred per cent to the profession, and this profession can only be done this way, despite the fact that many seem to get by without even giving it half of themselves'. Prey is very fortunate in having a stable private life. He married very young – indeed, he attributes great importance to the fact that this stability has left him free to put all his energies into his art – and he and his wife Barbara (Berbl) have two grown-up daughters and a son, all of whom are musical; and the son is training to be a baritone.

As a man, despite his friendly, gregarious side, Prey is also a loner and difficult to get to know. He has homes in the Bavarian countryside and on a North Sea Island off the German coast and deeply treasures his times alone, walking in the woods or on the shore, the times when his real inner preparation and journey into the works he interprets takes shape. Like his beloved Schubert, he delights in every aspect of nature and is insatiably curious about anything that arouses his interest, displaying the same precision he applies to his work. He admires this kind of precise, meticulous knowledge wherever it's to be found: the only man he is known to refer to as 'my friend', for instance, is an old clock-maker and collector on his North Sea Island, whose minute knowledge of the mechanism of any known brand of clock escapements fascinates him.

Prey admits that this essential duality in his nature, at once gregarious and solitary, corresponds directly to the two sides of his profession: the excitement of the theatre and the inward-looking dimension of *Lieder*-singing. 'As a human being I need both those things: opera and *Lied*. But if you were to hold a gun to my head and say that, in the future, I should devote myself only to one of them, it would be *Lied*.'

BERND WEIKL

'Although few people realized this at the time, I first sang all my big roles at the top places: my first Wolfram, Amfortas and Hans Sachs at Bayreuth, my first Ford at La Scala and my first Mandryka at the Metropolitan Opera. I like that dangerous edge, the sensation of walking on a tightrope without an acrobat's net underneath', grinned Austrian-born Bernd Weikl on the day after the premiere of *Arabella* at the Metropolitan Opera, in February 1983. His booming, broad baritone voice and burly good looks make him a natural for Mandryka, Richard Strauss's rustic aristocrat hero, and his performance, vocally excellent, oozed just the right kind of bravura, gusto and a larger than life, 'outdoor' aura typical of a certain breed of provincial aristocracy.

Weikl admits that, in a repertoire ranging from Eisenstein in Johann Strauss's operetta *Die Fledermaus* to heavy Wagnerian roles like Hans Sachs in *Die Meistersinger von Nürnberg*, Mandryka is the character he identifies with most closely: 'he is almost like me: half-Hungarian, half-Slav, from the provinces that constituted the eastern half of the Austro-Hungarian Empire. Warm-hearted – like me! – contemptuous of Viennese decadence, in which he feels lost, and with good reason; intelligent but also a bit stubborn and not too quick-witted. If he's got the line, he can go through a wall, but it takes a bit of time. One can still come across people like him in northern Dalmatia and places like that, unspoilt by the industrial world, where one can live surrounded by woods and rolling hillsides.

'Vocally, the role is perfectly written for the voice, down to the minutest detail. One cannot change a thing, nor should one wish to. Like all Strauss baritone roles, it has a high *tessitura*. But this is no problem for me because I have an easy top. So, both vocally and dramatically, I feel very comfortable with this character, who, as I said, resembles me a great deal. The real me, in fact, is somewhere between Mandryka and Eugene Onegin, which I have sung over two hundred times all over the world, and recorded under Sir Georg Solti, and which is also beautifully written for the voice; it has a special kind of *Italianità* that Tchaikovsky invented for himself and it's a joy to sing his long, flowing, *legato* lines.' Weikl's close identification with these two roles seems paradoxical because Onegin is the polar opposite of Mandryka: ultra-sophisticated, blasé and disdainful of country gentry. When this was pointed out to him he replied that, like Onegin, he too is always too late at grasping opportunities. 'In Scenes 5 and 6 Onegin realizes he has missed a chance for happiness and realizes it was all his own fault. I, too, always understand too late.... I'm always dreaming and often blind to what is there, under my very eyes. Sad, but true.'

Weikl can afford to take a gamble on singing big roles like Mandryka and Sachs for the first time at the top festivals and opera houses because he is excellently trained and has, over the years, been very careful about the choice and timing of his repertoire. He was born in Vienna in 1942 but left the city with his parents as a baby, and grew up in a small town of 4,000 inhabitants near the German–Czech frontier. The community consisted mostly of farmers and miners who had never left the confines of their valley, spoke a strange dialect that is neither Czech nor German and always seemed to be singing something or other, usually from a vast variety of folk songs. Weikl thus grew up surrounded by the streams and mushroom-filled woods of this lovely part of the world, and says he spent most of his early childhood with a fishing rod in his hand. He didn't much care for this kind of life at the time, 'but I enjoy it now, in retrospect. I wish I could get away from the career for a while and withdraw into this kind of pastoral bliss and spend hour after hour lying in a fishing boat on a quiet lake, with lots of books, because reading is my passion – not fiction but mostly medicine, science and psychology – and meditating. I have now trained myself to concentrate hard enough to control the blood flow to any part of my body. This kind of body-awareness is very important and also helps control nerves, stage fright and so on.'

Apart from reading, other hobbies include painting and cooking, 'especially spicy foods, strange, exotic recipes like sausages made out of crabmeat, or duck stuffed with chestnuts. I have loved cooking ever since my student days, and find that preparing an interesting dish has a lot in common with preparing an operatic role! My wife greatly enjoys the meals I prepare.' They have no children, because the pressures of operatic life would mean that either the child would have to be alone for long stretches of time, or the two of them would have to spend a long time apart – a sure recipe for marital disaster. They did foster a child once but were heartbroken when it was eventually taken away and have never tried it since. His wife is from Hanover, with a Polish gypsy great-grandmother, and worked as a secretary in the Hanover Conservatoire where Weikl spent five years as a student.

As a child he had always enjoyed singing and, after the family left the little country town when he was ten years old to settle in Mainz, he went to school there and made a habit of singing at all the school fêtes and special events. He also learnt how to play the guitar, the violin and jazz piano and, as he got near to matriculation, everyone urged him to have his voice professionally assessed. But his intention was to study economics at Mainz University, and he thought there was little point in the exercise. Finally, after singing at the school ceremony that followed the final *Abitur* examination, someone insisted on taking him to a local singing teacher who immediately offered to take him on as a pupil. For the fun of it he agreed, but still without any intention of pursuing a professional career in music. 'But after a while I discovered I had no real love for economics, which is truly the most boring subject imaginable, especially for a musically inclined person. However, I forced myself to complete my course. At the same time I also did two semesters each of Italian, criminology and Chinese culture and history, while continuing my singing lessons.'

His love of music grew in inverse proportion to his declining enthusiasm for economics, and soon after completing his studies at Mainz University in 1965, he enrolled as a full-time music student at the Hochschule für Theater und Musik in Hanover, where the director was a family acquaintance, and where he remained for the next five years. He enjoyed the course, which offered ample scope to develop both his musical and his dramatic skills: during his first year, for instance, he appeared as an actor in several straight plays – including one by Tennessee Williams, and Peter Weiss's *The Assassination of Marat*, in which he played the title role – and in his third year, 1967, he took part in the film *The Life of Anna Magdalena Bach* (recently screened on Britain's Channel 4). The following year he was engaged by the local opera house after its Intendant heard a cassette of him singing Valentin's aria from Gounod's *Faust* and one of Renato's arias from Verdi's *Un ballo in maschera*. He continued making regular appearances there during the remaining two years of his course at the Hochschule für Musik.

Upon graduation in 1970 he was engaged by the Deutsche Oper am Rhein in Düsseldorf, where he sang Figaro in Rossini's *Il barbiere di Siviglia* and the title role in Tchaikovsky's *Eugene Onegin*. The milestone year of his career was 1972 when, at the age of thirty, he made four successive international debuts: Melot in von Karajan's production of *Tristan und Isolde* at the Salzburg Easter Festival, Don Giovanni at the Hamburg State Opera, the Rossini Figaro at the Vienna State Opera and Wolfram von Eschenbach at the Bayreuth Festival. In 1973 he also sang Figaro for his Covent Garden debut and in 1977 he made his Metropolitan Opera debut, as Wolfram.

Wolfram was his first big Wagnerian role and he immediately felt comfortable with it both vocally and dramatically. 'It's tailor-made for a baritone with an easy top because the *tessitura* in Act III is very high and rather dramatic – in fact more suited to a Heldentenor than a baritone. Therefore, as in *Eugene Onegin*, one should guard against pushing the voice in Act I, where the *tessitura* is lower. If one starts pushing right from the start, one will simply have no top left for Act III. Of course, this is something one learns from experience, which is why [as Thomas Allen, who excels in both these roles, also stresses in his chapter] these parts become easier every time one sings them.'

As far as the dramatic content of the role is concerned, although, as he explained, his portrayal tends to vary slightly not only from production to production, but also according to the taste and cultural receptivity of the audience in question, he is more inclined towards an introverted portrayal. 'I even sing Wolfram's big Act III aria, "O du mein holder Abendstern", softly and rather introspectively because, first, it isn't *really* an aria but virtually integrated into Elisabeth's Farewell, which it immediately follows. Second, because Wolfram knows she will soon die, as certainly as if he were already holding her body in his arms, therefore he could hardly be expected to sing this joyfully, could he?

'In any case, the most interesting things on stage are always sung *piano* or *pianissimo*. The "Schwerter" ensemble [the scene where the knights draw their swords to attack Tannhäuser in the Great Hall, in Act II] should sound like an angry whisper, like a pack of snakes hissing. Even declarations of love are made in a whisper, and all good composers understood this and marked some of the most important passages *piano* because these are the moments when people really concentrate and listen intently. [Like the *pianissimo* markings at the end of Don José's Flower Song in *Carmen*, as Carreras explains in his chapter.] Otherwise, there can be no real climaxes, because there is no build-up of tension that can culminate in a resounding crescendo.' Herbert von Karajan heartily agrees and is one of the very few conductors who insists on his singers observing all *piano* and *pianissimo* markings religiously. 'If people start to shout when they should be singing *piano*, or speaking *piano* because, in Wagner, so many things are spoken on the notes, they lose their reserves of dynamic scale. And it's odd, but if you start with almost nothing, with minimal volume, people concentrate much more on hearing what you have to say. Then, when the outbreak comes, it makes far greater impact', he told me when I spoke to him for my previous book, *Maestro*.

The production of *Tannhäuser* that Weikl most enjoyed working in was Götz Friedrich's at the Bayreuth Festival. 'It was a very profound, psychological production that paved the way for Patrice Chéreau's controversial Bayreuth centenary production of *Der Ring des Nibelungen*. Like all historic productions, it was ahead of its time and, true to pattern, it was first derided and later hailed as a masterpiece. I was passionate about it and fought tooth and nail for it, because I feel that being ahead of time is particularly crucial in Wagner, who was himself light years ahead of his day and never afraid of revolutionary innovations like covering the orchestral pit and even building a new type of theatre for his works. I'm sure that if he were alive today he would want to experiment with laser beams, which, so far, nobody – apart from Günther Schneider-Siemssen, I think – seems to have tried to use in an operatic production. Imagine how effective lasers would be in, say, *Der fliegende Holländer*, where images of the Dutchman could be flashed to Senta alone, thus making it immediately obvious that nobody else understands or knows what's going on, and that only she lives with this obsession'. *Opera* magazine hailed Friedrich's production as 'the most vivid and stimulating since Wieland Wagner's death . . . it made it clear from the start that the Venusberg, a respite from the pallid, authoritarian court of the Landgrave, exists only in Tannhäuser's mind and that Venus is merely Elisabeth in a more erotic form. Yet the sado-masochistic dances of the Venusberg are in themselves a degrading form of sexuality and Tannhäuser is unable to achieve the synthesis of both these lurid imaginings and the harsh reality of courtly life where he is required to sing appropriately chaste songs. . . . ' The review went on to add that 'Bernd Weikl as Wolfram produced some of the best singing of the evening'.

Weikl's other favourite role is Hans Sachs, which he first sang at the 1981 Bayreuth Festival, and which is the longest role in his repertoire. Memorizing the text alone is a mammoth task, in which Weikl says he was greatly helped by the fact that he had spent a long time working on German *parlando* in his student days. Again, it was Wolfgang Wagner, whom he says he adores and who was instrumental in launching and establishing him as a Wagnerian singer, who persuaded him he was ready for this monumental role and 'who gave me the benefit of his tremendous knowledge of this work, explaining the role minutely, step by step with the help of his grandfather's letters'.

Weikl has great affection for the role, which he hopes to go on singing and perfecting throughout his career. 'I love Sachs and play him as a mixture of sensitive poet and earthy, village philosopher. Even though he is well-educated enough to speak Latin and be so knowledgeable about music, he is not a savant or some kind of "professorial" character but a man of the people, a cobbler rooted in popular tradition. Without this earthy side his popularity among the townsfolk would be hard to explain (because they don't generally warm to those who don't speak their language); and so would his instinctive antipathy for Beckmesser, a genuine, "dry" intellectual. This instinctive antipathy is crucial and reveals several important facets of Sachs's character, which is far from being as saintly or goody-goody as it's often portrayed.

'To be sure, he is a good and warm-hearted man, but he is also tricky and cunning enough to indulge in intrigue after intrigue on stage, and egocentric enough to crave and enjoy authority and power *per se*. When Beckmesser, alone among the masters, who accept his authority unques-tioningly, dares to challenge him, Sachs becomes quite nasty and sarcastic – not just out of a poet's genuine, wholehearted response and admiration for Stolzing's fresh, novel approach to composition, but also out of pique, I think. Together with the strong pragmatism evident in Sachs's realistic acceptance of the fact that he is too old for Eva, I think that this egotism is a significant characteristic. Like Wagner himself, Sachs was deeply conscious of what he saw as his mission in life.'

Weikl's interpretation, which perfectly demonstrated the dramatic points he has just made, drew high critical praise at the time. The influential German monthly magazine *Opernwelt* wrote that 'Bernd Weikl rose to the highest Bayreuth standards. His was a temperamental, direct, popular Sachs, oozing vitality and with a touch of irony and enigmatic humour. He proved very impressive in his first contact with this complex role, with his excellent vocal qualities, musical and dramatic intelligence and the subtle expressive nuances he brought to Sachs's two monologues.'

Since then Weikl has sung Sachs in several places, including the Bavarian State Opera, the Metropolitan Opera, the Hamburg and Vienna State Operas, and in Florence. Yet, vocally speaking, nowhere did he find singing the role as easy as in Bayreuth, where the acoustic is unique and where 'an orchestral *piano* is a *real piano* – not a soupy *mezzoforte*! Mind you, singing Sachs in Munich under Sawallisch was also a great joy because he was incredibly supportive and, in a role like Sachs, this is crucial! A conductor who can't, or who won't, follow you can be sure to dry you out, for it goes without saying that you can't follow *him* for five hours or so. If you did and if, because you need an extra second or two for a certain phrase, you had to look down at his baton and think technically instead of concentrating on the drama, the power of your interpretation would vanish and be instantly ruined.'

As well as being the longest role in Weikl's repertoire, Sachs also has the lowest *tessitura* he has ever had to cope with, which is why it can be sung both by baritones and basses. As in Wolfram, the crucial point to bear in mind is not to start pushing and giving out too much vocal power in the first two acts, because that would mean that by the time Act III, with its very high *tessitura*, is reached the singer would have no top left. 'This spot, with its high, baritonal *tessitura* is where basses usually come unstuck. In order to be able to sing the finale with full power one must remember to keep the voice very light, and very baritonal in Acts I and II. This becomes easier with experience, which is why Sachs demands great vocal and artistic maturity.'

Weikl rightly feels that the reasons why there is such a tragic shortage of singers capable of tackling big roles like Sachs with distinction nowadays are, first, because nobody takes the trouble to build them up, and secondly, because singers themselves are too impatient and greedy, sing too much and embark on big roles long before they are ready for them. 'Today, everybody does too much. In the old days singers were given a fixed salary and were expected to spend years in an ensemble theatre where they sang three or four times a week. Now, if they are to enjoy the kind of income that I, for one, have become accustomed to, they have to work very hard indeed. I suppose they also feel that if they are to put up with this extraordinarily demanding life – no smoking, very little drinking, taking constant care of one's voice and body in general – they might, at least, enjoy all the rewards they can get. So, they don't say "no" as often as they should.

'This is why, although fabulous voices do still emerge regularly, they tend to get prematurely ruined and we have no Verdi mezzos, no Heldentenors and no Heldenbaritones capable of singing Wotan, either. I know what I'm talking about, because people have been practically trying to *force* me to take on this damned role for years! But I cannot and will not do it, not now, anyway. I have promised to look at it, with a view to doing it in 1988. Of course this means having to decide, by instinct, which way the voice is likely to go during the next few years. Usually I've been lucky with hunches, but one cannot be absolutely sure. What I know for certain is that it will become darker and deeper — voices always do with age — but in no way would I wish to force it, because that would mean losing my top. For, while I have now shed the Rossini Figaro because I felt the voice is too heavy for it, I still have an excellent top range and can sing Eisenstein's high C in *Die Fledermaus* with ease!

'At the moment, the voice is perfect for the Italian *Fach*, the Wagnerian roles I already mentioned, and Richard Strauss, who wrote in the highest *tessitura* in the baritone range. I can take on dramatic roles, but only if they have a high *tessitura*. When it goes down by a quarter or a third of a semitone, while I can still sing the notes, the voice loses its brilliance. When I sang the title role in *Don Giovanni*, for instance, it was impossible for me to make the Champagne aria sound brilliant in the same way that I can make Figaro's *cavatina* in *Il barbiere di Siviglia* sound brilliant. It was just that bit too low, and, had the conductor allowed me to, I would have transposed it up!

'Wotan would pose the same problem at present, because it is a dramatic role with a low *tessitura*. I have his range, but it's lyric, not dramatic. Even when the voice is ready for it I would always want to sing certain passages lyrically, though, to make him human and draw out the public's sympathy and compassion for this defeated figure, no longer a god. At the moment, I'm just curious to see exactly which way the voice will go. The late Beniamino Gigli and Hans Beirer, who is still alive and living in Vienna, both retained their top notes to the end, while the rest of their voice got lower and deeper and more and more baritonal.

'Of course, this kind of baritonal sound but with resounding top notes was the real "Heldentenor sound" that Melchior and all great Heldentenors of the past used to have [as Sir Reginald Goodall defines the term in René Kollo's chapter]. Nowadays tenors with voices just about suited for Tamino embark on Heldentenor roles and are then aghast when their voices collapse. "But what went wrong? I *could* sing it!" Well, I could probably sing it, too, but the question is, should I? And the answer to that is a firm "no" because in so doing I would be endangering my future career by forcing the voice to do something for which it is not yet physically, biologically, ready. There *is* no such thing as a twenty-five-year-old Tristan. There cannot be. You have to be at least forty for Tristan and for Tannhäuser, which is even more demanding because of its even higher *tessitura*, but especially for Siegmund which, as all singers realize only after they have sung it, is *the* hardest of all Heldentenor roles. A tenor who sings Siegmund too early is sure to forfeit his chances of ever singing Siegfried because Siegmund is very baritonal, with a low *tessitura* which tenors find very hard to grapple with. (I or any other Wagner baritone could sing the role.) In the process, they start pushing their voice, thereby instantly damaging their top range.'

When asked to explain why forcing the voice damages the higher range, Weikl replied that this was a physical thing, like an elastic band snapping. 'When you force the middle range up you lose the top, which should sound smooth and light; because at a certain age the physical possibilities for the voice to stretch naturally don't exist, so the voice simply snaps. When the middle range becomes *naturally* more solid and massive with age, like Gigli's and Beirer's did, then one can produce those big sounds fearlessly, without danger of the voice snapping. It's a question of patience and natural, gradual vocal maturity. There is no substitute for time and no way one could speed this process up and jump from light-lyric to heavy Wagnerian parts, just as there is no way a young pianist could embark on the Tchaikovsky Piano Concerto without first spending several years on Czerny's *études*, and no way a painter could paint great abstract pictures without first being a good draughtsman and naturalistic painter.'

Like most singers in this book, Weikl thinks that the ideal way for tenors to begin is with Mozart and light-lyric Italian roles, and then gradually progress to some of the heavier Italian lyric, *lirico-spinto* and dramatic roles. This kind of background forms a solid foundation from which they could then progress to the Wagnerian repertoire 'like Domingo who, after years of singing both the lighter and the heavier Italian roles, has now sung an exemplary Lohengrin, vocally impeccable! His only problem is with the language, not the notes, and I understand he is working on that, too, with great success.

'The same is true for baritones. They should begin, as I did, with the Mozart roles like Papageno and Guglielmo plus some of the Italian *bel canto* parts like the Rossini Figaro or Belcore in Donizetti's *L'elisir d'amore*. They will find, again as I did, that this kind of solid foundation is a tremendous help in tackling Strauss roles like Mandryka or Wagner roles like Sachs. Still, like a sportsman who waits and judges the moment for beating his own record at 200 or 500 metres, I reserve my answer as to if, and when, I'll take on Wotan, or indeed Telramund in *Lohengrin*, which at present also lies beyond my vocal capabilities, unless, of course, I were to sing it under a conductor like Herbert von Karajan or Carlos Kleiber, capable of producing genuinely transparent orchestral sound which in turn allows us singers to paint with a very subtle palette of vocal colours. For I would like my portrayal of Telramund to be different from the usual, crude characterizations which make him out to be rather stupid, constantly ranting at the top of his voice and being so obvious that his devious schemes wouldn't fool anyone. I would like to interpret him in a more introverted, intelligent and vocally more lyrical way.'

Weikl, whose Italian repertoire includes Gérard in *Andrea Chénier*, Tonio in *I pagliacci*, the Conte di Luna in *Il trovatore*, Germont in *La traviata*, Ford in *Falstaff* and Iago in *Otello*, says he wouldn't attempt Scarpia in Puccini's *Tosca* yet. 'In the future, maybe. Scarpia is certainly an interesting role but a bit heavy for me. It has to sound nasty, and it has to sound ironic, arrogant and sadistic, all of which, vocally, I cannot do. I'm not born for it. And one good thing I have discovered is that, having already done quite a bit in my career, I am now in a position to pick and choose. This is a great help because it gives me the freedom to refuse roles I don't wish to do and to embark on important new ones in my own good time.'

After his successful portrayal of Ford in Giorgio Strehler's La Scala production in 1980, conducted by Lorin Maazel, Weikl was asked to sing Falstaff; but he refused, because he felt he needed a lot of time to think about and work out this role in his mind, and to prepare for it, musically and stylistically. He started off by listening to Toscanini's recording before taking it to his voice teacher and a special Italian voice coach, Ubaldo Gardini (who has worked in the greatest opera houses, like the Metropolitan Opera and Covent Garden and coached the most distinguished artists of our day), to work on vowels. 'Because in Falstaff you really have to sound Italian. You cannot make do with an approximation, which you could get away with, just, in *Un ballo in maschera* or *L'elisir d'amore*. You really have to steep yourself in the Italian mentality, what is called *Italianità*, otherwise it wouldn't work. So this is what I'm trying to do.'

Weikl draws a parallel between Falstaff and Hans Sachs – 'both larger-than-life personalities who dominate and arrange the lives of those around them, both winners and both easy to identify with' – and is struck by the fact that at the end of their lives, both Verdi and Wagner should have composed the most lighthearted works in their long careers. 'Both *Falstaff* and *Die Meistersinger von Nürnberg* are mature works of very great composers and I always see each as a kind of counterpart for the other. There must be something about their way of looking at life in advanced years: with a smile, with humour, and the realization that, after all, the world is not to be taken seriously!'

THE BASS-BARITONE

A male singing voice with a range slightly lower than the baritone's but not as low as the bass's, stretching from G below the stave to F or F sharp above.

SIMON ESTES

'With a voice as beautiful as yours, why do you want to sing Wagner?' asked an eminent conductor, well known for his Wagnerian affiliations and recordings, when Simon Estes went to audition for him in Bayreuth. 'Can you imagine anything so absurd?' added the six-foot-one black American bass-baritone, whose repertoire includes all the major Heldenbaritone roles, roaring with laughter. 'This man's remark explains everything that's wrong about Wagnerian singing as we have come to know it. Unfortunately, we have got used to those huge, Scandinavian voices that have the volume but not the warmth and people have got so mixed up they have come to think that "biggest is best". I don't think that's correct. I'm sure Wagner wanted his music sung by singers who sang *bel canto* and knew how to spin long, subtly shaded lines. Yet when one attempts to sing Wagner with the same beauty of tone that one would apply to Verdi, even those who should know better seem genuinely surprised. A young conductor in Bayreuth once stopped the orchestra at rehearsal and exclaimed: "But Simon, you sing so *musically!*".'

Singing musically has always been one of Estes's top priorities, and he attributes his musicality to the fact that at the beginning of his career he sang a lot of *Lieder*. 'Singing too much opera is dangerous. I'm always telling my students at the Juilliard, where I am now a full member of the faculty, that singers who start with *Lieder* have longer operatic careers, because *Lieder* are much more exposed: there's just you, the piano and the audience so you learn a great deal about vocal discipline, concentration, depth of interpretation, singing with subtly graded dynamics and colouring the voice. And once you have learnt all of this, you will make a much more interesting opera singer because your singing will be more musical instead of being just loud.'

Estes possesses a powerful, resonant, darkly coloured voice that, in a less sensitive singer, could have become just loud and monotonous. The fact that it hasn't and that his Wagnerian singing is known for its subtlety is also due to the fact that he first sang Wagner in theatres where acoustic conditions were perfect and allowed him to paint with a very fine brush. He performed his first Wagnerian role – the title role in *Der fliegende Holländer* – in 1977 at the Zurich Opera, a small theatre posing no acoustic problems, and the following year at Bayreuth, where the acoustic is ideal. (Estes was the first male black singer to appear there. He longs for the day when his colour will be irrelevant and when he will be referred to simply as a bass-baritone, for he rightly feels that in music the only colour should be in the voice – 'look at a score! The composer has written "soprano", "tenor", "bass"; there is no mention of colour or nationality, he has written for a voice' – but is resigned to the fact that this day has not yet come.)

His appearance was a sensation and his was hailed 'as the finest Heldenbaritone singing heard at Bayreuth since Hotter' (*Opera*), while *Opernwelt* called him 'the ideal interpreter of this role', which he has since sung at most major opera houses, including the San Francisco and the Hamburg State Opera, Covent Garden and the Paris Opéra. He is deeply attached to this work, which proved so significant for his career, but finds the Dutchman the most taxing of all his Wagnerian roles, including Amfortas and Wotan, 'because of the way it's written. Wagner was still young and inexperienced and the orchestra is terribly loud, especially in the first aria, "Die Frist ist um", which the Dutchman has to sing "cold" the moment he first walks on stage. Although the part contains a strong *bel canto* element, which is always a pleasurable thing to sing, Wagner didn't "have it all together" yet. By the time he came to write the *Ring*, *Tristan und Isolde* and *Parsifal* he did, and while the roles of Wotan, King Marke and Amfortas demand a great deal of you, the way they are written makes them easier to sing.'

From the dramatic point of view, he finds the Dutchman a very complex figure. 'On the one hand he wants salvation, and on the other hand he doesn't. He wants to find a woman who'll be true to him, and then he doesn't. He's probably very masochistic with a tendency to feel rather sorry for himself. He keeps going out to sea and one wonders whether he is subconsciously looking for an excuse to leave each of the women he gets involved with. At one point he really hopes Senta will be the right one. But the mere fact of seeing her *talking* to a man, Erik, is excuse enough for him to flee. It's almost as if he half expects to be betrayed. He's probably so insanely jealous that no woman could live with him. Who knows, maybe he, himself, has been doing a lot of sleeping around during those boat trips around the world and judges the world accordingly. . . .

'The interesting thing about both the Dutchman and Amfortas is that they're both looking for salvation, but the Dutchman doesn't want it as much as Amfortas does. There is something very tender, too, about the Dutchman. I think at one point, where he sings "du bist ein Engel, eines Engels Liebe Verworf'ne selbst zu trösten weiss", he has almost fallen in love with Senta. The excitement in the music seems to say he's quite sold on her. If he hadn't found her talking to Erik he would have had to marry her. So maybe this is why he was so ready to believe the worst of her: because it's a way out. But – like Wotan in his Farewell to Brünnhilde – he shows some tenderness because he says he'll let her live, that she's the only one he'll allow to stay alive.'

Wotan in *Die Walküre*, which Estes first sang at the Deutsche Oper in Berlin in 1985, is perhaps the most 'total' operatic character in the repertoire. 'He's a mythical being: he's God, and he's human, too: a married man, obviously unfaithful and, to put it mildly, rather promiscuous; tremendously proud, very chauvinistic but on the other hand also very tender: chauvinistic with his wife and tender with his daughter, Brünnhilde, whom he really, really loves. With his wife he's a typical husband who doesn't want to be bothered with what he considers to be trivial problems like Siegmund and Sieglinde's incest and her adultery, because so what, it's spring, let them enjoy themselves. He wants to dominate Fricka and thinks he's going to be able to do it. But in the end, she wins. There were certain vows to which all the gods adhered and she was the one to look after the marriage contract. Wotan knows this. And he tries everything in the world to get around her, but in the end she says: "You *have* to fulfil your responsibilities, otherwise you'd no longer be God. You have no choice." So he breaks down to his wife.

'Then Brünnhilde, his favourite daughter, comes along. I don't think at this point Wotan wants to reveal to anyone that he's been weak and given in to his wife. But she says, "tell me, that's what I'm here for". He's still reluctant but finally says, "all right, but I'll really be talking to myself, thinking aloud". So he starts to tell her. She knows he doesn't want to have to kill Siegmund so she says she'll take care of the problem. But he says, "you can't, don't you see, you *can't*". That's what's so frustrating: that he wants her to but knows he can't possibly let her help Siegmund and Sieglinde. His frustration then turns to anger and he gets really mad at her and says, "if you interfere, you're *really* going to get the wrath of God on you the way nobody has before".

'And, of course, she disobeys him, returns and has to face the consequences. The only moment in the whole of *Die Walküre* where Wotan shows any tenderness is just before his Farewell to her, where he softens and becomes really human. He loves his daughter *so* much that he wants the best for her and says: "I have to punish you, but at least I'll make it so that whoever rescues you – and I hope somebody does – will be a great hero, a great man, because anybody who isn't would be frightened away by the fire with which I'll encircle you." This is his act of great love, great tenderness, for his daughter.

'Vocally, Wotan is a tremendously demanding role, ranging from F below up to G above. There are spots – like the end of his narration in Act II, and the scene in Act III when he is angry with his daughters, the Valkyries, for sheltering Brünnhilde – where the orchestra is very loud. The *tessitura*, on the other hand, is comfortable. It's a real bass–baritone role. Neither baritones nor basses can sing it.' Bernd Weikl, a baritone, and Kurt Moll, a bass, both agree and have so far solidly refused to sing Wotan, which happens to be one of Estes's three favourite Wagnerian roles, along with King Marke and Amfortas.

He considers that *Parsifal* contains the most beautiful music ever written. 'Although *Tristan und Isolde* is magical too, with passages of incredible beauty, *Parsifal* is the ultimate. The whole theme of the Grail is a religious experience and, being a religious person, this opera is very special to me; something very personal and special happens every time I sing Amfortas. My only regret is that I have never sung it with Herbert von Karajan, whose recording is unsurpassable and whose recordings of all Wagner operas are the only ones I want to listen to.'

From the vocal point of view, the most difficult part is Amfortas's Act I aria 'Wehvolles Erben', which is very dramatic and has a high *tessitura* stretching up to G above the stave, i.e. into the domain of the baritone. Indeed, Amfortas is basically a baritone role and this makes this aria in particular hard for a voice like Estes's, especially towards the end. 'But there is also a nice, tender part, where he sings "Nach ihm, nach seine Weihegrüsse muss sehnlich mich verlangen", which should be sung very tenderly, and if you have a conductor who lets you sing it that way the whole aria becomes much easier.'

Amfortas's Act III aria, 'Ja Wehe! Wehe', Weh' über mich', is the one Estes most enjoys singing, 'because it's almost as beautiful as the one in the first Act. At this point life is very, very painful for him and he wants to die, but doesn't want to kill himself. So he grabs a sword and wants the others to do it. Of course, his wound is more of a psychological guilt torment than a real, physical pain. He feels, desperately, mortally guilty because he sinned, betrayed the Grail and the brotherhood and caused his father's death. The music is very funereal at this point and reminds me a bit of Siegfried's funeral music. Amfortas feels *he* should have been the one to die. It's terrible to live with this guilt, this knowledge that one is weak. Wagner himself was very weak, of course, perhaps the weakest of all composers. Verdi wasn't, and it shows in his music. There's a vigour, a virility, a pulse beating through his music, even at the most tragic moments, that one doesn't find in any other composer.'

Estes explains that, despite the difficulty of his first aria, Amfortas is one of the easiest Wagnerian roles to sing because Wagner's writing was so accomplished by this stage that he made even the approaches to the high notes smooth and easy. 'The same is true of the vocal writing in Verdi's *Don Carlos*, also a very mature work. Philip II is much easier to sing than early Verdi roles like Zaccaria in *Nabucco* or the title role in *Attila*, both of which are as difficult as the Flying Dutchman and for the same reasons.' He finds Amfortas also a fascinating role to portray. So is Jokanaan in Strauss's *Salome*, which he first sang at the Zurich Opera in January 1986. 'I absolutely *adore* singing it. I love the story and I love the character. He's strong, he's possibly the strongest operatic character in the repertoire. He never falters for a moment, not for a second! Vocally it's a real baritone role, but I found it very easy to sing. If a role doesn't seem easy, i.e. doesn't come naturally, I flatly refuse to sing it.' (*Opera* wrote that, vocally speaking, Estes's 'was a Jokanaan of honey and sulphur'.)

Estes also sang the title role in Verdi's *Macbeth* recently – again at the Zurich Opera – and considers his performance to have been one of the greatest successes of his career: despite the fact that it is one of the most dramatic of all Verdi baritone roles, it posed no vocal problems and seemed easier to sing than either Wotan or the Flying Dutchman. One of the pluses of having sung so much Wagner is that every other composer now seems easy in comparison, because his exposure to Wagnerian roles has given him a tremendous reservoir of strength and stamina. His future plans include a systematic expansion into the Verdi baritone repertoire: he will sing Macbeth again at the Bavarian State Opera and Iago at the Hamburg State Opera, as well as continuing to sing his principal Verdi bass roles like Attila (at the Vienna State Opera in 1987), Zaccaria and Philip II.

The reason he found Macbeth easy to cope with is that his voice is now mature enough to sustain the *tessitura* of a higher repertoire. He says he always had the high notes because his voice is unusually wide-ranging, but when he was younger he couldn't *sustain* the higher notes. 'Now I'm going to sing more and more Verdi baritone roles, along with my Wagnerian roles of course. I will sing Wotan again in a new production of *Die Walküre* conducted by James Levine, produced by Otto Schenk, with Hildegard Behrens as Brünnhilde, and the Wanderer in *Siegfried* for the first time, both at the Metropolitan Opera.'

Estes has already sung Amonasro in *Aida* (at Leontyne Price's farewell performances at the Met and at the San Francisco Opera), one of the heavier Verdi baritone roles, with great success. 'It's not difficult because it isn't long. But you need a very strong, a very "present" and substantial voice for it. He is a king, so he requires an important-sounding voice. The *tessitura* is no problem, and although the role is short it is one of the most rewarding and beautiful short roles Verdi ever wrote: the pleasure of singing phrases like "rivedrai le foreste imbalsamate" and so on, is indescribable.'

The title role in *Attila*, on the other hand, is in Estes's words 'an ungrateful role to sing', and most of the basses in this book seem to agree with him. It is a bass role and harder to sing than any of the Verdi baritone roles because the *tessitura* is uneven. 'It's almost baritonal, but not quite. It contains no real low notes to speak of – the range is from C below to F sharp above the stave – but baritones obviously couldn't sing the notes at the bottom end. Verdi had some trouble in those early years in sorting out who was a bass and who was a baritone, and most of his early bass roles, like Zaccaria in *Nabucco*, contain some very high notes like F sharps – which is why I agree with the European way of classifying certain voices as "bass-baritones". Ezio Pinza, Cesare Siepi, Giorgio Tozzi and, from the current generation, Ruggero Raimondi, José Van Dam and myself all fall into this category. We all have different timbres, of course, and darker or lighter shades of colour. Timbre and colour are crucial factors in choosing repertoire. But some voices also have a long range that allows them to "fish" in a greater variety of waters.' (Estes, for instance, has sung the bass part in Mahler's Symphony no. 8, which goes from C below the stave to F sharp above.)

He cannot explain why black voices, which are usually rounder, warmer and more sensual than most white voices, should also often be more wide-ranging. 'I really cannot explain it. It must have something to do with biological factors, because the voice is a physical, anatomical thing. This is why I always urge singers to take plenty of physical exercise to build up their muscles and diaphragm. I myself learnt all I know about breath control from my passion for sports, especially high-jumping [at school he

used to high-jump six feet two inches, an inch higher than his own height]
and basketball. It has stood me in very good stead.'

Estes was one of the best basketball players in his home town, Center-
ville, Iowa. He was born in 1938, the son of a coal-miner and the grandson
of a slave who had been sold in the South for five hundred dollars. He
was one of five children – two boys and three girls – in a very close-knit
and extremely religious family. From the age of eight he sang solos in the
town's Second Baptist Church and as a chorister in the school choir. At
the time, he says, he had a high C 'that just wouldn't stop!'. There was
tremendous racial discrimination in the area he grew up in: 'We weren't
murdered physically, but we were murdered in every other way. What
helped me learn to live and cope with this was my parents' deep religious
faith. They taught me that if a white person called me a dirty nigger or
insulted me in any other way, I was to feel sorry for them, love them and
pray for them. Being a member of a minority group can make a child
either very strong or very bitter, and I'm not bitter. I've learnt to be
tactful and diplomatic, but strong.' His mother, brother and sisters went
to church every Sunday and once read through the whole Bible – three
chapters a day and five on Sundays. It took a whole year to read through
both the Old and the New Testaments.

Estes's voice broke late. Suddenly, during his senior year in high school,
he noticed he couldn't sing his high notes any more, and his voice was
gone virtually overnight. He thought there was something wrong with
his throat and went to a doctor, who told him his voice was changing.
For two or three years he couldn't sustain anything, but gradually the
voice came back. At the time, 1963, Estes, who was studying psychology,
theology and pre-med at Iowa University with the intention of pursuing
'some sort of career in the behavioural sciences', thought he was a tenor
and joined the University's Old Gold Singers. There he met the man who
was to discover him and set him on the road to becoming an opera singer:
a naturalized Greek-American called Charles Kellis, who classified him as
a bass-baritone and has remained the only teacher Estes has had in his life.
'I'm sure this man was sent from God. He is entirely responsible for
discovering my voice and teaching me the basics of vocal technique,
pronunciation of vowels and interpretation. I was naive enough to think
I was a tenor, but he knew better. This is why having a good teacher is
crucial for young singers.'

As soon as Kellis discovered this promising voice he played Estes some
operatic records – for prior to that day Estes had never heard of opera –
of Leontyne Price and some of the other great voices of the day. The bait

worked. Estes got hooked and, with Kellis's encouragement, applied and was accepted by the Juilliard School of Music. Two years later, with the help of a grant from the Martha Baird Rockefeller Foundation and funds from the New York Community Trust Fund, Estes travelled to Europe where, with very little notice, he was asked to sing Ramfis in *Aida* at the Deutsche Oper in Berlin. This was his stage debut, in 1965. The following year he won the bronze medal at the Tchaikovsky Competition in Moscow.

His career started slowly, and for some time he did a great many of those *Lieder* recitals he mentioned earlier. After he returned from Moscow he made his San Francisco Opera debut singing the four villains in Offenbach's *Les Contes d'Hoffmann*, which he has continued singing throughout his career. He finds this work interesting 'because you have four characters in one opera, all musically very different, to sing and to play. The easiest of all is Lindorf, in the Prologue and Epilogue, a clever businessman, very cold, who makes but a brief appearance. Coppelius, in the Olympia Act, is the lightest, a bit of a show-off who has only one aria to sing. Dappertutto, in the Giulietta Act, is more difficult: he is a shrewd, cynical Don Giovanni type and has a very famous aria, the Diamond aria, which is very difficult, especially if you sing it in the original key of A flat, which I don't. I transpose it down to F sharp. But the hardest of all four is Dr Miracle in the Antonia Act, because he has a lot of very dramatic, very loud, hard singing, against a loud orchestration and at a high *tessitura*, because a lot of the time he is singing alongside the tenor and the soprano. And he needs "clout" because he is a kind of devil, a Mephistopheles, and that at the end of the opera, when you are quite tired.' (Estes agrees with director John Schlesinger and disagrees with Domingo about the sequence of the acts in this opera. Domingo favours the Olympia-Antonia-Giulietta sequence, for reasons he explains in his chapter, while Schlesinger prefers the Olympia-Giulietta-Antonia sequence favoured by Estes.) Estes agrees with Hermann Prey and Kurt Moll that vocal technique remains the same regardless of the style of the composition one is singing, whether this be by Wagner, Verdi, Berlioz, Schubert, Brahms or Mozart. What changes is the singer's expressive approach, which is determined by his own musicality, sensitivity and familiarity with certain idioms and musical epochs.

After his San Francisco debut Estes headed for Europe. The way was not yet altogether smooth for male black singers in America – to this day, he points out, there are four male, as against sixteen female, black singers on the staff of the Metropolitan Opera – but things were more encouraging in Europe. He made his Hamburg State Opera debut in 1967, in Günther Schuller's *The Visitation*, but his big break came ten years later when he sang the Flying Dutchman in Zurich and in the historic Bayreuth production by Harry Kupfer in 1978. In 1980 came his debut at the Bavarian State Opera as Philip II, closely followed by his debut at the Vienna State Opera. His Metropolitan Opera debut was in 1982, as the Landgrave in *Tannhäuser*, and since then he is a regular annual visitor. In 1983-4 he sang the Flying Dutchman at the Paris Opéra and, in March 1986, at Covent Garden. His career has not been altogether free of setbacks and disappointments, one of the biggest of which was not singing Wotan in the Solti/Peter Hall 1983 Wagner centenary production of *Der Ring des Nibelungen* at Bayreuth. He feels this was because he is black, and he has voiced his disappointment in the press and elsewhere.

'My teacher Charles Kellis, who knows that in some instances it took me longer to get the best parts because of my colour, always says to me "Simon, if I were you, I'd be angry, I'd be militant". I'm not and I'm not bitter, either. I feel sorry for the people concerned. Obviously I'm hurt, but I don't want sympathy because sympathy is for the weak and I like to think I'm a strong person. All I want is for people to be aware and to understand. As I said, I get my strength from my religion and my upbringing [also from his own family, his Swiss wife and two infant daughters]. I'm very grateful to God for giving me this great gift of singing and for making it possible for me to share it with people.'

Estes says that his quiet strength, which is part of a wider philosophical outlook, also prevents him from being nervous before performances or important debuts. On the contrary: 'On a performance day I'm like a horse that *has* to race. I'm excited, I'm full of energy, I can't *wait* to go out there and sing! If my health is good, if I'm well-prepared, which I usually am, then any mistake can be attributed only to the fact that I'm human and not a computer. Like secretaries who might make typing errors or doctors who also make mistakes, I, too, must be allowed, and forgiven, an accidental slip. So why waste energy being nervous? I want to save all my energy for my performance! I also don't believe in wasting energy in having arguments with conductors, managements or colleagues. If there is any problem it should be discussed and solved quietly, in private. In fact, some of my colleagues are always telling me: "Simon, you don't belong to the operatic world, you're too *normal*!" '

RUGGERO RAIMONDI

'Ruggero Raimondi is "the Italian Chaliapin": the most sensitive singing-actor in the profession, along with Placido Domingo, and the only male Italian singer with a truly outstanding dramatic gift. He also possesses a great voice and cuts a fascinating figure on stage with his splendid physique,' declares director Piero Faggioni, who has staged some of the most imaginative productions featuring Raimondi over the years: *Faust*, *Boris Godunov* and *Don Quichotte* at the Teatro La Fenice in Venice and *Carmen* at the Edinburgh Festival, the Paris Opéra and La Scala. 'But perhaps most important, he is an exceptional, profound soul and if, as a director, one succeeds in plumbing those depths and drawing out all the emotion he's capable of, the results can be incredible.'

Not every singing, or indeed straight, actor possesses the wherewithal for being remarkable on film as well. Raimondi does and has won high acclaim with his haunting, white-faced portrayal of the title role in the late Joseph Losey's film of *Don Giovanni* and for the manly, swashbuckling bravura with which he invested the usually cardboard character of the toreador Escamillo in Francesco Rosi's *Carmen*. His photogenic features and ability to adapt to the cinematic medium and the economy of film technique so impressed the distinguished French film director Alain Resnais that he offered Raimondi a role in a straight film, *La Vie est un roman*.

Both on stage and screen, Raimondi's performances exude strong visceral power and a degree of identification with the role at hand that sometimes amounts to total surrender. Combined with his big, sonorous yet subtly coloured voice and imposing, six-foot-six good looks, these qualities help explain the impact of his performances and the almost hypnotic power they exert over large sections of the female members of the audience. In Germany and France especially, Raimondi's appearances are often followed by backstage scenes of the kind of hysterical adulation usually reserved for pop stars. Yet according to the coach and accompanist

Janine Reiss, who taught him most of his French roles and regularly accompanies his solo recitals, Raimondi himself is blithely unaware of possessing such strong magnetic power or of the effect this can have on his female admirers. 'After some of Ruggero's recitals I have seen women behaving almost like animals or Bacchantes or something, the way women can when they are no longer able, or willing, to control themselves. This kind of hysteria arouses incredulous stupefaction in him and both frightens and bores him to death.'

Yet the powerful, magnetic presence so characteristic of Raimondi today was apparently not innate. Both he himself and several colleagues and acquaintances testify that, in his youth, he was 'paralysed' by a crippling shyness that caused him to blush every time anyone addressed a word to him. Soprano Mirella Freni and her ex-husband, the coach Leone Magiera, remember standing on the same railway platform time after time and making bets as to whether the young Raimondi would muster up enough courage to say hello! Piero Faggioni, who first encountered the twenty-two-year-old Raimondi shortly after the latter was hired by the Teatro La Fenice in 1964, recalls that every time he stepped on stage he froze and stood around with his arms rigid, 'like a robot'. Gradually, largely thanks to Faggioni's influence, he began, as he explains later, 'to open up, find and liberate' himself through his roles.

Perhaps this is why he states that one of the most interesting projects he has ever been involved in was the television entertainment he made with choreographer Maurice Béjart titled *Six Arias in Search of a Singer*. The protagonist of this surrealist-ironic game was a singer who seeks and finds himself and the idealized love of an imaginary woman, who eventually brings him death, through each of the following arias: the death of Boris Godunov, Escamillo's Toreador Song from *Carmen*, the death of Don Quichotte, Mephistopheles's Serenade from *Faust*, Iago's 'Credo' from *Otello* and the Champagne aria and Cemetery scene from *Don Giovanni*.

After working on film Raimondi finds it takes him a few days to adapt back to the theatre, which requires larger, 'more amplified' gestures and movements. While he enjoys the concentration, discipline and extreme economy of gesture and expression demanded by the cinema, he dislikes the piecemeal fashion of shooting takes. 'You rehearse for hours and then shoot for maybe three seconds, during which you must transmit all the tension that on stage you can take three hours to establish and develop. The "takes" usually bear no relation to what you've shot before, so you get no sense of continuity or developing tension. And while, on the whole,

I can say that my experience of working in the cinema has been exalting, this side of it I found boring and traumatic.' He regrets that his encounter with Joseph Losey came so early in his film career, when he was totally inexperienced, and could not get 'the maximum' out of his collaboration with this 'extraordinary man'.

At the time of our last conversation, August 1985, Raimondi was recording the role of Count Almaviva in Mozart's *Le nozze di Figaro* for Phonogram. He had no film projects in view for the foreseeable future, but in the theatre one of his 'most cherished dreams' was to sing consecutive performances of Mozart's three Da Ponte operas, beginning with the title role in *Don Giovanni*, then Count Almaviva and finally Don Alfonso in *Così fan tutte*. 'This way one could highlight the common denominator in this trilogy: the destruction of love and triumph of social convention. For the real protagonist in these operas is social, moral convention which, despite the strongly ironic way it's treated by both Mozart and Da Ponte, always comes up trumps in the end.'

Raimondi would place *Don Giovanni* first, because the hero personifies the most idealized form of love to be found in this trilogy. As Giovanni explains in the exposition of his philosophy of love to Leporello in Act II, 'women never spurn my great nature's gift but only call it deception when I bestow it on others'. He would place Don Alfonso last, because he is 'the ultimate role of this parable: the man who, in *Così fan tutte*, brings home the fact that life is basically a question of accommodation and adaptation to the social conventions of the day. At the end of this opera, those four people – Guglielmo and Fiordiligi, Ferrando and Dorabella – who don't love each other and who have already abandoned and been unfaithful to one another, decide to bow to convention and come together again. Who knows what will happen in the long run? In any case, they are destroyed people. I always imagine them as youngsters who met and liked each other socially, casually, and got engaged without really knowing one another. And through their partial knowledge of each other, they discover the people who really suit them. Yet despite this, they feel honour-bound to return to social ties and obligations. But the huge question mark remains.'

Raimondi has not yet sung Don Alfonso on stage and is still in the process of thinking about this role. He views Alfonso as a 'demonic, almost Mephistophelean character, a puppeteer who, in his cynicism, really knows the foibles of human nature and takes pleasure in manipulating the lives of others, to the extent that, for the sake of a bet, he is prepared to play havoc with the lives of his friends. I always think that, bet apart,

Alfonso also *enjoys* disillusioning others, possibly because, like a latter-day Don Giovanni, he has returned from hell and no longer has any stake in life. His detached, realistic knowledge of human nature places him almost outside life. For him, everything is finished and all that remains is cynicism. And perhaps this is his hell: having to experience other people's hell.' From the vocal point of view, Don Alfonso's *tessitura* presents no problems for Raimondi, who is struck by its 'interesting, nervous dynamics': *piano* immediately followed by *forte* and then down to *piano* again, continuously up and down.

He would place *Le nozze di Figaro* – which he considers far from being the light opera it is often made out to be – in the middle of the trilogy. Like Richard Strauss's great librettist, the poet Hugo von Hofmannsthal, who wrote that 'in Figaro there is little to make one laugh and much to smile at', Raimondi stresses that the comedy and irony are in the situations rather than in the characters themselves. 'Because the main theme of this opera is the beginning of the end of a great love. Two people – the Count and Countess – who once shared a tremendous love story have now reached a point where they have nothing to say to each other. And both are beginning to look elsewhere for the love they've lost. The Count is trying to compensate by displaying an insatiable appetite towards the female form and chasing every woman in his household, while the Countess is more troubled by Cherubino than she cares to admit – look how she snaps at Susanna when the latter pays Cherubino too many compliments and fondles him too closely in Act II.

'Yet all these situations are far from clear. They are not happening on the surface, in the open, but underlie the plot in a sub-text sort of way and this ambiguity should be implied and suggested in the way the characters are portrayed. The only one outside this shadowy tangle of relationships is Figaro, who tries to get what he wants by his wits, his cunning and counter-intrigues. But at the end he is the principal loser in this game, even though *all* the characters lose out. The opera ends with "Contessa, perdono", but far from signifying its rehabilitation, this finale marks the end of love for both couples. Although outwardly, again for hypocritical reasons of social convention, everything returns to normal, the love between the Count and Countess is dead. They find themselves at the onset of a routine phase in a relationship that has lost all meaning and contains no seeds for growth into anything worthwhile. As far as the other two are concerned, one already senses a certain bareness in the character of Figaro as well as Susanna's subconscious attraction to the Count's sensuality. Of course, one knows Beaumarchais later carries the

Count-Susanna and Countess–Cherubino relationships to their logical conclusion in *Cherubin*. And the seed for the future is there, in the finale of *Le nozze di Figaro*.'

Raimondi sings Figaro as well as Count Almaviva – his portrayal of this role in Jean-Pierre Ponnelle's production at the Metropolitan Opera in autumn 1985 drew generally excellent reviews – but finds the Count infinitely more interesting, both vocally and dramatically. The Count's continuous search for love (which Raimondi sees also as an attempt to cling to his youth, challenged by the constant presence of Cherubino) and awareness of being inside the web of an enormous intrigue that somehow eludes him means that he is reacting to new situations all the time. 'This requires a great multitude and variety of vocal colours. In fact the secret of interpeting this role well lies in colours and in dynamics, which should vary, vary, vary constantly because every note expresses a different mood and state of mind. This is why this opera requires sensitive, enlightened directors and singers who understand Italian and can do justice to the complete cohesion between Mozart's music and Da Ponte's libretto. For Mozart, in his genius, understood there was an etymology to be exploited in Da Ponte's text, which contains a metaphor in every sentence, and wrote those wonderful recitatives in which the real drama and tension of the work take place. It is therefore absolutely crucial that the director and the singers understand every word they are singing.'

To those able to appreciate the subtlety of the text the Count emerges as a sad, rather than a comic, character who requires a thorough psychological preparation. 'For every time he comes close to unravelling the intrigue he senses around him, it eludes him even further. He has this horrible suspicion of wearing horns, not just as a husband but also as a representative of a certain class. Take Act II, when the Count is heard approaching the Countess's bedroom and Cherubino is quickly hidden in her closet. Far from being funny, it is a very dramatic moment, with the Countess, who is on the point of being repudiated, feeling extremely insecure. This should be reflected in all her movements, and more so as the Count proceeds to question her in a brusque, inquisitorial manner. When she admits Cherubino is hidden in her closet the Count explodes into a murderous rage, livid at the constant presence of this young page whom he keeps bumping into everywhere and who is chasing all the girls with the vigour of a young Almaviva, thus reminding the Count of the truth he would rather not face: that his own youth is beginning to fade away. His explosion of rage should therefore be doubly terrifying and certain to strike the fear of death in the Countess. At the climax of his wrath, after he has fetched a spare key, he unlocks the closet and out comes ... Susanna!

'This is where a note of comedy comes in. But it is the situation that's funny, not the Count, who is so surprised he feels his head spinning and doesn't know how to react: he looks at the Countess, who he knows will nag and roast him about this for at least a fortnight and who, although equally stupefied, feigns assurance and outrage. Then in bursts Figaro. The Count, sensing they are all in league, hopes he can now trap them into revealing their plot through the business of the foglio and the seal. But then the gardener walks in and announces someone has jumped off the balcony, and the Count realizes his suspicions about Cherubino were right in the first place. He knows it and, although he cannot prove it, the game has now become quite serious. So, far from being a buffoon, he is a character of great complexity and dramatic possibilities.'

This is why Raimondi takes such pleasure in singing this role, which is really a baritone's part, but with a *tessitura* that lies very comfortably for his voice. However, he points out that, after singing Almaviva, it would be impossible to sing any of his *basso-profondo* roles, like Boris Godunov, Mephistopheles or Philip II, right away. He therefore tries to schedule it next to roles with a similar, rather high, *tessitura* like Figaro, or Don Profondo in Rossini's *Il viaggio a Reims*, as he did in summer–autumn 1985.

Raimondi's favourite role in the Da Ponte trilogy is the title role in *Don Giovanni*. In fact he says that, along with the title roles in *Boris Godunov* and *Don Quichotte*, this is his favourite role in his entire repertoire, which includes (apart from those already mentioned or discussed) Verdi parts like Silva in *Ernani*, the title role in *Attila*, Fiesco in *Simon Boccanegra* and Procida in *I vespri siciliani*; the title role in Rossini's *Mosè in Egitto*; French roles which, apart from Don Quichotte and Escamillo, include Mephistopheles in both Gounod's *Faust* and Berlioz's *La Damnation de Faust*; and Russian parts like Boris, and Khovanshchy in Mussorgsky's *Khovanshchina*. (Only on record and the concert platform, sadly, Raimondi's repertoire also includes one of the most riveting interpretations of Scarpia since Gobbi.) Originally, he hadn't expected to find Don Giovanni as interesting as Boris and Don Quichotte, and says that his relationship with this role was one of 'slow, gradual discovery, but on a very profound level .

'Everybody sees the external side of Don Giovanni, the wooer and seducer of women. But I've come to the conclusion that Don Giovanni is a great hole: a legend, a character who exists only by reflection, through other people's reactions and desires, a legend who dies a spectacular, mythical death so he can be reborn and constantly renewed through various authors.' Jeremy Caulton, Director of Opera Planning at English National Opera, makes exactly the same point about Giovanni, which he calls 'almost a con trick', and stresses that every time it is discussed at planning meetings it becomes almost embarrassing because everyone is projecting their most private fantasies in their conception of it.

Raimondi also agrees with Sir Peter Hall's view of Don Giovanni (explained by Thomas Allen in his chapter) as a man who challenges God. 'This theme lies at the very crux of the opera. Don Giovanni cannot be an atheist. He *has* to be a believer who resists and challenges God right to the end. Without this dimension the story and character of Don Giovanni would lose the grandiose element that makes him so special, and become ordinary. The essence of Giovanni's greatness is the contrast between his totally unconventional, devil-may-care nature and the other characters, all of whom abide and are crushed by the mores and conventions of the day. But he, while remaining within the bounds of the law, breaks all the rules and conventions that average, mediocre people live by. This makes everyone mad with envy and desire for him. He is the man they would all like to, but dare not, be. He is also a catalyst who throws light on and exposes everybody's weaknesses, the problems they would rather hide from themselves and others and the sham of the situations they are locked in. Which is to say he plays havoc with the lives of everyone whose path he crosses: through him, Anna realizes Ottavio is not the man for her, Elvira enters a convent, Zerlina tastes something she didn't know existed, but she and Masetto decide to muddle on with a relationship in which there can be no pleasure and no trust.

'Another main characteristic of his is that he is a chameleon who changes his colour with every note and every situation and according to whom he is with: with the mild he is charming, with the strong he is even stronger and with the weak he is bored. Therefore, even more than Count Almaviva, the secret for bringing him fully to life lies in a myriad vocal colours which should change by the minute, to match the situations and characters he is confronted by. Each vocal colour – different for Zerlina, Anna, Elvira, Masetto, the peasants or Leporello – represents a different language, and the fact that instinctively he senses what tone to use for everybody is what makes him so exciting and irresistible in their eyes. This, along with the fact that he has an orgasm, every few seconds, is what stops him from being boring. The director Franco Enriquez put his finger on it when he said that Don Giovanni should have a "spermatozoic voice", and I was particularly flattered when he added "you, Ruggero, would make a good Giovanni because you *do* have a spermatozoic voice!". '

Raimondi agrees with the other famous interpreters of this role that, from the strictly vocal point of view, it is not particularly difficult. It is a 'hybrid' role that can be sung both by baritones and basses, although not surprisingly he feels the ideal voice for it is a bass-baritone. (Prey and Milnes disagree and, again, it's interesting that every singer projects himself as the ideal Giovanni!) 'Baritones tend to find the *tessitura* tricky in certain passages, like the Champagne aria, which is rather low but which has to be sung ferociously fast – because it's orgiastic – but with a full, rich voice that should project to the last row of the gallery, which is easier for basses with a good top than for baritones. Basses, on the other hand, have difficulty with the Serenade, which demands finesse and a light voice, something basses have to work extra hard at. But they have an easier time with the ending, which has a low *tessitura* and a loud orchestration. I would like to experiment with singing this opera with original instruments, to see if they would help in finding the right orchestral and vocal colours; because, as I said, from the vocal point of view the whole interpretation of Don Giovanni hinges on colours, colours, colours in a vast variety of shades and nuances.'

Like Milnes and Allen, Raimondi feels that, from the dramatic point of view, it is vital to highlight the character's tremendous vital force and state of constant tension. The action centres on Giovanni's last day on earth, a day that began badly, with the Commendatore's murder, and has gone from bad to worse: Elvira arrives and proceeds to slander him to all and sundry, his wooing of Zerlina is interrupted three times, Anna and Ottavio enlist his help in tracing the Commendatore's murderer, and then Anna – furious, in my view, at what Elvira has revealed about Giovanni's track record with women – recognizes him as the murderer. In his own words, Giovanni senses that 'today, the demon is amusing himself extra hard'. Therefore he is in a state of extreme tension, ready to spring to action and to react to any situation at all times. 'This should be reflected in all his movements – the way he looks at people, the way he glances over his shoulder, the way he walks, the way he talks, holds his glass or draws his sword – and communicated to the audience. The tension and sheer adrenaline he exudes should be such that when he's on stage everyone should *feel* he's on stage and when he isn't they should feel his absence. This makes him an especially exhausting role that eats away at your nerves. [Again Allen and Milnes both agree.] Very few singers are capable of sustaining this degree of tension right up to the end.'

Yet sustain it they must because the finale, the Supper scene, demands extreme vocal power and should make a terrific impact: it is, in Raimondi's words, 'a duel of Titans' in which Giovanni is finally overwhelmed, or rather removed, by extra-terrestrial forces, unrepentant, unrelenting and, although he knows the odds, resistant to the end. 'In fact, from the moment the Commendatore's statue spoke to him Giovanni realized, and this is expressed in his music, that the moment has acquired an unreal dimension that touches on the mysterious, and suspects that, from now on, things can only go against him. But he still wants to fight. Mockingly, he invites the statue to dinner, it replies "yes" and this is the penultimate call. At the Supper scene he behaves first with the grace and debonair manners of an excellent, aristocratic host and then, as the confrontation mounts in tension, refuses to compromise or repent and dies as legends should: in a mythical, abnormal way so they can go on living. The difficulty here is to establish credibility for the death, which is by no means the end, of a legend.'

A character who, in Raimondi's opinion, missed her chance of becoming a legend, too, is Donna Anna who, he is sure, had enjoyed a night of love with Giovanni before the action begins. 'There is something special about the bond between those two, and this is reflected in their music, which suggests a strong attachment. But, come the morning, she probably began to pester him with demands for a permanent, or at least a regular, attachment and to revolt against his extreme need to be free and to flee from the everyday. There is great ambiguity in the music of Giovanni's flight – which has interesting dynamics, *forte*, *piano*, *forte*, as she screams "gente, servi" – in which there is an implicit desire to maintain contact. This undercurrent of strong mutual attraction underlies all their exchanges and should be reflected in strong eye contact. Anna knows perfectly well it was Giovanni who had burst into her room and killed her father. But it is significant that she only chooses to "recognize" him just after she has heard of his record with women from Elvira!'

In spring 1986 Raimondi – who after his retirement from the operatic stage in the distant future would like to try his hand at directing opera and plays – sang this role in his own production of *Don Giovanni* at Nancy. Raimondi stated that his production has no pretence of delivering *the* truth on *Don Giovanni* but only reflects *his* truth on this work, today, in 1986. The premiere drew crowds from all over Europe and was extremely favourably reviewed in the French press: 'A Don Giovanni bursting with vitality, in fact super-endowed in his domain, who draws into his orbit all he encounters, in whom he liberates the same devouring energy. There is not a moment's void in this production: everything is in constant motion. Out of this hurry to change places, clothes, partners, to get close to and liberate bodies of their inhibitions, emerges a sense of urgency and openly expressed sensuality. There's no question of tenderness or fear, but of life triumphant and avid for love. And as in this case there was perfect accord between the producer and the principal singer, who are one and the same, the title role has never been better sung. . . . Through his force, Don Giovanni reveals the other characters to themselves by bursting apart their taboos.' (*Le Matin.*)

An idea he was particularly looking forward to experimenting with was a new insight for the Cemetery scene: 'in the eighteenth century it was customary in northern Spain to picnic in graveyards and eat and drink next to the graves of dead relatives. Leporello, a man of the people rooted in local traditions, should therefore be doing just that when Giovanni climbs over the railings in an attempt to flee from his latest conquest. This startles Leporello so much that he drops his bottle of wine, and I think it would be effective to have an overturned bottle rolling about.' Raimondi hoped this first attempt at operatic production would be successful because, much though he has enjoyed many of the productions he has sung in, none of them allowed him to perform the role *exactly* as he sees it.

Despite its complexity and the demands it makes on the performer's nervous system, Don Giovanni is not the most difficult role in Raimondi's repertoire. 'The hardest of all is Boris Godunov, because here you cannot cheat. Unlike Giovanni, who exists as a reflection of other people's reactions and desires, Boris has to be constructed slowly, step by step from within, out of your own feelings. Yet the character is so anguished and emotion-packed that if you abandon yourself to its emotion completely and allow yourself to cry and sob with him, you risk closing your throat and blocking the voice', explains Raimondi, who first sang Boris in 1972 at the Teatro La Fenice, in a historic production staged by Piero Faggioni of Mussorgsky's original version – which had never been staged in Italy before. 'You should always try to be one step removed from the character, which is very difficult indeed because certain moments, like the Clock scene, are written in so powerful and realistic a way that you almost feel yourself suffocating. It's practically impossible not to get completely involved. . . . I always sleep particularly badly after performing Boris, for example.'

Raimondi points out that the clue to Boris's character is contained in the opening chord of the Coronation scene, which is marked *tenuto*, and this terrible note of doubt encapsulates everything in Boris's character: the ambition, the thirst for, and then reality of, power, the intrigues and the death, or rather suicide, by remorse. 'All this is in Boris's head the moment he steps out of the cathedral. After so many intrigues, his ambition to be Tsar is finally realized. Yet at this moment, bang, in creeps a note of doubt, a presentiment or warning about this man who will ultimately condemn himself to a slow death by remorse for the murder of a child. This doubt, this seed of what is to be, must be suggested in your voice for a brief moment before Boris pulls himself together and addresses his people.'

In Act II Boris first shows his warmest, most humane side in the scene with his children, and then his strongest, most threatening side in the scene with Shuisky. But Shuisky's account of the murder of the former Tsarevitch drives Boris's guilt-ridden conscience to a frenzy – he chooses to interpret the prevailing famine and great fire of Moscow as God's punishment for his crime – and he has a hallucination in which he sees a bloodstained child. 'This obsession weighs on him more and more and almost brings him to the brink of madness. Gradually you must work yourself into this state of mind and build up this load of anguish inside you, so the audience can feel it too. Yet at the same time you must strive to keep your involvement under control, so you don't lose contact with reality. Otherwise you'd be finished. Because this scene is also very difficult from the vocal point of view: it is rhythmically imprecise, and while going through the excruciating emotions I've described you have to keep counting in order to stay within the measures.'

The most difficult technical demand of this role is the variety of vocal effects it requires: groans, gasps, sighs and choking sounds which every interpreter must invent according to his abilities. The *tessitura* itself is not uncomfortable and the most difficult moment from this point of view is that passage in the death of Boris which contains an E above the stave that has to be sung *pianissimo*. 'This is an agonizing moment, both vocally and dramatically, because Boris is dying of a broken, destroyed heart. A bell tolls and the chorus of monks enter, according to tradition, to dress him in a monk's habit and carry him to the altar for his death. At that precise moment the words change and he says he sees a child again, then, bang, comes the cerebral haemorrhage that kills him. All this is so harrowingly, so overwhelmingly intense that at the end you yourself feel dead, totally spent.'

Piero Faggioni remembers that the first time Raimondi sang this scene he fainted and had to be carried off the stage. 'He cried real tears, experienced Boris's agony and gave so much of himself that he was in a state of trance. Afterwards he told me he couldn't go on working like this, he had to find a way of protecting his health and his sanity, because at this depth he couldn't defend himself. I conceded he had a point. There is a mysterious balance, poised halfway between genuine emotion and conscious technical control, that every singer must discover for themselves.'

Raimondi's capacity for total immersion in his roles renders his own and other people's testimony that at the beginning of his career his dramatic ability was nil all the more astonishing. His total inability to link and co-ordinate sound production with any kind of body movement was, Faggioni explains, due both to psychological reasons and to the fact that he lacked any sort of dramatic training, having, like many other young singers, studied only with singing teachers.

Born in Bologna in 1942 to parents who were ardent opera lovers and who possessed a large collection of records, Raimondi started taking piano lessons at the age of seven but loathed them and soon gave them up. But he loved singing and learnt all the big arias he heard on his parents' records by heart. His voice broke and settled into its present register early and was first spotted on a Roman beach, where the thirteen-year-old Raimondi was singing Iago's 'Credo' from *Otello* to himself. Two music-loving Roman gentlemen promptly approached his parents and told them they should have their son's voice assessed professionally. Two years later his grandmother, who was of the same opinion, arranged for him to audition for the well-known conductor Francesco Molinari-Pradelli, who declared he was prepared to bet on Raimondi's having a big career.

So, at his family's instigation – especially that of his father, who saw the possibility of fulfilling his own unrealized dreams through his son – Raimondi abandoned his plan to become an accountant and started taking singing lessons with Ettore Campogalliani in Mantua, to prepare for the entrance exams to the Milan Conservatoire. He passed them, but as he was only sixteen he was only allowed in for the first year as a listener. This meant a daily ride by train to and from Bologna, getting up at five every morning, because his parents felt he was too young to live alone in the city. Not surprisingly he got fed up with this exhausting drill and at the end of the year persuaded his parents he was now old enough to live and study in Rome, where he spent the next four years studying with Teresa Pediconi and Antonio Piervenanzi and relishing life in the Italian capital, 'a marvellous place to grow up and spend one's formative years in during its golden age in the early sixties'.

In 1964 he won the Adriano Belli Singing Competition in Spoleto singing Colline in *La Bohème* and this led to an immediate invitation by the Rome Opera to understudy the famous bass Nicola Rossi-Lemeni in the role of Procida in *I vespri siciliani*. As the latter fell ill before the last performance, Raimondi got the chance to make his professional debut in this important role. 'Actually I was ill as well,' he remembers, 'but my eagerness and enthusiasm for grasping this golden opportunity were such that I kept quiet about it and sang the performance with bronchitis', fortunately also with great success and far-reaching results. For Raimondi's father had invited the husband of soprano Maria Chiara to attend the performance and the latter was so impressed by the young man's potential that he arranged an audition with the Intendant of the Teatro La Fenice, Mario Labroca, who was to become Raimondi's mentor and the man responsible for launching his career by offering him a five-year contract on the spot. It was at La Fenice, thanks to Labroca's unswerving faith in him, that Raimondi sang all his big roles like Mephistopheles, Boris Godunov, Don Giovanni, Count Almaviva and Don Quichotte for the first time.

During his years at La Fenice Raimondi was coached from time to time by Leone Magiera, who remembers that 'his voice was already there: strong, sonorous and resonant. I didn't have to work on technique. What I did have to do was instil the rudiments of interpretation, because at the time Ruggero used to sing everything loud. I had to teach him first the need and then the way to sing *piano* and *pianissimo* at times, and how to colour the voice according to the content of each phrase. And believe me, it is very, very difficult to discipline a large voice and learn to render it "smaller" at will so that it can sing Don Giovanni's Serenade as beautifully as Ruggero now does. Strangely enough, the technical way to do this is by supporting and sustaining the breath even more and go for a smaller, but sustained, sound because even a *piano* sound should have "body", otherwise it wouldn't be heard. Ruggero, who is an extremely intelligent and sensitive man, understood this and gradually succeeded in making his voice the subtle, richly shaded instrument it now is. As a human being he was always special, interested in everything and always searching for new insights, for the truth behind the works. He is a great researcher and now a profoundly artistic temperament.'

Janine Reiss, who met and came to work with Raimondi a bit later on in his career, says he is 'a candid, almost naive and totally transparent man, and it is this real and deep human simplicity, rather than his equally real musical and cultural sophistication, that he brings to his roles. This is why his interpretations ring so true and why he practically *becomes* the characters he portrays.'

Thinking back to those days, Raimondi says that his motive in acceding to his parents' wish that he become a singer was the hope that, through the various roles, costumes and make-believe of the theatre, he might lose his crippling shyness and liberate himself from his complexes. But this didn't begin to happen until his encounter, at the Teatro La Fenice, with the man who 'changed my life and taught me how to use my hyper-sensitivity in a creative way': Piero Faggioni.

Faggioni vividly recalls his first meeting with this 'enormously tall, taciturn young man just out of music school, with his huge brown eyes and awkward movements, stiff and rigid like a Frankenstein'. Faggioni was Jean Vilar's assistant at the time, charged with rehearsing the latter's production of Verdi's *Jérusalem* for a forthcoming German tour. Raimondi at one point had to kill a man with a knife. Faggioni showed him various ways of doing this with verve and élan, but he just couldn't manage any of them. 'His arms seemed nearly paralysed. Like many young singers who have spent years in front of the piano doing breathing exercises but who have had no dramatic training, he was totally unable to co-ordinate his body movements with sound production.' But his voice was remark-able indeed, and after singing his second role at La Fenice, Pistola in *Falstaff*, Labroca felt it was time for bigger things and was determined to cast him as Mephistopheles in Faggioni's forthcoming production of Gounod's *Faust*. 'I liked Ruggero and found him immediately *simpatico*,' says Faggioni. 'I also knew that he admired my ideas and way of working, so I resolved to try and help him develop some dramatic skill. I told Labroca I would accept him as Mephistopheles provided I could take him home with me to Rome for a fortnight of intense training.'

Faggioni had never before, or indeed has never since, undertaken to train anybody in this way, but the experience proved 'extraordinary' for both artists and forged a lasting link of friendship and professional collaboration. Faggioni remembers that the training began with some exercises he thought up intuitively, on the spot: 'In my tiny room, I put on a record of Faust and had him listen to a few bars of Mephistopheles's music at a time, asking him to co-ordinate those with specific body movements – raising an arm, bending his knees, turning his head, etc. – because I could see that his psychological block was not due to total inhibition but to the strain imposed on his body by the muscle contractions involved in voice production. I knew he loved sports, so after a couple of days, when we came to Mephistopheles's aria "Le Veau d'or", I asked him to imagine we were two drunken friends ski-ing down a mountain slope, because I sensed he'd feel freer and more relaxed if trying to link sound to the body movements of a specific sport. Indeed, he found this exercise enjoyable and I soon discovered he had natural, built-in body rhythm and could move his body musically, i.e. succeed in co-ordinating certain movements to specific musical phrases. So I asked him to begin humming them to himself while "ski-ing". After five or six days, when I saw his movements were well-co-ordinated to the phrases he was humming, I felt it was time for him to begin singing them out loud. The experience was very much like watching a hedgehog rolling and unrolling from its ball. And every day he ventured out a bit more. I shall never forget the look of gratitude on his face the moment when he realized for the first time that he was now able to come out of himself and experience the freedom singers feel when sound production can relate naturally to body movements: the whole body becomes like a gigantic lung that can expand and contract at will and the voice becomes capable of producing vocal nuances and colours that would be inconceivable if they were standing up straight and rigid.'

When it came to the 'Kermesse' scene at the tavern, where Mephistopheles has to jump on tables and run around the place in circles, there was no room to experiment in Faggioni's tiny studio. So he decided to take Raimondi out into the street, to the Foro Italico and, in full view of the passing crowds, asked him to 'spring, saunter, run and spin around'. To his horrified reply that people were watching, he replied: 'Who cares? Pretend we're drunk!' Raimondi nearly had a heart attack and wished the earth would open up and swallow him. 'But Piero who, as you know, has never been an inhibited character, insisted and little by little he succeeded in unblocking the tensions that made me freeze whenever confronted by people.'

After getting over his initial shock at this unorthodox method of preparing a role, Raimondi began to enjoy himself: 'I had never had so much fun in my life. I always retain a special affection for Mephisto, the role that changed my life and freed me from my shyness and my complexes. Piero gave me this idea of Mephisto as a swashbuckling, Douglas Fairbanks type of figure with an athlete's physique and an acrobat's agility, who runs and jumps around, indulging in all manner of gymnastics and who enjoys showing off his body and physical dexterity.' The two rehearsed every movement minutely and, seeing how much Raimondi was enjoying himself by then, each day Faggioni made him do a bit more. When they returned to Venice to begin rehearsals in the theatre, the chorus greeted the news that Raimondi was to sing Mephistopheles with amazement and incredulity because they felt sure he could never cope with the dramatic demands of the role. But after seeing him whirl around and jump from tables over a metre high at the first rehearsal, they burst into equally stunned applause.

It was this production of *Faust*, in 1965, that launched Raimondi's career. Soon after that, he was asked to sing in a new production of *Faust* by Luca Ronconi, in Bologna, in 1967, and the title role in *Don Giovanni* in a production by the late Herbert Graf in Geneva in 1968. This was attended by Peter Diamand, then Director of the Edinburgh Festival, who was impressed enough to recommend Raimondi to the Glyndebourne Festival Opera, where he made his debut in the same role in 1969. Yet Raimondi says that during those Geneva performances he was still 'so full of Mephistopheles' that Graf didn't fully succeed in imposing his conception of Don Giovanni on him.

Mephistopheles is a role with extremely interesting expressive possibilities. And while Raimondi's interpretation is still based on Faggioni's idea of a 'gymnastic' character inspired by Douglas Fairbanks, he feels in retrospect that his original interpretation had perhaps been too physical. The role also presented some vocal problems in those days because he sang it 'with a young voice and all the cockiness of youth, with enormous power and without conscious calculation. I thought nothing of missing a breath while jumping off a table, for instance. Naturally I couldn't have gone on singing it this way, because certain natural resources diminish, if not vanish altogether, with maturity. So, one begins to *think* about technical things – like finding the right position for singing certain notes consciously.'

The most crucial moment from the vocal point of view is Mephisto's entry, 'Me Voici', in the prologue, which contains a central C. It is also the character's first appearance and should therefore make an impact and have a certain vocal weight which Raimondi feels it didn't in early days. 'Then you have to climb to an F above the stave which is not written in the score but interpolated by so-called tradition but which I can manage because I am a bass-baritone, not a *basso profondo*, and the *tessitura* of this role has always suited me particularly well. There are some more vocal difficulties in the 'Kermesse' scene, where you suddenly have to plunge down to F below the stave, and the aria "Le Veau d'or" contains some difficult trills which one always feels like singing "open" rather than "covered" [i.e. well-sung!], but whether you manage to do this depends on the state of your breath and general vocal condition on each particular evening. And in this aria in particular, my training with Piero proved invaluable: it allows me to feel vocally secure while moving around in a highly gymnastic fashion. Because you couldn't sing "Le Veau d'or" standing still! It's a demonic aria in which Mephisto proceeds to hypnotize and lay everybody bare. So he should *behave* like a magician and circle around people both with his eyes and with his body – all of which demands long breath and tremendous physical stamina.'

After his first, intensely physical interpretation of Mephistopheles at the Teatro La Fenice, Raimondi next sang the role in Bologna, in a controversial production by Luca Ronconi which placed the action in the nineteenth century and in which Mephistopheles was portrayed as a rather demonic cardinal with vast business interests that included a high-class brothel with can-can dancers! This conception opened up even greater possibilities for vocal colour and refinement. 'This is when I began to be aware of the ironic streak in Mephisto's character, who now became drier, more cynical, critical and introspective. While retaining his high mobility and almost balletic quality, he began to use these ultra-physical qualities to become more dominant. Because essentially Mephisto is a being with a deep need to show off his power and demonstrate what he can do, for both his own and other people's amusement. First, he proceeds to stun Faust in the Prologue with a succession of tricks – conjuring up visions of wealth, power and physical gratification – and then he does the same for the crowds in the tavern in the "Kermesse". In giving it, he almost experiences pleasure himself, but in a rather critical way, underlining sensual, ironic, wicked undertones. In the church with Marguerite he is evil – perhaps his only really evil moment – then in the Serenade he is ironic, assuming the posture of a jester, and he almost savours Faust's lust for Marguerite, because of course Faust and Mephisto are two opposite sides of the same character, like Jekyll and Hyde.'

Raimondi stresses that the vocal and physical demands of this role require considerable physical preparation because the total independence of vocal production from body movements so essential to the role is quite difficult to achieve, even for experienced singers. 'I do lots of breathing exercises – breathing in and holding my breath for five, ten, fifteen seconds and regulating it rhythmically – as well as straightforward gymnastics and long walks to get myself fit, because this sort of role requires it. So does Don Quichotte, which paradoxically enough also demands terrific physical effort, despite the fact that the character has to look old.'

Raimondi first sang the title role in Massenet's *Don Quichotte* at the Teatro La Fenice in 1982–3, again in a production by Piero Faggioni, with whom he had rather lost touch after that historic production of *Boris Godunov* which had been followed by a less happy collaboration in *Le nozze di Figaro*. Since then Raimondi's career has assumed international importance, with a string of acclaimed debuts: La Scala, in 1970, as Procida in *I vespri siciliani*; the Metropolitan Opera as Silva in *Ernani* and, ten years later, as Procida. (His portrayal of this role is considered a masterpiece. After Raimondi sang it at the Metropolitan Opera in 1980, the critic of *Opéra International* wrote: 'To say Raimondi was the triumph of the production would be to utter an understatement! His return to the Met was hailed with an enormous ovation after the aria "O tu Palermo" that will remain memorable. An intense and accomplished actor, he makes of Procida, the fanatical patriot, a magisterial scenic and vocal composition.') He has sung in the Verdi *Requiem* in St Paul's Cathedral and the Albert Hall in London; Covent Garden, in 1972, as Fiesco in *Simon Boccanegra*; Paris Opéra, in 1975, again as Procida; the Losey film of *Don Giovanni* in 1978; his Salzburg Festival debut, in 1980, as the King, and later Ramfis, in *Aida* and also the Verdi *Requiem*, both under Karajan. What had hurt Faggioni was Raimondi's agreeing to sing Boris Godunov at the Paris Opéra in 1979 under Seiji Ozawa in a production that was originally meant to be directed by him but which, because of disagreements over the choice of designer, was finally given to Joseph Losey.

Fortunately, Raimondi and Faggioni's friendship and mutual regard for each other were strong enough to survive this difference of opinion and their next encounter, in 1982, resulted in a fascinating production of *Don Quichotte*. This came about through Raimondi's insistence on doing this opera, which he liked, but which Faggioni didn't because, while he found the character of Don Quichotte himself extraordinary, the rest of the opera struck him as rather 'fragile'. But the more he thought about the character, the more parallels he found between Don Quichotte, himself and Raimondi. 'Both of us have remained fairly naive and idealistic: people who love and carry out our profession because of the possibility it affords for communicating ideas and principles through bringing these works to life, rather than for reasons of glory. While Ruggero is not quite as naive and idealistic as I, there are, nevertheless, in him the remains of an idealist whose dreams have remained unfulfilled inside him and who is wounded by the world he has come to live in.'

Having thus found a point of identification with the opera, Faggioni proceeded to stage the work in a way that poised it halfway between the real historical character of Don Quichotte and the 'quixoticism' involved in being part of the theatrical and operatic professions. The action didn't take place in sixteenth-century Spain but in the early part of the twentieth century, the time of Massenet, who composed this role for Chaliapin. It showed a great singer – like Chaliapin or an earlier-day Raimondi – performing this role on tour in Spain. The setting is a rather dingy Spanish courtyard, and Don Quichotte's first entry is on a wooden horse pulled by children, obviously part of the theatrical props. Then the lights dim, and he begins to sing the love-duet; but there is an electrical fault, so he steps outside the character and shouts, 'eh, lights', and as they are put right and dim, again, assuming a more nocturnal, subtle hue, he slips back into the character of Don Quichotte, into which Raimondi and Faggioni have poured all their own unfulfilled dreams and frustrations of battling against the routine in their profession. Here, as Faggioni remembers and the critics concur, Raimondi produced 'some wonderfully subtle shades of vocal colour'. *Opera* referred to 'Ruggero Raimondi's masterly portrayal of the title role, notable for finely controlled and perfectly judged dynamic and for the cantabile quality of a spendidly coloured voice. Raimondi, a singer of undisputed international stature, seems once again to have been stimulated by an interesting character.'

Raimondi considers this production one of the greatest dramatic experiences of his career and is deeply attached to the role, despite its enormous vocal and dramatic demands. 'As I mentioned before, you have to be very fit to sing Don Quichotte, otherwise you'd risk running out of breath halfway through, or even in the middle of a phrase. Certain scenes like the duel, for instance, demand that you prepare yourself very well in advance, because once you're on stage and lost in the heroic verve of the character you are apt to forget to exercise the control necessary for the physical act of singing, and this is a big problem. If you forget to breathe in the right place, a note that has always seemed easy suddenly becomes difficult, even impossible, to cope with, because you forgot to prepare your mechanism for hitting that note. Again, as in Boris, it all hinges on the interplay between abandon and control. However lost you might be in the character, you must remember to count, one, two, three, and take care how you jump off the horse because, in the passage you're supposed to be singing while jumping off, there is a high note. So you must find a way of being in a state of ecstasy without ever being out of control. But the ideal balance between the two is never reached. . . . You never succeed in controlling yourself one hundred per cent.'

Thomas Allen, another great singing-actor, agrees, but it is interesting that singers who are not known for the dramatic power of their interpretations never seem to experience, or refer to, this problem. For, as Raimondi rightly stresses, there are two kinds of opera singers in the world: 'those who sing high notes and those who interpret, and I am aware of belonging to the latter category. But this is something you pay for, because you tend to forget about technical control, throw yourself into the role and thus get very, very tired. Still, you arrive at certain depths of insight that the other kind of singers never touch. . . . '

He recalls some two- to three-minute sequences in Losey's film of *Don Giovanni* where he 'touched certain inner chords of sensitivity I didn't know I had. Losey called them a "flash", and after they were over it was very hard to find those depths again and to recapture the mystery of those moments. I am quite psychic, deeply attracted to and at the same time frightened by the occult, and have travelled quite far in a psychic sense, almost to the point of losing myself. I am what the French would call *journalier*, i.e. I have certain days of heightened sensitivity when I have the sensation, not of becoming the character I'm singing, but of actually hearing his voice. In moments like this I totally lose the battle for technical control and abandon myself wholly to the character and the sensations and emotions he is experiencing. It's a wonderful feeling of dying and then being reborn again. . . . But moments like this are very special and don't happen very often. In my experience, they have happened only in *Don Giovanni*, *Boris Godunov* in both Venice and Paris, and *Don Quichotte*.'

Piero Faggioni says that, in moments like this, he has the impression of a soul in the process of self-liberation through singing, thanks to the genius of a composer who sensed that a certain musical note evokes and releases the maximum expression of a given emotion or sensation, like a painter who instinctively knows what colours will evoke certain responses in the onlooker. Musical notes and phrases perform the same function. Yet there is a crucial difference between the two. The latter are not concrete, and until a singer comes along and turns them into a certain vocal colour they remain simply a breath, a vibration. 'But if this singer is capable of arriving at, and re-creating, the same emotion the composer imagined, then a miracle happens, and it is this kind of miracle that makes opera great. And it is thanks to artists like Raimondi and Domingo, who *can* perform such miracles, that I find the courage to continue in this profession.'

JOSÉ VAN DAM

Belgian-born José Van Dam is a refined, intelligent and immensely musical singer who combines stylistic sensitivity with a profound, reflective, artistic temperament and one of the most beautiful bass–baritone voices around: warm, mellow, well-rounded and aptly described in *Gramophone* as 'strong, expressive, keenly focussed, truly a *basso cantante* with a remarkable baritone upper extension'. The dramatic power of his interpretations is enhanced by a sense of economy and sobriety, in the ancient Greek sense of the words, that enable him to contain even the most intense and extreme passions within the bounds of good taste. This innate feeling for measure and pacing, which ensures that the full impact of his performance is always saved for the *real* climax of the work at hand, is as characteristic of Van Dam as his disdain for cheap, applause-begging pyrotechnics. Yet there are some who, while never disputing the musical excellence of his interpretations, accuse him of a certain 'coldness' on stage and feel that the absence of facile thrills detracts from the dramatic impact of his performances.

Nothing could be further from the truth. In fact, one seldom leaves a Van Dam performance of one of his great roles – which include Amfortas in *Parsifal*, Jokanaan in *Salome*, the title roles in *Der fliegende Holländer* and *Wozzeck*, and his unforgettable portrayal of Don Alfonso in *Così fan tutte*, to name but a few – without the conviction of having had each role revealed in its true dramatic essence and sung with the consummate skill of a mature artist at his peak.

Our first conversation took place at the 1982 Salzburg Easter Festival, during rehearsals for Herbert von Karajan's production of *Der fliegende Holländer*, which I had heard him record a few months before, in Berlin, when he had complained that 'there is something antiseptic about the atmosphere of a recording studio. It's a bit like being in an operating theatre or being asked to make love in public. I'm self-conscious and acutely aware of everybody present whereas on stage I feel alone and

264

completely private. When singing the love-duet with Senta, for instance, I'm conscious only of us two. Nothing else exists at the moment. Which is why I feel that my real interpretation of any role begins not before a recording, but during rehearsals for a stage production.'

On stage, Van Dam's portrayal of Wagner's tormented hero was, and I suspect will remain, the most moving and convincing I have seen: all inner fire and brooding despair, totally devoid of unnecessary histrionics. But although it was generally pronounced a resounding success and praised for 'perfectly focussed tone and eloquent phrasing, based on clear enunciation and long breath' (*Opera*), some critics were disappointed by its brooding esotericism and yearned for a more extrovert, possibly more Mephistophelian, performance. Van Dam understands their point of view but explains that such a thing would be completely at odds with his view of the role.

'I see the Dutchman as a very tense, very dramatic yet wholly introverted character, and these contradictory characteristics make it an exceptionally difficult and demanding part, even though, by Wagnerian standards, it is not particularly long. Hans Sachs in *Die Meistersinger von Nürnberg*, for example, is much longer yet considerably easier because it is more lyrical and the character is calmer and more poised. But the Dutchman is a turbulent and insecure soul with a fiery side to him which is written into the music and must therefore be expressed. Yet this is only one side of the coin. The other is a very solitary, introspective side which must be brought out, too. It's easy enough to stress the fiery, at the expense of the introverted, side. In fact, I fell into this trap myself when I started singing the role and realize, in retrospect, that my portrayal used to be *too* dramatic.'

But as the role grew on him, he began to modify his interpretation because he gradually became aware of a very human side to the Dutchman's character. This tendency always to search for the most human side of every role is, he says, an obsession of his; which is why he fundamentally disagrees with those who feel his Dutchman is not demonic enough. 'Why should he be? He is not the devil, but merely a man who once made a pact with the devil, a pact he has now come to regret bitterly. For over four hundred years he has been roaming the seas, searching for salvation. If one cares to look beyond the legend, one will find a man searching for his twin soul, his other half, what every human being is searching for, consciously or not. And when, after many years at sea, he is allowed to go ashore to look for the woman who might redeem him, he feels almost like an extra-terrestrial, so solitary, introverted and uncommunicative has he become: this withdrawn side of his nature must be expressed. But *only up to a point*, otherwise it would automatically become extroversion. I *could* express it more than I do. I just don't *want* to. Exactly the same interpretational point, if I may digress for a moment, that underlies my restrained and at times subdued singing in the baritone aria, 'Herr, lehre doch mich', in Brahms's *Ein Deutsches Requiem*, which is an intimate, mystical prayer. Therefore to degrade it by using it as a vehicle for a display of vocal bravura would amount to a betrayal of its very essence. But this is part and parcel of a choice facing every artist at the onset of his career: either to aim at pleasing everybody or to try and serve his art as honestly as possible, true to his inner vision of every work he interprets.

'From the purely vocal point of view, the Dutchman presents few problems. It's a well-written role which, despite the anguished nature of the man, contains a strong *bel canto* element, a great line, something I always enjoy, and the *tessitura* is very comfortable for me. In fact, there are only two strictly *vocal* problems: first, having to sing through a very large orchestra, which is always hard for deep, rounded voices like mine, or most baritone and bass voices. This is difficult to understand, because it has to do with frequencies. But it's a fact that high voices would have no difficulties in riding above this kind of orchestration, even if they happened to be smaller. Second, the fact that, the moment the Dutchman walks on stage, he has to plunge into the long and difficult aria "Die Frist ist um" without a chance to warm up except backstage, which is not the same thing. Having to sing an important aria "cold" is always hard, whether you happen to be singing the Dutchman or Escamillo. But in the former case the aria in question is so tense and powerful that the prospect is enough to fill you with panic.'

Apart from these strictly vocal difficulties, he explained that there are some additional technical problems, well known in the profession, which stem from the role's specific dramatic demands. One of them occurs in the Senta-Dutchman duet in Act II, 'Wie aus der Ferne', which starts off quietly but contains one or two very dramatic, and musically very loud, outbursts 'which call for your vocal maximum or almost (for the *absolute* maximum must always be conserved for the finale) but which are followed by quieter passages where you have to pull back your forces almost instantaneously. And once in a crescendo this is very, very hard to do and it took me a long time to learn how to. But once I had, the role became somewhat easier.

'From the purely *dramatic* point of view, the toughest challenge comes just *before* "Wie aus der Ferne" when Daland introduces the Dutchman to Senta with an aria, "Willst du, mein Kind", which lasts about five minutes. And during those five minutes he has to stand there, silent and motionless, yet in a state of white-hot, one hundred per cent focussed concentration, which is one of the hardest things to do on stage, both for singers and straight actors. He has to gaze at Senta with an intensity that almost sends one's head spinning, so unusual and unnatural is it – for in real life one doesn't go about staring at people in such persistent and hypnotic fashion – trying to convince her to accept him, but without saying or doing anything. And all the time he's gazing at her, he is in a state of inner turmoil, wondering whether she is the one who will save him yet not daring to believe it and thinking, "I would like it to be you, but is it?". And this anguish of simultaneous longing and doubt can only be communicated to the public, who must feel it too, through your own almost superhuman concentration. If you just stood there, waiting for your turn to sing, nothing would happen.'

And as if that weren't enough, just as he feels like relaxing after all the bravura and concentration of this duet, he has to start all over again, in the trio that immediately follows Daland's re-entry. And the Erik-Senta-Dutchman trio at the finale of Act III, 'Verloren, verloren', is difficult, too, because it's quite spread out and comes at the end of the evening, when he is feeling tired. All these various technical and dramatic demands, but most of all the character's state of constant inner tension, combine to make the Flying Dutchman one of the most taxing and wearing roles in his repertoire. The other is Wozzeck. 'And they happen to be among my very favourites.'

To my surprise, this short list does not include one of Van Dam's most famous roles, Amfortas in *Parsifal* (which he has sung on record and on stage at the Salzburg Easter Festival under Karajan), a character that can easily be reduced to a monotonous bore at the hands of anyone but a first-class singer. Van Dam is considered to be not only its greatest *living* interpreter, but one of the greatest in the hundred-year history of the role, as those who have seen some of his distinguished predecessors testify. His interpretation is permeated by an unusual degree of empathy and compassion that endows Amfortas with a dignity and humility seldom experienced before and lifts him above the merely pitiful by offering us a glimpse of the man as he must have been before his fall. And, as several critics were quick to note, this makes all the difference: 'Van Dam voiced Amfortas's self-pity with an eloquence the character hardly deserves and a top register worthy of a hero', were John Higgins's perceptive remarks in *The Times*. From the vocal point of view, every word and phrase is coloured with different shades and nuances from an extraordinarily wide palette of vocal colours which bring life to every line of Amfortas's long monologues. The critic of the *Guardian* noted that the long lament in Act I, 'Wehvolles Erben', was 'enormously wide in its dynamic and expressive range'.

Why, then, does Van Dam consider this role, which so few succeed in bringing fully to life, easier and less draining than the Flying Dutchman? 'First of all, because all the time Amfortas is on stage he has to sing. No long silences here. And second, because he is an extrovert. He is fed up and lets you know he is fed up whereas the Dutchman keeps a lot inside which you can only *suggest* but not fully express. Again, there are no difficulties as far as the *tessitura* of the role is concerned. In fact the single vocal problem worth mentioning is the fact that, despite Amfortas's successive outbursts, your vocal maximum must be conserved for the finale of Act III where, just before Parsifal's return, he sings his most important lines: "mit seiner Qual, von selbst dann leuchtet euch wohl der Gral!".'

In dramatic terms the real challenge, which is great indeed, is to unveil the man's spiritual world; 'because Amfortas is wavering between sainthood and frailty. He is saint and man in one, the possessor of the Grail and, before his fall, of the spear, i.e. the equipment for sainthood. But he is also prone to human weakness, which prompted him to succumb to temptation and stigmatized his holy side, symbolized by the Wound. Since then, he has had to live a life of suffering for the sake of others and submit to the torture of having to uncover the Grail, knowing he has betrayed it. And there is nothing he can do about it except wail and wait for death. Essentially a suicidal type who would have killed himself long ago were it not for his mystical side, a core of which still exists inside him, despite everything.'

Van Dam is fascinated by the link, both musical and spiritual, between *Parsifal* and *Der fliegende Holländer* and feels that these two works are part of the same quest. 'Musically, both are permeated by a strong lyrical element which, apart from a few well-known passages, is largely absent from the *Ring*. And spiritually, because every time Wagner – an exalted sort of individual, prone to ecstatic inspiration – touches on the mystical, he succeeds and is at his best, while in the labyrinthine politics of the *Ring* he takes himself too seriously and is less successful, in my opinion. Maybe he sensed that *Parsifal* was to be his last work and, at the end of his life, wanted to return to some of the issues that had preoccupied him in his youth. This often happens in life. There are things one knows instinctively, subconsciously, right from the beginning but only succeeds in understanding clearly and fully consciously after a long and sometimes roundabout journey. This is true both of the personal and of the creative, intellectual and spiritual spheres of one's life.'

When asked if he shares any of Wagner's mystical spiritual beliefs, such as reincarnation and the re-meeting of deeply linked souls through successive lives to resolve any issue left unconcluded in previous incarnations, he replied that this is a question he often asks himself. 'And I'm still not sure of the answer; because there is an element of mystery in music, especially in great music like Wagner's, Mozart's or Bach's, music which transcends the human limitations of the geniuses who created, but were sometimes unworthy of, it and which goes *beyond* any personal beliefs the composers themselves might have held. I haven't read all that much about Wagner, because as a human being he interests me less than other composers, but I *have* read a great deal about Mozart. And the more I read about him, the less I understand him. In everyday life he seems to have been a rather ordinary sort of person; but this incomparable, celestial music kept pouring out of him. Earlier on this summer [1983], while in Aix-en-Provence, I saw *Mitridate, rè di Ponto*, an opera he composed at the age of fourteen! And at other times he wrote some of his greatest masterpieces in the most extraordinary circumstances. The overture to *Don Giovanni*, for instance, was composed on the eve of the premiere, when he rushed home after the dress rehearsal and told his wife: "Listen, I have to write an overture, talk to me while I'm doing it so I don't fall asleep!" So, you see, this man and his relationship to his music is a phenomenon not wholly human in the sense that it is *super*human and quite inexplicable. One should therefore conclude that these great geniuses were simply channels for something transmitted to their brain and their hands from somewhere else, from other spheres, by a sort of ray or beam.

'To a small extent the same is true of us interpreters. Needless to say, we, too, are unworthy of the music we interpret, but occasionally also subject to moments of ecstatic inspiration when the same "something" that was transmitted to its creators is also transmitted to us. Especially in those *Sternstunden* when you have a Karajan in the pit and he creates an atmosphere where you find yourself so "in" the character, so inside and part of the music that without your realizing it something strange and mysterious happens. All of you – he in the pit and you on stage – merge and become parts of a sort of transmission unit communicating this music, with great pleasure and deep joy, to the public who alone can experience it in its entirety. *We* can't. We can only play our part in its transmission. Which is why I feel that a singer's, or any artist's, life is a life lived for others, a life light-years removed from the mirage of glamour and glitter that the public sometimes associates with it. We make gifts of ourselves, we toil, we struggle to perfect our voice and technique so that it can serve the composers with ever-growing skill, but the result is not for us to enjoy.'

Yet he also pointed out that, naturally, interpreters cannot 'give' what they do not possess, and that those performances in which the role eludes them because they have to grapple either with vocal or health problems are extremely frustrating. So are those that find them on stage with colleagues or conductors they have no rapport with. For Van Dam, the ultimate is working with Karajan, 'whose rapport with his singers amounts to a metaphysical marriage'. For Karajan's sake, this careful and astute singer knowingly made one of the few mistakes of his career: he agreed to sing Rocco, a role with a *tessitura* much too low for him, at the 1978 Salzburg Easter Festival production of *Fidelio*, because he didn't want to miss the chance of working with Karajan again and had already refused his offer to sing Pizarro. He always refuses to sing Pizarro, and most of the villains in the repertoire, first because he is not nasty by nature and has found that, however hard he tries, it is difficult to establish an imaginary link and bring out the full villainy in roles like Pizarro or Scarpia, which he also keeps turning down. His second reason is purely vocal: he possesses neither the right kind of 'white' voice nor the special vocal colours required by such roles. Besides, Pizarro and Telramund in *Lohengrin* (which, again, he consistently refuses to sing) are known in the profession as 'killer roles' because every time those characters walk on stage the orchestra is unleashed with no holds barred, thus making it necessary to ride over it while at the same time trying to add 'ugly' colours to the voice. For both these reasons he turned down Karajan's offer of Pizarro, then 'weakened enough' to accept his alternative suggestion of Rocco. 'But it was a mistake and I'll never sing it again.'

A rare mistake indeed in a career built on a repertoire wide and versatile enough to include, as well as the roles of Amfortas in *Parsifal*, Jokanaan in *Salome*, and the title roles in *Der fliegende Holländer* and *Wozzeck*, parts as varied as Philip II in Verdi's *Don Carlos* and the title roles in *Attila* and *Simon Boccanegra*; the title role in Puccini's *Gianni Schicchi*; the title roles in *Prince Igor* and *Boris Godunov*; Mephistopheles in *Faust*, the four villains – Lindorf, Coppelius, Dr Miracle and Dapertutto – in *Les Contes d' Hoffmann*, and Escamillo in *Carmen*. (It was with this last warhorse that he made most of his important international debuts, including the ones at La Scala, Covent Garden and the Metropolitan Opera; he sings the role extremely well but dislikes it because he considers it 'one-dimensional and lacking in depth and humanity' and possibly because dramatically he lacks the extrovert bravura essential to the role.) He has sung several Mozart roles, like Sarastro in *Die Zauberflöte*, Don Alfonso in *Così fan tutte*, Figaro in *Le nozze di Figaro* and Leporello in *Don Giovanni* (which he also sang in Joseph Losey's superb film), as well as the title role in Messiaen's *St François d'Assise*, which had its world premiere at the Paris Opéra in November 1983, under Seiji Ozawa, and which required him to be on stage for a full four and a half hours. This is two and a half hours longer than Hans Sachs in *Die Meistersinger von Nürnberg*, which was the next role in Van Dam's agenda at the time.

After he first sang Hans Sachs at the Théâtre de La Monnaie, Brussels, in early 1986, *The Times* wrote that 'Van Dam's comfortable figure, the quizzical lift of the eyebrows and the benign curve of the lips make him a natural for Wagner's cobbler [just as they fitted him ill for Escamillo in Salzburg last spring]. The warm, easy flow of the voice never seems to tire. Most Sachses have to hold back a bit in the third act [as Weikl points out in his chapter], so that the final celebration of traditions teutonic is given its full weight. Van Dam has no such need.' The critic went on to add that 'the interpretation still lacks a little weight' from the dramatic point of view, but attributed this to the idiosyncratic production that updated the work to the middle of the nineteenth century.

Van Dam considers this versatility – the ability to excel in both Wagner and Mozart roles and in the French, Italian and Russian as well as the German *Fach* – to be 'what an international career is all about: not rushing hither and thither, seemingly without stop'. But he points out that if, after singing Hans Sachs, he can still sing Figaro and Boccanegra (i.e. Mozart and Verdi), something very few singers can do, he will profess himself more than satisfied with his career. In 1985 he sang the title role in Verdi's *Simon Boccanegra* at the Théâtre de La Monnaie for the first time. The role is usually sung by baritones, yet Van Dam's superb vocal technique and versatility proved him more than equal to the task: 'José van Dam, who had already sung the part of Fiesco, was singing his first Simon, and his command of the role, both vocally and dramatically, is already so certain that it is scarcely possible to imagine a better interpretation. Van Dam's voice has always been remarkable for definition of focus and range of dynamic, and on this occasion the beauty of the *legato*, the immense, burnished power, the delicacy of the *mezza voce* were quite overwhelming.' (*Opera*.)

Sadly, he seems adamant that his repertoire will never include Wotan in *Der Ring des Nibelungen*, mainly because he considers it a very dangerous role that has ruined many a voice. 'From the vocal point of view it's very long and not at all lyrical. You have to sing hours and hours of dialogue and power politics, and the single reward is the farewell to Brünnhilde. From this dramatic point of view I find it a bit too Germanic for me.' Having devoted most of his 'study-time' in 1983 to learning St Francis, he was looking forward to spending a great deal of 1984 'throwing myself into' Hans Sachs.

Memorizing St Francis was one of the main difficulties in this mammoth role; 'the music itself was no problem, but those phrases, repeated either with the same music but different words or vice versa, were. And, in performance, so were those constant changes of measure that necessitated my looking at the conductor all the time: and, of course, its length. But the role is very well-written for the voice and has a strong vocal line, something rare in contemporary music which, on the whole, tends to be anti-vocal and which I generally don't enjoy singing. Even Wozzeck is anti-vocal. But the character is so interesting dramatically that this more than compensates for the lack of vocal and musical satisfaction.'

Surprisingly, the portrayal of a spiritual giant like St Francis didn't have any lasting effects on his own spiritual development or psyche. Like most artists, he has the capacity of shedding his roles when he walks off stage, 'be they saintly, like St Francis or John the Baptist, or satanic, like Mephistopheles', otherwise he simply couldn't do the job. The mention of St John brought about a discussion of Jokanaan in Richard Strauss's *Salome*, which Van Dam recorded and later sang to universal acclaim at the 1977 Salzburg Festival under Karajan and, in spring 1986, at Covent Garden. 'Although both are holy men, Jokanaan is a totally different character and a totally different role from St Francis. It is very sharp and requires considerable bravura and a strong vocal and dramatic presence. The opera is about the confrontation between a primitive and an illumined being – an ascetic who has never before been confronted by, and is ignorant of, things like Salome's overwhelming and insatiable physical desire. Their confrontation comes to a head in their duet, which is the climax of the opera. But, although a duet, it is not a real dialogue, because each is really talking to himself and totally unable to see or comprehend the other's attitude and point of view. This is why Salome says, in the final scene when she is singing to Jokanaan's severed head, that "you never saw me, why did you never see me?" This sort of irreconcilable confrontation between very strong characters – also found in the duet between Philip II and the Grand Inquisitor in *Don Carlos* – is something that particularly excites Karajan and I think we succeeded in bringing out the drama of the work very strongly in the Salzburg production.'

As well as Jokanaan, Amfortas, the Flying Dutchman, Philip II, Escamillo and Rocco, Van Dam's collaboration with Karajan includes one of his most famous Mozart roles: Figaro, both on stage and on disc, in both cases generally to mixed reviews. He is aware that his interpretation of Figaro is controversial and not to everybody's liking. Peter Jonas, Managing Director of English National Opera, feels that Van Dam 'sings the aria "Tutto e tranquillo e placido" in the last act better than anybody. He lets it just ... unfold before you and it is an extraordinary moment.' Yet some people – probably the same as those who find his Dutchman insufficiently demonic – complain that his Figaro, although vocally marvellous, isn't funny enough. Van Dam's reply to them is that 'five minutes after the beginning of the opera Figaro discovers that his master, the Count, wants to make love to his fiancée. I find nothing funny in this! For up to now he has always thought of the Count, whom he had helped to woo his own bride, as much a friend as a master and knows all about his present peccadillos. The fact that the Count now wants to turn his attention to Figaro's bride-to-be wounds him through and through. All this is not at all funny. The only reason why Figaro has to use humour and cunning is that, because of his position, he is powerless to do anything else. He can only win or lose by his wits.

'The same is true of Leporello in *Don Giovanni*: in the balcony scene, Leporello is forced against his will to pretend to be his master and serenade Donna Elvira. It's easy enough to turn him into a grimacing clown, and many people do. But I think Leporello is intelligent and sensitive enough to be embarrassed by Elvira's humiliation, and his heart isn't in it. So, I feel it would be wrong to insert a comic element in this scene. After all, it's easy to make people laugh. But that's not the main reason why you're there, unless of course you are singing a comic role like Gianni Schicchi, which I sang with great joy at the Deutsche Oper in Berlin.'

Van Dam is a very quick learner, capable of memorizing Leporello in a fortnight and Wozzeck in three months. Yet he likes to spend a very long time on new roles – ideally a year between learning and performing – so that all its layers can filter through and become part of him. This probably accounts for the depth of reflection he brings to them, although the *kind* of preparation partly depends on the nature of the role at hand.

If it's based on a historical or literary character he will read all the available literature before starting his musical preparation. For example, when he 'felt the urge' to sing Philip II he read several historical biographies, as well as Schiller's play, on which Verdi's *Don Carlos* is based.

'But there is quite a difference between the real Philip II, Schiller's Philip II and Verdi's. And although my task is to interpret Verdi's, who happens to be the most human of the three, it is both interesting and useful to have this repository of background knowledge because it helps you gain insights into the character which you might not necessarily find in the libretto. For example, by reading Schiller I found out a lot about Philip's struggle with the Inquisition and the fact – never stated in the libretto – that Posa was a Protestant and that Philip knew it; and this helped my approach to the Philip II-Posa duet, one of the most beautiful Verdi ever wrote.' When Van Dam first sang this role, in Brussels in 1981, he showed his home town just why he is one of the most sought-after voices today. His range of dynamics, the focus and quality always superbly maintained, is truly astonishing and he gave a magnificent performance. Van Dam repeated his 'outstanding performance' (*Opernwelt*) of Philip II at the 1986 Salzburg Easter Festival.

Similarly, reading Goethe's *Faust* before singing Mephistopheles in Gounod's opera was immensely helpful. 'I was very curious to find out what this great classic was like, and I found it full of wonderful things, like Mephisto's extraordinary, acerbic retorts of which there is no trace in the libretto used by Gounod and barely a hint in the text of Berlioz's *La Damnation de Faust*. But this discovery, in Goethe, of Mephisto's pronounced ironic streak helped crystallize my view of him as someone out to amuse himself. Being Satan, the god of Evil, he is omniscient and therefore knows the future in advance. But his sarcastic, sardonic side makes him want to amuse himself by seeing it happen. So, although it's true that the clues to every operatic character are contained in the score, this kind of pre-preparatory work helps form a sort of underpinning for your interpretation.'

After completing any necessary literary or historical research Van Dam begins his musical preparation, and usually works alone until he has memorized both text and score. Then he sings through the score with a coach, to see if his judgement of tempi is correct. Text and score are memorized simultaneously and in some cases, including most Italian roles, the music helps the memorization of the words, while the reverse is true of Amfortas and most German roles. While studying, he tries to concentrate on *what* he is singing without bothering too much about any potential vocal difficulties, because he feels that once he understands *how* the part should be sung the vocal side usually takes care of itself. But when tackling an exceptionally difficult role, like Wozzeck, he works with a coach *while* actually memorizing it. Then he tapes those sessions and later works on them alone, listening, criticizing and correcting himself.

'Wozzeck is undoubtedly *the* most taxing and wearing role in my entire repertoire,' he sighs. 'Even more difficult than the Dutchman, because of the enormous emotional strain it imposes on the interpreter. Vocally, it's easy, for the simple reason that there's hardly anything to sing. It's more of an actor's part than a singer's, and its single *technical* difficulty is its length, because Wozzeck is present in all but two of the fifteen scenes, which means that, if you are singing in a house where the dressing-rooms are far from the stage, you have to hang around and never leave the stage during the entire performance.

'From the dramatic point of view, however, the role is a colossal challenge. You have to portray a man at the end of his tether, on the verge of a breakdown, who only manages to keep himself together through an almost superhuman effort at self-control. This is obvious right from the first scene in which he is shaving the Captain. Every time the latter addresses him and calls his name, "Wozzeck", he snaps, or rather jerks, to attention as if hit by a whip. You sense that it would only take a trifle to trigger off a complete collapse; and what does eventually trigger it off is by no means a trifle. For Wozzeck's entire existence revolves around Marie and their child, for whose sake he submits to a life of victimization and intimidation at the hands of his superiors, just to be able to bring her a little extra cash. And when he finds out that she is unfaithful – even though the Drum-major might be her umpteenth lover, he is the first that Wozzeck himself knows about – his whole world crumbles and he goes to pieces. Despite the tragic ending, the sheer strength and intensity of this man's love makes Wozzeck one of the most beautiful love stories in all opera. I love it most especially. But it takes a lot out of me. I would certainly hate having to unwind all alone afterwards.'

Being away from home and frequently alone after a performance is a sacrifice most singers have to make, for no one has managed to carve an international career by staying at home. But Van Dam finds that it was a sacrifice that seemed much easier twenty years ago, when he was young; because about seven years ago, after two broken marriages, he suddenly re-met and married his first love, the woman whom he had been in love with at the age of seventeen. Life had separated them, both of them had got married, each had had a child and then got divorced. Then after all those years, they met again and felt just the same as before, 'as if', Van Dam says, 'my emotional life had stopped at the age of seventeen and was resumed after I found Christiane again.

'Now I feel that at last I have attained a certain balance, because an artist's life is a peripatetic life, a life of dreams. What we lack and desperately need is reality, something we can be sure of and rely on, an anchor. I was conscious of this need even twenty-five years ago, at the beginning of my career; and finally, I have found it. But the problem is that, having found it, I am loath to leave home and travel on my own. I just miss it too much. My wife cannot always travel with me because we have a big farmhouse outside Brussels where we live with our two children – hers and mine – and a huge menagerie of cats, dogs, goats, cows and horses. On top of which she actually *hates* travelling. So, because both parties should get what they need out of a marriage, we compromise a little. But for me, who used to set off for anywhere quite lightheartedly, these separations are a real trauma, and if, for example, I'm singing at the Paris Opéra, I'll drive all the way to Belgium after the performance, just to be at home, something I never used to do before. I'm conscious of having found, or refound, or discovered something that many singers may never find . . . and since our re-meeting, I'm aware of having grown and developed both as an artist and as a man. I love my work as much as ever. In fact, as I mentioned before, those *Sternstunden* I am sometimes lucky enough to be part of are the greatest joy in my life. But now I'm aware that there are other things in life besides a career and that it would be nice to experience some of them sometime – maybe in about ten years' time, around the age of fifty-five, when it will be time to start retiring and gradually limiting my engagements to about fifteen a year. The rest of the time I would spend at home, teaching and trying to pass on some of the experience I have gained after so many years in this profession.'

Van Dam's own first singing teacher was the Jesuit priest who ran the choir in his neighbourhood church in Brussels. A family friend who heard José, then aged eleven, singing in his room, convinced his parents that the boy was good enough to sing in public. They were simple folk – his father was a carpenter and there had never been musicians in the family before – but as soon as the priest took José into his choir and recommended piano lessons and *solfège*, they acquiesced and henceforth did everything in their power to encourage and help their son. At the age of thirteen José was taken to Professor Frédéric Anspach of the Brussels Conservatoire, who nursed him through his voice break and subsequent years as a student at the Conservatoire, where he received his Diploma in Lyric Art in 1960.

Almost immediately after his graduation he was hired by the Paris Opéra, where he remained for four years and sang small but important parts like Marcello and Colline in *La Bohème* and Angelotti in *Tosca*. Then, in 1965, he joined the Geneva Opera for two years and then went to the Deutsche Oper in Berlin, where he sang most of his major roles for the first time. While still a young singer, he did some radio and television work in his spare time. When he listens to tapes of some early broadcasts today, he is struck by the fact that his voice was already that of a man of thirty, even though its range, from a low F to C, was considerably narrower and shorter at both ends than now. It has since stretched by about a third at each end and stabilized to its present range about fifteen years ago. He will be forever grateful to Professor Anspach for dissuading him from trying to stretch it forcibly and for pointing out that this would happen by itself, with time.

'He was absolutely right. With the natural expansion that comes from singing regularly the voice got both broader and bigger, something that should always be allowed to happen naturally. You should never *force* a voice by trying to make it bigger. What you *can* do, but only very gradually and very carefully indeed, is to stretch and broaden its range, semitone by semitone, through specific vocal exercises, a little bit like trying to stretch an elastic band. Try to visualize pulling at either end of an elastic band: as long as it "gives" it's all right. But as soon as it's fully stretched, you should stop pulling at once, or it will snap and lose elasticity at the opposite end. It's the same with the voice. If you forced it, you would automatically lose some notes either at the top or the bottom. You should develop it very, very gently and very, very gradually. This may take years, which is why I sometimes feel that the greatest gift young singers can possess is patience; for they cannot expect their voice to follow them. It is *they* who must follow their voice. And instead of thinking "I want to sing this or that role" they should first wait until they have the voice for those roles and *then* sing them!'

THE BASS

The lowest male singing voice, with a compass from F below to F above the stave, in the bass clef. Basses are usually divided into basso cantante *and* basso profondo, *the latter being ideal for Russian roles, while the former (which literally means a singing bass) denotes a bass voice especially suited to melodic delivery and lyric roles.*

PAATA BURCHULADZE

In June 1984 Covent Garden mounted an expensive, star-studded new production of *Aida* conducted by Zubin Mehta and directed by Jean-Pierre Ponnelle, with Luciano Pavarotti as Radames and Katia Ricciarelli in the title role. But Pavarotti caught a virus and had to sing the premiere with a temperature, Ricciarelli got booed and so did the producer, and almost everything about the project was judged to be a disaster. Except for one thing: a young, unknown Georgian bass in a secondary role who, in a classic case of 'a star is born', became an overnight sensation. For, as the editor of *Opera*, Harold Rosenthal, wrote in his review, echoing the verdict of the first-night audience who gave the young unknown an ecstatic ovation, 'the evening's best singing came from the Russian bass Paata Burchuladze, making his Covent Garden debut as Ramfis. He possesses a huge, beautifully produced voice allied to an imposing stage presence. He dominated every scene in which he appeared and was by far the best Ramfis I have heard since Ezio Pinza.' The *Guardian* hailed 'a thrilling promise for the future'.

It was on the strength of this single, extraordinary performance that, on the spot, I decided to include Burchuladze in this book. It is rare indeed for an unknown, twenty-nine-year-old singer to arrive at an international opera house for a secondary role and end up dominating a cast of major stars. It is equally unusual for such a house to sign up a young unknown, also on the spot, at the end of their audition. Yet this is precisely what Covent Garden – to whose principals belongs the credit of launching Burchuladze's international career – did, a year before, and the reason is obvious. Here, at last, is a glorious, firm, resonant bass voice huge in size and dark in colour – *The Economist* referred to it as 'coal-black' – capable of thrilling even the most jaded critic or opera buff.

In an age when opera has made huge dramatic strides but the shortage of good, let alone great, voices is such that singers often have to be cast in roles for which they are ill-suited, inadequate and ill-equipped, the emergence of a great voice is a major and exhilarating event. The exhilaration is intensified when the great voice in question is also capable of interpretation, as was the case with Burchuladze, whose 'bullet-headed Ramfis, sonorous and malevolent, impassively watched his opponents destroy themselves' (*The Times*).

How did he manage to make such an impact and render a secondary role so important and dominant? 'Because Ramfis *is* important!' answered Burchuladze. 'He is the power behind the throne and controls everything in Egypt. It is he, rather than Pharaoh, who decides when war should be declared, what the punishment for treason should be, and who endorses Amneris's wish to marry Radames. In the opening scene he is on his way to the palace to announce *his* choice of leader for the Egyptian armies to Pharaoh, and all the latter has to do is ratify this choice. Throughout the opera, he is given plenty of time and scope to demonstrate his dominance: the Nile scene, the trial scene, his confrontation with the repentant and distraught Amneris. The only instance where Pharaoh is seen to override his wish is the triumph scene, where he supports Radames's request for clemency towards the Ethiopian prisoners. In everything else Ramfis is victorious and his power should be reflected and be made apparent in his singing. This crucial point is the most interesting thing about the role, which presents no vocal problems. But it should be sung not just with a beautiful voice. What it needs is an *important* voice that mirrors Ramfis's omnipotence.' Burchuladze's highly individual interpretation – which introduced a hitherto unknown 'political' dimension by emphasizing this theme of power and its manipulation into an opera usually presented as a tragic love story and a clash between public duty and private passion – was developed during rehearsals with Jean-Pierre Ponnelle.

Since this historic triumph at Covent Garden, Burchuladze has been hailed as 'the second Chaliapin' by no less a man than Herbert von Karajan, who signed him up to sing the Commendatore in his recording, and forthcoming 1987 Salzburg Festival production, of *Don Giovanni*. At the time of writing Burchuladze was singing Walter in Verdi's *Luisa Miller* at the Vienna State Opera and had just sung *I lombardi* at La Scala, where he will also open the 1986-7 season as Zaccaria in a production of *Nabucco* conducted by Riccardo Muti, which will subsequently be taken to the 1987 Berlin Festival. He will also return to London for three concerts in 1986 – two Verdi *Requiems*, one under Maazel and one under Giulini, plus an Albert Hall Prom – and in 1987 for Don Basilio in *Il barbiere di Siviglia* and 1989 for Silva in *Ernani* at Covent Garden. In January 1987 he will also make his debut at the Paris Opéra in a performance of the Verdi *Requiem* with Luciano Pavarotti.

Thirty-one-year-old Burchuladze, born in Tiflis, is proud of his Georgian origins and of everything Georgian: the language, the landscape, the wine, the countryside and the local opera house. According to his mother, a singing teacher, he began to sing almost before he could speak. He studied the piano for seven years at school, while also taking singing lessons for three years, enrolling at the Tiflis Conservatoire. At the time he had no intention of pursuing a professional career in music and, while spending his days at the Conservatoire, he also studied engineering at night classes at the local technical university. He also got married at the time, and now has two sons, aged thirteen and four.

The first role he sang at the opera workshop of the Conservatoire was Mephistopheles in Gounod's *Faust*, at the age of twenty-two which, according to everyone, was too young for such a demanding role. Indeed, Burchuladze confesses that a cassette he has of this performance 'makes me laugh!'. Nevertheless it was considered a great success at the time and helped draw attention to him. 'Despite my youth, I obviously sang it correctly. Because if you weren't singing this role correctly, you couldn't get through it to the end. It's a fascinating part, full of irony and subtle jest. Naturally, at twenty-two I experienced a lot of vocal problems which are now non-existent. The Garden scene, for instance, demands a great deal of professionalism which of course I lacked. Another major problem was the end of the "Serenade", where Mephistopheles has to burst into ironic laughter. In my experience only Boris Christoff does this exactly the way it's written: not as straightforward laughter, but a sort of laughter sung on the notes.'

In 1978, at the age of twenty-three, Burchuladze was one of a handful of four or five Soviet singers chosen annually to study at the singing school of La Scala in Milan, as part of an exchange that allows six Italian dancers to study at the Bolshoi. Burchuladze points out that Italian singing is very different from Russian, and 'while the Russian style comes naturally to me, I had to work terribly, terribly hard at perfecting my Italian singing. I needed to be steeped in it and my time in Italy was invaluable. For you cannot sing Philip II in *Don Carlos* the Russian way. It would sound awful! And that's exactly what I was doing when I arrived in Italy!'

One of the main problems encountered by Russian singers when singing Italian roles is, according to Sir John Tooley, General Director of the Royal Opera House, Covent Garden, their tendency to waffle a bit, because they are taught in a way that makes them want to push the voice back, in order to make a bigger sound, instead of focussing and centring it. 'This relates to the fact that Russian singing requires a very big, rather than a focussed, slimmed-down sound which is what is needed for the perfect singing of Italian opera. In wanting to make the voice bigger, Russian singers tend to push it back so they can fill it sideways. But in doing this they lose some of the sharp focussing and forward projection, and what actually happens is that, in trying to make a bigger sound, a voice that isn't well-centred will go even further back and the sound will come out waffly. It's all a question of centring: this centring can mean a slimmer sound than perhaps they want to hear. But this is exactly the kind of sound the Italians – and I, too – want to hear.' This is a point which, according to many, Burchuladze, who as Sir John also points out 'has a truly amazing voice', still has to come to grips with more fully.

In Milan he studied the entire Verdi bass repertoire with Giulietta Simionato and Professors Beltrami and Müller, who pointed out that Verdi basses and baritones should have big, important voices to enable them to sing long, flowing lines effortlessly, with full power but without ever forcing the voice. They also taught him how to produce those long lines and the evenness of colour essential to Italian singing, and worked on interpretation. He remarks that for Verdi and Puccini in particular 'a *beautiful* voice is a must, whereas in Bellini one could get away with just singing very well. From the vocal point of view, the easiest to sing is Verdi because his music is very beautiful and well written and because he understood singers. It is easier, for example, for a bass to sing an F above the stave in Verdi than in any other composer because, with his understanding of the voice, he makes it easier for you to climb up to it.'

Since then, Burchuladze has studied several Verdi roles, including Silva in *Ernani*, Zaccaria in *Nabucco*, Banquo in *Macbeth*, Philip II in *Don Carlos*, Fiesco in *Simon Boccanegra*, which he will sing at the 1987 Maggio Musicale Fiorentino, and Padre Guardiano in *La forza del destino*, which he has also recorded for Deutsche Grammophon and which he particularly enjoyed singing because 'he is a very clean, unique person who always thinks high thoughts and has the truth and the good of others at heart. Everything he does is motivated by altruism and the desire to smooth other people's paths, console and guide them. His music is also very serene and it's important to sing it in a way that radiates tranquillity and inner peace.'

Burchuladze points out that the Italian style is 'very melodious and differs drastically from Russian singing, where the drama contained in certain words dictates they should be emphasized at the expense of the musical line and evenness of colour. This is something you should never do when singing Philip II or any Italian role. But you *must* do it when singing Boris. In fact one shouldn't even talk of singing Boris but of "doing" Boris because the role doesn't contain all that much singing, in the classic sense of the word. One can talk of singing a role like Silva in *Ernani* which contains long, melodious *bel canto* lines. But Boris is different. A lot of his phrases shouldn't be sung at all, but gasped, shrieked or uttered with an anguished groan. [Other great interpreters of this role, like Nicolai Ghiaurov, disagree.] It's a highly dramatic role and the anguished nature of Boris demands sounds that cannot be classified as "singing". Of course, in this sense, Boris is an exceptional case. But even more lyrical Russian roles, like Prince Gremin in *Eugene Onegin*, should never be sung in an even, belcantistic, Italianate way. This would be as wrong as singing Verdi in the Russian style; because although the music is by Tchaikovsky and consequently softer, more romantic and more melodious than Mussorgsky's, Gremin is still a Russian role and should therefore be sung more dramatically, with uneven emphasis placed on certain words and a lot of *rubato*.'

Burchuladze greatly enjoys singing this role because Gremin's single aria in Act IV is long, important and consists of beautiful music. Also because 'Gremin is a good man, a good person. His aria is all about love, his love for his wife, and should be sung with great feeling and sincerity. Technically, it should be sung more lightly than the heavier Russian roles, which is rather difficult for me especially when, as in this case, the *tessitura* is rather high. From the dramatic point of view I see him as a wise, sophisticated man of the world who realizes Tatyana doesn't love him in the same way that he does, because when an old man marries a much younger woman he is prepared and ready for everything. Yet he is sure of her and of her behaviour because the Russian aristocracy were very intelligent about observing certain conventions regardless of personal feelings.' Burchuladze first sang Gremin at the Tiflis Opera – and will do so at the Rhenische Staatsbühne in Bonn in 1987 – where, on his return from Italy, he was engaged as a full-time member. It was there that he also sang the title role in *Boris Godunov*, for the first time, at the age of twenty-nine.

He realizes Boris is a role he will probably go on singing and developing throughout his career, because 'it is the kind of role you can keep on exploring without ever plumbing its depths fully. This is why there are as many interpretations of Boris as there are basses. I have read a lot about the history of the period and don't see him as a bloodthirsty tyrant, as he is sometimes portrayed. I see him as a humane and solitary man, weighed down by the burden of power and unable to sleep because of his guilt about the part he may have played in the murder of the young Tsarevitch. But I don't think he was directly responsible for this murder. If he were, it wouldn't haunt and drive him to the brink of madness in this way. I see him as a patriot who loves his country passionately and wants to serve it by putting an end to the lawlessness generated by the endless power struggles among the nobles, and who is concerned about the plight of the people. I think what actually happened was that Boris – like Henry II of England, whose casual remark "will no one rid me of this troublesome priest" led to the murder of Thomas Becket – probably made some inadvertent remark about it being expedient for the young heir to be removed, and that this was enough for some minions to take the law into their own hands and murder the child. I'm quite sure this is what must have happened because it explains both the *kind* and the extent of Boris's guilt. For he is clearly a very emotional man and this very human side of his predominates in my interpretation.'

Burchuladze stresses that singers should have solved all vocal and technical problems before tackling this role. 'The voice should be fully developed and you should be in full technical command of it. If you were to start worrying about hitting this or that high note, everything would be ruined because you would immediately find yourself outside the character instead of being wholly immersed in his anguish. This is why Boris is not a part for young singers.' (Burchuladze sang it at twenty-nine!) 'Like Verdi's Otello, it requires psychological as well as vocal maturity. Of course, there is always the danger that, by the time you've matured as a man, the voice may no longer be intact, or there at all! But you must judge when the right balance between the two has been reached. That is the right moment to sing Boris.'

Burchuladze feels that Mussorgsky is the most difficult Russian composer to sing, along with Rachmaninov. Tchaikovsky is easier, because he is more melodious. In September 1985 Burchuladze gave a recital at London's Wigmore Hall consisting of Mussorgsky and Rachmaninov songs – plus the Clock scene and the Death of Boris. He had spent three years preparing those songs, which he had included in several recitals, and says that after one has sung them *any* operatic role seems easy in comparison. 'That's how difficult they are. Rachmaninov in particular demands great finesse because you have to sing *piano* and *legato* even in phrases containing high or low notes, which is always more difficult than singing such phrases with full power and requires tremendous voice control. But while Rachmaninov is more difficult vocally, Mussorgsky is more emotional and difficult psychologically and dramatically, if you want to communicate the full meaning in those songs [the *Songs and Dances of Death* cycle], which are all about death.'

The composition of a recital – i.e. the sequence in which the songs are placed – is crucial to its success, especially, explains Burchuladze, when the songs deal 'with gloomy subjects. It's always important to begin and end "crescendo", which is why I chose to end my Wigmore Hall recital with something gay like "The Goat" and "The Flea".'

The recital drew reviews as enthusiastic as those that greeted his London debut. 'The young Georgian bass stunned and delighted a full house with an all-Russian programme. We were stunned simply by the gigantic size, the prodigious range and the thick, rich timbre of his voice. The delight came later, as he dropped the solemn mask and revealed a winning, indeed grinning, personality in Mussorgsky's "The Goat" and, inevitably as an encore, "The Flea", both done with stylised but undeniably comic gestures', wrote *The Times*. Burchuladze considers this recital an important moment in his career and cannot understand singers who don't enjoy singing *Lieder*. 'One should be a musician as well as an opera singer. A song recital requires greater finesse and delicacy than an operatic performance because you have to concentrate even harder and pack a great deal of emotion into a song lasting only a few minutes – and this without the aid of a plot, sets or costumes.'

The chain of events that led to Burchuladze's British debuts and the consequent launch of his international career began in 1981, when he returned to Italy from Tiflis to take part in the Voci Verdiane Competition at Busseto, where he was the youngest contestant and won second prize (no first prize was awarded that year). The following year he won first prize and the Gold Medal at the Tchaikovsky Competition in Moscow, where a British member of the jury, James Robertson, was so impressed that on his return to Britain he told some friends at Ibbs & Tillett about him. It was this respected firm of agents who arranged Burchuladze's first trip to Britain in 1983, when he sang a recital at the Warwick Arts Trust, a performance of Elgar's *The Dream of Gerontius* at the Lichfield Festival and gave that all-important audition at Covent Garden.

Burchuladze has now been principal bass at the Tiflis Opera, which remains his base, for several years. His contract stipulates that he sing four different operas a month. He is allowed to travel freely, as long as he makes up for his quota on his return. Sometimes this means six or seven performances a week. As Tiflis is one of the two Soviet opera houses where everything is sung in the original language – the other is the opera house at Talinn in Estonia – this can mean singing Boris in Russian one night, followed by Leporello in Italian and Jokanaan in German in quick succession.

Away from singing, the principal passion of this amiable, barrel-chested *bon viveur*, once an accomplished rugby-player, is hunting – bears, wild boar, pheasants and moorhens – in the reputedly breathtakingly beautiful Georgian mountains.

Burchuladze is also on the teaching staff of the Tiflis Conservatoire. He greatly enjoys this part of his work and feels pride in being able to repay, to some extent, the great debt he feels he owes the Soviet educational system, which encourages and nurtures budding talent by providing it with all the means it needs in order to grow. He is therefore happy to give young singers the benefit of his own experience and is particularly enthusiastic about one of them, a twenty-five-year-old bass-baritone called Sandro Tomadze, a graduate from the Georgian Academy of Dramatic Art who, he is convinced, will also embark on a major career within two years.

From the technical point of view, Burchuladze feels that the most important aspect of vocal training is correct voice placement, because resonators are crucial to good singing. 'I could sing a performance with a sore throat but never with catarrh congestion, because that would block the resonating cavities,' he points out. As far as breathing is concerned he is, like Carlo Bergonzi, an advocate of natural breathing and does not recommend complicated or exaggerated methods of breath support. 'It is better to breathe normally than to take huge intakes of breath, because all this extra air needs more time to be exhaled. I recommend normal breathing even for high notes. It's always best to breathe normally and not *think* about them, but just sing them from love, because you are lost in the music. This way, you will never encounter vocal problems in any roles.' (Herbert von Karajan made precisely the same point when discussing voices in his chapter in my previous book, *Maestro*.)

One of the most difficult things for Russian students to learn and come to terms with is classical singing in general and Mozart in particular for, according to Burchuladze, 'the tradition for it doesn't exist here. Mozart is the polar opposite of Russian music, and his style is even more difficult for us, Russians, to master than the Italian. Russian singing allows you to give out any amount of emotion. But Mozart demands that all emotion be contained within a strict classical form, both technically and dramatically. His style is totally pure, precise and crystalline and all the emotion is there, in the music. You cannot change a single note and you cannot add anything. A certain decorum must be observed at all times and even the most extreme feelings must be expressed within the confines of good taste and the convention of the times, all of which amounts to a very tight corset. And this is something, very, very difficult for us Russians.'

Burchuladze's two Mozart roles to date are Leporello – which he studied with Simionato in Italy, has sung many a time at Tiflis, and is due to sing at the Bolshoi – and the Commendatore in *Don Giovanni*, on disc with Karajan. He has strong ideas about Leporello and dislikes portrayals that make him too much of a buffoon. 'The role wasn't written to be exaggerated. Leporello is funny in certain moments, of course, but he is not a clown. If he were the vulgar creature he is often made out to be his loyalty and concern for Don Giovanni at the finale wouldn't make sense. He would, in fact, have left his service long ago. As it is, he's always talking about leaving, but never actually does so for the simple reason that he *can't*. He can't live without Don Giovanni, who is a magnet to which he is drawn, indeed glued, by some very potent force. But he is not afraid of pointing out the errors of his behaviour to him, because he has a strong conventional moral sense. Vocally it is a difficult role because Leporello never stands still. He's always running around and at the finale he has to crouch under the table and sing from this awkward position, which is always hard.'

The Commendatore he considers more of a Verdian than a Mozartian role, and as such it presents no problems for a big voice like his. 'The Commendatore is a man who speaks with the authority of Heaven and therefore, like Ramfis in *Aida*, requires a big, resonant voice projected with full power. The *tessitura*, which is not very low, presents no problems.' Burchuladze relished the experience of recording this role with Karajan, whom he idolizes and who, at the end of his audition, had burst into loud applause and declared he was looking forward to working with Burchuladze 'for many years'!

Apart from the forthcoming production of *Don Giovanni* at the 1987 Salzburg Festival, Burchuladze is also due to sing Silva in *Ernani* with Zubin Mehta, has just recorded Ramfis in *Aida* for Decca – who after his triumph in that role at Covent Garden immediately recorded a disc of Verdi and Russian arias, released in 1985 – and is greatly looking forward to singing the title role in Boito's *Mefistofele* in Tiflis, in a production directed by Ramaz Chkhikvadze, the celebrated actor and director of the world-famous Rustaveli Theatre Company (whose performance and production of Shakespeare's *Richard III* at London's Round House in

1980 was one of the most memorable theatrical events of the past decade). He is also learning Fiesco in *Simon Boccanegra* and Philip II and looks forward to singing all the Verdi bass roles in the future. He would like to sing some Bellini, including Oroveso in *Norma* and Count Rodolfo in *La sonnambula*. One day he would also like to sing the title role in *Don Giovanni*, 'perhaps in the way Siepi performed him' which, as he told *The Times*, 'was always the best'. He is certainly aware that his voice is growing and developing all the time. 'It is constantly changing. It is different now, at thirty-one, than it was two years ago and will go on changing and developing for at least another ten years. If it had already reached its peak, I'd be finished!'

NICOLAI GHIAUROV

'The point of arrival, the climax, in the career of every bass is singing Boris Godunov. Because of the extreme complexity of the character, the role requires an artist with considerable stage experience, both vocal and dramatic. Someone once rightly said that inside Boris there is the equivalent of a Hamlet and two Macbeths and it takes maximum emotional and dramatic concentration, plus the fullest range of vocal colours at a singer's disposal, to express this state of mind,' explained Bulgarian-born Nicolai Ghiaurov, the celebrated bass, after giving a profoundly moving performance of this role (for the umpteenth time in his long and distinguished career) at the Vienna State Opera in 1985, at the age of fifty-six.

Not surprisingly, he felt rather worn after delivering such an emotion-packed performance and recalled his singing teacher, the former baritone Christo Brambarov, who told him that after singing Boris he was barely able to speak, not because he was vocally tired but because of the extreme emotional exhaustion involved in bringing this anguished character to life. 'And, I must say, I found this to be absolutely true. When I first started singing Boris I used to give so much of myself that after the Clock scene I had great difficulty in finding the necessary strength to continue to the end. But gradually, with experience, I managed to find a way of controlling myself. It's crucial for every artist to strike the right balance between total abandon to a character's emotion and the detachment necessary for maintaining technical control of one's performance. In youth, one tends to allow oneself to be totally swept away by the emotional surge suggested by the music and the dramatic action and it's all too easy to exhaust and burn oneself out before the end.'

All great singing-actors – like Domingo, Vickers, Allen and Raimondi – experience this problem and have to guard against the over-involvement so natural to truly dramatic animals and all stress the need for every artist to find a solution for himself. Feodor Chaliapin, one of the greatest singing-actors in operatic history, was also plagued by this tendency to over-immerse himself in the characters he portrayed and explained in his memoirs, *Pages from my Life*, that, whenever he came to the kind of scene that sends shivers down the spines of the audience, he tried to single out someone in the wings and smile at them, in order to stop himself from getting too involved in the action; because if he did, he might begin to cry. And the moment *that* happened, he pointed out, the audience would begin to laugh! 'Chaliapin was dead right,' adds Ghiaurov. 'Our task is not to display our *own* emotion to the public, but to draw just enough of it out of ourselves to make the necessary imaginative link that will make a character like Boris real to *them*.'

Ghiaurov is himself a great singing-actor in the Chaliapin/Callas mould whose portrayals never fail to illumine and bring his roles to life in a most compelling way. As Sir John Tooley puts it, he is 'a great, great artist. His voice is not, perhaps, one of the most *beautiful* bass sounds. But what he did, and still does, with it is quite amazing.' Ghiaurov has sung Boris Godunov in every major theatre and most music festivals in the world, and is renowned as one of the role's great interpreters. He felt particularly proud and gratified by the fact that he was still able to sing it with distinction at the age of fifty-six because, artistic satisfaction apart, he feels that his vocal longevity – like that of Carlo Bergonzi, Nicolai Gedda, Alfredo Kraus and Jon Vickers – vindicates the solid foundations on which he based his career: six years of vocal training (first with Christo Brambarov in 1949-50 and then five years at the Moscow Conservatoire), and readiness to follow his teacher's advice about choice and timing of repertoire.

'Those of my generation who still sing big roles at our age are only able to do so because we allowed ourselves time, a lot of time, before embarking on them in the first place. When I first went to study with Brambarov, for instance, we spent an entire year working on just one octave of the voice – just vocal exercises. Today, most teachers think their pupils can start working on interpretation straight away, before their voices are ready or adequately trained. Of course, singers themselves are partly to blame for this. They are avid for rapid results and a hasty rise to fame, something they are neither prepared nor equipped for. But it never works in the long run, which is why nowadays so many careers tend to be short-lived.'

In 1985 Ghiaurov celebrated twenty-five years on the stage. Born in 1929 in the small provincial town of Velingrad in Bulgaria, he loved singing and had a good treble. His parents, who were too poor to afford a musical instrument, encouraged him to show off, sing and play his mouth-organ at parties. When his voice broke, his teachers at school advised him to stop singing for a while. But his love of, and interest in, music continued. He learnt to play the clarinet, the violin and the trombone by borrowing instruments from friends, as his parents's poverty meant he couldn't have his own. His main ambition at the time (surely significant in view of the great dramatic gift he brings to operatic interpretation), was to become an actor and he appeared in several plays, including Sardou's *Tosca* and Daudet's *L'Arlesienne*, at the tiny local theatre of his native town.

His voice was 'discovered' during his national service, when he played the clarinet in the small army orchestra and also helped rehearse the army chorus. During the course of a rehearsal he sang a few phrases as an example to the chorus, and an officer who had a good tenor voice asked Ghiaurov if he would like an introduction to a good singing teacher, Christo Brambarov, then a celebrated baritone at the Sofia Opera House. Ghiaurov duly sought Brambarov out and auditioned for him. But, much to his disappointment, although Brambarov's verdict was that the young bass certainly had the potential for a professional career, he was himself too busy to teach him, and advised him to go to the Conservatoire. Fortunately, at the last army concert before demobilization, Ghiaurov was the soloist in a cantata by the blind Bulgarian composer Petko Staikov. The composer was so impressed by Ghiaurov's voice that he personally called the Conservatoire and arranged for his admittance. Confronted with this news, Brambarov relented, agreed to teach the promising young bass at the same time and has remained his mentor and adviser throughout the years.

Brambarov had the advantage of being steeped in the tradition of Italian singing. He had studied for seven or eight years in Milan, heard all the greats of the past like Aureliano Pertile, and carried the tradition of the old Italian *bel canto* school to Bulgaria. Such familiarity with Italian singing is rare in Slav countries, as Paata Burchuladze points out in his chapter, so Ghiaurov was especially fortunate in his teacher. Indeed when, many years later, he gave a charity recital at the Casa Verdi in Milan (a charity institution founded by Verdi for old retired singers) an aged tenor walked up to him and asked: 'Tell, me, did you study in Italy? You sound as if you did!' Equally important was Brambarov's psychological sensitivity and knack for penetrating and getting to know his pupil's character well. He warned Ghiaurov not to expect to become a second Chaliapin overnight but to study hard and patiently for at least five years, not by himself but *with* his teacher. His methods were vindicated by the result at the examinations held at the Conservatoire at the end of the first year, when Ghiaurov's exemplary rendition of a church canon – Brambarov still felt it was too early for operatic arias – so impressed the jury that they decided to give this promising pupil a scholarship for study in an even better academy: the Moscow Conservatoire.

Ghiaurov spent five years, 1950–5, in Moscow and this was a crucial time not only for his vocal development but also for his overall artistic growth. 'I tried to enlarge and enrich my cultural horizons as much as possible by sampling the rich and varied cultural life Moscow had to offer: first-rate theatres, the Bolshoi Ballet, symphonic and chamber concerts, museums and galleries. I also became friendly with many of the great artists around, actors, authors and musicians alike, such as the Armenian composer Aram Khatchaturian, the violinists David Oistrakh and Leonid Kogan and the eminent stage and film actor Cherkassov, who starred in Eisenstein's films *Alexander Nevsky* and *Ivan the Terrible*. My close contact with artists of such calibre helped me mature as an artist.' He also relished the stimulating atmosphere at the Conservatoire, steeped in the heritage and tradition of Tchaikovsky and boasting excellent chamber groups and an active opera workshop where pupils were taught by eminent theatrical and operatic stage directors of the day. It was here that he sang Don Basilio in Rossini's *Il barbiere di Siviglia* for his final examination, after which he was awarded the Conservatoire's highest distinction, the Gold Medal, on his graduation.

After a short spell in Leningrad, Ghiaurov returned to Sofia to begin his professional career and resume his studies with Brambarov, who taught him 'the science of singing. He told me the conductors I would soon begin working with would tell me how they wanted me to sing this or that and it was his duty to give me the instrument with which to fulfil their wishes' (*Opera*). This was in 1955, which was to prove a crucial and lucky year for Ghiaurov: he won a *grand prix* at a singing competition in Paris and this opened the eyes of the bureaucracy-ridden Bulgarian Ministry of Culture who, on Ghiaurov's return from Moscow – despite his Gold Medal from the Moscow Conservatoire and Brambarov's protests – had assigned him to a third-rate provincial theatre. Now they changed their minds and Ghiaurov was immediately engaged as a principal bass at the Sofia Opera House, where he made his debut during the same year as Basilio in a production of *Il barbiere di Siviglia* that was subsequently filmed. At the same time he also made some recordings of Russian songs which, according to the British critic Alan Blyth, author of *Opera on*

Record, 'reveal the rich, steady quality of his tone, the evenness of emission, evidence and reward of his long training' (*Opera*).

After a year in Sofia Ghiaurov was invited back to Moscow where, in 1957, he made his Bolshoi debut as Pimen in *Boris Godunov* and also sang Mephistopheles in Gounod's *Faust*, in Russian. The following year he also sang this role, in Italian, in Bologna. In 1960 he made his debut at La Scala as Varlaam in a production of *Boris Godunov* with fellow-Bulgarian Boris Christoff in the title role, and his Vienna debut in a recital. 1962 was another crucial year that saw his Salzburg Festival debut in the Verdi *Requiem* and his Covent Garden debut as Padre Guardiano in *La forza del destino*, followed by his American debut, in 1963, as Mephistopheles at the Chicago Lyric Opera. The Hamburg and the Vienna State Operas followed suit and his now fully fledged international career culminated with his Metropolitan Opera debut and his assumption of the title role in *Boris Godunov* at the Salzburg Festival, both in 1965.

Ghiaurov had followed Brambarov's advice diligently and refrained from tackling Boris during the first ten years of his professional career. By the time he sang it in 1965 he already knew the work well, first because during his student days in Moscow he had attended numerous rehearsals and performances at the Bolshoi Theatre – which boasts a traditional, fifty-year-old 'museum piece' production preserved as a relic of the authenticity of the period – and second because, as already mentioned, he had sung the roles of Pimen and Varlaam. Indeed, when he made his debut at La Scala in the latter role the administration also asked him to sing the title role in the final performances, after Christoff's departure. 'But I said no, I prefer to wait.'

It proved a wise and fortunate decision, for five years later Ghiaurov was to sing Boris at the Salzburg Festival in a production conducted and directed by Herbert von Karajan, 'a stupendous occasion that gave me enormous joy. Karajan was passionate about this work and the character of Boris and his musical interpretation was simply breathtaking. During rehearsals he took all the cast to see Eisenstein's film of *Ivan the Terrible* so they could steep themselves in the atmosphere of the period. His concentration, down to the minutest detail, was such that he understood the work to the limits of what is possible for a non-Russian speaker. Mussorgsky managed to interpret and take Pushkin's text a stage further, through his music, and no translation ever wholly captures the cohesion between his score and the original text. But Karajan's genius and extreme emotional sensitivity overcame this handicap and helped him find just the right orchestral colours and accents.'

Karajan's Salzburg production was very different from the Bolshoi staging and was characterized by extremely brilliant orchestral sound, especially in the Polish and the Revolution scenes, when Ghiaurov remembers that 'the splendid sonorities emerging from the orchestra literally sent shivers down one's spine. There was also a huge, augmented chorus that emphasized the view that the real protagonist of this opera is the people. I was surprised and impressed by Karajan's emotional state at the end of those performances. After the death of Boris he was almost in a trance, especially at the premiere.... Never, in my long career, have I seen a conductor as deeply moved and affected by the drama as he was. He had already amazed me at the end of the dress rehearsal, when he came up to me with tears in his eyes and kissed my hand. Needless to say, I was speechless and presumed this was intended as a homage to the dead Boris. Now that I have worked closely with him over many years, I know him to be an intensely emotional and sentimental man. And as a conductor he is, of course, in a class of his own.'

Ghiaurov's interpretation of Boris is musical rather than declamatory. Unlike many a colleague, he tries to interpret the role by *singing* it rather than resorting to recitation and excessive para-musical vocal effects like gasps, groans, shrieks and suchlike which, he feels, have little to do with Mussorgsky's musical line and instead of enhancing the dramatic power of the role only succeed in rendering it less interesting. 'Mussorgsky's music is *so* interesting that there is no need to go beyond it in order to make an impact. I follow his score and written indications meticulously and I don't think that this profoundly "musical" approach detracts from the power of my interpretation.' Anyone who has seen or heard Ghiaurov's vivid characterization of Boris on stage or record, so rich in dramatic detail, will agree.

From the vocal point of view, the role does present some difficulties. It was, he explains, originally written for a baritone and although it was later transposed down a quarter semitone Rimsky retained the higher version of Boris's monologue. 'This is always a difficult spot for me, as is the beginning of the Coronation scene, where you have to climb up to an F, the highest note in the bass range and as difficult as the tenor's high C. Even my teacher, who was a baritone, found this a headache because this note occurs at a moment when you are standing on stage, as if on an empty plate, when, after the resounding *fortissimo* of the chorus, Boris enters and begins to think aloud. He prays to God to bless and protect his reign but is overcome by a sad premonition that he and his people will be overtaken by disaster. His doubts and sense of foreboding are strengthened by the fact that he wasn't the legitimate heir but merely a powerful Boyar who accepted the crown in order to end the lawlessness that was plunging Russia into chaos.'

Ghiaurov agrees with Raimondi and Burchuladze that the essence of Boris's character is the relentless remorse and stricken conscience that destroy and drive him to his death. His soul is in a state of turmoil and this must be suggested right from the beginning, the Coronation scene, and then given full vent in his monologue, where he says that, although he has done everything in his power to help his people – saved them from anarchy, fed and protected them – they curse him in the streets and squares. 'The problem is that you have only three comparatively short scenes – the Coronation, Clock and Death scenes – with which to create and develop a portrayal of this exceptionally anguished and tormented man, and this is why I said earlier that this role requires an amazing degree of concentration and the skills of a mature and experienced artist.'

The only point in the Salzburg production about which Ghiaurov had reservations was the fact that Karajan made some substantial cuts to the score, which, like all other productions of this opera that Ghiaurov had sung to date, was in Rimsky-Korsakov's edition. Unlike some younger colleagues, like Claudio Abbado and Riccardo Muti, Karajan is not fanatic about textual authenticity and, as in the case of *Don Carlos*, leans towards the traditional as opposed to the original versions of well-known works, mainly because he thinks that there was usually some good reason for those alterations. Ghiaurov, too, tends to prefer Rimsky's version to Mussorgsky's original, but felt in this case that Pimen's scene in particular had been shortened too much.

Fifteen years later, in December 1979, he had the opportunity to sing the title role in Mussorgsky's original version for the first time, at the opening of La Scala's season, under Claudio Abbado. The production was directed by the Soviet producer Yuri Lyubimov, who now lives in the West. Initially Ghiaurov was apprehensive about accepting the assignment, first because he was quite attached to, and convinced by, Rimsky's version, which had become an integral part of his career, and second, because he was frightened by Abbado's youth and by the fact that he understood no Russian. 'Mussorgsky demands great maturity from a conductor. I later found out that Abbado has a veritable passion for his music and I was surprised by the profoundness and meticulousness with which he approached the score, and by the power and subtlety of the orchestral sound he produced.' (Indeed, Abbado is known to consider Rimsky 'a criminal' for what he did to Mussorgsky's original score by rendering the orchestration over-brilliant to the point where, he feels, it obscures some of the work's depth and introspection.) 'Of course, this was a different Boris from the one I was used to singing. The essence and inner substance of the character remain the same but in this version they are expressed in a much simpler, less spectacular and "theatrical" way – down to Boris's costumes, which were much more modest than usual – and this requires even greater concentration and inner power.' 'Nicolai Ghiaurov still manages the great part with authority, even if he did not always appear completely convinced either by the production or this edition' (*Opera*).

Ghiaurov's Russian repertoire also includes Prince Khovanshchy in Mussorgsky's *Khovanshchina*, Prince Gremin in Tchaikovsky's *Eugene Onegin*, and Ivan Susanin in Glinka's *A Life for the Tsar*. Like Hermann Prey he doesn't think one should speak of different 'styles of singing', because 'vocal emission and technique are one and the same regardless of what one is singing. What changes is the language, and what is normally described as "stylistic" detail – like vocal colours, the lightening or darkening of sound – is a natural by-product of the language, the words and their correct pronunciation. What I think of as "style" is the distillation of a people's musical and cultural heritage. The land of his birth bestows certain national sensibilities on each composer and these are, in turn, reflected in his score and the language of his libretto. Mussorgsky's music is steeped in the Russian folkloric tradition and reflects the immensity and profound melancholy of the Russian soul. French music, which belongs to a different land and cultural heritage, naturally has quite different characteristics.

'This is why my portrayals are based entirely on the musical score. I cannot go beyond, or outside, what the composer has written because I *feel* a character right from the opening orchestral bars. Boris, for example, is summed up in his entirety, in all his depth, in those sombre themes and harmonies that precede his first entry. [Ruggero Raimondi mentions this very point, too, in his chapter.] Similarly, those rapid, galloping orchestral bars that herald Mephistopheles's first entry in Gounod's *Faust* outline all the elegance and cavalier fashion with which this character is viewed, through French eyes. Both in the case of Boris and of Mephisto, those bars immediately suggest what lines your interpretation should take, as do the melancholy bars before Philip II's aria "Ella giammai m'amo" in *Don Carlos*. There are certain arias – "Le Veau d'or" and the Serenade in *Faust*, "Finch' han dal vino" in *Don Giovanni* and Philip II's aria, already mentioned – which encapsulate the entire character in cameo and which I always think of as points of departure, columns which it is up to me to ornament, according to the details supplied by the dramatic situation and his relationships to the other characters.'

Ghiaurov tries to observe a sense of measure in his portrayals and to refrain from exaggerations or cheap effects, like hanging on to certain high or low notes longer than necessary. In any case, he doesn't think an artist can build a career solely on his facility for high or low notes and feels grateful that, unlike tenors, basses tend to be judged by their overall interpretation and relative success in bringing characters to life rather than on the impact of certain difficult notes. 'Naturally, high notes have a dramatic reason for being there. Composers use them to indicate the emotional climax of a given aria. In the bass range, which should span two octaves from F below to F above the stave, the top F is our limit, in the same way that the high C is the top note in the tenor range. Very, very seldom will you find a bass capable of reaching up to F sharp – this is as rare as a tenor who can sing C sharp (or, as it's usually called, D flat), i.e. a minor miracle!'

Composers tend to vary a great deal in their vocal writing. Some are great orchestrators whose vocal writing leaves something to be desired, while others have an innate understanding of the voice, which can make a singer's life much easier. 'Rimsky was a great orchestrator who knew the sonority and possibilities of each instrument and exploited the splendour of the bassoon or clarinet or violin perfectly in his colourful orchestrations. Verdi, on the other hand, was a vocal genius, a man of the theatre who understood and wrote extremely well for the voice. He knew how to find just the right sonorities for expressing the dramatic essence of every character and situation and his genius is so individual that it can be instantly identified in every note he wrote.'

Verdi's flair for vocal writing grew with experience and reached its apogee in his later works: *Don Carlos*, *Aida*, *Otello* and *Falstaff*. But it was already in evidence in his earliest operas like *Attila*, where the title role contains some phrases that require the bass to sing some lines spanning the entire bass range. 'Those lines, however, are not as well thought and worked out as, for example, Philip II's last line in his duet with the Inquisitor in *Don Carlos*, which also spans the entire bass range. That kind of mellowness came with experience. In *Attila* you also find a few low notes that don't sound right and are inadequate for expressing the emotions inherent in the given dramatic situations. [Simon Estes agrees.] Still, it's a well-written role, and so is Zaccaria in *Nabucco* and most other early Verdi bass roles. [The best Verdi had to say about *Attila* when he wrote to Contessa Maffei was that 'it is not inferior to the others', while he damned another of his early efforts, *Alzira*, as 'really terrible'.] The single exception is Silva's *cabaletta* in *Ernani*, which is so bestially difficult and contains such uncomfortable approaches to high notes that anyone familiar with Verdi's work would have guessed this couldn't have been written by him. Apart from musical ineptitude, it also lacks dramatic depth and credibility, because a man like Silva, the way he is delineated by Verdi, could *never* behave in the way suggested by the lightweight character of this inane *cabaletta*! Well, now we *know* it wasn't written by Verdi, because it doesn't exist in his original score (and because he wrote no *cabalettas* for the baritone, but just for the tenor), but was added later for a bass called Marini. The conspicuous absence of Verdi's vocal ability and instinctive dramatic flair from this *cabaletta* was eloquent and revealing. For, as I said, both in his early and his middle operas his vocal writing is that of a natural man of the theatre.'

As Ghiaurov has already mentioned, Verdi's vocal genius reaches its zenith in *Don Carlos* and in the masterly way he sketches the character of Philip II, which is the most important bass role in the Verdi repertoire (and, along with the title role in Boito's *Mefistofele*, in the entire Italian repertoire), in the same way that Boris is in the Russian. Vocally, the role is ideally suited to Ghiaurov's voice and he has sung it all over the world, throughout his career. After a Covent Garden performance the *Daily Telegraph* wrote: 'One was torn between pity and enchantment as this great singer traversed the whole gamut of human emotion, from the *mezza voce* of the brooding opening to the violent outbreaks of grief which were yet completely mastered by his grandiose voice.'

Ghiaurov is fascinated by this character, 'so interesting and so complex in his richness, solitude, pain, bitterness and sense of betrayal which are all encapsulated in his big aria, "Ella giammai m'amo", one of the most beautiful Verdi ever wrote. I read Schiller's play and tried to find out as much as possible about the historical Philip, because all this underpinning helps me get beneath the skin of the character. But there is no point in dwelling too much either on Schiller's or on the real historical Philip, because the Philip I have to interpret is Verdi's, the musical character, as he emerges out of the score.' José Van Dam made the same point in his chapter, and it was interesting to find out, in Marcello Conati's fascinating book *Interviews and Encounters with Verdi*, that Verdi himself complained about the fact that he was bound by Schiller's view of Philip, which he found typical of the latter's tendency to idealize characters: '"If the real Philip II had encountered a man like the Marquis of Posa, he would have crushed him, instead of warning him to beware the Grand Inquisitor", remarked Verdi. Yet he followed Schiller and surpassed him in creating a character so moving and sympathetic in his solitude and in the isolation which must needs accompany great power.'

By the time he wrote *Don Carlos* Verdi's vocal expertise was such that he 'dared write that phrase at the end of Philip's duet with the Grand Inquisitor – "Dunque il *tro*no dovra piegar sempre al al*tare*" – which contains both an F above and an F below the stave, i.e. both the highest and the lowest note in the bass range within a single line, and has become a sort of barometer according to which basses are judged and measured. The role as a whole is deeply thought out and beautifully written. Verdi found just the right *tessitura* for the impressions and states of mind he wished to convey. In the aria "Ella giammai m'amo", for instance, one finds lines where every note is perfectly chosen to convey each nuance from a wide variety of emotions: the line "dormiro sol", which goes from A to B flat, instantly conveys beauty, tranquillity and sweetness of sound. But had Verdi chosen to write a *tessitura* from C to D flat instead, not only would the feeling of peace be destroyed, but the line would also be impossible to sing.'

As well as Philip II and the parts already mentioned, Ghiaurov has sung all the major Verdi bass roles, including Fiesco in *Simon Boccanegra* and Procida in *I vespri siciliani*. This repertoire also includes the title role in *Don Giovanni* and all the major French and Russian bass roles. One of the greatest joys in his career was singing for the first time, in 1960, the title role in Massenet's *Don Quichotte*, which he also recorded, to mark the fiftieth anniversary of the world premiere of the work, at the Monte Carlo Opera in 1910. 'The opera is the last work in the career of a mature and experienced composer and the title role was written for Chaliapin. The result is a beautifully written role, full of comfortable sonorities and marvellous music for the bass voice. It demands a good command of French and a wide palette of vocal colours. The climax of the work, and the part where Massenet's genius is at its greatest, is Don Quichotte's death, which is incredibly difficult, profound and moving and very close to the character of any idealistic singer or actor who sees the world as a better place than it is, and whose perception of reality and fantasy is blurred and ambiguous. This floating state of mind and thin dividing line between the real and the imaginary requires a very special quality of sound and it's very, very hard to explain *how* one finds and achieves those colours. Could Rostropovitch explain the different way he pulls this or that string when playing Dvorak or Shostakovich, for instance? I doubt it. The right colours must be found intuitively as part of one's search for, and perception of, the character. Our problem as singers is that we don't have an instrument to play on. We, ourselves, are the instrument; therefore we must look for these colours inside ourselves and our own psyche. I think you will find that any singing-actor who sings this role tends to identify a great deal with the character of Don Quichotte. [Ruggero Raimondi agrees.] It is very close to, and a sort of homage to, the character of Chaliapin himself, an idealistic artist who perceived the world very much along the lines I have indicated. . . .'

Chaliapin was so moved when Massenet first played Don Quichotte's Death scene on the piano that he started to sob and had to leave the room to regain his composure. '*Calme toi*. Or at least wait until the end. *Then* you can cry', snapped the composer, echoing Ghiaurov's opening remarks about an artist's need to protect himself from his own over-sensitivity to the great works he is fortunate enough to interpret.

KURT MOLL

'The two roles I love, and identify with most are Gurnemanz in *Parsifal* and Ochs in *Der Rosenkavalier*. I never tire of singing them! They represent and fulfil two opposite sides of me and every time I perform them I find new details to savour and play with,' smiled Kurt Moll, tall, jovial, one of the best mimics in the business and, at forty-eight, one of the most celebrated basses of our day, specializing mainly in the German repertoire. Gurnemanz, the contemplative Knight of the Grail in Wagner's mystical drama and Baron Ochs, Strauss's breezy, earthy, *bon viveur* provincial aristocrat are diametrical opposites as far as the bass repertoire is concerned. Yet it was hardly surprising to learn they are Moll's favourites: he is, today, *the* foremost interpreter of both roles and his special identification and affection is evident in his superb portrayals.

Moll is an accomplished comic on stage, and his performance of Ochs – and indeed of Osmin in *Die Entführung aus dem Serail* – sparkles with brio, gusto, bonhomie and an overall lightness of touch that prevents it from ever lapsing into slapstick or vulgarity. 'This character is neither a buffoon nor unsuitably noble, but a bluff figure between the two.... Moll is totally vocally secure, with each note firmly placed' (*The Times*). His interpretation of Gurnemanz, which won high praise both on disc and in Karajan's 1980-81 Salzburg Easter Festival production, is based on perfect diction and the skilful use of varied dynamics and shades of colour, even in the long *parlando* passages, and he succeeds in making Gurnemanz's long narration the riveting story it really is. As Wagner surely intended, one doesn't want to miss a word, nor does one. Herbert von Karajan observed at the time that 'a great deal in *Parsifal* depends on how it's sung. The text is crucial and especially so in the role of Gurnemanz: everything hinges on the pronunciation of the words and the way they are moulded and blended into the sound. But granted the artist we had – Kurt Moll – the rehearsals were more of a joy than work.'

Moll explains that the most difficult spots in *Parsifal* are Gurnemanz's long, *legato* passages – the Swan music in Act I and the Good Friday music in Act III – which are so beautiful that the singer could easily lose himself in it and forget to pay attention to certain crucial technical details. Otherwise, it presents no vocal problems. The *tessitura* is comfortable and the length no problem for a singer of his experience and sophistication. 'Gurnemanz is one of the first Knights of the Grail and the only person in the drama who knows the significance of everything and has lived through the whole fiasco of Kundry's spell and Amfortas's fall. In his long narration, he recounts the story to the young squires, like a teacher passing on his knowledge. Those passages are not very difficult: they are almost entirely *parlando* (spoken on the note), and there are many spots where the orchestra is extremely soft, almost barely audible, so one needn't use too much voice. It was Karajan who first pointed this out to me, by asking: "Why do you want to sing those passages in full voice? Wagner certainly didn't intend you to!" And he is dead right. On examining the score I realized there are lots of stretches where one can hold back and exercise considerable vocal economy. This way the climactic moments make far greater impact, instead of going virtually unnoticed in a narration that can easily become boring.

'The key passages to watch for, and make sure one retains sufficient vocal resources for, occur in Act I, in the scene where Gurnemanz upbraids Parsifal for slaying the swan. There are stretches of *legato*, *cantabile* music, so beautiful one could easily forget oneself and give out more voice than one should, or needs to. This would be very dangerous, because these passages are immediately followed by an outbreak: the sentence "Dem stauntest du nicht? Dich lockt' es nur zu wild kindischem Bogengeschoss?" ['Did this not impress you? Did it only tempt you to a wild, childish shot from your bow?']. This demands considerable vocal power which, at this stage, is possible only if you have paced yourself correctly in the preceding passages. I always feel that if I can sing this phrase, after all Gurnemanz has already sung, with no signs of vocal strain or fatigue, then Act I has gone quite well.' (It was interesting to hear a good but inexperienced singer get rather unstuck at precisely this phrase in a recent performance of *Parsifal* in London.)

In Act III the tricky moments occur again after Gurnemanz has sung a long stretch of *parlando* phrases. Parsifal's return is followed by two long, *cantabile* passages, the washing of his feet by Kundry, and his anointing by Gurnemanz. This moment is so rousing and moving that, as Moll points out, it is easy for singers to get carried away and sing 'too massively, too thickly and give out too much volume and intensity, which would be wrong and make the thing sound like an Italian aria. The same is true of phrases in the Good Friday music – "Will ihr Gebet ihm weihen" and "Das merkt nun Halm und Blume auf den Auen" ['and dedicates to him its prayer' and 'now grass and flowers in the meadow know'] – which, again, could easily sound too thick and too meaty if one has let oneself go, and not prepared the voice accordingly. These are the two key passages by which I judge my performance in Act III. Without sufficient experience and familiarity with the work, it's all too easy to come unstuck. Mind you, singing this role with Karajan automatically made it easier: he is *the* exponent *par excellence* of transparent conducting, of the great, *legato* line and of *piano* singing, so I was able to paint with a very fine brush. He also seemed to agree with my basic interpretation of the role and when this happens, when you really see eye-to-eye with a conductor, miracles can happen.'

The Salzburg Easter Festival production of *Parsifal* was one of the occasions forever lodged in that special personal treasure-house of one's greatest operatic memories, and so is the much acclaimed recording which preceded it and was awarded the *Gramophone* 'Record of the Year' Prize and the *Deutscher Schallplattenpreis*. 'The finest of all principal singers is surely the Gurnemanz of Kurt Moll, a wonderful blend of *bel canto* and *Lieder* singing, the voice a true bass, perfectly poised and projected, finely nuanced, ever attentive to the colour and meaning of the words' (*Gramophone*). After the Salzburg performances *The Times* referred to 'the splendid cast of singers, starting with Kurt Moll's Gurnemanz, a vivid narrator, ardent servant of the Grail, his powerful, wide-ranging *basso* a joy to hear'.

Moll is equally renowned for his portrayals of King Marke in *Tristan und Isolde* and Pogner in *Die Meistersinger von Nürnberg*, which Peter Jonas, Managing Director of English National Opera, would instance as one of *the* performances that have given him greatest pleasure and which Moll considers the hardest role in his entire repertoire. 'In Act I, in Pogner's address to the Masters, the *tessitura* is basically the same as Hans Sachs's: it begins lyrically, in the best and most comfortable position for my voice, and then proceeds to spiral slowly and steadily higher, culminating in an F. This is like climbing a mountain, more and more slowly, always in second gear, never in full steam because then you would certainly get worn out halfway. This is truly very, very hard to do and it takes a very experienced singer to make it appear effortless.' Moll succeeds in singing the role impeccably and endowing Pogner with just the right measure of both paternal concern and ambition – a trait he also achieves admirably in another Wagnerian 'father', Daland in *Der fliegende Holländer*.

Less difficult than Pogner and less tiring, yet more psychologically wearing than Gurnemanz, is the role of King Marke in *Tristan und Isolde* which Moll first sang in 1964 in Mainz and has since performed in most of the great theatres and festivals and also on record, under Carlos Kleiber. The reason why – despite the fact that the role consists of one long scene lasting about twenty minutes, plus a brief appearance at the end of Act III – it is so emotionally taxing is because of the character's intensity and introspection. 'Marke's big scene in Act II is a huge outburst of pain, the greatest part of which, as he himself says, can never be fully absorbed or expressed. This contributes not just tremendous inner, psychological tension but also a considerable degree of physical, bodily tension, which must be communicated to the audience. This is a very tiring thing to have to do and leaves me kind of steamed up afterwards. . . .'

One of today's great interpreters of the role of Tristan – Jon Vickers – has stated that he despises the character he portrays so movingly and considers him 'a deplorable man' because of his betrayal of the benefactor to whom he owed everything in this world. 'I think that Tristan is a despicable man and his behaviour shocking, absolutely disgraceful! King Marke adored him, had indicated he was grooming him to be his heir and that, for him, the young man fulfilled all his filial instincts. It is therefore disgraceful that Tristan shouldn't have remembered all this before betraying his benefactor, that he should not have been restrained by feelings of gratitude or the realization that the exalted position to which he had been elevated at court was not due only to his own prowess and heroism but also, largely, to Marke's benevolent affection. And, to me, forgetting this, whatever the temptation, seems unforgivable. For there is a higher love than that between man and woman – if *that's* the height of man's understanding of love then mankind is in a sad mess, and mankind *is* in a sad mess! – and there are sacrifices that man is called to make, sacrifices like the agony of Aeneas at having to leave Dido when called to serve something other than himself. I have great respect for Aeneas – and little respect for Tristan.'

So, when singing the role he tries to bring out the beauty, 'and there is great, great, exquisite beauty', of the love relationship between Tristan and Isolde, as depicted in Wagner's music, downplay 'the sordidness' of their situation and, in the death of Tristan, convey the feeling that his great love for her brings her to him in his hour of need in such a way that it doesn't matter to him whether it's fact or whether she simply exists in his heart and mind. 'What matters is that he is conscious of her presence and thus finds solace and joy.... I try to portray him as any dying soldier in a trench, cut off from those he loves and whose overwhelming love for one who is absent brings her to his heart and enables him to die in peace. Those are the aspects I wish to convey. The philosophical aspects I disagree with, I leave out.'

I wondered what Moll, who has to experience this benefactor's agony at his double betrayal at the hands of the two people he loves most, feels towards Tristan. 'I don't despise him, no, and I don't think Marke does, either. If he did, he would probably have asked Melot to kill him right away. But that, of course, would turn him into a kind of Ivan the Terrible and this is certainly not the way his personality emerges from Wagner's score, which depicts him as a deeply civilized, humane and honourable man. He retains his trust and faith in Tristan until the last possible moment, even when confronted with the most flagrant evidence of his betrayal, and with tears in his eyes he asks "Tristan, is it true you are no longer my friend?". This is the truly tragic dimension of his character and what he dwells upon most in his outburst.

'He is far more reticent and introspective about his feeling towards Isolde, and here I was greatly helped by the insights and sensitivity of Carlos Kleiber during our collaboration at Bayreuth and during the preparation of our recording. He pointed out several crucial details like, for instance, the passage where Marke refers to his feelings for her beginning with "Dies wundervolle Weib" and so on, which is merely a thought expressed in music and which would normally never be spoken out loud and should therefore be sung *pianissimo* and *legatissimo*. This contrast between the more extrovert parts where he confronts Tristan's betrayal and this very personal, "thinking aloud" section is essential for drawing an accurate and human portrait of Marke. It was wonderful to sing this role with Kleiber, who feels and experiences the work very deeply. Although he knows a great deal about it – and about a great many other things – and rehearses minutely and analytically, the end result emerges not out of "intellect" but from his heart and feelings. That's what I love about him.' *Opera* remarked that Moll's portrayal at the Bavarian State Opera 'radiated warmth, humanity and understanding' and hailed his performance at the Bayreuth Festival, under Kleiber, as 'a performance in a thousand'. Moll adds that the only technical difficulty in the role is the fact that when Marke arrives at Tristan's castle in Brittany at the end of Act III he usually has to sing from the very back of the stage, which always poses problems of projection, even for big voices like his.

Although Moll had sung some of the smaller Wagnerian roles in his twenties under the constant supervision of his voice teacher, he didn't embark on the big roles until fifteen years into his career. Like most of the artists in this book he, too, recommends Mozart as the ideal composer for young singers to begin their careers with, because 'Mozart demands singing in its purest form and is therefore the best possible training for the voice. One cannot hide behind the orchestra and the voice has to come out clean, pure and technically perfect. The reason why Wagnerian singing can be dangerous for young voices is the huge size of the orchestra, which is a temptation: singers, especially when they are young and inexperienced, feel inclined to compete with it and produce a big, loud, beefy sound. Needless to say, this would be disastrous in the long run and in any case it is the wrong way to sing Wagner! One should never try to compete with the orchestra. One should sing Wagner with the same clarity and purity of sound that one applies to Mozart – without tricks and without vulgarity. But the only living conductors to understand this and produce the kind of transparent orchestral sound that allows singers to be heard without shouting or producing the kind of relentless, monochromatic sound so often mistaken for Wagnerian singing are Karajan and Kleiber.'

Moll learnt the basics of Wagnerian singing, and indeed of all singing, from his teacher Emmy Müller, who guided his development with great care and responsibility and whom he considers 'God's gift to me'. He was born in Buir near Cologne in 1938, learnt to play the cello as a child and studied at the Cologne Conservatoire and privately, in nearby Krefeld, with Emmy Müller, who continued supervising his progress throughout his years at the Conservatoire and long after the onset of his professional career.

He made his professional debut in Cologne as Lodovico in Verdi's *Otello* and in 1961 was engaged by the Aachen State Theatre, where he remained for two years. In 1963 he moved on to Mainz and a year later joined the Wuppertal State Theatre, where he remained for five years before joining the Hamburg State Opera in 1970. At the time he sang mostly Mozart roles, like Sarastro in *Die Zauberflöte*, Leporello in *Don Giovanni* and Bartolo in *Le nozze di Figaro*, plus some *bel canto* parts like Basilio in Rossini's *Il barbiere di Siviglia*. He explains that his vocal range – from C below to C above the stave – was there from the beginning, but the voice was lighter and not supported properly from the diaphragm. So, when it came to Daland, which the Aachen Theatre asked him to sing, his teacher agreed he could try it but only under her constant supervision. 'We learnt it together, phrase by phrase, analysing every word and learning how to cope with its vocal demands. She then came to every rehearsal and performance, to make sure I was singing it correctly, without pushing, and that the voice wasn't being damaged. This is the right way to proceed. Without a sound technical basis one wouldn't get very far in Wagner. Sadly, today's singing teachers don't have the same sense of responsibility. Everything tends to depend more on financial considerations. . . .'

Moll himself would like to become a singing teacher after his eventual retirement. He already knows, judging from the stream of singers who ask him for advice and from the gratitude they express for any guidance, how sorely needed good teachers are. He hates to do anything half-heartedly and, as at present his operatic commitments do not allow enough time for serious teaching, he prefers to wait until the time when he is able to devote 'one hundred per cent' of his energies to it. (What little time he has, he likes to spend with his family – his wife, their teenage daughter and small adopted Columbian son and daughter – at home in Munich.)

Like most great singers whose careers rest on a solid foundation, Moll is quick to pinpoint the dangers facing young singers today: inadequate guidance and time devoted to vocal training – even in Conservatoires, where, in his opinion, too much time is wasted on inessential things as opposed to pure vocal training, which tends to be neglected but should be re-established as a daily routine – a serious dearth of good teachers and careers that start and develop too fast. 'Singers hit the big theatres much too soon. In earlier days they began in small theatres and proceeded step by step, embarking on certain roles only when the head of the music staff judged they were ready for them, and gradually they progressed to the big international houses. Nowadays ensemble theatres don't exist any more. The unprecedented proliferation of opera – which in recent years amounts almost to an explosion – combined with financial considerations means that everyone embarks on roles before they are ready for them, with disastrous results, both for themselves and for the unfortunate composers whose works tend to get massacred.'

Moll's own international career began at about the same time that he joined the Hamburg State Opera, in 1970. The same year he made his debuts at the Bavarian State Opera (as Pogner) and the Salzburg Festival (as Sarastro). The following year he made his debut at the Vienna State Opera as Gurnemanz. In 1972 he sang Osmin at La Scala, in Strehler's famous production, and in 1973 Bartolo in *Le nozze di Figaro* at the Paris Opéra, where he also returned for Gurnemanz. In 1977 came his Covent Garden debut as Kaspar in *Der Freischütz* and in 1978 he sang the Landgrave in *Tannhäuser* at the Metropolitan Opera. Apart from the Mozart, Wagner, Strauss and Weber roles already mentioned, his repertoire includes Massenet's *Don Quichotte*, Padre Guardiano in Verdi's *La forza del destino* and both Pimen and the title role in *Boris Godunov*.

Moll's fabulous voice, described in *Grove's Dictionary of Music* as a 'true, strong, flexible' (and, one would add, resonant) 'bass' ensures that his performances are always vocally distinguished. In addition, they always seem to be dramatically interesting and stylistically impeccable. Yet, like all great artists, Moll is an intuitive, instinctive animal, and despite his great technical skill he arrives at his interpretations through feeling rather than conscious, analytical thought. He therefore found it hard to analyse and pinpoint exactly what is meant by the elusive term 'style' as applied to singing and music and, like Hermann Prey, Nicolai Ghiaurov and Simon Estes, was quick to stress that, whatever it is, it has nothing to do with vocal production as such. 'One cannot speak of different "singing" styles because sound emission and vocal technique are one and the same whether one is singing Mozart, Wagner, Strauss or musical comedy. Take Baron Ochs's long conversational passages in *Der Rosenkavalier*, for instance, which are delivered in a light *parlando*. As far as the vocal instrument *itself* is concerned they are not so very different, in terms of sound emission, from the recitatives in Mozart operas. Yet one would never sing them in the same way, because it goes without saying that singing in Mozart's day was very different from singing in Strauss's.

'This is where "style" comes in and I think it consists of the sum total of the special characteristics of each work, both musical – like phrasing and the way the recitatives are declaimed or spoken – and spiritual, i.e. the place of the particular work within the composer's entire output and within its time. [Again, Nicolai Ghiaurov makes a similar point in his chapter.] This is where a singer's innate musicality comes in. If a singer is musical he will intuitively sense how to shape a Mozart phrase, where the borderline is that should never be crossed when singing a Mozart aria, how to colour Gurnemanz's narration and how to find the right accents and inflections for Baron Ochs. If he can't feel this or realize that it goes without saying that these roles cannot be sung in the same way, then he is simply not musical.'

Moll's own stylistic sensitivity is displayed to perfection in his comic roles like Osmin and Baron Ochs. He has sung Osmin in Giorgio Strehler's production of *Die Entführung aus dem Serail* at both La Scala and Salzburg and considers it one of the most interesting views of this work he has ever seen or sung in, very much centred around the character of Osmin and highly original in the sense that the arias, which were sung in full light, seemed to be superimposed on to the dialogue and recitatives which were treated as a straight play and took place in the semi-shaded lighting. Moll says he learnt a great deal about Osmin – the right vocal colours and character details to highlight – from this production, which was performed in Salzburg and elsewhere for some twelve years until about 1978.

My chance to see Moll's hilarious and lovable Osmin came in the autumn of 1979, in John Dexter's production, conducted by James Levine, at the Metropolitan Opera. He insists that his Osmin is intentionally portrayed as a lovable character. 'It is utterly wrong to try and turn him into some kind of sadistic brute. He is a baroque character, both vocally and dramatically. The whole work is rooted in the baroque style. It's Mozart but a Mozart who had not yet moved into the classical form. The *fioriture* in Osmin's music are typically baroque but it is nevertheless important *not* to sing every phrase the same: each should be sung *slightly* differently, to bring the thing to life and invest it with interest and sparkle. From the dramatic point of view, the important thing is not to allow Osmin to become *really* nasty! He is a baroque character, a Commedia dell' Arte figure of a braggart, a dog that barks very loud but doesn't bite! Even in his famous "Vengeance" aria, "Ha. Wie will ich triumphieren", he makes those ferocious statements mainly because he's enjoying the sound of his own voice and relishing the beautiful music and the coloraturas he's been given to sing! Otherwise the whole work would lose the gaiety of a *Singspiel*.' This is what I meant by saying one should be aware of the place of each work within a composer's output.

Despite the stylistic differences between the two roles, Osmin has exactly the same *tessitura* as Baron Ochs, which Moll sang for the first time in 1966 in Wuppertal, Hamburg in 1977, and Salzburg in 1978 before he went on to sing it just about everywhere. He sang it again in Salzburg in 1983–4 in Herbert von Karajan's production, which was recorded and filmed on videodisc. Although Osmin and Ochs are now among Moll's best portrayals, he says both characters were very difficult for him to come to grips with at first. 'In Ochs in particular, the most difficult thing for me to achieve was the charm and lightness of touch so essential to the character. Being light-hearted and charming is, perhaps, easier for southerners than for northerners like me, to whom characters like King Marke and Gurnemanz come more easily.' Indeed, the lightness of touch and Austrian charm now so characteristic of Moll's portrayal of Ochs was apparently conspicuously absent from his early performances: 'Kurt Moll sang an ill-tempered Ochs with a powerful bass and un-Vienna-like intonation', wrote *Opera* after Moll's performance at the Hamburg State Opera in 1977; and the same magazine noted after his first Salzburg performances, under Christopher Dohnányi, that 'Kurt Moll, the Ochs, was in splendid voice, complete with low C firmly sung and not just grunted. But he is not much of an actor, physically or vocally. The words were roundly and clearly voiced but not filled out with much meaning or character.'

The man who helped Moll achieve the charm, lightness of touch and authenticity for which his portrayal is now famous was, again, Herbert von Karajan, who has a special affection for this role – which, he says, resembles him a little – and relishes its mordant, Austrian humour. According to Richard Osborne, who interviewed both artists during the recording of *Der Rosenkavalier* for *Gramophone*, this offered Moll a veritable lexicon of inflections, accents and tones which he has down to a fine art. Karajan stated that 'to some extent Ochs is a "type" and there were many Ochses living in Austria between the wars, living in their castles in a style that was far from elegant – these were not good times for such people. But Ochs is not a buffoon, he has been at court, he is an educated man. He has the smell of the country about him, but he knows how to behave. Like Falstaff he has his little failings, his women and so on. In Act III he realizes the world is against him, but he is intelligent enough to know he is the victim of his own weaknesses.' No one who saw this production is likely to forget Moll's performance in Act II, while his wound was being tended to, or his rendition of the famous waltz! The critics were also quick to notice the difference. *Opera* now remarked: 'One of the finer elements in the production was the ebullient Ochs of that delightful singer, Kurt Moll, never descending to the vulgar gags other productions have required of him.'

The recording was also singled out for high praise. The American magazine *Ovation* wrote: 'Towering over everyone else is Kurt Moll as Baron Ochs. Commentators never tire of pointing out that this role should not be played with too much vulgarity – for all his loutishness, Ochs is still an aristocrat. Moll finds an easy solution to this problem: he *sings* aristocratically, pouring out tones of baronial splendour that seem to emerge from some vast, princely reservoir, spanning the vast reaches of the *basso* range with patrician ease and a noble *legato*. Nor does Moll sound like an aged lecher: the robust power of his upper range fits right in with the forty-ish character envisaged by the opera's creators.'

During the last three years Moll began a gradual, careful expansion into the Russian repertoire. He sang Pimen first, in Russian, at the Vienna State Opera during the 1982–3 season and the title role in *Boris Godunov* at the Hamburg State Opera in 1983–4, in German, much to his regret, because in singing Pimen he had discovered that 'Russian is simply the best language for the bass voice, because it has those marvellous consonants which produce their own resonance in the head. I don't speak the language and consequently had to learn the role of Pimen phonetically, with a cassette and a phonetic transcription. But I think that, as a result, I now understand the Russian mentality, and the reason why Russians usually speak so slowly and deliberately: the language demands it. Those Russian roles are composed for, and out of, that language.'

Not surprisingly it proved fiendishly difficult to memorize Pimen, because as he doesn't speak Russian it was impossible at that stage to make an imaginary link with *what* he was actually singing. Gradually he learnt to sight-read the score and the phonetic transcription of his cassette and then went to a Russian language coach, who remarked that Moll seemed to have a natural flair for the Russian language; to which he replied that, after listening to any language for any length of time, one begins to pick up certain nuances and inflections. Then he started trying to learn it by heart and, after working on it for weeks, suddenly it happened: the whole text was there, in his mind, from one moment to the next, seemingly overnight. He then went to Vienna to work with a Russian-born coach who showed him all sorts of details about the way Russians pronounce their consonants, and especially the letter *l*. The labour of love was then completed by his having the whole libretto translated word by word, indeed syllable by syllable, so he knew *exactly* what he was singing all the time, and could make the connection between the phonetic text he learnt and the real language.

When it came to his singing the title role in *Boris Godunov* – which, he explains, has the same *tessitura* as Pimen but simply *sounds* darker – he found the experience of singing it in German different and less satisfactory than it would have been had he sung it in the original language, 'because the German mentality is different from the Russian, which is right there, in the language and lodged in the text. Those Russian consonants say it all, with that tremendous resonance of theirs.' Our conversation took place before the Hamburg premiere, and he pointed out that he was aiming to make his German come across softer and more Slavic-sounding, hoping it would make a difference. The performance was very well reviewed. 'Kurt Moll's Boris was sung with a sumptuous, rounded, even and powerful voice, resounding with cavernous sounds that reflected a deeply introspective characterization', wrote *Opéra International*.

He doesn't plan to take on many more roles or expand upwards into the domain of the bass-baritone. He has been asked, again and again, to sing Wotan and Hans Sachs but keeps declining, because 'I am a real bass and these two are bass-baritone roles. I have no ambition to expand beyond my natural range. To be sure, I would *like* to sing Hans Sachs but I know my voice isn't right for it and that I would have to push, something I'd rather not do.' Moll looks after his voice and health – as its superb condition at the age of forty-eight testifies – but doesn't believe in singers living neurotically, in perpetual fear of catching chills and sore throats. 'One should live as normally as possible and not render oneself neurotic on account of one's voice or go around perpetually wrapped in mufflers, forever avoiding proximity to smokers and never having a drink. That kind of mentality produces extra strain for the nervous system and is therefore automatically counter-productive. As far as I'm concerned, the most essential thing is sufficient sleep. And this is sometimes difficult to accomplish with the peripatetic lives we singers live, moving from hotel room to hotel room and missing out on afternoon sleep because of rehearsals. This *can* be very tiring – which is why I'm trying to cut down on travel and sing more in places reasonably close to home.'

Moll enjoys painting, reading and going to the theatre. He also relishes singing *Lieder* recitals and has discovered a great many unknown songs by Löwe. He stresses that it's difficult to capture the right kind of intimate 'chamber style' essential to *Lieder* evenings between operatic performances, 'because this is chamber theatre and corresponds to an orchestra playing a string quartet. Very rewarding. . . .'

Moll doesn't sing many Italian roles. He has sung the Inquisitor in *Don Carlos* plus a few other Verdi roles, but points out that once a singer gets associated with a particular repertoire he tends to be asked to sing the same roles most of the time. He would, one day, like to sing Philip II in *Don Carlos*, in a new production by a very good producer, and at the time of our conversation was planning to sing Padre Guardiano in *La forza del destino* at the Bavarian State Opera under Giuseppe Sinopoli. Does his predominantly German repertoire mean that he enjoys and is more fulfilled by German opera? He replied that this isn't necessarily so because 'in all great works, the music and the text are inextricably interwoven. It doesn't matter to what extent I, Kurt Moll, identify with any spiritual belief or credo expressed in those works. It would matter a great deal, though, if I were singing a mediocre work. If I had no personal point of contact with a second-rate work then I certainly couldn't perform it because there is nothing there to carry me away and out of myself. But great works encapsulate a world of their own and the music and text *compel* you to make the necessary imaginary link with the character. Therefore I wouldn't say I feel more fulfilled after singing King Marke in *Tristan und Isolde* than after singing Padre Guardiano in *La forza del destino*. When a work is that great and that cohesive, it has a value of its own.'

SAMUEL RAMEY

'As a young singer, I never dreamt my career would take me to the places it has,' mused American-born Samuel Ramey, one of the outstanding basses of our day and the most distinguished interpreter of Rossini in many a decade. 'At the time, I thought I'd be happy if it could get me a contract with New York City Opera and make it possible for me to support myself through singing. But I never thought someone from western Kansas would get to sing at La Scala, Covent Garden and places like that! It was nice to dream about, but I never seriously thought it would happen.'

Ramey's international career began in earnest after his appearance as Assur in Rossini's *Semiramide* at the 1980 Aix-en-Provence Festival with Marilyn Horne and Montserrat Caballé. His dark, beautifully focussed bass voice with its phenomenal facility for *coloratura* drew ecstatic reviews. 'Of course, one suspected that these ladies would be sensational,' wrote *Opera*. 'What came as more of a surprise was the assured mastery of the florid style by Samuel Ramey as Assur. How powerfully he sang "Ah, la sorte ci tradi", and how agile the voice in the big duets with Semiramide and Arsace – a real command of *roulades*!'

Ramey is a serious singer who studies hard and works hard. His seemingly effortless mastery of *fioriture* and the note-perfect performances he delivers almost as a matter of course are the result of meticulous preparation and a will to illuminate the music and find the dramatic reasons behind the florid style. He was, therefore, well-prepared for the invitations that began to pour in after his triumph as Assur at Aix. In 1981 he repeated his success in this role in the Aix production of *Semiramide* at the Théâtre des Champs-Elysées in Paris, and made his La Scala debut in the title role in *Le nozze di Figaro*; the following year he sang the same role at Covent Garden, and soon all the major opera houses followed: the Deutsche Oper in Berlin, the Théâtre de la Monnaie in Brussels, the Chicago Lyric, San Francisco, Hamburg and Vienna State Opera. He opened the 1983–4 season at the Paris Opéra in the title role of Rossini's *Moïse* (the French version of *Mosè*), and during the same season also made his Metropolitan Opera debut as Argante in Handel's *Rinaldo*. Herbert von Karajan has chosen him to record and perform the title role in *Don Giovanni* at the 1987 Salzburg Easter and Summer Festivals.

Ramey has also made regular appearances at the Rossini Festival at Pesaro, where he sang Douglas in *La donna del lago*, Mustafa in *L'italiana in Algeri*, Selim in *Il turco in Italia*, Lord Sidney in *Il viaggio a Reims*, the title role in *Maometto II* and the bass part in *Edippo a Colonno*. Indeed, it was another Rossini role – the tutor in *Le Comte Ory* – that triggered off the chain of events that led to his triumph at Aix-en-Provence: Marilyn Horne was so impressed when she heard him sing this role with New York City Opera that she insisted he be engaged to sing Mustafa in her recording of *L'italiana in Algeri*.

Despite his uncontested mastery of Rossini, Ramey has steadfastly refused to limit himself to Rossini roles or *bel canto* in general: 'I love and experience great pleasure in singing Rossini and *bel canto* music and will always want to go on doing so. They suit my technical possibilities and are very healthy for the voice. But I refuse to be known just as a Rossini specialist. That would be far too restricting when there is so much wonderful repertoire, so many more roles and styles, that I also love singing. I like to think that having a versatile repertoire is one of my calling cards.'

Sir John Tooley, General Director of the Royal Opera House, Covent Garden, heartily agrees and adds that 'Ramey's fluency and flexibility are quite breathtaking. He can rattle off practically *any* bass role, on top of his staggering mastery of the Rossini repertoire. He also has the gift of creating a character successfully with the voice in a way many singers find difficult. This makes him independent of production, to a large extent, by enabling him to override and transcend indifferent stagings through his ability to establish the characters vocally.' Ramey's repertoire also includes the title role in Verdi's *Attila* and Philip II in *Don Carlos*, the title role in Boito's *Mefistofele*, Nick Shadow in Stravinsky's *The Rake's Progress*, plus several French roles like the four villains in Offenbach's *Les Contes d'Hoffmann*, Mephistopheles in Gounod's *Faust* and the title roles in Massenet's *Don Quichotte* and Meyerbeer's *Robert le diable*.

The hallmarks of Ramey's interpretations, whatever the style or the role, are elegance, finesse and good taste. Nothing is ever allowed to go over the top and there is never a trace of gimmickry or vulgarity in his portrayals. Ramey, himself an elegant, lean, nattily dressed forty-four-year-old, was pleased to know 'this shows' because finesse is something he works and works at during his preparation, smoothing, polishing and refining all rough edges, both vocally and dramatically.

Ideally, when he has the time and is not rushed or pressured, which, alas, is often the case, Ramey likes to prepare a role by first sitting down with the text, going through it and translating his role – because despite the word-perfect performances he delivers in those languages, he doesn't speak French or Italian – then learning the notes by pounding away alone at the piano. When he has some idea of the music and how to sing it, he goes to his voice teacher or a coach to work on interpretation. He likes to work for three to four hours a day, 'otherwise the voice gets tired. I went through a couple of periods in my life when I had a lot of music to learn so I was working longer every day and got sick. The vocal cords got swollen, so the whole thing proved thoroughly counter-productive.'

Ramey's training took place in his native Kansas. Born in the small town of Colby in 1942, he decided during his late teens that 'music was going to be my life' after joining the chorus of a visiting touring opera company. His music teacher at school started teaching him some music theory, piano, and some of the basics of singing, like breath support and so on, in preparation for his college entrance exams. He passed them and for the next four years studied singing at Wichita State University where his singing teacher was a retired baritone, Arthur Newman, who proved a 'very stabilizing influence' and is responsible for laying the foundations for Ramey's technical mastery.

'One of the luckiest things in my life was the fact that I never had a teacher who harmed my voice. Both my high school teacher and Arthur Newman gave me a solid base on which to build, and the latter also gave me the benefit of his stage experience and steered me in the right direction as far as repertoire is concerned. This was fortunate indeed, because college age can be very dangerous for singers. That's when the voice is beginning to gel and grow and when it's so easy for it to be pushed in the wrong direction. Some of the large colleges have big opera workshops and being pushed into singing Verdi or Puccini at this early stage can be very dangerous indeed. But I was lucky to have this man guide and advise me about what I should and what I shouldn't do.'

Ramey says that, technically speaking, his voice then was pretty much the same as today, with the same wide range from D below the stave to G above. As far back as he can remember he always had this unusually wide range and could also sing *coloratura*. The necessary agility and flexibility were there, innate. What he had to work on was focussing his voice, that is centring it on a narrow focus, 'so that it isn't too spread'. Some contemporary basses with remarkable voices have still not managed to achieve this focus which, as Arthur Newman rightly pointed out to Ramey, is particularly important for low voices. Newman also helped Ramey develop his innate agility and flexibility by introducing him to an Italian exercise book by Vaccai which contained a great many *coloratura* exercises as well as others designed to develop a long line. Ramey always recommends this book to young singers who come to ask his advice, especially if they would like to tackle Rossini roles, 'for Rossini demands the ability both to sing *coloratura* – the *sine qua non* of a Rossini singer – and to spin a long line. Most singers tend to be able to do one or the other. This is why so few can sing Rossini.' So when, after he began his professional career, the opportunity arose to sing a Rossini role, it seemed like an ideal choice for his voice.

This happened some years later, in New York. As soon as he graduated from college Ramey took the Greyhound bus to New York City, where he stayed with friends who had preceded him to the city by a few months, until he found a job, as a copy-writer at an advertising agency. For the next three and a half years he worked at this, while also studying with Armin Boyajian, who remains his teacher to this day, and singing in church or synagogue choirs. At the same time he met and married his wife, Carrie, to whom he is very close and who accompanies him on all his travels. He didn't feel ready for a professional career until 1973, when he entered the Metropolitan Opera auditions and made it to the final ten. At the same time he auditioned, for the fourth time, for New York City Opera and was signed on as a full company member.

He made his professional debut later in 1973, as Zuniga in *Carmen*, and, apart from a couple of seasons, continued to sing there for a decade. His roles included Colline in *La Bohème*, Henry VIII in *Anna Bolena*, Raimondo in *Lucia di Lammermoor*, Basilio in *Il barbiere di Siviglia*, the Tutor in *Le Comte Ory* and the title roles in Boito's *Mefistofele*, *Don Giovanni* and *Le nozze di Figaro*. In 1976 he made his European debut at Glyndebourne as Figaro and returned in 1977 for Nick Shadow in *The Rake's Progress*. In 1978 came his French and German debuts, in Bordeaux (as Don Giovanni) and at the Hamburg State Opera (as Arkel in *Pelléas et Mélisande*) respectively. A year before the triumphant appearance as Assur in *Semiramide* already referred to, he had made his debut at Aix-en-Provence as Figaro.

The first Rossini role Ramey ever sang, Basilio, is the one he enjoys least, because on the whole he prefers dramatic to comic characters. He was more interested in the second, the tutor in *Le Comte Ory*, because it is more difficult: 'It has a slow, marvellous, wide-ranging aria without too much *coloratura*. Wide-ranging roles are always more difficult, because once the voice is set to go up it is very hard to bring it down. [Sherrill Milnes makes precisely the same point in his chapter.] But, of course, the crux of any Rossini role is *coloratura*. No one could sing Rossini without an agile, flexible voice. The challenge of *coloratura* music, however, is how to make it into something more than a mere vocal display; because unless one finds the *reason* for all those *fioriture*, Rossini operas can degenerate into people just standing on stage singing scales! And this nightmarish spectacle of people standing on stage and just singing is something I always objected to in opera, ever since my student days.'

Ramey's innate ability to establish character through his voice serves him particularly well in Rossini roles, which so easily lend themselves to cardboard interpretations. This is also partly due to the extreme difficulty of the music, which inhibits a wide variety of stage movements. One of the most difficult is the very role that launched Ramey's international career, Assur in *Semiramide*, which he was singing for the first time, at Aix. 'This was one of the high points, the greatest experiences in my career. It was also one of the most demanding pieces of music I had ever sung! Definitely not something you can just step into, because it demands tremendous give-and-take between the two voices: there are two long and very difficult duets – one with the mezzo and one with the soprano – where you have to match exactly what they do. You can't have two different ideas and styles going on at the same time. So, you have to rehearse very carefully and work out the cadenzas absolutely perfectly – at least, one should always *aim* for perfection. But in this case, everything went well. We also had a wonderful orchestra, under Jesús López-Cobos, who had done his homework meticulously and proved a terrific ally in the pit.'

Equally exciting but marginally less difficult is the role of Mustafa in *L'italiana in Algeri*, which, as Ramey rightly points out, has usually been sung by a character-singer, almost to the point where it wasn't even *sung* in the strict sense of the word (a fate that frequently befalls the roles of Papageno in *Die Zauberflöte* and Beckmesser in *Die Meistersinger von Nürnberg*, as Hermann Prey explains in his chapter). But Ramey thinks of Mustafa not so much as a buffoon as a *cattivo* (wicked) character and so, when invited to sing this role at Pesaro, he decided to find a way of being funny without resorting to vocal gimmickry. 'I refuse to play him as a buffoon because I want to *sing* the role. I want to sing *all* his music, which contains some very difficult passages with a lot of *fioritura* work which many of the singers who have sung it in the past didn't even *attempt* to sing! But I think that, above all in roles like this, the music and the composer must be served. The music was written to be realized and I greatly *enjoy* singing it. Other gimmicks are superfluous.'

The same principles underlie Ramey's interpretation of the role of Selim in *Il turco in Italia*, which is hardly as difficult or as satisfying as either Assur or Mustafa and which therefore interests him less, despite the fact that it contains some good duets. Nevertheless, he sings it with impeccable style, and the absence of gimmickry from his portrayal at the 1983 Pesaro Festival was singled out and praised by *Opera*. 'This great virtuoso singer with his opulent, wide-ranging voice conveyed in the role of Selim the true significance of the bass in comic opera: a genuine bass capable of fluent singing and a *diminuendo* without lapsing into *parlando* or clowning manner.'

Ramey's impressive artistry seems to have grown from strength to strength over the past few years. Perhaps the fact that his career began comparatively late – at the age of thirty-one – may have something to do with his vocal security, the assured mastery he displays in so many styles and his inability, so far, to put a foot wrong. Critics, used by then to Ramey's expertise at *coloratura*, were surprised to discover his ability to dominate the stage, both vocally and dramatically, in roles that have little call for *coloratura* when he sang the title role in *Moïse* at the Paris Opéra in the 1983–4 season. 'The cast was very much dominated by Samuel Ramey as Moses,' wrote *Opera*. 'I have in the past thought of him as a specialist singer, a fine *coloratura* bass, but this role contains little *coloratura* and Moses hardly gets an extended aria at all. It is far more difficult to dominate in recitative, *arioso* and ensemble, but Ramey did just that. His voice has grown tremendously, the low notes pour out in a rich flow. There are now few bass roles, I imagine, that he cannot conquer.' Ramey feels that the problem in this role lies in the fact that not all of Moses's music, which contains a great many declamatory recitatives, is as intense or on the same level as that of his confrontation scene with Pharaoh. And as he refuses 'to sing just for the sake of singing', he had to strive to bring something personal to the role.

He conceived of Moses not as a venerable patriarch but a young man, a very powerful character who has a special gift of communicating with God and who is chosen as a spokesman for his people. He was relieved to discover that this was also the idea behind Luca Ronconi's production and felt the latter did a wonderful job in coming to the aid of the music in some of its weaker passages (especially the long, 'oratorial' choruses that could easily have become dull) and compensating by providing a lot of interest on stage. This is something a good stage director should always be able to do. Vocally speaking, the role was not difficult by Rossini standards, and anyway Ramey is fortunate in being able to learn roles easily.

One of the most enjoyable Rossini roles he has sung is Lord Sidney in *Il viaggio a Reims*, at Pesaro where it was also recorded, and at La Scala in autumn 1985 under Claudio Abbado. This was his first opportunity to work with Abbado and he confesses that, despite his own impeccable credentials as a Rossini bass, he was 'somewhat in awe' at the prospect of working with the greatest living Rossini conductor, especially in pioneering a work pieced together for the first time. 'But I was amazed at how natural and approachable he is, and at his knack of putting young singers at ease. When I went up to him at the first rehearsal and addressed him as Maestro, he immediately asked to be called Claudio. And, believe me, there are very few conductors around who would say that or who ever come off their pedestal, even with singers of a certain standing. Working with him was also great from the musical point of view, first because this role is great fun and second because Claudio knows a great deal about the voice and could make useful vocal suggestions. For example, when I was having trouble with a passage where there was a jump of an octave on an "e" vowel, he said: "Listen, the 'e' vowel is not important on a high note like that. Caruso never sang 'e' on a high note. Just sing 'a'." So I tried it and it worked fine, because it's a more open sound and therefore easier to support.'

The performances at La Scala were also enormous fun, with jokes all the time, off stage and on, and everyone in a good mood. One of the unexpected delights came at the end of the last scene, where Lord Sidney has to sing 'God Save the Queen'. Abbado had casually suggested after one of the performances that Ramey might perhaps improvise a cadenza. He then forgot all about it; but Ramey didn't. He went home and wrote down a famous Verdi cadenza. He didn't remind Abbado or tell any of his colleagues what he intended to do, but at the next performance, just after he sang 'God Save the Queen', he stopped and plunged into this cadenza. 'Claudio covered his eyes in disbelief and started to laugh, Ruggero Raimondi couldn't believe his ears and the audience loved it!'

Ramey has now tackled most of Rossini's bass roles. In 1983 he successfully surmounted one of the biggest vocal challenges of his career: recording the title role in *Maometto II* (a work later revised by Rossini and usually performed under the title of *L'assedio di Corinto*), which he subsequently sang in 1985 and which is the most difficult part he has sung to date. 'Maometto makes Assur look simple! Although it has a wide range – from G above to F below the staff – the overall *tessitura* is very high, which is why baritones can sing it, too. I only knew the role in *L'assedio di Corinto*, where it is similar but shorter by two arias, and I must say I can see why! Because in this edition it is quite staggeringly difficult. As it had never been performed before, we were all gold-mining our roles, in a sense, and I found myself wondering if I could ever manage to sing it on stage. On balance I feel that, granted enough time to prepare and get it into the voice and provided I can schedule it between the right roles, I might just be able to do it.'

The ideal thing would be to sing it between Mozart roles, because he thinks Mozart is always the best partner for Rossini as both these composers make similar vocal and stylistic demands. Of course, Rossini roles are more exposed because the orchestra is thinner, whereas in Mozart the orchestration is 'so fabulous that everything you sing is almost a duet with the orchestra. Even Figaro's aria "Non più andrai" and Don Giovanni's Champagne aria I think of as duets because the orchestration is every bit as important as the vocal line. One never feels threatened by the orchestration, despite the fact that the *tessitura* of both those roles is not easy. [The ideal voice for both roles is a bass-baritone. Baritone and bass voices experience some problems in certain passages, as Thomas Allen, Sherrill Milnes and Ruggero Raimondi all explain in their chapters.] And although both Rossini and Mozart demand utmost precision, they differ in specifics like, for example, the fact that Mozart *coloraturas* are more *legato* and require absolute evenness, whereas in Rossini *coloraturas* there is more give and take – almost the feeling of *rubato* – within each measure. The beat doesn't stop, but there is a more flexible feeling in the vocal line. In this sense Mozart is the more difficult of the two.'

Ramey's two Mozart parts are the title roles in *Le nozze di Figaro* and *Don Giovanni*. Figaro suits him better, from both the vocal and the dramatic points of view. The character is, he says, among all the roles he sings, the one closest to his own personality. 'I hardly have to "act" at all. Everything seems to happen naturally and, again, I tend not to overdo the buffoonery. Vocally the role fits me like a glove because although the *tessitura* lies high in places, it always allows enough time for you to plunge down to the lower passages. Figaro also has the bass line in the ensembles, whereas Giovanni's is always a third of a semitone above Leporello's.'

Don Giovanni's *tessitura* is more problematic for a bass, which is why baritones also enjoy singing it. All the interpreters of this role agree that the Serenade is one of *the* most problematic spots for a bass voice, and Ramey confesses that 'this is what I spend the night before thinking about! And during the performance, what worries me most is the prospect of the Serenade getting closer and closer. After it's over, I heave a sigh of relief. The Champagne aria doesn't worry me so much. I've worked it out quite well with the breathing and consequently don't find it all that difficult.'

Ramey's portrayal of this role is vocally more lyrical and dramatically softer and more romantic than the more demonic portrayals favoured by some of his colleagues. He explains that it is easier for him to identify with, and bring out, 'the elegance in the character than his more sordid aspects. I see Don Giovanni as someone who simply *loved* women, not as an animalistic character with a constant, insatiable sexual hunger or as a Mephistophelian sadist. I feel that, in his way and for the moment, at least, he is in love with and appreciates each of the three women – Anna, Elvira and Zerlina – quite genuinely.' To date, although Ramey has sung this role in most major opera houses, the only time he did so in a new production was at New York City Opera, where he didn't quite agree with the conception of the director, John Cox, who saw Don Giovanni as 'actually in league with Satan. All he had to do was *look* at the Commendatore in the opening scene, like a snake hypnotizing a bird, for the latter to drop his sword. There was no fight at all. Giovanni simply ran his sword through the old man. I found it hard to identify with this conception because I see Giovanni as a less sinister and more elegant man.'

It will therefore be interesting to see Ramey's interpretation when he performs the role at the 1987 Salzburg Easter and Summer Festivals under Herbert von Karajan. When he came to record the role with him, after a successful audition in the summer of 1983, Ramey was in a highly nervous state because it was a long time since he had had to audition for anybody, and anyway he had never been much good at it. On top of this he got ill and had to postpone it for a couple of days. When he finally came face to face with the great Maestro, he was intrigued by the fact that he didn't ask for the Champagne aria, but only for the Serenade and Giovanni's third aria, 'Meta di vuoi qua vádono'. 'But surprisingly enough he asked for Giovanni's first entry and the entire opening scene, complete with recitatives and ensembles – for which a score had to be found – because he is one of the few to understand that, in Mozart, this is where the *real* drama takes place.' Even though Ramey hadn't slept a wink the night before and felt he didn't sing the Serenade as well as he can, Karajan was highly complimentary and impressed enough to sign him up.

Apart from this forthcoming production of *Don Giovanni*, Ramey's future plans include some of the Verdi bass roles for which he feels his voice is now ready. It is still developing, settling down deeper, and he feels that for the next few years most Verdi bass roles would be ideal. So far he has only sung Attila at the New York City Opera in 1980 and Venice in 1986, and Philip II in *Don Carlos* in Brussels in 1983 in a production that compared the situation in Philip's Spain to that of contemporary Iran and drew a parallel between the struggle between him and the Grand Inquisitor and that between Bani Sadr and the Ayatollah. 'Not surprisingly, I'm longing to sing the role again, hopefully in a new production!' He will in fact sing Philip in new productions in Geneva in 1988, Chicago in 1989 and in a revival at Covent Garden in 1989.

Until recently Ramey didn't feel ready for the big bass roles of Verdi's middle and later periods – like Fiesco in *Simon Boccanegra*, Procida in *I vespri siciliani* or Philip II – because they are typically *basso-profondo* parts with characteristically long Verdi lines. Attila and the early Verdi bass parts, on the other hand, have a very high *tessitura* and could almost be considered bass–baritone roles. 'But early Verdi is almost Rossini-like, both because of the higher *tessitura* and of the formula of aria-followed-by-cavatina that he adheres to. I would have no qualms about singing Attila at the same time as Assur or Maometto, for instance. His *tessitura* is high, mostly above the stave and therefore much easier for someone with a Rossini background. But I would hate to have to sing Assur or Maometto at the same time as Philip II! This role has a low *tessitura* that sits down on the voice and demands a great deal from its middle part – all those wonderful long lines of his are written in the middle voice. By some unlucky coincidence, I had to learn Maometto for the recording while preparing Philip II and it was awkward. I had to work very, very hard. Usually, when scheduling my roles, I try not to mix styles or *tessituras* because the voice then wonders what on earth is going on and which way it's supposed to be going. When I vocalize for Rossini, for instance, I do so entirely on fast scales. But when preparing Philip II, while always doing a *few* scales to get the voice going, I concentrate largely on slow, *legato* exercises aimed at getting the middle voice nicely focussed and at achieving a smooth, long line.'

Ramey greatly enjoys singing French roles, too, which he finds similar to Rossini because they require lightness of touch, long lines and quite a bit of *fioritura*. Although he doesn't actually speak French he loves singing in this language, which seems to bring out a particular quality in his voice. His teacher feels that some of Ramey's best singing is in French roles, like Mephistopheles in Gounod's *Faust*, and the title roles in *Don Quichotte* and *Robert le diable*. 'Ramey's French was magnificently projected,' noted *Opera* after the premiere of *Moïse* in Paris.

The experience of Ramey's Mephistopheles in Gounod's *Faust* at Covent Garden in February 1986 fully justified his teacher's view. His performance – in a revival of an archaic production that had little else to offer – was a rare *tour de force*: stylistically impeccable and note-perfect from start to finish. Ramey has also sung the title role in Boito's *Mefistofele* and points out that there are considerable musical and dramatic differences between the two: in *Faust* Mephisto is a much more elegant character, first because the French language demands, and indeed dictates, a more refined vocal and dramatic approach; and second because, throughout this work, Mephisto doesn't appear as himself: he is not really the devil, but the devil in disguise, out to amuse himself. 'He is charming, light-hearted and cavalier and only becomes really nasty for a couple of moments, with Marguerite in the church scene. Otherwise he is a *bon viveur* having a good time and it's important to establish this lightness of touch right from his first entry – his aria "Me Voici" in the Prologue – without hamming and being too demonic.'

Vocally the role does present some difficulties. One of its special features is the contrast in the style of writing. Many a time Mephisto sings certain phrases twice, and one of the interesting secrets is getting a vocal contrast in the colouring of the words the second time they are repeated. A more serious difficulty lies in the *tessitura*: a lot of Mephisto's music is written in the *passaggio* zone, the place where the gears change, and this, as Ramey points out (and all the singers in this book agree), is very tiring for the voice. 'For my voice one of the hardest spots in this opera is the aria "Le Veau d'or", which is easier for bass-baritones but tricky for basses because it contains three high notes – a C, a D and an E flat – that lie right in the *passaggio*, and yet require full vocal power to project through a heavy orchestration. Once this aria is over, I feel I can relax a bit. The Serenade I find much easier, because it consists of flowing, *cantabile* singing, something I always enjoy.' Some singers tend to go over the top at the end of the Serenade, where Mephisto is required to laugh sarcastically and indulge in exaggerated snarls and so on. Ramey doesn't. He produced just the right kind, and amount, of vocal effects. 'Samuel Ramey's well-cast vocal prowess properly hypnotizes the ear with its superb command of Gounod's devilish writing,' wrote *The Times*.

The title role in Boito's *Mefistofele* – which Ramey first sang at the New York City Opera in a production by Tito Capobianco and will sing again at the 1989 Maggio Musicale Fiorentino – is dramatically very different and vocally much more difficult. 'He has to be interpreted quite differently from Gounod's. Here, Mefistofele is himself, the devil, almost throughout. The opera starts with the aria "Ave Signor", a dialogue with God in which Mefistofele is immediately nasty and sarcastic, and we also see him in a witches' Sabbath, being himself, i.e. demonic, all the time. He is in disguise only for a couple of moments – the garden scene and his meeting with Faust – which do require a certain lightness of touch and humour. The fact that there are so few moments where you can lighten the voice makes it much more difficult to sing than Gounod's even though, technically, it's better written for the voice. The *tessitura* is variable and generally high-lying. But there are passages where you suddenly have to plunge to very low notes, for a whole scene, which is one of the hardest things for the voice to have to do. Most of the time the role also requires real power-singing: you have to give a lot of volume and the orchestration is heavy and largely centred on the brass section. This, combined with its length, makes Boito's Mefistofele one of the most tiring and draining – in fact probably *the* most draining – roles in my repertoire. Still, I greatly enjoy singing it. It is, after all, a title role and a real *tour de force*.'

One of Ramey's many accomplishments is his mastery of the baroque style. His exemplary singing of the role of Argante in Handel's *Rinaldo*, with which he made his Metropolitan Opera debut in January 1984, showed his command of this style to be on a par with his Rossini, Mozart and French singing. *Rinaldo* is the only Handel opera Ramey has sung on stage. He hopes that after his success in this production he may, one day, get a chance of singing *Giulio Cesare*. Stylistically, he considers Handelian singing even more difficult than Mozart or Rossini, mainly because of the differences in pitch between then and now, and the mathematical precision demanded by the baroque style. In Rossini *coloraturas*, for instance, there is a bit of give and take, whereas Handel's have to be utterly precise and exact: consequently they are more difficult. 'Handel operas are almost as difficult for producers as they are for singers, because it is very hard to find something for them to do while we are singing all those *da capo* arias, so fiendishly difficult to sing that you couldn't possibly hope to combine them with complicated stage movement. But despite its difficulties, I find baroque music very exciting and exhilarating to sing.' Peter Jonas, Managing Director of English National Opera, feels that hearing

Ramey singing Handel *coloratura* has been one of the outstanding musical experiences of his life.

Apart from a new production of Boito's *Mefistofele* at the 1989 Maggio Musicale Fiorentino, Ramey's future plans include the title role in *Le nozze di Figaro* under Riccardo Muti in 1987 at La Scala, as well as a complete Mozart cycle there, again under Muti, in 1989. As he has mentioned, some of the big Verdi bass roles, like Procida in *I vespri siciliani*, lie in the near future, while Fiesco in *Simon Boccanegra* can, he feels, wait a bit longer. So far, Ramey has avoided mistakes in his choice of repertoire and gives some of the credit for this to his erstwhile agent and manager Matthew Epstein (who was largely responsible for steering his career in the right direction and whom he still rings up for advice), and to his European agent Tom Graham. But it takes a good brain to recognize and accept good advice and the credit for that is Ramey's alone.

For instance, there is a proposal for him to sing the title role in *Boris Godunov* in 1990: despite the fact that this is years ahead, he is still not sure whether he will agree to do it. 'Boris is a dangerous role. You can get so dramatically involved in the action that this can detract from the vocalism. [A point Ruggero Raimondi makes in his chapter.] "I have discussed this at length with my teacher, Armin Boyajian, who pointed out that many singers' voices have never been the same after singing Boris, especially if they sang it too young. So I must decide whether to attempt it in 1990 or whether to leave it for the very end of my career. Matthew Epstein doesn't want me to sing Boris and feels sure I never will!'

People are always suggesting that one day Ramey will make a great Flying Dutchman or a Hans Sachs in *Die Meistersinger von Nürnberg*: but again he doesn't know, because he has always felt more suited to the Italian repertoire and it would be impossible to sing Wagner next to Rossini roles! 'Even though I don't think Wagnerian singing would endanger the agility in my voice – which has always been there – I always remember Astrid Varnay once coming up to me and saying: "I think you have a wonderful bass voice. But take my advice and don't ever let anybody talk you into singing Wagner." And this coming from a great Wagnerian singer!'

BIBLIOGRAPHY

Berlioz, Hector, *Memoirs,* translated and edited by David Cairns (Gollancz, Knopf, 1969)

Blyth, Alan (ed.), *Opera on Record,* 3 vols (Hutchinson, 1979, 1983, 1984)

Budden, Julian, *The Operas of Verdi,* 3 vols (Cassell, OUP, 1973, 1978, 1981)

Caruso, Dorothy, *Enrico Caruso, his Life and Death* (Laurie, 1946; Simon and Schuster, 1945)

Celleti, Rodolfo, *Memorie d'un ascoltatore* (Il Saggiatore, 1985)

Celleti, Rodolfo, *Le grandi voci* (Instituto per la collaborazione culture, 1964)

Chaliapin, Feodor, *Man and Mask: Forty Years in the Life of a Singer,* translated by Phyllis Mégroz (Gollancz, 1932)

Conati, Marcello, *Interviews and Encounters with Verdi,* translated by Richard Stokes (Gollancz, Cornell University Press, 1984)

Del Mar, Norman, *Richard Strauss: A Critical Commentary on his Life and Works,* 3 vols (Barrie & Rockliff, Cornell University Press, 1962, 1969; Barrie & Jenkins, Cornell University Press, 1972)

Domingo, Placido, *My First Forty Years* (Weidenfeld & Nicolson, Knopf, 1983)

Falkner, Sir Keith, *The Voice* (Yehudi Menuhin Music Guides/Macdonald & Co., 1983)

Gobbi, Tito, *Tito Gobbi on his World of Italian Opera* (Hamish Hamilton, 1984)

Grove's Dictionary of Music and Musicians, edited by Eric Blom, 9 vols, fifth edition (Macmillan, 1954)

Kobbé, Gustave, *Complete Opera Book,* edited and revised by the Earl of Harewood, ninth edition (Bodley Head, Putnam, 1976)

Liebermann, Rolf, *Actes et entractes* (Stock, 1976)

Matheopoulos, Helena, *Maestro: Encounters with Conductors of Today* (Hutchinson, 1982; Harper & Row, 1983)

Pavarotti, Luciano, *My Own Story* (Sidgwick & Jackson, Doubleday, 1981)

Pleasants, Henry, *The Great Singers, From the Dawn of Opera to our own Time* (Gollancz, Simon & Schuster, 1967)

Robinson, Paul, *Opera and Ideas* (Harper & Row, 1985)

Rosenthal, Harold, *Two Centuries of Opera at Covent Garden* (Putnam, 1958)

Rosenthal, Harold, *My Mad World of Opera* (Weidenfeld & Nicolson, 1982)

Bibliography

Schwarzkopf, Elisabeth, *On and Off the Record: A Memoir of Walter Legge* (Faber & Faber, Scribners, 1982)

Scott, Michael, *The Record of Singing*, 2 vols (Duckworth, Scribners, 1977 and Duckworth, Holmes & Meier, 1979)

Snowman, Daniel, *The World of Placido Domingo* (Bodley Head, McGraw-Hill, 1985)

Wagner, Cosima, *Diaries,* edited and annotated by Martin Gregor-Dellin and Dietrich Mack, translated by Geoffrey Skelton, 2 vols (Collins, Harcourt Brace, 1978 and 1980)

Wagner, Richard, *The Diary of Richard Wagner – the Brown Book 1865–1882,* presented and annotated by Joachim Bergfeld, translated by George Bird (Gollancz, CUP, 1980)

Wagner, Richard, *My Life,* edited by Mary Whittall, translated by Andrew Gray (Cambridge University Press, 1983)

Weaver, William (ed.), *Verdi: A Documentary Study* (Thames & Hudson, 1977)

INDEX

compiled by Frederick Smyth

The more important references are indicated by bold figures. '*n*' refers to a footnote; '*bis*' means that there are two separate references on the page; 'q' stands for 'quoted'. Use has been made of the following abbreviations: spr – soprano; mspr – mezzo-soprano; tnr – tenor; bar – baritone; bsbar – bass-baritone; bs – bass; accomp – accompanist; adm – administrator (comprehending also opera house intendants and managers); cdr – conductor; dir – (stage-) director or producer; libr – librettist; tchr – teacher.

Index

Index